FAIR AND EQUITABLE BENEFIT-SHARING IN INTERNATIONAL LAW

Fair and Equitable Benefit-Sharing in International Law

ELISA MORGERA

OXFORD
UNIVERSITY PRESS

OXFORD
UNIVERSITY PRESS

Great Clarendon Street, Oxford, OX2 6DP,
United Kingdom

Oxford University Press is a department of the University of Oxford.
It furthers the University's objective of excellence in research, scholarship,
and education by publishing worldwide. Oxford is a registered trade mark of
Oxford University Press in the UK and in certain other countries

Public sector information reproduced under Open Government Licence v3.0 (http://www.nationalarchives.gov.uk/doc/open-government-licence/open-government-licence.htm)

Published in the United States of America by Oxford University Press
198 Madison Avenue, New York, NY 10016, United States of America

British Library Cataloguing in Publication Data
Data available

Library of Congress Control Number: 2023948643

ISBN 978–0–19–886213–0

DOI: 10.1093/oso/9780198862130.001.0001

Printed and bound by
CPI Group (UK) Ltd, Croydon, CR0 4YY

Per Margherita e Tommaso

Acknowledgements

This book has benefitted from a multitude of opportunities for learning, collaboration, and conversations over ten years. In many ways, it is the culmination of a five-year research programme on fair and equitable benefit-sharing in different areas of international law (BENELEX, 2013–2018), which was funded by the European Research Council. I am extremely grateful to all the colleagues, students, and advisors that support the BENELEX project. First of all, I am indebted to the BENELEX researchers that engaged in a truly transformative process of peer-learning and peer-review as part of the project. Elisa Tsioumani, Louisa Parks, and Annalisa Savaresi greatly contributed to the conceptualization of the project and the co-development of its methods. We were then joined over time by other co-researchers: Daniela Diz, Mitchell Lennan, Mika Schroder, Wim Peters, and Kim Bouwer. I am also grateful to the colleagues that joined the BENELEX Advisory Board and engaged in in-depth exchanges of ideas for five years: Professors Francesco Francioni, Duncan French, Ellen Hey, Kati Kulovesi, Andre Nollkaemper, Jérémie Gilbert, and Colin Reid; Dr Claudio Chiarolla, Dr Lorenzo Cotula, Kathryn Garforth, Dr Harry Jonas, Maria Socorro Manguiat, Julia Oliva, Dr Shakeel Bhatti, and Tomme Young.

The BENELEX Project also offered us an opportunity to learn from local community members and NGOs that supported our interactions, whose contributions to our thinking are gratefully acknowledged and are fully discussed in Louisa Parks' monograph *Benefit-sharing in Environmental Governance: Local Experiences of a Global Concept* (Routledge, 2020). I am grateful to Maria Gaglia-Bareli and Frosini Koutsouti of the Ikarian Documentation and Research Center (Greece); the late Rodney Sibuye of the Kukula Association of Traditional Health Practitioners of Bushbuckridge, Cath Traynor and Gino Cocchiaro at Natural Justice, Marie-Tinka Uys at the Kruger to Canyons Biosphere Reserve, and Professor Wayne Twine of the University of the Witwatersrand Rural Facility (South Africa); Lesle Jansen at Natural Justice and Friedrich Alpers at Integrated Rural Development and Nature Conservation (Namibia); Ana di Pangracio and Pia Marchegiani at the Foundation for the Environment and Natural Resources (Argentina); Professor Poline Bala of the University of Sarawak; and—last but definitely not least—Dr Harry Jonas at Natural Justice (Malaysia).

Many colleagues and students at the University of Edinburgh, where the project was based until 2017, also generously contributed to our research conversations and to our blog post: Prof Neil Walker, James Harrison, Elizabeth Bomberg, Tim Hayward, and Doreen McBarnett; Dr Elizabeth Cripps, Dr Laura Jeffrey, Dr Genevieve Patenaude, Dr Liliana Riga, and Dr Meriwether Wilson. Many colleagues and students at the University of Strathclyde, where the project was based for the final years, have also greatly contributed to the project and its blog post: Dr Saskia Vermeylen, Dr Stephanie Switzer, Dr Miranda Geelhoed, Dr Maria Ntona, and Naomi Kenny. Many sincere thanks also to Leonie Breeuwer, LLM student at Strathclyde University, for her editorial assistance in completing the manuscript of this book.

Several visiting researchers have also joined our intellectual efforts and contributed with their independent research: Dr Margherita Brunori (who is also the artist of the book cover and several art works on the BENELEX website), Dr Adriana Bessa, Dr Lalanath de Silva, Dr Maria Peterson, Dr Komlan Sangbana, Dr Dimitri Pag-Yendu, Dr Marie-Catherine Petersmann, and Dr Núria Reguart-Segarra.

The research for this book continued well beyond the BENELEX project, and was enriched with the work undertaken under other grants. One was the research project MARINE BENEFITS (2015–2017, funded by the UK Ecosystem Services for Poverty Alleviation Programme), which investigated fair and equitable benefit-sharing in the context of international fisheries law and policy, with a view to connecting different sources of inequity concerning marine ecosystem services that contribute to poverty in small-scale fishing communities. I am grateful to my co-researchers Dr Daniela Diz and Dr Meriwether Wilson for the insights that arose from our collective work. The second is the One Ocean Hub (2018–2024), a collaborative research programme for sustainable development funded by UK Research and Innovation through the Global Challenges Research Fund (Grant Ref: NE/S008950/1), which supports continued research and engagement across natural and social sciences on fair and equitable benefit-sharing in the marine context. I am particularly grateful to Professor Rachel Wynberg, Dr Philile Mbatha, Dr Jessica Lavalle, Professor Kerry Sink, Professor Kerry Howell, Dr Kirsty McQuaid, Dr Giulia La Bianca, Dr Holly Niner, Prof Lynne Shannon, Dr Mat Upton, and Dr Sian Rees.

I am also grateful to the colleagues at the Secretariat of the Convention on Biological Diversity, the Food and Agriculture Organization of the United Nations, the Organization for Economic Cooperation and Development, and the European Commission for the invitations to carry out consultancies that have contributed to my understanding of international processes on fair and equitable benefit-sharing. Additionally, I extend my gratitude to all the international delegates that shared their concerns, questions, and ideas with me over the course of twenty years on the sidelines of international negotiations on fair and equitable benefit-sharing.

I am also grateful to the UN Special Rapporteurs on Human Rights and the Environment, Professors John Knox and David Boyd, for the invitations to contribute to their expert groups on biodiversity and human rights (in 2017 and 2020 respectively) and in particular for reflecting some of my key research findings in Principle 15 of the 2018 Framework Principles on Human Rights and the Environment.

As always, my infinite gratitude goes to the friends who have always been there for me, Francesca and Lorraine, and to my family.

Elisa Morgera
Edinburgh
7 August 2023

Contents

Table of Cases

INTERNATIONAL COURT OF JUSTICE (ICJ)

HUMAN RIGHTS COMMITTEE (HRC)

INTER-AMERICAN COURT OF HUMAN RIGHTS (IACTHR)

AFRICAN COMMISSION ON HUMAN AND PEOPLE'S RIGHTS

AFRICAN COURT ON HUMAN AND PEOPLE'S RIGHTS

PERMANENT COURT OF ARBITRATION

Table of Treaties and International Materials

List of Abbreviations

ABMTs	Area Based Management Tools
ABNJ	Areas Beyond National Jurisdiction
ABS	Access to genetic resources and fair and equitable benefit-sharing
AHTEG	Ad Hoc Technical Expert Group
BBNJ	Biodiversity of Areas Beyond National Jurisdiction
CAO	Compliance Advisor Ombudsman
CBD	Convention on Biological Diversity
CERD	Committee on the Elimination of Racial Discrimination
CFS	Committee on Food Security
CIME	Committee on International Investment and Multilateral Enterprises (OECD)
COP	Conference of the Parties
DSI	Digital Sequence Information
ECOSOC	Economic and Social Council (United Nations)
EEZ	Exclusive Economic Zone
EIAs	Environmental impact assessments
ESIL	European Society of International Law
FAO	Food and Agriculture Organization of the United Nations
FPIC	Free prior informed consent
GCRF	Global Challenges Research Fund
GISRS	Global Influenza Surveillance and Response System
GLIS	Gobal Information System
HRC	Human Rights Council
HRCtte	Human Rights Committee
IACtHR	Inter-American Court of Human Rights
ICESCR	International Covenant on Economic, Social and Cultural Rights
IFC	International Finance Corporation
IGC	Intergovernmental Conference
IHR	International Health Regulations (WHO)
IISD	International Institute for Sustainable Development
ILA	International Law Association
ILC	International Law Commission
ILO	International Labour Organization
IMO	International Maritime Organization
INSDC	International Nucleotide Sequence Database Collaboration
IOC	Intergovernmental Oceanographic Commission
IPBES	Intergovernmental Science-Policy Platform on Biodiversity and Ecosystem Services
IPCC	Intergovernmental Panel on Climate Change
IPRs	Intellectual Property Rights
ISA	International Seabed Authority
ITLOS	International Tribunal for the Law of the Sea

ITPGRFA	International Treaty on Plant Genetic Resources for Food and Agriculture
IUCN	International Union for Conservation of Nature
LDCs	Least Developed Countries
MAT	Mutually Agreed Terms
MGRs	Marine genetic resources
MNEs	Multinational enterprises
NGOs	Non-governmental organizations
NIEO	New International Economic Order
OAS	Organization of American States
OAU	Organization of African Unity
OBIS	Ocean Biogeographic Information System
OECD	Organisation for Economic Co-operation and Development
OHCHR	Office of the High Commissioner for Human Rights
PIP	Pandemic Influenza Preparedness
PRAI	Principles of Responsible Agricultural Investment That Respects Rights, Livelihoods and Resources
R&D	Research and development
REDD +	Reducing Emissions from Deforestation and Forest Degradation (Programme)
SDGs	Sustainable Development Goals
SEA	Strategic environmental assessment
SERAC	Social and Economic Rights Action Centre
SMTA	Standard Material Transfer Agreement
SSF	Small-scale fisheries
TRIPS	Trade-Related Aspect of Intellectual Property Rights (WTO)
UDHR	Universal Declaration of Human Rights
UKRI	UK Research and Innovation
UN	United Nations
UNCLOS	United Nations Convention on the Law of the Sea
UNCTAD	United Nations Conference on Trade and Development
UNDRIP	United Nations Declaration on the Rights of Indigenous Peoples
UNDROP	UN Declaration on the Rights of Peasants and Other People Working in Rural Areas
UNECE	United Nations Economic Commission for Europe
UNEP	United Nations Environment Programme
UNESCO	United Nations Educational, Scientific and Cultural Organization
UNFCCC	United Nations Framework Convention on Climate Change
UNFSA	United Nations Fish Stocks Agreement
UNGA	United Nations General Assembly
UNIDROIT	International Institute for the Unification of Private Law
UNPFII	UN Permanent Forum on Indigenous Issues
VCLT	Vienna Convention on the Law of Treaties
VGGT	Voluntary Guidelines on the Responsible Governance of Tenure of Land, Fisheries and Forests
WHO	World Health Organization
WIPO	World Intellectual Property Organization
WTO	World Trade Organization

An International Law Phenomenon

1. Introduction

Fair and equitable benefit-sharing is a diffuse legal phenomenon in international law that remains perplexing with regard to its general nature, extent, content, and implications. In broad terms, fair and equitable benefit-sharing has been included in international treaties, case law, and interpretative materials to address complex questions of environmental sustainability and equity among States, as well as among different sectors of society. In principle, it serves to recognize, encourage, and reward in innovative ways[1] sustainable human relations with the environment, by focusing on equity issues arising from the most intractable challenges of our time (biodiversity loss, climate change, poverty, global epidemics). Despite being fragmented, the increasing empirical evidence indicates that in practice benefit-sharing rarely achieves its stated fairness and equity objectives, and actually ends up entrenching or worsening inequitable relationships, with little or no benefit for the environment.[2]

The continued proliferation of benefit-sharing clauses in international law can in effect be explained by its intuitive appeal as an optimistic frame.[3] It emphasizes the advantages (the positive outcomes or implications) of tackling challenges in conservation, natural resource use, and knowledge production so as to help motivate participation by different actors. As Nollkaemper aptly explained, frames 'play an essential, though not always recognized, role in the development of international law' and they 'have distinct normative and regulatory implications'.[4] Actors with particular agendas and powers use frames strategically to single out and 'emphasize certain aspects of reality over others to promote a particular problem definition or approach to its solution'.[5] As a frame, benefit-sharing holds the promise of facilitating agreement upon specific forms of cooperation, with different parties being motivated by their perception of the benefits that would derive from it.[6]

[1] Based on empirical studies, Wynberg and Hauck, for instance, believe that benefit-sharing may denote 'a new way of approaching natural resource management and spreading the costs and benefits of using and conserving ecosystems and their resources across actors': R Wynberg and M Hauck, 'Sharing Benefits from the Coast' in R Wynberg and M Hauck (eds), *Sharing Benefits from the Coast: Rights, Resources and Livelihoods* (UCT Press, 2014), 1, at 6.

[2] A Martin et al., 'Just Conservation? On the Fairness of Sharing Benefits' in T Sikor (ed.), *The Justices and Injustices of Ecosystem Services* (Routledge, 2013) 69, at 84–88.

[3] This concept will be discussed in more depth in the following methodological section, based on L Parks and E Morgera, 'The Need for an Interdisciplinary Approach to Norm Diffusion: The Case of Fair and Equitable Benefit Sharing' (2015) 24 Review of European, Comparative & International Environmental Law 353.

[4] A Nollkaemper, 'Framing Elephant Extinction' (2014) 3 European Society of International Law (blogpost).

[5] ibid.

[6] CW Sadoff and D Grey, 'Cooperation on International Rivers: A Continuum for Securing and Sharing Benefits' (2005) 30 Water International 420, at 420 (emphasis added).

Fair and Equitable Benefit-Sharing in International Law. Elisa Morgera, Oxford University Press. © Elisa Morgera 2024.
DOI: 10.1093/oso/9780198862130.003.0001

On the other hand, empirically, benefit-sharing has been seen as a 'disingenuous win-win' framing, which is premised on global public goods and 'dominating knowledge approaches', which in practice leads to the loss of control and access over resources by the vulnerable.[7] Benefit-sharing negotiations often put pressure to 're-negotiate' communities' human rights or put a price tag on them.[8] The costs and losses that may be associated with certain benefits[9] tend to be downplayed, or left out completely in these framings.

These dynamics also arise in benefit-sharing negotiations among States. There, the tensions between economic and non-economic benefits, as well as between their immediate and long-term relevance, and their local and global relevance, remain unclear. On the one hand, non-monetary benefits such as technology transfer and capacity building, can be essential to enhancing the ability of beneficiaries to share in and produce monetary benefits in the long term.[10] On the other hand, they may create dependency on external, pre-packaged solutions that may not fit particular contexts or that may allow for the exertion of undue influence by donor countries[11] and the long-term co-development of technology.

On the whole, the body of empirical research on benefit-sharing points to the critical weight that power asymmetries have in all of the relations to which benefit-sharing applies, and document numerous instances in which benefit-sharing has been used 'as a semantic sticking plaster for harmful practices, as a superficial means to garner social acceptability for certain natural resource developments or regulations, and even to rubber-stamp inequitable and non-participatory outcomes that benefit "stronger" parties'[12] (such as rich and technology-exporting countries and powerful foreign investors).[13] Empirical studies so far, however, have not engaged in a systematic reflection on the opportunities and limitations of international law to prevent, address, and remedy the injustices that may be brought about in the name of benefit-sharing.[14] The implication is that as an aspirational and optimistic frame, benefit-sharing remains to be assessed from a healthily sceptical and legally robust perspective.

Why has there not been more progress in understanding fair and equitable benefit-sharing as an obligation under international law, against the evidence of multi-actor practice at different levels of implementation? A key reason is that fair and equitable

[7] Martin et al. (n. 2), at 84–88.

[8] M Orellana, 'Saramaka People v Suriname Judgment' (2008) 102 American Journal of International Law 841, at 847.

[9] From an intra-State benefit-sharing perspective, see Wynberg and Hauck (n. 1), at 158.

[10] e.g. Nagoya Protocol on Access to Genetic Resources and the Fair and Equitable Sharing of Benefits Arising from Their Utilization (Nagoya, 29 October 2010, in force 12 October 2014), preambular recitals 5, 7, and 14.

[11] E Morgera, E Tsioumani, and M Buck, *Unraveling the Nagoya Protocol: Commentary on the Protocol on Access and Benefit-sharing to the Convention on Biological Diversity* (Brill, 2014), at 313, 331.

[12] Parks and Morgera (n. 3).

[13] See, e.g., P Schwartz, 'Corporate Activities and Environmental Justice: Perspectives on Sierra Leone's Mining' in J Ebbeson and P Okowa (eds), *Environmental Law and Justice in Context* (Cambridge University Press, 2009), 429, at 438.

[14] See, e.g., R Wynberg and M Hauck, 'People, Power, and the Coast: A Conceptual Framework for Understanding and Implementing Benefit Sharing' (2014) 19 Ecology and Society 27; E van Wyk, C Breen, and W Freimund, 'Meanings and Robustness: Propositions for Enhancing Benefit Sharing in Social-Ecological Systems' (2014) 8 International Journal of the Commons 576.

benefit-sharing has predominantly been studied in sub-specialist areas of international law, in isolation from one another. The most extensive area of research focuses on fair and equitable benefit-sharing as the cornerstone of the composite international legal regime on bioprospecting (research and innovation based on access to genetic resources and traditional knowledge) comprising the Convention on Biological Diversity and its Nagoya Protocol on Access to Genetic Resources and the Fair and Equitable Sharing of Benefits Arising from Their Utilization, the International Treaty on Plant Genetic Resources for Food and Agriculture, and the World Health Organization's Pandemic Influenza Preparedness Framework.[15] Legal scholarship under the law of the sea on the regimes on non-living resources in the Area and outer continental shelf has also addressed benefit-sharing, but to a limited extent due to the partial development of international standards on deep-seabed mining.[16] Some limited scholarship has also emerged on benefit-sharing and the use of outer space and its resources.[17] However, a growing number of international legal materials refer to benefit-sharing from more widespread and traditional use of other natural resources (terrestrial mining,[18] forest,[19] water,[20] tourism,[21] fisheries,[22] as well as land use[23]); environmental protection (biodiversity conservation[24] and the fight against climate change[25]); as well as broader knowledge production. [26] Only some of

[15] Such an 'international regime' was identified in Convention on Biological Diversity (CBD) Decision X/1 (2010), preambular, para. 6, as comprising the Convention on Biological Diversity (Rio de Janeiro, 5 June 1992, in force 29 December 1993); the Nagoya Protocol; the International Treaty on Plant Genetic Resources for Food and Agriculture (Rome, 3 November, in force, 29 June 2004); and CBD, Bonn Guidelines on Access to Genetic Resources and Fair and Equitable Sharing of the Benefits Arising out of Their Utilization, CBD Decision VI/24 (2002) Annex. Specialist legal scholarship is abundant. See, e.g., EC Kamau and G Winter (eds), *Genetic Resources, Traditional Knowledge and the Law: Solutions for Access and Benefit Sharing* (Routledge, 2009); G Singh Nijar, 'Traditional Knowledge Systems, International Law and National Challenges: Marginalization or Emancipation?' (2013) 24 European Journal of International Law 1205.

[16] JE Noyes, 'The Common Heritage of Mankind: Past, Present and Future' (2011–2012) 40 Denver Journal of International Law and Policy 447, at 451, 469–470; J Frakes, 'The Common Heritage of Mankind Principle and the Deep Seabed, Outer Space, and Antarctica: Will Developed and Developing Nations Reach a Compromise?' (2003) 21 Wisconsin International Law Journal 409, at 417.

[17] F Xu and J Su, 'Towards a Legal Regime of Benefits Sharing for Space Mining: With Some Experience from the Area' (2022) 76 Resources Policy 102627; E Paxson, 'Sharing the Benefits of Outer Space Exploration: Space Law and Economic Development' (1993) 14 Michigan Journal of International Law 487.

[18] e.g. Inter-American Court of Human Rights (IACtHR), *Case of the Saramaka People v. Suriname*, Judgment of 28 November 2007 (Preliminary Objections, Merits, Reparations and Costs).

[19] e.g. UN Reducing Emissions from Deforestation and Forest Degradation (REDD) Programme, Social and Environmental Principles and Criteria, Criterion 12 (2012).

[20] e.g. Ramsar Convention on Wetlands of International Importance, Res X.19: Wetlands and River Basin Management: Consolidated Scientific and Technical Guidance (2008), Annex, para. 25.

[21] e.g. Guidelines on Biodiversity and Tourism, CBD Decision V/25 (2000).

[22] e.g. Food and Agriculture Organization (FAO), Voluntary Guidelines on the Responsible Governance of Tenure of Land, Fisheries and Forests in the Context of National Food Security, UN Doc CL 144/9 (C 2013/20) (2012).

[23] e.g. UN Rapporteur on the Right to Food, Large-Scale Land Acquisitions and Leases: A Set of Minimum Principles and Measures to Address the Human Rights Challenge, UN Doc A/HRC/13/33/Add.2 (2010).

[24] e.g. African Commission on Human and Peoples' Rights, *Endorois Welfare Council v. Kenya*, Communication no. 276/2003, 25 November 2009.

[25] e.g. Adaptation Fund Board, Adaptation Fund Environmental and Social Policy (2013), para. 13.

[26] UN General Assembly (UNGA), Universal Declaration of Human Rights, Res 217 A (III) (1948), Art. 27(1); Report of the Special Rapporteur in the Field of Cultural Rights: The Right to Enjoy the Benefits of Scientific Progress and Its Applications, UN Doc A/HRC/20/26 (2012); and UN Committee on Economic,

these developments have been analysed in the context of scholarship on Indigenous peoples' human rights and the environment.[27]

Both from an international law-making and implementation perspective, the proliferation of references to benefit-sharing has been accompanied by a remarkable lack of conceptual clarity, to the point that it has been rightly asked whether there is just one concept of benefit-sharing or many.[28] Benefit-sharing is employed in international law to connote a treaty objective,[29] an international obligation,[30] a right,[31] a safeguard,[32] or a mechanism.[33] However, there is no instance in which it has been unequivocally understood,[34] fully developed,[35] or made satisfactorily operational.[36] To address these shortcomings, international negotiations are ongoing on the clarification or reform of benefit-sharing under the Nagoya Protocol, the International Plant Treaty, and the International Seabed Authority.[37] In addition, a new international benefit-sharing regime under the UN Convention on the Law of the Sea on marine genetic resources in areas beyond national jurisdiction was agreed in 2023,[38] and another is likely to emerge from ongoing negotiations of a new treaty on pandemics by the World Health Organization (WHO).[39] While some cross-regime reflections have occurred in policy and academic literature, this has not been a systematic effort from the perspective of general international law. Against the backdrop of this intense and multi-faceted international law-making process, what has not yet been assessed is the extent to

Social and Cultural Rights, General Comment No 25 (2020) on science and economic, social and cultural rights (Arts 15(1)(b), (2), (3), and (4) of the International Covenant on Economic, Social and Cultural Rights, UN Doc E/C.12/GC/25 (2020).

[27] e.g., UN Special Rapporteur on the Issue of Human Rights and the Environment John Knox, Framework Principles on Human Rights and the Environment, UN Doc A/HRC/34/49 (2018), Principle 15; J Gilbert, *Natural Resources and Human Rights* (Oxford University Press, 2018). These advancements in scholarship built on the research for this book: author's correspondence with Professors Knox and Gilbert.

[28] B de Jonge, 'What Is Fair and Equitable Benefit-Sharing?' (2011) 24 Journal of Agricultural and Environmental Ethics 127; D Schroeder, 'Benefit-Sharing: It's Time for a Definition' (2007) 33 Journal of Medical Ethics 205, at 208.

[29] CBD, Art. 1; ITPGRFA, Art. 1; Nagoya Protocol, Art. 1.

[30] CBD, Arts 15(7) and 8(j); Nagoya Protocol, Art. 5.

[31] International Labour Organization's (ILO) Convention no. 169 Concerning Indigenous and Tribal Peoples in Independent Countries (Geneva, 27 June 1989, in force 5 September 1991), Art. 15(2); ITPGRFA, Art. 9.

[32] *Saramaka* (n. 18), para. 129; *Endorois* (n. 24), para. 227; Rapporteur on Indigenous Peoples' Rights, Study on Extractive Industries and Indigenous Peoples, UN Doc A/HRC/24/41 (2013), para. 52.

[33] United Nations Convention on the Law of the Sea (UNCLOS) (Montego Bay, 10 December 1992, in force 16 November 1994), Art. 140; ITPGRFA, Art. 10; Nagoya Protocol, Art. 10.

[34] For the interpretative divergences and ongoing negotiations under the Nagoya Protocol, see Morgera, Tsioumani, and Buck (n. 11).

[35] e.g. International Seabed Authority (ISA), Towards the Development of a Regulatory Framework for Polymetallic Nodule Exploitation in the Area, Doc ISBA/19/C/5 (2013).

[36] An inter-sessional process is currently underway on enhancing the functioning of the ITPGRFA Multilateral System. ITPGRFA, Res 2/2013 (2013).

[37] D Wilde et al., 'Equitable Sharing of Deep-Sea Mining Benefits: More Questions Than Answers' (2023) 151 Marine Policy 105572.

[38] Agreement under the United Nations Convention on the Law of the Sea on the Conservation and Sustainable Use of Marine Biological Diversity of Areas beyond National Jurisdiction (New York, 19 June 2023, A/CONF.232/2023/4, not yet in force) [BBNJ Agreement].

[39] WHO Convention, agreement or other international instrument on pandemic prevention, preparedness and response (A/INB/1/12) (draft outline published 14 June 2022).

which international law has already clarified how fair and equitable benefit-sharing should be interpreted and implemented in ways that align with its equity rationale. In other words, how can benefit-sharing be interpreted to provide 'new perspectives and potentially fresh solutions to tricky legal problems' to the benefit of all, not just to the advantage of the powerful.[40] Such an enquiry will be undertaken both from the perspective of specific international regimes, and general international law. The latter is particularly useful to shed new light on the interpretative barriers that have been identified within specific regimes.

2. An Initial Overview of the Emergence of Fair and Equitable Benefit-Sharing in International Law

The following sections will provide an overview of the emergence of fair and equitable benefit-sharing across different areas of international law, with a view to identifying a normative core and conceptual distinctions that can provide elements for deeper analysis in the following chapters.

2.1 When Did Fair and Equitable Benefit-Sharing Emerge in International Law?

Benefit-sharing is best known within the realm of international biodiversity law, but it made its first appearance in international human rights law. The 1946 Universal Declaration of Human Rights referred to everyone's right to share in the benefits of scientific advancement.[41] The 1986 UN Declaration on the Right to Development referred to States' duty to ensure the 'active, free and meaningful participation in ... the *fair distribution of the benefits* resulting' from national development for their entire population and all individuals.[42] What benefit-sharing means in either context, however, remains unclear, although there are indications that these human rights are connected to international environmental law, notably technology transfer obligations.[43] Leaving aside the debate on the value of solidarity rights,[44] these references to benefit-sharing express dissatisfaction about the current level of cooperation in relation to financial and technological obligations under international environmental

[40] C Burke, *An Equitable Framework for Humanitarian Intervention* (Hart, 2014), at 250–251.

[41] Universal Declaration on Human Rights, Art. 27(1) (emphasis added), which is reiterated in slightly different wording in Art. 15 of the International Covenant on Economic, Social and Cultural Rights (ICESCR) (New York, 16 December 1966, in force 3 January 1976).

[42] UNGA, UN Declaration on the Right to Development, Res 41/128 (1986), Art. 2(3) (emphasis added).

[43] Report of the Independent Expert on Human Rights and International Solidarity to the General Assembly, UN Doc A/68/176 (2013), para. 27(d); Report of the High-level Task Force on the Implementation of the Right to Development on its Sixth Session: Right to Development Criteria and Operational Sub-criteria, UN Doc A/HRC/15/WG.2/TF/2/Add.2 (2010), criteria 3(b)(i); UN Special Rapporteur in the field of cultural rights, Report on the Right to Enjoy the Benefits of Scientific Progress and its Applications, UN Doc A/HRC/20/26 (2012), paras 1 and paras 25, and 30–43.

[44] P Alston, 'A Third Generation of Solidarity Rights: Progressive Development or Obfuscation of International Human Rights Law?' (1982) 29 Netherlands International Law Review 307.

law, particularly the international climate change regime. However, there is no explicit reference to intra-State benefit-sharing in the international climate regime and little practice in international biodiversity law with regard to finance and technology.[45] However, progress has been made internationally since the 2010s to clarify the content of the human right to science.[46]

Benefit-sharing is also embedded in the 1989 ILO Indigenous and Tribal Peoples Convention No. 169, which provides that Indigenous and tribal peoples 'shall, wherever possible participate in the benefits' arising from the exploration and exploitation of natural resources pertaining to their ancestral lands. Notwithstanding its vagueness[47] and the limited membership of the ILO Convention,[48] this provision has become quite prominent in the interpretation of other international instruments (the American Convention on Human Rights,[49] the African Charter on Human and Peoples' Rights,[50] the UN Convention on the Elimination of Racial Discrimination,[51] and the UN Declaration on the Rights of Indigenous Peoples[52]) in connection with the free prior informed consent of Indigenous peoples over developments concerning their territories.[53] On the human rights side, regional case law has built on the ILO Convention No. 169 to clarify that benefit-sharing is triggered by the exploitation of traditionally owned lands and natural resources necessary for the survival of Indigenous and tribal peoples or by the establishment of environmental protection measures negatively affecting them.[54] Other human rights processes have increasingly relied on this interpretation.[55] Benefit-sharing has been invoked in relation to Indigenous peoples' right to property and natural resources,[56] culture and non-discrimination,[57] and their right to development,[58] as well as in the context of

[45] e.g. CBD Decision VII/29 (2004), Technology Transfer Work Programme, paras 3.2.8 and 3.2.9.

[46] Committee on Economic, Social and Cultural Rights, General Comment No 25 (2020) on science and economic, social and cultural rights (Arts 15(1)(b), (2), (3), and (4) of the International Covenant on Economic, Social and Cultural Rights, UN Doc E/C.12/GC/25 (2020).

[47] L Swepston, 'New Step in the International Law on Indigenous and Tribal Peoples: ILO Convention No. 169 of 1989' (1990) 15 Oklahoma City University Law Review 677, at 703–706.

[48] The Convention has twenty-four ratifications as of June 2023: https://www.ilo.org/dyn/normlex/en/f?p=1000:11300:0::NO:11300:P11300_INSTRUMENT_ID:312314, accessed 25 June 2023.

[49] American Convention on Human Rights (San José, 22 November 1969, in force 18 July 1978).

[50] African Charter on Human and Peoples' Rights (Banjul, 27 June 1981, in force 21 October 1986).

[51] International Convention on the Elimination of All Forms of Racial Discrimination (New York, 7 March 1966, in force 4 January 1969).

[52] UNGA, Declaration on the Rights of Indigenous Peoples, Res 61/295 (2007) (UNDRIP).

[53] e.g. *Saramaka* (n. 18) and subsequent case law cited below.

[54] ibid; *Endorois* (n. 24); IACtHR, *Case of Garífuna Community of Triunfo de la Cruz and its members v. Honduras*, Judgment of 8 October 2015 (Merits, Reparations, and Costs); IACtHR, *Case of Garífuna Punta Piedra Community and its members v. Honduras*, Judgment of 8 October 2015 (Preliminary Objections, Merits, Reparations and Costs); IACtHR, *Case of Kaliña and Lokono Peoples v. Suriname*, Judgment of 25 November 2015 (Merits, Reparations and Costs).

[55] e.g. UN Indigenous Peoples' Partnership, Strategic Framework 2011–2015, available at http://www.ilo.org/wcmsp5/groups/public/---ed_norm/---normes/documents/publication/wcms_186285.pdf, accessed 25 June 2023; Report of the Special Rapporteur on the Implications for Human Rights of the Environmentally Sound Management and Disposal of Hazardous Substances and Wastes to the Human Rights Council, UN Doc A/HRC/21/48 (2012), paras 36 and 69(h).

[56] UN Permanent Forum on Indigenous Issues (UNPFII), Review of World Bank operational policies, UN Doc E/C.19/2013/15 (2013), para. 27; *Saramaka* (n. 18), para. 138.

[57] Report of the Special Rapporteur on Indigenous Peoples' Rights, UN Doc A/HRC/12/34 (2010), paras 50–52.

[58] *Endorois* (n. 24), paras 294–295.

large-scale investments in farmland impacting on their right to food.[59] Overall, however, limited attention has been paid specifically to benefit-sharing in human rights policy and academic circles, possibly because it is seen as an '*additional* safeguard'[60] to the complex and still unsettled notion of free, prior, and informed consent (FPIC).[61] Therefore, much remains to be clarified about the interactions between benefit-sharing and FPIC. On the one hand, benefit-sharing may serve as a condition for the granting of FPIC, thereby contributing to culturally appropriate and effective consultations and affecting the scope of environmental and socio-economic impact assessment.[62] On the other hand, benefit-sharing may represent the end result of an FPIC process, thereby providing concrete expression of the accord granted by Indigenous peoples on the basis of their own understandings and preferences.[63] It also remains to be determined whether benefit-sharing could be required when FPIC is not.[64]

Early benefit-sharing obligations can also be found in the law of the sea. The 1982 UN Convention on the Law of the Sea (UNCLOS) created a complex international approach to the '*equitable sharing of* financial and other economic *benefits* derived from' mining activities in the deep seabed ('the Area'),[65] as part of the regime on the common heritage of humankind.[66] UNCLOS also includes another benefit-sharing obligation concerning areas within national jurisdiction:[67] it mandates States to share, through the multilateral benefit-sharing mechanism of the Area, revenues deriving from mining activities in the outer continental shelf.[68] Precise rules and procedures on benefit-sharing in both contexts are yet to be developed.[69] That said, the International Seabed Authority has already engaged in non-monetary benefit-sharing in relation to exploration in the Area.[70] As part of the common heritage regime, benefit-sharing was

59 Report of the UN Special Rapporteur on the Right to Food, Large-Scale Land Acquisitions and Leases: A Set of Minimum Principles and Measures to Address the Human Rights Challenge, UN Doc A/HRC/13/33/Add.2 (2009), paras 30–33.

60 Rapporteur on Indigenous Peoples' Rights, Study on Extractive Industries and Indigenous Peoples, UN Doc A/HRC/24/41 (2013), para. 52 (emphasis added).

61 e.g. the lengthy monograph by E Desmet, *Indigenous Rights Entwined with Nature Conservation* (Intersentia, 2011) does not mention benefit-sharing.

62 Expert Mechanism on the Rights of Indigenous Peoples, Follow-up Report on Indigenous Peoples and the Right to Participate in Decision-making with a Focus on Extractive Industries, UN Doc A/HRC/21/55 (2012), para. 43.

63 Report of the Special Rapporteur on Indigenous Peoples' Rights, UN Doc A/HRC/12/34 (2010), para. 43.

64 JM Pasqualucci, 'International Indigenous Land Rights: A Critique of the Jurisprudence of the Inter-American Court of Human Rights in Light of the United National Declaration on the Rights of Indigenous Peoples' (2009–2010) 27 Wisconsin Journal of International Law 51, at 91.

65 UNCLOS, Art. 140(1) (emphasis added).

66 UNCLOS, Arts 136–141.

67 UNCLOS, Art. 82(1) and (4).

68 A Chircop, 'Commentary on Article 82' in A Prölss (ed.), *The United Nations Convention on the Law of the Sea: A Commentary* (Hart, 2017)

69 UNCLOS, Art. 160(2)(f), (i), and (g); ISA (n. 35); and Issues Associated with the Implementation of Article 82 of the United Nations Convention on the Law of the Sea, International Seabed Authority Technical Study No. 4 (2009).

70 Regulation 27 of the Regulations on prospecting and exploration for polymetallic nodules and Regulation 29 of the Regulations on prospecting and exploration for sulphides and crusts; and Annex 4 of these regulations; Recommendations for the guidance of contractors and sponsoring States relating to training programmes under plans of work for exploration, Doc ISBA/19/LTC/14 (2013); see J Harrison, The Sustainable Development of Mineral Resources in the International Seabed Area: The Role of the Authority

associated with natural resources that cannot be appropriated to the exclusive sovereignty of States. These resources must be conserved and exploited for the benefit of mankind, without discrimination and for peaceful purposes, and are subject to international management.[71]

As anticipated above, more substantial developments on fair and equitable benefit-sharing have occurred in the context of international biodiversity law. The 1992 Convention of Biological Diversity (CBD) includes benefit-sharing obligations, elucidated through a series of consensus-based, soft-law decisions adopted by 196 Parties,[72] and the legally binding Nagoya Protocol on Access to Genetic Resources and Benefit-Sharing (Nagoya Protocol).[73] Most attention has focused on fair and equitable benefit-sharing in relation to bioprospecting, that is, transnational bio-based research and development (R&D). This has relied, in the context of the CBD and its Nagoya Protocol, on *bilateral*[74] contractual arrangements for sharing benefits arising from R&D conducted in another country with the country providing genetic resources, and with the Indigenous peoples and local communities providing genetic resources held by them and associated traditional knowledge. The operability of these provisions remains a matter of international debate and academic research.

Furthermore, multilateral benefit-sharing approaches in relation to bioprospecting have emerged in more specialized areas. The International Treaty on Plant Genetic Resources for Food and Agriculture embodies the most sophisticated elaboration of benefit-sharing as a *multilateral* system for listed crops of global importance for food security (such as rice, potato, and maize). At the crossroads of biodiversity and health, the World Health Organization (WHO) 2011 Pandemic Influenza Preparedness Framework (PIP Framework) embodies a multilateral system for sharing samples of pandemic influenza viruses, and benefits arising from it, most notably the sharing of vaccines produced from research on the viruses.[75]

While several commentators saw benefit-sharing from minerals in the Area as the most controversial element of common heritage, and, as such, responsible for the very cautious use of this principle in international law,[76] the uptake of benefit-sharing as a self-standing approach in the international regime on bioprospecting has proven that the concept is capable of adapting to the legal specificities of genetic resources under the sovereignty of third countries (under the Nagoya Protocol) or being held in trust by an international network of collections (under the International Plant Treaty).[77] Benefit-sharing has now come full circle. Its normative development under

in Balancing Economic Development and Environmental Protection (Edinburgh Law School Working Papers; no. 2014/50).

71 UNCLOS, Arts. 136–138 and 140–141.

72 As opposed to the limited membership of the ILO Convention (twenty countries).

73 See Morgera, Tsioumani, and Buck (n. 11).

74 Although note the possibility for a multilateral benefit-sharing mechanism to be established under Nagoya Protocol, Art. 10: see Morgera, Tsioumani, and Buck (n. 11), at 197–208.

75 World Health Organization (WHO), Pandemic Influenza Preparedness Framework for the Sharing of Influenza Viruses and Access to Vaccines and Other Benefits, WHO Doc WHA64.5, 24 May 2011.

76 See, e.g., SJ Shackelford, 'The Tragedy of the Common Heritage of Mankind' (2009) 28 Stanford Environmental Law Journal 109, at 128; Noyes (n. 16), at 451, and 469–470; Frakes (n. 16), at 417.

77 In effect, UNCLOS already included other articulations of benefit-sharing related to resources outside of the common heritage regime: UNCLOS, Art. 82(1), (4). It has also been argued that benefit-sharing is

the International Plant Treaty and the Nagoya Protocol influenced the further development of the law of the sea with regard to marine genetic resources of areas beyond national jurisdiction.[78]

Returning to international biodiversity law, benefit-sharing has also emerged under the CBD as a component of the ecosystem approach,[79] in conjunction with the benefit-sharing arising from the use of Indigenous peoples' and local communities' traditional knowledge.[80] This is in recognition of the relationship between the stewardship of traditionally occupied or used territories and natural resources and the production and inter-generational transmission of traditional knowledge.[81] Such knowledge embodies *traditional lifestyles*[82] (a *communal way of life*)[83] based on the link between communities' shared cultural identity, the biological resources that they use,[84] and their customary rules about knowledge and environmental stewardship.[85] In this connection, benefit-sharing serves as both *recognition* and *reward* for the use of knowledge and for the customary environmental management. Under the CBD, it is through interpretation in relation to the ecosystems approach that benefit-sharing has been developed as an incentive for the good management practices of Indigenous peoples and local communities[86] as well as of other stakeholders who are responsible for the production and sustainable management of ecosystem functions.[87] This has provided the conceptual departure point for developing soft law guidance on benefit-sharing both with regard to natural resource use[88] and with regard to conservation

foreseen in the regulation of marine scientific research under UNCLOS: see generally C Salpin, 'The Law of the Sea: A Before and an After Nagoya?' in Morgera, Buck, and Tsioumani (eds), *The 2010 Nagoya Protocol on Access and Benefit-Sharing in Perspective: Implications for International Law and National Implementation* (Martinus Nijhoff, 2013), 149.

[78] Agreement under the United Nations Convention on the Law of the Sea on the Conservation and Sustainable Use of Marine Biological Diversity of Areas beyond National Jurisdiction (New York, 19 June 2023, A/CONF.232/2023/4, not yet in force).

[79] Principles of the Ecosystem Approach, CBD Decision V/6 (2000), para. 9; E Morgera, 'Ecosystem and Precautionary Approaches', in E Morgera and J Razzaque (eds), *Encyclopedia of Environmental Law: Biodiversity and Nature Protection Law* (Edward Elgar, 2017)

[80] Bonn Guidelines on Access and Benefit-sharing, CBD Decision VI/24 (2002) Annex, para. 48; and Tkarihwaié:ri Code of Ethical Conduct on Respect for the Cultural and Intellectual Heritage of Indigenous and Local Communities, CBD Decision X/42 (2010), Annex, para. 14; Principles of the Ecosystem Approach (n. 79), Principle 8; Refinement and elaboration of the ecosystem approach, CBD Decision VII/11 (2004), Annex, rationale to Principle 4. For a discussion, see E Morgera, 'The Need for an International Legal Concept of Fair and Equitable Benefit-sharing' (2016) 27 European Journal of International Law 353.

[81] J Gibson, 'Community Rights to Culture: The UN Declaration on the Rights of Indigenous Peoples' in S Allen and A Xanthanki (eds), *Reflections on the UN Declaration of the Rights of Indigenous Peoples* (Bloomsbury, 2011) 434, at 434–435.

[82] On the basis of the wording of CBD, Art. 8(j).

[83] CBD Secretariat, How tasks 7, 10, and 12 could best contribute to work under the Convention and to the Nagoya Protocol, UN Doc UNEP/CBD/WG8J/8/4/Rev.2 (2012), para. 23.

[84] In the light of the placement of CBD, Art. 8(j) in the context of *in situ conservation* (CBD, Art. 8).

[85] See generally B Tobin, *Indigenous Peoples, Customary Law and Human Rights – Why Living Law Matters* (Routledge, 2014).

[86] Principles of the Ecosystem Approach (n. 79), para. 9.

[87] ibid, Operational Guidance 2, Annex, para. 9; CBD, Refinement and Elaboration of the Ecosystem Approach, Annex, para. 12.5.

[88] e.g. Addis Ababa Principles and Guidelines, Annex II: Practical Principle 12, CBD Decision VII/12 (2004).

measures (i.e. protected areas[89] and climate change response measures).[90] It has also led to the development of a specific benefit-sharing obligation owed to communities as stewards of genetic resources 'held by them' under the Nagoya Protocol.[91]

Along similar lines but based on different premises (human rights to property and to culture), benefit-sharing has been increasingly recognized by international human rights judicial and quasi-judicial bodies[92] as an implicit component of Indigenous peoples' rights to their territories and natural resources.[93] In the human rights context, however, benefit-sharing is mainly conceived as a tool to *protect* communities against third parties' natural resource development (mining and logging) or conservation measures that can negatively affect communities' way of life.[94] Similar concerns have been addressed under international human rights law for non-Indigenous communities, as captured in the 2018 UN Declaration on the Rights of Peasants[95] and the 2018 Framework Principles on Human Rights and the Environment.[96]

With regard to Indigenous and local knowledge, a qualified obligation to encourage intra-State benefit-sharing in the CBD[97] has been interpreted through a series of decisions to apply more broadly to communities' customary sustainable use of biological resources[98] across all of the Convention's thematic areas of work.[99] This interpretation has developed into a binding obligation under the Nagoya Protocol in relation to traditional knowledge that is more narrowly construed as being 'associated with genetic resources'.[100] While it has been acknowledged in a human rights context that benefit-sharing is also needed when the traditional knowledge of Indigenous peoples is threatened,[101] there has been no elaboration in this connection by human rights

[89] CBD, Work Programme on Protected Areas, Annex, paras 2(1) and 2(1)(4) (while the latter refers to both benefit-sharing and cost sharing, the focus on benefit-sharing is clarified in CBD Decision IX/18 (2008), Preamble, para. 5.

[90] This would be the justification for CBD Decision XI/19 (2012), REDD+, for example.

[91] Nagoya Protocol, Art. 5(2): Morgera, Tsioumani, and Buck (n. 11), at 117–126.

[92] African Commission on Human and Peoples' Rights, Centre for Minority Rights Development (Kenya), and Minority Rights Group International, *Endorois* (n. 24); *Kaliña and Lokono* (n. 54).

[93] Namely, UNDRIP, Arts 25–26: see Report of the UN Special Rapporteur on Indigenous Peoples Rights, UN Doc A/HRC/15/37 (2010), paras 76–77; and Framework Principles on Human Rights and the Environment (n. 27), where benefit-sharing is included under Principle 15.

[94] E Morgera, 'Under the Radar: Fair and Equitable Benefit-Sharing and the Human Rights of Indigenous Peoples and Local Communities Related to Natural Resources' BENELEX Working Paper no.10 (SSRN, 2016), available at https://papers.ssrn.com/sol3/papers.cfm?abstract_id=2887803, accessed 26 June 2023.

[95] UN Human Rights Council, 'United Nations Declaration on the Rights of Peasants and Other People Working in Rural Areas' (8 October 2018) UN Doc A/HRC/RES/39/12 (adopted by thirty-three votes to three—Australia, Hungary and the UK; eleven abstentions).

[96] n. 27.

[97] CBD, Art. 8(j). This understanding can also be found in other legal developments contemporary to the CBD, such as Agenda 21, paras 15(4)(g) and 15(5)(e).

[98] CBD, Art. 10(c).

[99] e.g. CBD, Revised Work Programme on Inland Water Biodiversity, Decision VII/4 (2004), Annex, para. 9; CBD, Work Programme on Island Biodiversity, Decision VIII/1 (2009), Annex, Target 9.2; CBD, Work Programme on Drylands, Decision VIII/2 (2006), Target 9.2.

[100] Nagoya Protocol, Arts 5(5) and 7. See the discussion in Morgera, Tsioumani, and Buck (n. 11), at 126–130. See also benefit-sharing from farmers' traditional knowledge, a combined reading of the ITPRGFA, Arts 9(2)(a) and 13(3), as discussed by E Tsioumani, 'Exploring Fair and Equitable Benefit-Sharing from the Lab to the Land (Part I): Agricultural Research and Development in the Context of Conservation and the Sustainable Use of Agricultural Biodiversity' (SSRN, 2014), available at http://papers.ssrn.com/sol3/papers.cfm?abstract_id=2524337, accessed 25 June 2023.

[101] UNPFII (n. 56), para. 27.

bodies.[102] This gap has been recognized by the CBD parties, who developed international guidelines on prior informed consent and on benefit-sharing from the use of traditional knowledge.[103]

In addition, because of the political emphasis placed on bio-piracy as the unlawful use of traditional knowledge for commercial innovation purposes, little attention has been paid to benefit-sharing from the non-commercial use of traditional knowledge, including pure research aimed at providing global benefits (such as advancing climate science).[104] Although the CBD text itself does not distinguish between commercial and other utilization of traditional knowledge, other international legal materials expressly link benefit-sharing to commercial use.[105] The issue has been treated with extreme caution by the CBD's Conference of the Parties (COP) through a voluntary 'code of ethical conduct', which is not intended to 'interpret the obligations of the CBD'.[106] However, a systematic reading of the Nagoya Protocol points to an obligation to share (arguably non-monetary) benefits arising from non-commercial research on traditional knowledge, even when the research is meant to contribute to the global goal of conserving biodiversity.[107]

Finally, it should be noted that benefit-sharing requirements related to the use of natural resources and traditional knowledge of Indigenous peoples and local communities have been increasingly reflected in the standards of international development banks,[108] the requirements of international climate initiatives,[109] and guidelines on land tenure and agricultural investment.[110] A further conceptual aspect that remains

[102] In comparison to the Nagoya Protocol, neither the ILO Convention No. 169, or the UNDRIP, link benefit-sharing and traditional knowledge. Committee on Economic, Social and Cultural Rights (CESCR), General Comment No. 21, UN Doc E/C.12/GC/21 (2009), para. 37, refers to prior informed consent but not to benefit-sharing, with regard to traditional knowledge. See Morgera, Tsioumani, and Buck (n. 11), at 127–130; D Craig and M Davies, 'Ethical Relationship for Biodiversity Research and Benefit-sharing with Indigenous Peoples' (2005) 2 Macquarie Journal of International and Comparative Environmental Law 31.

[103] CBD, Mo'otz Kuxtal voluntary guidelines for the development of mechanisms, legislation or other appropriate initiatives to ensure the 'prior informed consent', 'free prior informed consent' or 'approval and involvement', depending on national circumstances, of Indigenous peoples and local communities for accessing their knowledge, innovations and practices, the fair and equitable sharing of benefits arising from the use and application of such knowledge, innovations and practices and for reporting and preventing unauthorized access to such knowledge, innovations and practices, CBD Decision XIII/18, para. 6 (2016).

[104] Consider, e.g., Intergovernmental Panel on Climate Change, 'Climate Change 2007: Impacts, Adaptation and Vulnerability: Contribution of Working Group II to the Fourth Assessment Report of the Intergovernmental Panel on Climate Change' (2007), at 138, and 673; Paris Agreement, Decision 1/CP.21 (2016) Art. 7(5); UNESCO Declaration on Bioethics and Human Rights (2005), Art. 17.

[105] Convention to Combat Desertification in Those Countries Experiencing Serious Drought and/or Desertification, Particularly in Africa 1996 1954 UNTS 3, Art. 17; World Bank, Operational Policy 4.10 (2005), para. 19; International Finance Corporation, Performance Standard 8 (2012), para. 16.

[106] CBD, Tkarihwaié:ri Code of Ethical Conduct to Ensure Respect for the Cultural and Intellectual Heritage of Indigenous and Local Communities, CBD Decision X/42 (2010), paras 1, 14.

[107] Nagoya Protocol, Art. 8(a), read with Art. 5 and Annex, and Arts 16–17. See Morgera, Tsioumani, and Buck (n. 11), at 179–184.

[108] e.g. Inter-American Development Bank, Operational Policy on Indigenous Peoples (2006), para. VI(f); European Bank for Reconstruction and Development, Environmental and Social Policy (2014), performance requirement 7, para. 15.

[109] Notably climate finance and REDD (n. 19). A Savaresi, 'The Emergence of Benefit-Sharing Under the Climate Regime: A Preliminary Exploration and Research Agenda', BENELEX Working Paper 3 (SSRN, 2014), available at https://zenodo.org/records/1921902#.XAaRcuKYSUk, last accessed 6 March 2024.

[110] Food and Agricultural Organization of the United Nations (FAO), Voluntary Guidelines on the Responsible Governance of Tenure of Land, Fisheries and Forests in the Context of National Food Security (VGGT) (2012).

to be elicited in this connection is the linkage between benefit-sharing and land tenure, including as an essential pre-condition for the protection and preservation of traditional knowledge,[111] against the background of the growing relevance of international human rights and investment treaties for land disputes.[112]

In the realm of international law on transboundary watercourses, benefit-sharing has been seen as an extension of the general principle of equitable and reasonable utilization.[113] This approach challenges international cooperation as it has traditionally focused purely on quantitative allocations of water.[114] Accordingly, benefit-sharing has led to a consideration of more sophisticated forms of inter-State cooperation that factor in non-water-related benefits (economic, socio-cultural, and broader environmental benefits) arising from the enhanced stewardship of a shared watercourse, which would normally be undertaken by an upstream State.[115] Water lawyers and practitioners are increasingly looking into this development, but they have not fully investigated cross-fertilization with international biodiversity law with regard to the role of communities in the conservation of inland water ecosystems and related traditional knowledge, and possible synergies and tensions with the human right to water.[116]

2.2 Some Preliminary Distinctions

This brief, yet admittedly quite overwhelming, historical overview indicates that international benefit-sharing objectives and obligations have arisen at different points in time in a variety of contexts, and are currently characterized by different levels of sophistication. Overall, there are four triggers for international benefit-sharing obligations, namely:

- Bioprospecting (whether of a transnational character, under the Nagoya Protocol, International Plant Treaty, and the WHO,[117] or in areas beyond national jurisdiction,

[111] CBD, Tkarihw aié:ri Code (n. 106), paras 17–19; CESCR, paras 36 and 50(c).

[112] L Cotula, 'Land: Property and Sovereignty in International Law' in E Morgera and K Kulovesi (eds), *Research Handbook on International Law and Natural Resources* (Edward Elgar, 2016) 219.

[113] MM Abseno, 'The Concept of Equitable Utilisation, No Significant Harm and Benefit-Sharing under the River Nile Cooperative Framework Agreement: Some Highlights on Theory and Practice' (2009) 20 Journal of Water Law 86; R Paisley, 'Adversaries into Partners: International Water Law and the Equitable Sharing of Downstream Benefits' (2002) 3 Melbourne Journal of International Law 280.

[114] P Wouters and R Moynihan, 'Benefit-Sharing in International Water Law' in F Loures and A Rieu-Clarke (eds), *The UN Watercourses Convention in Force: Strengthening International Law for Transboundary Water Management* (Routledge, 2013) 321.

[115] O McIntyre, 'Benefit-Sharing and Upstream / Downstream Cooperation for Ecological Protection of Transboundary Waters: Opportunities for China as an Upstream State' (2015) 40 Water International 48, at 50.

[116] D Shelton, 'Water Rights of Indigenous Peoples and Local Communities' in L Boisson de Chazounes, C Leb, and M Tignino (eds), *International Law and Freshwater: The Multiple Challenges* (Edward Elgar, 2013) 69, at 80.

[117] e.g. Kamau and Winter (n. 15); G Singh Nijar, 'Traditional Knowledge Systems, International Law and National Challenges: Marginalization or Emancipation?' (2013) 24 European Journal of International Law 1205.

in the case of the Biodiversity of Areas Beyond National Jurisdiction (BBNJ) Agreement);

- Natural resource use, broadly conceived (be that beyond areas of national jurisdiction, such as deep-seabed mining our outer space, or within national jurisdiction, such as logging and terrestrial mining);
- Conservation measures that are proposed or put in place in Indigenous peoples' territories,[118] which are receiving increasing attention in international human rights debates on 'fortress conservation' practices;[119] and
- The production and use of knowledge: this is not only the traditional knowledge of Indigenous peoples and local communities (although this is the area that has attracted the majority of international law-making and scholarly attention), but also other forms of knowledge in the context of the human right to science (extending, for instance, to inter-State obligations of technology transfer).[120]

One challenge in determining whether this is a relatively uniform concept in international law derives from the fact that benefit-sharing is applied to a variety of resources that are qualified internationally in different ways: common heritage of humankind, shared resources, and resources under national sovereignty, the protection of which is considered a common concern of humankind.[121]

In other words, fair and equitable benefit-sharing is applied to relations that are addressed to different extents by international law and are characterized by different de facto power asymmetries. For the purposes of conceptual clarity, therefore, a distinction needs to be drawn among:

- Benefit-sharing *among* States (inter-State benefit-sharing) applying to relationships that are characterized by sovereign equality and, in key areas of international cooperation, by the controversial principle of common but differentiated responsibility;[122]
- Benefit-sharing *within* States (intra-State benefit-sharing) applying to relations between a government and a community within its territory, whose relationship is characterized by the State's sovereign powers and international obligations over natural resources and the relevance, to varying extents, of international human rights law;[123]

[118] CBD Work Programme on Protected Areas, CBD Decision VII/28 (2004), Annex; *Kaliña and Lokono* (n. 54); *Endorois* (n. 24).

[119] UN Special Rapporteur on Indigenous Peoples' Rights Victoria Tauli-Corpuz, Report to the General Assembly, UN Doc A/71/229 (2016); UN Special Rapporteur on Human Rights and the Environment, David Boyd, Policy Brief No. 1: Human rights-based approaches to conserving biodiversity: equitable, effective and imperative (2021).

[120] E Morgera, 'Fair and Equitable Benefit-sharing' in E Orlando and L Krämer (eds), *Encyclopedia of Environmental Law: Principles of Environmental Law* (Edward Elgar, 2018) 323, at 803.

[121] ibid.

[122] See, e.g., L Rajamani, *Differential Treatment in International Environmental Law* (Oxford University Press, 2006); E Hey, 'Common but Differentiated Responsibilities' in R Wolfrum (ed.), *Max Planck Encyclopedia of Public International Law* (Oxford University Press, 2010).

[123] E Morgera and E Tsioumani, 'The Evolution of Benefit-Sharing: Linking Biodiversity and Communities' Livelihoods' (2010) 19 Review of European, Comparative and International Law 150.

- *transnational* approaches (benefit-sharing between communities, private companies[124] that may be protected by international investment law and that, even when that is not the case, are increasingly understood in the light of business responsibility to respect human rights;[125] and/or NGOs in the context of international investment or development cooperation) in the light of non-State actors' responsibility to respect human rights; and
- *intra-community* benefit-sharing applying to relations within communities,[126] which raises questions of the interaction among communities' customary laws, and national and international law.[127]

2.3 Why Has Fair and Equitable Benefit-Sharing Emerged in International Law?

One important perspective to understand the evolution of fair and equitable benefit-sharing is that different historic matrices have been operating behind the proliferation of references to it in international law.[128] It is argued here that benefit-sharing developed in international law first under the umbrella of the New International Economic Order (NIEO) and its legacy for the global sustainable development agenda and, more recently, under the discourse on ecosystem services.

The NIEO can be described as newly independent developing countries' attempt in the 1970s at radically restructuring the global economic system by prioritizing the objective of development as part of the decolonization process.[129] The NIEO provided the context for the development of the concept of national sovereignty over natural resources to support the self-determination of States and of peoples to make decisions regarding the economic, social, and cultural aspects of human development.[130] In both cases, the NIEO called for international cooperation on the basis of necessity and to move away from legal techniques that serve to perpetrate economic domination by

[124] International Finance Corporation (IFC), Performance Standard 7 (2012), available at https://www.ifc.org/en/insights-reports/2012/ifc-performance-standards, last accessed 19 February 2024, paras 18–20; FAO, International Fund for Agricultural Development, UN Commission on Trade and Development and the World Bank, Principles for Responsible Agricultural Investment That Respects Rights, Livelihoods and Resources (PRAI) (2010), Principle 6; UN Global Compact Office, Business Reference Guide to the UN Declaration on the Rights of Indigenous Peoples (2013), at 76–77; Report of the UN Special Rapporteur on Indigenous Peoples' Rights (Indigenous Peoples' Rights Report), UN Doc A/HRC/15/37 (2010), paras 73–75.

[125] UN Human Rights Commission (UNHRC), Protect, Respect and Remedy, a Framework for Business and Human Rights, UN Doc A/HRC/8/5 (2008), endorsed by Res 8/7 (2008); UNHRC, Guiding Principles on Business and Human Rights: Implementing the United Nations 'Protect, Respect and Remedy' Framework, UN Doc A/HRC/17/31 (2011), endorsed by Res 17/4 (2011).

[126] This is intra-community benefit-sharing: e.g. PRAI, Principle 6; Committee on Food Security (CFS), Principles for Responsible Investment in Agriculture and Food Systems (2014), paras iv, 23.

[127] e.g. Nagoya Protocol, Art. 12(1).

[128] Morgera (n. 80).

[129] Declaration on the Establishment of a New International Economic Order, GA Res 3201, 1 May 1974; Programme of Action for the Establishment of a New International Economic Order, GA Res 3202, 1 May 1974.

[130] ME Salmon, 'From NIEO to Now and the Unfinishable Story of Economic Justice' (2013) 62 International and Comparative Law Quarterly 31.

a minority of States.[131] Against this background, benefit-sharing has been linked to the still controversial notion of a human right to development[132] and to the rights of Indigenous and tribal peoples to their territories and natural resources.[133] In addition, it has been encapsulated in the innovative construct of the common heritage of mankind with regard to the moon[134] and deep seabed minerals,[135] to prevent a few States from appropriating resources beyond the reach of those with fewer technological and financial capacities.

Since then, the NIEO has formally disappeared from the international agenda, its project of overhauling the international economic order having been abandoned following the creation of the World Trade Organization.[136] However, the discourses on equitable globalization and the principle of sustainable development have been seen as 'direct reminders' of the NIEO's call for equity among States[137] and for a rights-based approach to development.[138] To a still significant extent, the NIEO has thus evolved into a general approach to the making of international environmental law aimed at solidarity and cooperation to the benefit of the least-favoured countries.[139] Furthermore, it has been enriched by the recognition of cultural diversity among and within States, resulting in the protection of the rights of marginalized individuals and communities over natural resources in order to protect their cultural identity and livelihoods.[140] As a result, national sovereignty over natural resources has been progressively qualified by duties and responsibilities towards other States and towards communities[141] (including communities outside States' own borders[142]) and redefined as a commitment to cooperate for the good of the international community at large in terms of equity and sustainability.[143] This evolution provides the background for the references to both inter-State and intra-State benefit-sharing in the CBD, the International Plant Treaty, and the Nagoya Protocol.

The more recent spread of benefit-sharing in the areas of water, land, and climate change has in turn been attributed to the discourse on ecosystem services[144]

[131] C Rossi, *Equity and International Law: A Legal Realist Approach to International Decision-Making* (Martinus Nijhoff, 1993), at 200–201.

[132] UNGA, UN Declaration on the Right to Development, Res 41/128 (1986), Art. 2.3.

[133] ILO Convention No. 169, Art. 15.2.

[134] Agreement Governing the Activities of States on the Moon and Other Celestial Bodies (New York, 5 December 1979, in force 11 July 1984), Art. 11(7).

[135] UNCLOS, Art. 140.

[136] F Francioni, 'Equity', in Wolfrum (n. 122), 632, para. 21.

[137] E Tourme-Jouannet, *What Is a Fair International Society? International Law between Development and Recognition* (Hart, 2013), at 37 and 86–87.

[138] Salmon (n. 130), at 49.

[139] See, e.g., S Maljean-Dubois, 'Justice et société internationale: l'équité dans le droit international de l'environnement' in A Michelot (ed.), *Equité et environnement* (Oxford University Press, 2012) 355, at 358–359.

[140] Tourme-Jouannet (n. 137), at 121, 149.

[141] F Lenzerini, 'Sovereignty Revisited: International Law and Parallel Sovereignty of Indigenous Peoples' (2006) 42 Texas International Law Journal 155.

[142] Y Benvenisti, 'Sovereigns as Trustees of Humanity: On the Accountability of State to Foreign Stakeholders' (2013)107 American Journal of International Law 295.

[143] P Birnie, A Boyle, and C Redgwell, *International Law and the Environment* (Oxford University Press, 2009), at 192.

[144] See, e.g., BA Nkhata et al., 'A Typology of Benefit Sharing Arrangements for the Governance of Social-Ecological Systems in Developing Countries' (2012) 17 Ecology and Society 1.

or nature's benefits to people[145]—the multiple ways in which ecosystems contribute to human well-being.[146] Having gained global scientific and political traction in the lead up to the 2005 UN Summit,[147] this discourse has served to emphasize the devastating impacts on the vulnerable of ecosystems' decline.[148] The Millennium Ecosystem Assessment[149] was a global scientific process that facilitated intergovernmental endorsement of the term 'ecosystem services' as the benefits people obtain from ecosystems, namely: food, water, timber, energy and fibre ('provisioning services'); 'regulating services', which affect climate, floods, diseases, wastes, and water quality; 'cultural services', which provide recreational, aesthetic and spiritual benefits; and 'supporting services' such as soil formation, photosynthesis, and nutrient cycling. While the economic valuation of ecosystem benefits was already considered essential for more effective biodiversity conservation in early normative developments under the CBD,[150] the Millennium Ecosystem Assessment increased attention on the contribution of biodiversity to human well-being and to development.[151]

In particular, the Millennium Ecosystem Assessment led to further reflection on the need for appropriate and explicit accounting of the multiple links between biodiversity and human development, particularly through recourse to economics, to prevent other development objectives that conflict with biodiversity protection from continuing to take priority.[152] On the one hand, therefore, it conveyed that applying economic thinking[153] to the use of biodiversity could help clarify why poverty reduction depends on maintaining the flow of benefits from ecosystems.[154] On the other hand, it encouraged a greater use of economic and market-based instruments in the management of ecosystem services, where enabling conditions exist.[155] But reference to ecosystem services has raised divisive questions about the moral and cultural acceptability and the effectiveness of the pricing and marketing of ecosystem services,

[145] S Diaz et al., 'Assessing Nature's Contributions to People' (2018) 359 Science 270.

[146] Millennium Ecosystem Assessment, available at https://www.millenniumassessment.org/en/index.aspx, last accessed 12 April 2016.

[147] E Morgera, 'The 2005 UN World Summit and the Environment: The Proverbial Half-Full Glass' (2006) 15 Italian Yearbook of International Law 53.

[148] T Sikor et al., 'Toward an Empirical Analysis of Justice in Ecosystem Governance' (2014) 7 Conservation Letters 524.

[149] The Millennium Ecosystem Assessment, Ecosystems and Human Well-Being, Synthesis Report (2005), available at https://www.millenniumassessment.org/en/index.html accessed 28 July 2023. For a discussion of legal implications, see generally Morgera (n. 147).

[150] e.g. CBD Decision III/18 (1996).

[151] E Morgera and E Tsioumani, 'Yesterday, Today and Tomorrow: Looking Afresh at the Convention on Biological Diversity' (2011) 21 Yearbook of International Environmental Law 3, at 11–12.

[152] P Sukhdev, H Wittmer, and D Miller, 'The Economics of Ecosystems and Biodiversity (TEEB): Challenges and Responses' in D Helm and C Hepburn (eds), *Nature in the Balance: The Economics of Biodiversity* (Oxford University Press, 2014) and other materials available at http://www.teebweb.org/ accessed 26 June 2023.

[153] Note that increased efforts have also been made to advance the use of economic valuation to mainstreaming environmental protection more effectively into development planning in the areas of climate change and desertification: N Stern, *The Economics of Climate Change: The Stern Review* (Cambridge University Press, 2007) and the Economics of Land Degradation initiative, available at http://eld-initiative.org/, accessed 25 June 2023.

[154] Sukhdev, Wittmer, and Miller (n. 152), at 6.

[155] UNEP High-Level Brainstorming Workshop on Creating Pro-Poor Markets for Ecosystem Services: 10–12 October 2005, London, UK. The whole paragraph builds upon Morgera and Tsioumani (n. 151), at 9–12.

about inherent pressures towards their privatization, and more generally about the appropriate balance between ecosystem stewardship and ownership.[156] The proponents of ecosystem services, however, openly acknowledge the limitations of *monetary valuation* particularly when biodiversity values are generally recognized and accepted socially and culturally.[157] Rather, they have emphasized valuation in a broad sense in order to clearly address the drawbacks and limitations of economics as 'a means to achieving human well-being'.[158] Accordingly, the international discourse on ecosystem services has also served to underscore the need for rights-based strategies to prevent biodiversity loss and its negative impacts on the vulnerable.[159] In addition to *vulnerability*, it drew attention to the (largely overlooked) *merit* of ecosystem stewards in contributing to global human well-being.[160] As a result, the ecosystem approach embodies a balancing of economic and non-economic understandings of the relationship between human beings and the environment, as well as inherent tensions in that regard. These understandings are also reflected in the concept of benefit-sharing as the sharing of not only economic, but also socio-cultural and environmental benefits arising from biodiversity conservation and sustainable use.[161] The resolution of these tensions partly depends on further appreciation of the natural capital[162] and partly on the scientific basis available for decision making.

It has been argued that an economic valuation of ecosystems serves to prevent monetized objectives from taking priority in decision making more easily[163] and that ecosystem stewards should be rewarded (including through payments for ecosystem services) for contributing to human well-being. While ecosystem stewards may often be vulnerable, being the most exposed to unsustainable and inequitable environmental management decisions and practices,[164] this is not always the case, and the notion of ecosystem services does not necessarily aim to protect the vulnerable.[165]

Legal scholars, therefore, have focused on the moral and cultural acceptability, and the social and environmental effectiveness, of pricing and marketing ecosystem services,[166] with the limitations of purely monetary valuation being openly acknowledged in the discourse.[167] Whether ecosystem services can be fully or solely responsible

[156] See generally C Reid and W Nsoh, 'Whose Ecosystem Is It Anyway? Private and Public Rights under New Approaches to Biodiversity Conservation' (2014) 5 Journal of Human Rights and the Environment 112

[157] Sukhdev, Wittmer, and Miller (n. 152), at 11–12.

[158] ibid, at 9.

[159] For instance, CBD Decision X/4 (2010), paras 5(d) and (f), pointing to: enhancing the benefits of biodiversity to contribute to local livelihoods; empowering Indigenous and local communities; and ensuring their participation in decision-making processes to protect and encourage their customary sustainable use of biological resources.

[160] Sikor et al. (n. 148).

[161] This paragraph builds upon E. Morgera, 'Conceptualizing Benefit-Sharing as the Pursuit of Equity in Addressing Global Environmental Challenges', BENELEX Working Paper no. 1 (SSRN 2014), available at https://papers.ssrn.com/sol3/papers.cfm?abstract_id=2524003, accessed 26 June 2023, at 7–8.

[162] See Chapter 6 in this volume.

[163] The Economics of Ecosystems and Biodiversity (TEEB), *Challenges and Responses* (2014).

[164] UNGA, Strategic Framework for the Period 2012–2013, UN Doc A/65/6/Rev.1 (2011), para. 11(24)(b); UNGA, Strategic Framework for the Period 2014–2015, UN Doc A/67/6 (prog 11) (2012), para. 11(16).

[165] See generally Sikor et al. (n. 148).

[166] See, e.g., Reid and Nsoh (n. 156) 112.

[167] TEEB, *Mainstreaming the Economics of Nature: A Synthesis of the Approach, Conclusions and Recommendations* (2010), available at https://www.teebweb.org/, last accessed 26 June 2023, at 11–12.

for the diffusion of benefit-sharing or not, they raise conceptual questions that find clear correspondence in the debate on benefit-sharing as a 'post-neoliberal attempt to harness market-based activities ... to social and environmental ends'[168] or a preference for solutions based on financial transactions that may ignore or even reinforce injustices.[169]

Ecosystem services have been included in the CBD guidance on the ecosystem approach, which aims at integrating the management of land, water, and living resources, and balancing the three objectives of the Convention—conservation, sustainable use, and access and benefit-sharing.[170] Ecosystem services have also been referenced in international guidance on human rights and the environment to emphasize the dependence of basic human rights from healthy ecosystems,[171] as discussed below. The interpretation at the crossroads of international biodiversity and human rights law enables an assessment of the influence of both rationales for benefit-sharing—NIEO legacy, including in the Sustainable Development Goals (SDGs)[172] and ecosystem services.

3. What is Fair and Equitable Benefit-Sharing?

Notwithstanding the various articulations of benefit-sharing in different areas of international law, a common normative core can be arguably identified on the basis of converging interpretative materials. A common normative core of fair and equitable benefit-sharing has been identified for comparison and generalization purposes[173]—concerted and dialogic partnership-building in identifying and allocating economic, socio-cultural, and environmental benefits among States and non-State actors, with an emphasis on the vulnerable.[174] The concept will serve to identify normative elements that are shared among different treaties and other international legal instruments, based on the understanding that international law is often developed by building in an iterative process on previously agreed language.[175]

However, it is not intended to provide a holistic or exhaustive notion of benefit-sharing. Rather, it will allow for an appreciation of the variation and continuous evolution across regimes with different purposes, standards of protection, and interpretative approaches. On that basis, the following subsections will focus, in turn, on the act of sharing, fairness and equity, the nature of the benefits to be shared, and the beneficiaries. Subsequent chapters will then analyse the varied phenomenology

[168] C Hayden, 'Benefit-Sharing: Experiments in Governance' in R Ghosh (ed.), *CODE: Collaborative Ownership and Digital Economy* (MIT Press, 2006), 113.

[169] Sikor et al. (n. 148).

[170] CBD Decision V/6 (2000), Annex, para. 1 and Principle 5.

[171] UN Special Rapporteur on Human Rights and the Environment John Knox, Biodiversity and Human Rights, UN Doc A/HRC/34/49 (2017).

[172] UNGA Res 70/1 (2015).

[173] In the tradition of analytical jurisprudence, as defined by W Twining, 'Law, Justice and Rights: Some Implications of a Global Perspective' in Ebbeson and Okowa (n. 13) 76, at 80–82.

[174] Morgera (n. 80).

[175] C McLachlan, 'The Principle of Systemic Integration and Article 31(3)(c) of the Vienna Convention' (2005) 54 International Comparative Law Quarterly 279, at 284.

of benefit-sharing across different regimes with a view to ascertaining the extent to which benefit-sharing obligations contribute to clarify and progressively develop the international duty to cooperate on the basis of existing, overlapping international obligations, standards, and goals.

3.1 Sharing

The verb 'to share' arguably distinguishes international agreements that encapsulate benefit-sharing as a specific legal notion from hortatory references to the benefits arising from international cooperation more generally.[176] The difference is that 'to share' and 'to participate' in the benefits convey the same idea of agency, rather than the passive enjoyment of benefits.[177] The ways in which the action of 'sharing' is articulated in the relevant international materials, in effect, points to a concerted effort in co-identifying with beneficiaries and apportioning benefits through a dialogic process. In other words, benefit-sharing differs from unidirectional (top-down) flows of benefits and, rather, aims at developing a common understanding of what the benefits at stake are and how they should be shared, through iterative dialogue. In this connection, it has been argued that benefit-sharing is aimed at consensus building.[178]

Through dialogue, benefit-sharing entails an iterative process, rather than an one-off exercise, of good-faith engagement among different actors that lays the foundation for a partnership among them.[179] In the inter-State context, this arguably refers to the idea of a global partnership enshrined in the Rio Declaration on Environment and Development,[180] in terms of both a 'new level of cooperation' between developed and developing States[181] and a form of cosmopolitan cooperation[182] between States

[176] Although the ILO Convention No. 169 does not use the verb 'to share' (rather the verb 'to participate in'), successive interpretations of the Convention have repeatedly used benefit-sharing terminology. See, e.g., Observation of the Committee of Experts on the Application of Experts, adopted 2009, published 9th ILC session (2010), para. 11. In fact, the Inter-American Court of Human Rights (*Saramaka* (n. 18), para. 138) and former UN Special Rapporteur of Indigenous Peoples' Rights James Anaya (Report of the Special Rapporteur on Indigenous Peoples' Rights (Indigenous Peoples' Rights Report), UN Doc A/HRC/15/37 (2010), paras 67 and 76–78) have emphasized that 'benefit-sharing', as encapsulated in the ILO Convention, refers to an inherent component of Indigenous peoples' rights to land and natural resources that is implicit in the American Convention on Human Rights and the UNDRIP.

[177] M Mancisidor, 'Is There Such a Thing as a Human Right to Science in International Law?' (7 April 2015) 4 ESIL Reflections.

[178] Special Rapporteur on the Rights of Indigenous Peoples, Report to the Human Rights Council, UN Doc A/HRC/12/34 (2009), para. 53; Report of the Special Rapporteur on Indigenous Peoples' Rights (Indigenous Peoples' Rights Report), UN Doc A/HRC/24/41 (2013), para. 88.

[179] On the intra-State dimension of benefit-sharing, see, e.g., Review of Developments Pertaining to the Promotion and Protection of Human Rights and Fundamental Freedoms of Indigenous Peoples, UN Doc E/CN.4/Sub.2/AC.4/2001/2 (2001), para. 19. On the inter-State dimension, see, e.g., Report of the High-Level Task Force on the Implementation of the Right to Development on Its Second Meeting, UN Doc E/CN.4/2005/WG.18/TF/3 (2005), para. 82.

[180] Rio Declaration on Environment and Development 1972, 11 ILM 1416 (1972), Preamble and Principles 7 and 27.

[181] PM Dupuy, 'The Philosophy of the Rio Declaration' in J Viñuales (ed.), *The Rio Declaration on Environment and Development: A Commentary* (Oxford University Press, 2015) 65, at 69 and 71. See generally R Wolfrum and C Kojima (eds), *Solidarity: A Structural Principle of International Law* (Springer, 2010).

[182] Dupuy (n. 83), at 72; F Francioni 'The Preamble of the Rio Declaration' in Viñuales (n. 181), at 89.

and civil society that are inspired by a vision of public trusteeship.[183] With regard to the intra-State dimension of benefit-sharing, the term 'partnership' specifically refers to an approach to accommodate State sovereignty over natural sovereignty and Indigenous peoples' self-determination.[184]

The verb 'sharing' also implies that while not every actor may play an active part in a certain activity that triggers benefit-sharing, everyone should have the opportunity to participate in some of the benefits derived from it.[185] This is probably the least studied aspect of the treaties that include benefit-sharing. Beyond a mere logic of exchange, benefit-sharing serves to recognize, reward, promote, and renew/strengthen the conditions for the production of global benefits (such as scientific advancements for global food security and global health) that derive from specific activities that trigger benefit-sharing among certain parties. As discussed later, however, international rules on benefit-sharing have predominantly developed with regard to the sharing of benefits among those directly participating in the triggering activity and often enshrine the underlying production of global benefits in the treaty's objective.[186] Therefore, exhortatory or interpretative references to global benefits may arguably express the intention of providing a benchmark to scrutinize the suitability of implementing measures in sharing benefits beyond the specific parties involved in a triggering activity.

Occasionally, however, specific obligations concern the sharing of global benefits deriving from specific triggering activities, in which case vulnerable beneficiaries tend to be privileged. For instance, the International Plant Treaty foresees that benefits deriving from the use of plant genetic resources for food and agriculture flow directly and indirectly to farmers in all countries, particularly in developing countries, irrespective of whether they have contributed relevant genetic material to the international community, according to internationally agreed upon eligibility and selection criteria.[187] In other regimes, however, these obligations remain much more indeterminate.[188]

3.1.1 Inter-State Benefit-Sharing

In the inter-State dimension, there appears to be two fundamental ways to share benefits among States—multilateral and bilateral—with the latter being a residual solution and the former being confined to specialized ambits of application. The multilateral sharing of benefits, which has been resorted to in the context of natural resource use

[183] P Sand, 'Cooperation in a Spirit of Global Partnership' in Viñuales (n. 181), 617, who refers as a concrete example to the ITPGRFA.

[184] M Fitzmaurice, 'The Question of Indigenous Peoples' Rights: A Time for Reappraisal?' in D French (ed.), *Statehood and Self-Determination: Reconciling Tradition and Modernity in International Law* (Hart, 2013) 349, at 375; Report of the Special Rapporteur on Indigenous Peoples' Rights (Indigenous Peoples' Rights Report), UN Doc A/HRC/12/34 (2010), para. 53.

[185] W Schabas, 'Study of the right to enjoy the benefits of scientific and technological progress and its applications' in Y Donders and V Volodin (eds), *Human Rights in Education, Science and Culture: Legal Developments and Challenges* (Ashgate Publishing, 2007), at 276, referring to the *traveaux préparatoires* of Art. 27(1) of the Universal Declaration on Human Rights.

[186] CBD, Art. 1; ITPRGFA, Art. 1; Nagoya Protocol, Art. 1.

[187] ITPGRFA, Art. 13(3) and Annexes 1–3 to the Funding Strategy in 2007; FAO, Report of the Governing Body of the International Treaty on Plant Genetic Resources for Food and Agriculture (2007).

[188] Nagoya Protocol, Art. 8(b).

within the common heritage regime and in specialized areas of bioprospecting, occurs through multilateral decision making within an international organization leading to the determination of standard contractual clauses. Under the law of the sea, benefits from the minerals in the deep seabed have been shared in this way,[189] and the development of precise rules and procedures has been left to the International Seabed Authority,[190] which eventually turn on contractual agreements with private contracts. Under the International Plant Treaty, a standard material transfer agreement has been agreed upon, with two mandatory monetary benefit-sharing options for the commercial use of a specified list of plant genetic resources for food and agriculture (such as rice, potatoes, and maize).[191] In these cases, the applicable multilateral decision-making rules determine how State parties arrive, through dialogue, at a concerted determination of the sharing modalities.[192]

Compared to the circumscribed areas of deep seabed minerals and plant genetic resources for food and agriculture, the bilateral sharing of benefits[193] is envisaged under the CBD[194] and its Nagoya Protocol[195] as a residual regime with regard to transboundary bioprospecting.[196] In this case, benefit-sharing is operationalized through ad hoc contractual negotiations ('mutually agreed terms'), instead of standard contractual terms decided by an international decision-making body.[197] Thus, treaties incorporating a bilateral approach leave national rules to govern the contracts. These treaties have so far not provided specific substantive criteria in this regard,[198] or created an international mechanism specifically aimed at overseeing how benefits are shared in specific cases.[199] While contractual negotiations may in principle also be seen as being a consensus-building, dialogic way to share benefits, leaving partnership building to contractual freedom raises concerns in the face of the well-documented, unequal bargaining powers at stake.[200] In partial recognition of this challenge in the bilateral context, the gradual development of international guidance (likely to be of a soft-law nature) on the terms of sharing is foreseen, in dialogue with non-State actors, but to a lesser extent than in treaties supporting multilateral benefit-sharing.[201]

[189] UNCLOS, Arts 136–141.

[190] ibid, Art. 160(2)(f)(i) and (g).

[191] ITPGRFA, Governing Body Res 2/2006 (2006).

[192] But also in the World Health Organization (WHO), Pandemic Influenza Preparedness Framework for the Sharing of Influenza Viruses and Access to Vaccines and Other Benefits, WHO Doc WHA64.5, 24 May 2011.

[193] Although note the possibility for a multilateral benefit-sharing mechanism to be established under the Nagoya Protocol, Art. 10: Morgera, Tsioumani, and Buck (n. 11), at 197–208.

[194] CBD, Art. 15(7). See also Agenda 21: Programme of Action for Sustainable Development, UN Doc A/Conf.151/26 (1992), paras 15(4)(d), 15(4)(j), and 16(7)(a).

[195] Nagoya Protocol, Art. 5.

[196] Morgera, Tsioumani, and Buck (n. 11), at 85.

[197] As is explicitly foreseen in CBD, Art. 15(7), last sentence, and the last sentence of Nagoya Protocol, Art. 5(1), where reference is made to 'mutually agreed terms'.

[198] Nagoya Protocol, Art. 5(1–2) and (5), 10th preambular recital. See Tvedt, 'Beyond Nagoya: Towards a Legally Functional System of Access and Benefit-Sharing' in S. Oberthür and K. Rosendal (eds), *Global Governance of Genetic Resources: Access and Benefit Sharing after the Nagoya Protocol* (2013) 158.

[199] Morgera, Tsioumani, and Buck (n. 11), at 282.

[200] ibid, at 7.

[201] Nagoya Protocol, Art. 30 and Decision NP-1/4 (2012); as well as Arts 19(2) and 20(2).

3.1.2 Intra-State Benefit-Sharing

With the exception of the Nagoya Protocol, which refers to mutually agreed terms,[202] international treaties on intra-State benefit-sharing do not elucidate in any comparable way to inter-State benefit-sharing described above, how sharing is to be undertaken. This may be explained by the fact that appropriate benefit-sharing systems have to be established 'on a case by case basis, taking into account the circumstances of the particular situation of the Indigenous peoples concerned'[203] and 'can take a variety of forms'.[204] In the context of both biodiversity and human rights, a (domestic) public law approach could be used to share benefits, either through direct payments or through the establishment of trust funds by the government.[205] It could also take the form of the legal recognition of communities' customary practices, participatory planning, and/or shared or delegated natural resource management.[206] In addition, benefits can be shared through practical cooperation and support from the government to communities, by sharing scientific information, building capacity, facilitating market access, and providing assistance in diversifying management capacities.[207] When the private sector is involved, however, a private law contractual approach is needed for setting up joint ventures and licences containing preferential conditions with communities,[208] although it is possible that governments could decide to set standard contractual terms in this regard.

Since all of these sharing modalities could be put in place in a top-down fashion with disruptive or divisive effects on beneficiary communities,[209] both international human rights and biodiversity instruments point to the need for the sharing of benefits to be culturally appropriate and endogenously identified.[210] In other words, even if treaty law leaves significant leeway to States in determining appropriate forms of sharing benefits with communities, culturally appropriate sharing would be difficult to ensure in the absence of a good faith, consensus-building process with communities. Similarly, international developments on 'business responsibility to respect human rights' have clarified that benefit-sharing, as part of the due diligence of companies

[202] Nagoya Protocol, Arts. 5(2) and 5(5). Contrast with CBD, Art. 8(j); ILO Convention No. 169, Art. 15(2).

[203] ILO, Monitoring Indigenous and Tribal Peoples' Rights through ILO Conventions: A Compilation of ILO Supervisory Bodies' Comments 2009–2010, Observation (Norway), Canadian Environmental Assessment Research Council 2009/80th session (2009), at 95.

[204] ILO, *Indigenous and Tribal Peoples' Rights in Practice: A Guide to ILO Convention No 169* (2009), at 107–108.

[205] CBD Secretariat (n. 83), para. 23; *Saramaka* (n. 18), para. 201.

[206] e.g. CBD, Work Programme on Protected Areas, Decision VII/28 (2004), paras 2(1)(3)–2(1)(5); CBD, Addis Ababa Principles and Guidelines on the Sustainable Use of Biodiversity, Decision VII/12 (2004), Annex II, operational guidelines to Principle 4; CBD, Expanded Work Programme on Forest Biodiversity, Decision VI/22 (2002), paras 13 and 31.

[207] Akwe: Kon Guidelines, CBD Decision VII/16C (2004), Annex para. 40.

[208] CBD, Guidelines on Biodiversity and Tourism, Decision V/25 (2000), para. 23; Addis Ababa Principles and Guidelines, Decision VII/12 (2004), operational guidelines to Principle 12.

[209] IACtHR, *Kichwa Indigenous Communitiy of Sarayaku v. Ecuador*, Judgment of 27 June 2012 (Merits and Reparations), para. 194; *Endorois* (n. 24), para. 274; CBD, Guidelines on Biodiversity and Tourism, para. II(27); PRAI, Principle 12.

[210] *Saramaka* (n. 18), para. 25; CBD Decision VII/11 (2004), Refinement and Elaboration of the Ecosystem Approach, Annex, paras 1(8) and 2(1); CBD, Tkarihwaié:ri Code of Ethical Conduct on Respect for the Cultural and Intellectual Heritage of Indigenous and Local Communities, Decision X/42 (2010), Annex, para. 14.

operating extractive projects in or near Indigenous territories, entails good faith consultations with communities with a view to agreeing on benefit-sharing modalities that make them partners in project decision making, rather than only giving them a share in the profits (for instance, through a minority ownership interest).[211]

3.2 Fairness and Equity

Benefit-sharing is accompanied by the qualification 'equitable'[212] or 'fair and equitable'[213] in all of the treaties referring to it.[214] Consequently, former UN Special Rapporteur on Indigenous Peoples' Rights James Anaya concluded that 'there is no specific international rule that guarantees benefit-sharing for Indigenous peoples, aside from the consideration that such sharing must be "fair and equitable"'.[215] This also seems to be the case for inter-State benefit-sharing. It is thus argued that the rationale for the emergence of benefit-sharing in international law is the operationalization of equity. In other words, benefit-sharing should be counted among the specific principles deriving from equity as a general principle of international law, which serves to balance competing rights and interests[216] with a view to integrating ideas of justice into a relationship regulated by international law[217] in the face of power asymmetries.[218]

International treaties that contain benefit-sharing, however, leave the specific determination of what is fair and equitable to successive multilateral negotiations (in the context of multilateral benefit-sharing mechanisms) and contextual negotiations, including contractual ones, in the context of bilateral inter-State benefit-sharing and of intra-State benefit-sharing. Thus, it may be necessary to rely on legal theory to further investigate this tenet of the proposed conceptualization. Building upon Roland Klager's insightful interpretation[219] of Thomas Franck's seminal work on equity in international law,[220] it can be argued that the use of the two expressions 'fair and equitable' serves to make explicit both procedural dimensions of justice (fairness) that determine the legitimacy of certain courses of action as well as the substantive dimensions of justice (equity).[221] And while these are inextricably linked notions, they

[211] Report of the Special Rapporteur on Indigenous Peoples' Rights (Indigenous Peoples' Rights Report), UN Doc A/HRC/15/37 (2010), para. 46; Rapporteur on Indigenous Peoples' Rights, Study on Extractive Industries and Indigenous Peoples, UN Doc A/HRC/24/41 (2013), para. 75.

[212] UNCLOS, Art. 140; CBD, Art. 8(j).

[213] CBD, 1 and 15(7); ITPGRFA, Arts. 1, 10(2), and 11(1); Nagoya Protocol, Arts 1 and 5.

[214] With the exception of the ILO Convention No. 169, references to fair and/or equitable benefit-sharing have been made by the: Committee on the Elimination of Racial Discrimination, Concluding Observations on Ecuador, UN Doc CERD/C/62/CO/2 (2003), para. 16; UNPFII, Report of the International Workshop on Methodologies Regarding Free, Prior Informed Consent and Indigenous Peoples, UN Doc E/C.19/2005/3 (2005), para. 46(e); Inter-AmCtHR, *Saramaka* (n. 18), para. 140 ('reasonable equitable'); and African Commission, *Endorois* (n. 24), paras 269 and 297.

[215] Report of the Special Rapporteur on Indigenous Peoples' Rights (Indigenous Peoples' Rights Report), UN Doc A/HRC/15/37 (2010), paras 67 and 76–78.

[216] Burke (n. 40), at 197–198.

[217] R Kläger, *Fair and Equitable Treatment in International Investment Law* (Cambridge University Press, 2013), at 130.

[218] Burke (n. 40), at 250–251.

[219] Kläger (n. 217), at 141–152.

[220] TM Franck, *Fairness in International Law and Institutions* (Clarendon Press, 1995).

[221] Kläger (n. 217), at 141.

also point to an inherent tension: fairness supports stability within the legal system (predictable and clear procedures), whereas equity tends towards change (recognition or enhanced realization of rights and the (re-)allocation of power over resources).[222]

This tension can only be resolved through a 'fairness discourse'—a negotiation 'premised on the moderate scarcity of the world's resources and existence of a global community sharing some basic perceptions of what is unconditionally unfair' and that at the very least allows for 'meaningful scrutiny of whether or not a certain conduct is ultimately fair'.[223] Within this discourse, two substantive conditions apply for determining what would be unconditionally unfair. First, a 'no-trumping' condition, whereby no participant can make claims that automatically prevail over the claims made by other participants.[224] Furthermore, this condition also notably applies to claims based on national sovereignty, thereby overriding presumptions in favour of States.[225] Second, a maximum condition, whereby inequalities in the substantive outcome of the discourse (i.e. the sharing of benefits) are only justifiable if they provide advantages to all participants.[226] In the words of Klager, therefore, the use of the expression 'fair and equitable' is 'an invitation by international law-makers to proceed by way of a fairness discourse based on a Socratic method'.[227] This argument resonates with and supports the earlier finding that 'sharing' conveys the idea of an iterative, concerted, and dialogic process aimed at reaching consensus among actors across power divides.

It should be further emphasized that similarly to other equitable principles, fair and equitable benefit-sharing is open-ended and evolutionary.[228] Consequently, while it does not open the door to subjective notions of justice,[229] it can be filled with content by establishing a linkage with different international legal subsystems (through systemic integration[230] or mutually supportive law-making).[231] In this connection, it is instructive to consider the evolution of the similarly worded notion of fair and equitable treatment in international investment law,[232] for which the meaning of 'fair and equitable' was—similarly to benefit-sharing—not clarified in the relevant treaties. International adjudication has instead fleshed out fair and equitable treatment by relying on international human rights law notions such as procedural fairness,

[222] ibid, at 121, 123, and 130.

[223] ibid, at 144.

[224] ibid, at 163.

[225] Burke (n. 40), at 250.

[226] Kläger (n. 217), at 145.

[227] ibid, at 146.

[228] *United States – Import Prohibition on Certain Shrimp and Shrimp Products – Report of the Appellate Body*, 6 November 1998, WT/DS58/AB/R, para. 130. Kläger (n. 217), at 109; McLachlan (n. 175), at 302 and 312.

[229] It is not an expression of equity as decisions are made *ex aequo et bono*. Statute of the International Court of Justice (San Francisco, 26 June 1945, in force 24 October 1945), Art. 38(2).

[230] *North Sea Continental Shelf Cases*, Judgment, 20 February 1969, ICJ Reports 3, para. 88; R Wolfrum, 'General International Law (Principles, Rules and Standards)', in Wolfrum (n. 122), 344, para. 63; HWA Thirlway, *The Sources of International Law* (Oxford University Press, 2014), at 106.

[231] R Pavoni, 'Mutual Supportiveness as a Principle of Interpretation and Law-Making: A Watershed for the WTO-and-Competing-Regimes Debate?' (2010) 21 European Journal of International Law 649, at 649.

[232] The suggestion to draw on the evolution of fair and equitable treatment to better understand fair and equitable benefit-sharing was put forward by F Francioni, 'International Law for Biotechnology: Basic Principles' in F Francioni and T Scovazzi (eds), *Biotechnology and International Law* (Hart, 2006) 3, at 24.

non-discrimination, and proportionality.[233] The emerging cross-fertilization between international biodiversity and human rights law in relation to benefit-sharing may, similarly, be part of a 'global discursive practice of mutual learning'[234] with regard to equity and fairness that has so far elicited little attention across different areas of international law and legal scholarship.

3.3 Benefits

International treaties containing benefit-sharing obligations define the nature of the benefits to be shared to various degrees. The Nagoya Protocol is the only instrument that provides a detailed (non-exhaustive) list of benefits that may apply to both intra-State and inter-State benefit-sharing.[235] In all of these cases, a menu of benefits to be shared is offered, the nature of which is invariably both economic and non-economic. This choice arguably allows the consideration, through the concerted, dialogic process of sharing, of the beneficiaries' needs, values, and priorities, so that they can exercise agency in a relationship of power imbalance, and possibly their 'different understandings of justice', with a view to selecting the combination of benefits that forms the basis of the partnership.[236] While the nature of the benefits is predominantly defined with regard to the parties involved in the triggering activity, several immediate benefits shared among them are meant to preserve, restore, or enhance the conditions under which underlying global benefits (such as ecosystem services) are produced. The benefits to be shared are thus seen as contributing to human well-being.[237] That said, the interplay and tensions between economic and non-economic benefits, as well as between their immediate and global relevance, remain unclear and contentious.

The possibility of choosing among monetary and non-monetary benefits has the advantage of allowing the distribution of more immediately available (generally non-monetary) benefits while the monetary benefits are being accrued (although the challenge of obtaining stable financing, generally through voluntary contributions, for sharing non-monetary benefits may still be a significant issue). Non-monetary benefits are also aimed at increasing the capabilities of those countries unable to directly participate in the triggering activity.

In the case of the law of the sea, the nature of the benefits has become clear with practice. While the International Seabed Authority (ISA) is still working out how

[233] PM Dupuy and J Viñuales, 'Human Rights and Investment Disciplines: Integration in Progress' in M Bungenberg et al. (eds), *International Investment Law: A Handbook* (CH Beck, 2015) 1739.

[234] G Pentassuglia, 'Towards a Jurisprudential Articulation of Indigenous Land Rights' (2011) 22 European Journal of International Law 165, at 201.

[235] Nagoya Protocol, Art. 5(4) and Annex. The distinction between monetary and non-monetary benefits has emerged in the CBD's Bonn Guidelines on Access and Benefit-sharing and the Nagoya Protocol. See L Glowka and V Normand, 'The Nagoya Protocol on Access and Benefit-Sharing: Innovations in International Environmental Law' in Morgera, Buck, and Tsioumani (n. 77), 21, at 23.

[236] K Simm, 'Benefit-Sharing: An Inquiry Regarding the Meaning and Limits of the Concept of Human Genetic Research' (2005) 1 Genomics, Society and Policy 29, at 29–30.

[237] Report of the Special Rapporteur in the field of cultural rights Shaheed: the right to enjoy the benefits of scientific progress and its applications, UN Doc A/HRC/20/26 (2012), para. 22; *Endorois* (n. 24), paras 278–279; and ILO Conference 87th Session 1999, Report III (Part 1a), at 434.

to share monetary benefits from mining in the Area, as expressly provided for by UNCLOS,[238] it has already regulated the sharing of non-monetary benefits such as training, capacity building, scientific information, and cooperation,[239] which is implicit in the common heritage concept.[240] In addition, the ISA has created an endowment fund for marine scientific research in the Area,[241] which was initially filled with the balance of the application fees paid by pioneer investors and is currently dependent on donations.[242]

Along similar lines, under the International Plant Treaty, a benefit-sharing fund is at present filled with donations in order to contribute to capacity building and technology transfer,[243] as monetary benefits have been defined (as a percentage of the gross sales of the commercialization of products), but not yet materialized.[244] The challenges in accruing monetary benefits under the International Plant Treaty—the most sophisticated international benefit-sharing mechanism to date—cast a shadow over the feasibility of monetary benefit-sharing under other less sophisticated regimes such as the Nagoya Protocol (which identifies monetary benefits as profits in the form of access fees, up-front or milestone payments, royalties, or licence fees).[245]

Other significant benefits have also been identified by the CBD, including participation in biotechnological research and access to the results of that research.[246] These benefits were expanded upon in the Nagoya Protocol to include participation in product development and admittance to ex situ facilities and databases,[247] joint ventures with foreign researchers, and joint ownership of relevant intellectual property rights (IPRs).[248] While questions related to IPRs remain controversial and well studied, the trade-offs among different forms of non-monetary benefits have not been fully analysed.[249] Non-monetary benefits such as technology transfer and capacity building can be essential to enhance the ability of beneficiaries to share in monetary benefits in the long term,[250] and, in addition, they may facilitate agency in developing technology.

[238] UNCLOS, Art. 140. E Morgera and H Lily, 'Public Participation at the International Seabed Authority – an International Human Rights Analysis' (2022) 31 Review of European, Comparative and International Environmental Law 374.

[239] Harrison (n. 70).

[240] R Wolfrum, 'Common Heritage of Mankind', in Wolfrum (n. 122), 452, paras 18–19; M Lodge, 'The Common Heritage of Mankind' (2012) 27 International Journal of Marine and Coastal Law 733, at 740.

[241] ISA Assembly, Resolution Establishing an Endowment Fund for Marine Scientific Research in the Area, Doc ISBA/12/A/11 (2006).

[242] Harrison (n. 70).

[243] Tsioumani (n. 100), at 31–33.

[244] N Moeller and C Stannard (eds), *Identifying Benefit Flows: Studies on the Potential Monetary and Non-Monetary Benefits Arising from the International Treaty on Plant Genetic Resources for Food and Agriculture* (FAO, 2013).

[245] Nagoya Protocol, Annex, 1(a–e).

[246] CBD, Arts 1, 15(5), 16, and 19.

[247] Nagoya Protocol, Annex, 2(a–c), I.

[248] ibid, Annex, 1(i) and (j).

[249] For this very reason, the question was eventually set aside in the negotiations of the Nagoya Protocol. See the discussion by R Pavoni, 'The Nagoya Protocol and WTO Law', in Morgera, Buck, and Tsioumani (n. 77), 185, at 200–205.

[250] e.g. Nagoya Protocol, preambular recitals 5, 7, and 14.

3.4 Beneficiaries

Fair and equitable benefit-sharing primarily (albeit, not exclusively) targets vulnerable beneficiaries, notably developing countries, Indigenous peoples, and local communities. It should also be noted that these conceptual difficulties add to the immense practical challenges in the contextual identification of beneficiaries within groups (of both State and non-State actors) that are non-homogenous and whose circumstances vary significantly across time and space. In this connection, the co-identification of beneficiaries and the connected risks of exclusion are tightly linked to the concerted and dialogic process of sharing discussed above and to the purposes of realizing fairness and equity discussed below.

The international treaties that include intra-State benefit-sharing obligations refer to beneficiaries in different terms, although they all place special emphasis on developing countries. Under UNCLOS, benefits should be shared with humankind without discrimination but 'taking into particular consideration the interests and needs of developing States'.[251] Similarly, the International Plant Treaty foresees benefit-sharing with all parties, specifically pointing to developing countries as beneficiaries of technology transfer, capacity building, and the allocation of commercial benefits.[252] Along similar lines, under the CBD and the Nagoya Protocol, beneficiaries are the 'provider countries' with the understanding that all countries can be both users and providers of genetic resources,[253] but provisions on technology transfer, funding, and sharing of biotechnological innovation specifically target developing countries.[254]

In both international biodiversity and human rights law, intra-State benefit-sharing most clearly targets Indigenous and tribal peoples as beneficiaries,[255] but also non-Indigenous local communities[256] in as far as their human rights to subsistence and culture[257] may be negatively affected by interferences with their customary relations with land and natural resources.[258] Along similar lines, the International Plant Treaty considers 'farmers' to be beneficiaries,[259] and recent international soft law initiatives have expanded the meaning of beneficiaries to include 'tenure right holders' (i.e. those having a formal or informal right to access land and other natural resources for the realization of their human rights to an adequate standard of living and well-being)[260] and small-scale fishing communities.[261] The latter, incidentally, appears to point to the

[251] UNCLOS, Arts 140 and 160(2)(f)(i).

[252] ITPGRFA, Art. 13(2)(b)(ii-iii), 13(2)(c), 13(4).

[253] CBD Decision VII/19 (2004), 16th preambular recital.

[254] CBD, Arts 16(3), 19(1–2), and 20(5), (7); Nagoya Protocol, Arts 8(a–b), 22–23, and 25(3–4).

[255] CBD, Art. 8(j); Nagoya Protocol, Art. 5(2) and (5); ILO Convention No. 169, Art. 15(2); *Saramaka* (n. 18); *Endorois* (n. 24).

[256] Morgera, Tsioumani, and Buck (n. 11), at 383.

[257] A Bessa, 'Traditional Local Communities in International Law' (PhD dissertation, European University Institute, 2013); inconclusive CBD Decision XI/14 (2012).

[258] O De Schutter, 'The Emerging Human Right to Land' (2010) 12 International Community Law Review 303, at 324–325 and 319.

[259] ITPGRFA, Art. 9.2: see generally E Tsioumani, *Fair and Equitable Benefit-sharing in Agriculture: Reinventing Agrarian Justice* (Routledge, 2022).

[260] VGGT (n. 110), Art. 8.6.

[261] FAO, Voluntary Guidelines for Securing Sustainable Small-scale Fisheries in the Context of Food Security and Poverty Eradication (2013), para. 5.1.

emergence of intra-State benefit-sharing under the law of the sea.[262] This is confirmed in the 2023 Agreement on Biodiversity of Areas Beyond National Jurisdiction, with regard to Indigenous and local knowledge holders.[263]

4. Aims and Approach to the Study of Fair and Equitable Benefit-Sharing

Against the backdrop of the history, conceptual distinctions, and normative areas of convergence of fair and equitable benefit-sharing in different areas of international law outlined in previous sections, this book seeks to provide the first systematic analysis of fair and equitable benefit-sharing from the perspective of general international law. It builds on an original comparison of international law-making and implementation practices across different regimes in the areas of international environmental law, international human rights law, and international law of the sea.[264]

Understanding more systematically fair and equitable benefit-sharing from the combined perspectives of different areas of international law that are increasingly interacting with one another, seeks to shift the investigation from current sectoral/technical approaches to the perspective of general international law, with a view to overcoming the limitations inherent in individual international regimes and addressing the shortcomings in benefit-sharing implementation that have arisen. In addition, a more general reflection can contribute to future research in other areas such as international health law,[265] international law on outer space,[266] and international economic law.[267]

[262] Note that intra-State benefit-sharing could also arise in the context of the negotiations on marine biodiversity in areas beyond national jurisdiction with regard to the use of traditional knowledge. Submission from the Federated States of Micronesia (14 March 2016), para. 8, available at http://www.un.org/depts/los/biodiversity/prepcom_files/Federated_States_of_Micronesia.pdf, accessed 25 June 2023.

[263] BBNJ Agreement, Arts 7(j) and (k), 13, 19(3), 24(3), 31(1)(a)(ii), 35, 37(4)(a), 41(2), 48(3), 49(2), and 51(3)(c).

[264] There are currently no books focusing on fair and equitable benefit-sharing from a general international law perspective, or from the combined perspectives of international environmental law, international human rights law, and the international law of the sea. There are several monographs and edited collections on fair and equitable benefit-sharing in international biodiversity law, which take a narrow approach to the subject-matter and are predominantly aimed at specialized international law scholars and practitioners, such as: Kamau and Winter (n. 15); EC Kamau and G Winter (eds), *Common Pools of Genetic Resources Equity and Innovation in International Biodiversity Law* (Edward Elgar, 2013) R Wynberg, D Schroeder, and R. Chennells (eds), *Indigenous Peoples, Consent and Benefit Sharing: Lessons from the San-Hoodia Case* (Springer, 2009); M Ruiz and R Vernooy (eds), *The Custodians of Biodiversity: Sharing Access to and Benefits of Genetic Resources* (Earthscan, 2012); B Fedder, *Marine Genetic Resources, Access and Benefit-Sharing* (Routledge, 2013).

[265] There is already a body of research on benefit-sharing in this area, but with limited engagement with other areas of international law. M Wilke, 'A Healthy Look at the Nagoya Protocol: Implications for Global Health Governance' in Morgera, Buck, and Tsioumani (n. 77), 123.

[266] See n. 17.

[267] There appears to be no literature examining the impact (or lack thereof) on international economic law of the UN General Assembly's calls for sharing the benefits of globalization. See, e.g. Res 63/230: Second UN Decade for the Eradication of Poverty (2008–2017), para. 12 or earlier references to benefit-sharing in the Charter of Economic Rights and Duties of States, GA Res 29/3281, 12 December 1974, Art. 10.

4.1 Mutually Supportive Interpretation of International Biodiversity and Human Rights Law

A recurrent question that will be analysed in this book is the relevance of international human rights law in all these configurations, noting in particular the complexities of applying international human rights law in the inter-State context. In that connection, a paradox should be kept in mind. Even if earlier references to benefit-sharing can be found in various areas of international law, conceptualizing benefit-sharing today should take international biodiversity law as a reference point in its interactions with international human rights law. The reasons for this stance is that the CBD has contributed to significant normative development of benefit-sharing, gradually building consensus[268] among 196 parties on both its inter- and intra-State dimensions across different triggering activities (bioprospecting, the use of knowledge, and natural resource management).[269] International human rights law has focused mainly on intra-State benefit-sharing and on a narrower range of triggers, which may explain the explicit reliance by international human rights bodies on the normative development of benefit-sharing under the CBD.[270] In turn, the law of the sea has focused on inter-State benefit-sharing.

The value of the CBD to provide relevant and applicable norms for the interpretation of other international treaties through systemic integration[271] is often underestimated. The CBD's membership is virtually global, and its subject matter is remarkably wide: it covers the variability of life on earth,[272] non-living resources that form part of ecosystems,[273] and all human activities that may affect biodiversity conservation as a common concern of humankind.[274] Admittedly, however, the open-ended and heavily qualified rules contained in the CBD may not, in and of themselves, provide sufficient guidance to the interpreter. Decisions of the CBD's COP,[275] as subsequent practice establishing agreement on the interpretation[276] of relevant CBD rules on benefit-sharing, need to be relied upon.[277] Notwithstanding the continued reluctance

[268] On the law-making power of consensus, see A Boyle and C Chinkin, *The Making of International Law* (Oxford University Press, 2007), at 260.

[269] The whole international community is party to the CBD, with the notable exception of the United States.

[270] e.g. CBD Art. 8(j) was relied upon in Review of Developments pertaining to the Promotion and Protection of Human Rights and Fundamental Freedoms of Indigenous Peoples, UN Doc E/CN.4/Sub.2/AC.4/2001/2 (2001), para. 15. CBD, Akwé: Kon Voluntary Guidelines, Decision VII/16C (2004), Annex was relied upon as a pre-condition for benefit-sharing by the Inter-American Court of Human Rights in *Saramaka* (n. 18), para. 41; by the UN Special Rapporteur on Indigenous Peoples' Rights, UN Doc A/HRC/15/37 (2010), para. 73; and by the UN Expert Mechanism on the Rights of Indigenous Peoples, UN Doc A/HRC/15/35 (2010), para. 37, which also referred to the CBD, Work Programme on Protected Areas, Decision VII/28 (2004).

[271] Vienna Convention on the Law of Treaties (VCLT) (Vienna, 23 May 1969, in force 27 January 1980), Art. 31(3)(c).

[272] See the definition of biological diversity under CBD Art. 2.

[273] See the definition of ecosystems under CBD Art. 2.

[274] CBD, preambular, para. 3.

[275] J Brunnée, 'COP-ing with Consent: Law-Making under Multilateral Environmental Agreements' (2002) 15 Leiden Journal of International Law 1.

[276] VCLT, Art. 31(3)(b): First and Second Report on Subsequent Agreements and Subsequent Practice in Relation to Treaty Interpretation, UN Doc A/Cn.4/660 (2013) and UN Doc A/CN.4/671 (2014).

[277] Morgera and Tsioumani (n. 151).

to use explicit human rights language,[278] this normative activity has contributed to clarifying the implications of the CBD obligations for the protection of the human rights of Indigenous peoples and other communities in the context of the technicalities of environmental decision making and management processes.[279]

Despite this, relevant interpretative guidance is dispersed in a myriad of CBD decisions and has not been subject to any significant monitoring or compliance processes, which explains why the status and broad implications of relevant and applicable CBD rules on benefit-sharing have not been appreciated.[280] In addition, there is some scope for concern about the position of certain CBD Parties with regard to human rights:[281] the CBD has provided a forum in which States' reticence on certain human rights questions has emerged.[282] Negotiations under the CBD, for instance, highlighted continued opposition to the right to 'free prior informed consent' of Indigenous peoples[283] and tepid language merely 'noting'[284] the relevance of the UN Declaration on the Rights of Indigenous Peoples, notwithstanding its intervening universal endorsement.[285] And yet, even in the face of continued reluctance by some CBD Parties to use explicit human rights language,[286] international human rights bodies have recognized that the CBD COP normative activity has contributed to clarifying the application of Indigenous peoples' human rights, including for the purposes of business due diligence.[287] These tensions will be analysed in detail in the following chapters.

The ecosystem approach has provided a conceptual and normative basis for the CBD COP to address questions arising in other international environmental agreements,

278 E Morgera, 'Against All Odds: The Contribution of the Convention on Biological Diversity to International Human Rights Law' in D Alland et al. (eds), *Unity and Diversity of International Law. Essays in Honour of Professor Pierre-Marie Dupuy* (Martinus Nijhoff, 2014) 983. Kumming-Montreal Global Biodiversity Framework 2021–2030, CBD Decision 15/4 (2022), paras 7(a), 7(g), and Target 22.

279 Morgera (n. 278).

280 Morgera and Tsioumani (n. 151), at 23–25.

281 For instance, the more significant CBD provision from a human rights perspective (Art. 8(j) on traditional knowledge) is heavily qualified, notably by a clause 'subjecting' it to 'national law'. Subjecting compliance with international law as expressed in the CBD to national law was considered unusual at the time of the Convention's adoption but has become a common feature in the development of soft law under the CBD. This type of reference to national law seems to point to the negotiators' intention to preserve the legal relationship between a State and the Indigenous peoples within its territory based on pre-existing, but possibly also future, national law. L Glowka et al., *A Guide to the Convention on Biological Diversity* (IUCN, 1994), at 48–49.

282 Indigenous peoples' representatives and the UN Special Rapporteur on Indigenous Peoples' Rights, expressed disappointment that negotiations of a new legally binding protocol under the CBD did not sufficiently respect Indigenous peoples' rights: Report of the Special Rapporteur on the Rights of Indigenous Peoples to the General Assembly, UN Doc A/67/301 (2012), para. 58.

283 Resulting in the adoption of the ambiguous expression 'prior informed consent or approval and involvement' in the Nagoya Protocol, Art. 7. Note that the UN Permanent Forum on Indigenous Issues noted that the term 'consultation' cannot replace or undermine the right of Indigenous peoples to prior informed consent: UNPFII (n. 56), para. 36.

284 Nagoya Protocol, preambular recital 26.

285 The adoption of the Declaration by the General Assembly was initially opposed by Australia, Canada, the United States, and New Zealand. All these countries had reversed their position by 2010 (see UN Office of the High Commissioner for Human Rights, press release 'Indigenous rights declaration endorsed by States' (23 December 2010).

286 Morgera (n. 278), at 983.

287 See generally E Morgera 'Dawn of a New Day? The Evolving Relationship between the Convention on Biological Diversity and International Human Rights Law' (2018) 54 Wake Forest Law Review 691–712.

thereby serving to ensure mutual supportiveness among them[288] as well as a basis to expand relevant science to socio-cultural dimensions with international human rights law.[289] Thus, on the basis of the ascertained limitations of extant international law on benefit-sharing, this book proposes an evolutive interpretation of benefit-sharing across the examined regimes that is based on mutually supportive interpretation of international biodiversity and human rights law. This is substantiated on the findings that international biodiversity law has provided the most sophisticated consensus guidance on the operationalization of benefit-sharing in the context of the governance of natural resources (and related knowledge) taking into account ecosystem services. In turn, international human rights law has clarified the minimum content of international benefit-sharing obligations, both substantively and procedurally, thereby providing a clearer sense of the limitations of State discretion in exercising sovereignty over natural resources.

The opportunities for cross-compliance that synergize the normative detail of international biodiversity law and the justiciability of international human rights remains to be critically assessed. So too are the tensions between different premises and interpretative approaches in these two areas of law, including in light of perceived 'unrealistic expectations regarding the conservationist behaviour of Indigenous peoples [that] may have detrimental consequences for the recognition and respect of their rights'.[290] In addition, as clearly demonstrated by the debate on IPRs, international economic law may present opportunities and challenges concerning the realization of fair and equitable benefit-sharing both from an environmental and human rights perspective.[291] In particular, the growing relevance of fair and equitable benefit-sharing to natural resource use, including in relation to the responsibility of businesses to respect human rights, highlights the need to fully investigate opportunities and tensions with international investment law.[292]

Three lenses will enrich this doctrinal analysis. First, treaties and other international frameworks will be understood as 'incompletely theorized agreements',[293] due to the ongoing (re)elaboration of fair and equitable benefit-sharing approaches in various areas of international law. Second, treaties and other international frameworks will be understood as integral components of global law—a 'heavily overlapping, mutually connected and openly extended' pattern of normative developments.[294] This will require a selective reading of the sources of international law, their areas of impact, and their perceived limits, with a view to determining evolving trends and understanding the 'capacity of law, drawing upon deep historical resources, to recast the ways in which

[288] See generally Pavoni (n. 231).

[289] Morgera (n. 278), at 983.

[290] Desmet (n. 61), at 41.

[291] See, e.g., LR Helfer, 'Toward a Human Rights Framework for Intellectual Property' (2007) 40 University of California Davis Law Review 971.

[292] So far, benefit-sharing and investment have only been researched in the context of bioprospecting: J Viñuales, *Foreign Investment and the Environment in International Law* (Oxford University Press, 2012), chapter 8.

[293] CR Sunstein, 'Incompletely Theorized Agreements' (2005) 108 Harvard Law Review 1733; S Switzer, 'Liminal Spaces: Special and Differential Treatment as an Incompletely Theorized Agreement' (2018) 15 Manchester Journal of International Economic Law 62.

[294] N Walker, *The Intimations of Global Law* (Cambridge University Press, 2015), at 11–12.

it addresses some of the problems of an interconnected world'.[295] Third, reflections on equity in international law will be connected with the ongoing scholarly debate on environmental justice, as fair and equitable benefit-sharing appears to respond (at least in principle) to multiple dimensions of justice, which in turn can support a variety of interpretations and applications. Ultimately, legal analyses of benefit-sharing still remain systematically connected to ongoing theoretical discussions of different concepts of justice and possible trade-offs among them,[296] emphasizing interpretations that support coherence in international law. These three lenses will be introduced in the following subsections.

4.2 Incompletely Theorized Agreements

As Sustain and colleagues have explained, the concept of incompletely theorized agreements captures the phenomenon that an agreement is reached on a principle without the parties necessarily agreeing on what it entails in a particular case. So the agreement is 'incompletely specified' allowing for stability and flexibility over time, while concealing disagreement regarding specific cases.[297] Fuller theorization, on the other hand, would illuminate problems, bias, confusion, or inconsistency,[298] thereby potentially leading to unnecessary antagonism.[299] Therefore, this concept serves to explain agreement on fundamental principles that is achievable by offering 'relatively narrow or low-level explanations of it'.[300] This may be because 'relevant actors are *clear on the result* without being clear, either in their own minds or on paper, on the most general theory that accounts for it'.[301] Actors would still articulate reasons for their differing positions but are unable or unwilling to choose between them due to the diversity of international community members who may try to 'live together, avoid error to the extent possible and show each other mutual respect'.[302] Ultimately, incomplete theorization allows for the continuation of mutual respect and cooperation while allowing for 'moral evolution over time' and 'openness to new facts and perspectives'[303] that can help address the areas of persistent disagreement.

This perspective allows for the investigation as to what extent international benefit-sharing provisions are under-developed because of: (1) lack of consensus due to fundamentally divergent agendas, as well as power and information asymmetries, among States (and how this divergence has affected ensuing implementation practices); and (2) objective difficulties in fully theorizing benefit-sharing as a novel legal approach to a more intense and cosmopolitan form of cooperation (and how this has led to the

[295] ibid, at 11–12, 14, 112–113, and 152.
[296] E Morgera, 'Justice, Equity and Benefit-Sharing under the Nagoya Protocol to the Convention on Biological Diversity (2015) 24 Italian Yearbook of International Law 113, at 113.
[297] Sunstein (n. 293), at 1739.
[298] ibid, at 1745.
[299] ibid, at 1746.
[300] ibid, at 1736.
[301] ibid, at 1737 (emphasis added).
[302] ibid, at 1739.
[303] ibid, at 1749.

creation of spaces for gradual development through learning by different actors at different levels, and across different regimes).

The lens of incomplete theorization will be applied first to systematically analyse the limitations of extant international law to prevent benefit-sharing practices on the ground from achieving equity objectives or even contributing to documented injustices such as loss of control over resources and knowledge by vulnerable groups.[304] Second, the positive side of incomplete theorization will help identify actual and potential opportunities for different international benefit-sharing regimes to build on one another's lessons learnt from a practical perspective, as well as contribute to a mutual supportiveness from a normative perspective.

4.3 Global Law

Following Neil Walker's reflection on global law,[305] this book will analyse fair and equitable benefit-sharing through the 'iterative, reflexive, and decentralized approaches' that are increasingly relied upon in the development and implementation of international law.[306] In effect, understanding fair and equitable benefit-sharing in international law is only part of the picture, as it is also shaped by national laws, private law contracts, corporate codes of responsible conduct, protocols developed by Indigenous peoples or local communities, eligibility requirements for international funding, and project-specific guidelines—and by reciprocal interactions among all these elements.[307]

In line with Walker's understanding of global law scholarship, this book thus attempts to 'gauge incipient trends and articulate future projections, as part of an iterative process of mapping, scanning, schematizing, and (re)framing' legal phenomena related to benefit-sharing,[308] with a view to understanding the 'capacity of law, drawing upon deep historical resources, to recast the ways in which it addresses some of the problems of an interconnected world'.[309]

To that end, the broader global law scholarship has drawn on the multi-disciplinary literature on norm diffusion, which can support the understanding of how benefit-sharing has become embedded in various contexts, while developing an awareness of the role of power and politics in this connection.[310] As William Twining[311] discussed, the sociological and constructivist international relations literature on norm diffusion helps to acknowledge the inherently political nature of studying norms as discourses (since discourses are necessarily displaced in these processes),[312] the role

[304] A Martin et al., 'Just Conservation? On the Fairness of Sharing Benefits' in Sikor (n. 2), at 84–88; Wynberg and Hauck (n. 1).

[305] Walker (n. 294), at 11–12, 14, 112–113, and 152.

[306] ibid, at 108.

[307] E Morgera, 'Global Environmental Law and Comparative Legal Methods' (2015) 24 Review of European Comparative and International Environmental Law 254.

[308] ibid, at 25–26, 112, and 143.

[309] ibid, at 110.

[310] Parks and Morgera (n. 3), at 365.

[311] W Twining, 'Social Science and Diffusion of Law' (2005) 32 Journal of Law & Society 203.

[312] S Engelkamp, K Glaab, and J Renner, 'Office Hours: How (Critical) Norm Research Can Regain its Voice' (2014) 10 World Political Science Review 33.

of actors—notably norm entrepreneurs[313]—(and their framing work) implicit in an acknowledgement of politics in order to avoid neglecting bottom-up perspectives in legal research. Twining demonstrates that the concept of norm diffusion is particularly apt to better understand the relations and mutual interactions between different levels of legal ordering (which are not necessarily static or clearly defined) of human relations at different geographical levels,[314] cautioning against 'naïve' and State-focused models focusing on the transplantation of law from developed to developing countries.[315] Awareness of bias, such as the assumption that all objects of diffusion are desirable, progressive, or innovative, or the assumption that all examples of diffusion of law fit neatly into a means-end, problem-solving framework, is thus called for.[316] This entails a move away from assumptions of the superiority or efficiency of norms that diffuse towards a logic where norms spread because they are seen to be appropriate in a specific context.[317]

There are a range of potential paths along which the norm of benefit-sharing may travel—from the top down, from the bottom up, or horizontally.[318] It is important to understand these paths, as discussions on benefit-sharing are ongoing, and therefore under social construction.[319] What today appears as an international legal concept of fair and equitable benefit-sharing may have originated elsewhere, for instance in the practices of Indigenous peoples and local communities at the local level[320] and it is continually influenced by legal developments and practices across scales. Depending on the different paths and actors involved, the framing of benefit-sharing can vary. Framing, as already mentioned, thus complements and strengthens studies of norm diffusion, as it provides tools for unpacking the different interpretations and meanings that may be attributed to a legal norm in different locations.[321]

Framing serves to reflect on the fact that 'meanings do not automatically or naturally attach themselves to the objects, events, or experiences we encounter, but often arise, instead, through interactively based interpretive processes'.[322] Benford and Snow provide key research tools on framing work: *articulation*, that is, 'the connection and alignment of events and experiences so that they hang together in a relatively unified and compelling fashion';[323] or *amplification*, stressing the importance of certain issues, events, or beliefs in order to increase salience. *Salience*, or *resonance*, is in turn what causes frames to be taken up by other actors.[324] Frame qualities affecting

313 EM Hafner-Burton et al., 'Political Science Research on International Law: The State of the Field' (2012) 106 American Journal of International Law 47.
314 ibid.
315 Twining (n. 311), at 203–205.
316 ibid.
317 Parks and Morgera (n. 3).
318 W Twining, 'Diffusion of Law: A Global Perspective' (2004) 36 Journal of Legal Pluralism 1, at 14.
319 Parks and Morgera (n. 3).
320 See, e.g., B Weston and D Bollier, *Green Governance: Ecological Survival, Human Rights and the Law of the Commons* (Cambridge University Press, 2013), at 221 and 237.
321 Parks and Morgera (n. 3).
322 DA Snow, 'Framing Processes, Ideology, and Discursive Fields' in DA Snow, SA Soule, and H Kriesi (eds), *The Blackwell Companion to Social Movements* (Blackwell, 2004), at 380.
323 RD Benford and DA Snow, 'Framing Processes and Social Movements: An Overview and Assessment' (2000) 26 Annual Review of Sociology 611, at 623.
324 ibid.

resonance include frame makers (their credibility), frame receivers (their beliefs and values), and the frame itself (cultural compatibility, consistency and relevance).[325] Accordingly, fair and equitable benefit-sharing can be studied as a frame for *articulation*, in that it connects ideas of equity and fairness in an arguably persuasive fashion. This is with a view to highlighting certain aspects of the norm that align with other norms already well embedded in a specific context (which could be anything from a village to an international organization) in order to secure the significance of the new norm. Benefit-sharing can also be seen as a frame for *amplification*, as it stresses the positive implications (rather than burdens and costs) of environmental cooperation in order to make this more salient. In either case, these efforts may fail, leaving room for the relabelling of an existing local norm (and thus the diversification of meaning attached to the norm) or indeed diffusion in a different direction, for example from the local to the international level, and subsequent re-definition of the meaning of the norm in another location.[326]

In the following chapters, the global law lens will allow reflection on fair and equitable benefit-sharing, as it finds itself 'somewhere between settled doctrine and an aspirational approach'.[327] The following chapters will discuss benefit-sharing as both 'framed' in different ways in different law-making contexts, and as a way of 'framing' the search for equitable responses to environmental challenges, namely by emphasizing the need to focus on benefits as opposed to burdens.[328] It has already been noted that benefit-sharing provides a 'social justice frame' to address questions of environmental management,[329] seeking to reconcile competing State and community interests by focusing attention on the *advantages* that derive from environmental protection and regulation, thereby facilitating shared understandings of benefits and allowing.[330] So far, however, the literature on benefit-sharing, while already making explicit reference to framing, predominantly points to a degree of confusion in the plethora of frames surrounding benefit-sharing and insufficient rigour in linking these frames to different notions of justice.[331] This is also one of the major shortcomings of global (environmental) law scholarship.[332] This book will therefore seek to explore equity from an international law perspective in a dialogue with literature on environmental justice (discussed below).

As Teubner has emphasized, the ambition of global law scholars to offer more than the impartial representation of observed facts and instead contribute to a transformative agenda[333] is an integral element of this book. In acknowledgement of the potential

[325] H Johnston and JA Noakes, *Frames of Protest: Social Movements and the Framing Perspective* (Palgrave Macmillan, 2005), at 12–16.

[326] Parks and Morgera (n. 3).

[327] ibid, at 18 and 21.

[328] ibid.

[329] See S McCool, 'Distributing the Benefits of Nature's Bounty: a Social Justice Perspective', Unpublished paper presented at the International Symposium on Managing Benefit Sharing in Changing Social Ecological Systems, Windhoek, Namibia, 2012.

[330] Sadoff and Grey (n. 6), at 420.

[331] McCool (n. 329).

[332] N Walker, 'The Gap between Global Law and Global Justice: A Preliminary Analysis', Edinburgh Law School Working Papers No. 2016/30 (SSRN, 2016), available at https://papers.ssrn.com/sol3/papers.cfm?abstract_id=2888557, accessed 26 June 2023.

[333] Global law, according to Walker, is 'an adjectival rather than a nominal category' that 'does not specify any particular source or pedigree, and so may account for itself in many different ways and may claim or

bias of global environmental law scholarship, this book will express awareness of the legitimacy implications of this project, and engage in self-reflection of the scholar's role, influence, and potential blind spots[334] that derive from professional experience, institutional culture and status, and the participation in epistemic networks. These factors are increasingly recognized as key determinants of international environmental law as a transnational and global legal field,[335] rather than an inherently universal and cosmopolitan one.[336] The original normative claims that are made in this book are backed by an original reflection within the well-established debate on human rights[337] and the environment.[338]

4.3.1 Global Law and Positionality

Discourses on global law also provide a channel for legal scholars and professionals to self-reflect on how they, in their own legal research, effectively 'reformulate what counts as a valid legal argument under conditions of globalization.'[339] As Walker highlighted, these 'specialists of global law ... become involved in "taking law to the world" through various different but mutually reinforcing modes and gradations of jurisgenerative activity'.[340] Thus, specialist (professional and academic) communities are not only 'sources of expertise and learning in matters of the emergent global law and as instruments of its application', but also 'active players in the fashioning and shaping of global law'.[341]

This is true of this book and its underlying research. This book is the culmination of a five-year research programme on fair and equitable benefit-sharing funded by the European Research Council (BENELEX, 2013–2018), and also benefited from continuous research under other externally funded programmes.[342] The BENELEX

assume authority on many different grounds'; yet at the same time, it 'modifies law's canonical forms' and 'claims a global warrant and makes a global appeal in the sense of claiming or assuming a universal or globally pervasive justification for its application'; thus, global law becomes defined by reference to 'its destination rather than its source', Walker (n. 294), at 19–22.

[334] Biases were highlighted as a key finding arising from examining international law as a profession: J d'Aspremont et al., 'Introduction' in J d'Aspremont et al., *International Law as a Profession* (Cambridge University Press, 2017), 1, at 1.

[335] A Roberts, *Is International Law International?* (Oxford University Press, 2017), at xxii, 16, and 25–26.

[336] ibid, at 6.

[337] e.g. F Francioni, 'International Human Rights in an Environmental Horizon' (2010) 21 European Journal of International Law 41; DK Anton and D Shelton, *Environmental Protection and Human Rights* (Cambridge University Press, 2012); A Boyle, 'Human Rights and the Environment: Where Next?' (2012) 23 European Journal of International Law 613.

[338] The UN Independent Expert on Environment and Human Rights briefly pointed to States' duty to ensure benefit-sharing from extractive activities in Indigenous peoples' land and territories: UN Independent Expert on Environment and Human Rights, Preliminary Report on the Issue of Human Rights Obligations Relating to the Enjoyment of a Safe, Clean, Healthy and Sustainable Environment, UN Doc A/HRC/22/43 (2012), para. 41; UN Independent Expert on Environment and Human Rights, Mapping Report, UN Doc A/HRC/25/53 (2013), para. 78. He also drew attention to benefit-sharing in the context of the right to science in the Preliminary Report, para. 21.

[339] Walker (n. 294), at 52.

[340] ibid, at 53.

[341] ibid, at 31 and more generally at 31–38.

[342] The five-year BENELEX research programme (2013–2018, funded by the European Research Council) that has shed light on how the normative advances on fair and equitable benefit-sharing under the Convention on Biological Diversity which have influenced other areas of international law (e.g. climate change, oceans, food and agriculture, and human rights). The other two externally funded projects are: the

research programme was a collaborative effort to examine fair and equitable benefit-sharing in different areas of international environmental law (biodiversity, climate change, agriculture, freshwater), in different areas of international human rights law (right to food, right to water, right to health, Indigenous peoples' rights to lands and natural resources, right to science), and in different areas of the law of the sea (deep-seabed mining, marine bio-prospecting, marine technology transfer).[343] In addition, the programme engaged in empirical inter-disciplinary research (law and political sociology) in five local-community case studies in Greece, Malaysia, Argentina, South Africa, and Namibia in different sectors (traditional pastoralism, traditional agriculture, mining on traditional lands, traditional medicine, and traditional wildlife and fire management in a protected area).[344]

BENELEX research findings have also been advanced and shared through consultancies with relevant international organizations that are involved in the clarification and further development of international law and guidance on fair and equitable benefit-sharing.[345] This in itself has contributed to a deeper understanding of the tensions and questions currently preoccupying the international community in this connection. But it has also influenced, to some degree, these processes.

Furthermore, BENELEX research has also benefited from participant observation of international environmental negotiations related to benefit-sharing since 2005, under the CBD (including the adoption of the Nagoya Protocol on Access to Genetic Resources and Benefit-sharing), the International Plant Treaty, the UN General Assembly process on marine biodiversity of in areas beyond national jurisdiction, and (since 2017) the International Seabed Authority, as well as invitations to

MARINE BENEFITS research project (2015–2017, funded by the UK Ecosystem Services for Poverty Alleviation Programme), which investigated fair and equitable benefit-sharing in the context of international fisheries law and policy, with a view to connecting different sources of inequity concerning marine ecosystem services that contribute to poverty in small-scale fishing communities; and the One Ocean Hub (2018–2024, a collaborative research for sustainable development project funded by UK Research and Innovation (UKRI) through the Global Challenges Research Fund (GCRF) (Grant Ref: NE/S008950/1).

343 Tsioumani (n. 259); A Savaresi and K Bouwer, 'Equity and Justice in Climate Change Law and Policy: A Role for Benefit-Sharing' in T Jafry (ed.), *Research Handbook on Climate Justice* (Routledge, 2018) 128; K Bouwer, 'Possibilities for Justice and Equity in Human Rights and Climate Law: Benefit- Sharing in Climate Finance' (2021) 11 Climate Law 1; K Bouwer, 'Insights for Climate Technology Transfer from International Environmental and Human Rights Law' (2018) 23 Journal of Intellectual Property Right 7.

344 L Parks, *Benefit-sharing in Environmental Governance: Local Experiences of a Global Concept* (Routledge, 2020).

345 CBD, Possible criteria for identifying a specialized international access and benefit-sharing instrument in the context of the Nagoya Protocol on Access to Genetic Resources and Benefit-sharing, UN Doc UNEP/CBD/ABS/A10/EM/2016/1/2 (2018); and a legal analysis of existing multilateral benefit-sharing mechanisms, and of the potential relevance of ongoing work undertaken by other international processes for Art. 10 of the Nagoya Protocol, UN Doc UNEP/CBD/ABS/A10/EM/2016/1/2 (2015); FAO and the Organisation for Economic Co-operation and Development (OECD), preparatory materials for the negotiations of new international standards on responsible investment in the agricultural sector (2012–2015) which resulted in the incorporation of fair and equitable benefit-sharing in the 2016 FAO-OECD Guidance on Responsible Agricultural Supply Chain and the 2014 Principles for Responsible Investments in Agriculture and Food Chains of the Committee on Food Security; and for the International Development Law Organization (IDLO) and CBD Secretariat, legal assessment tools were developed to support the mainstreaming of biodiversity (2016–2017) in the context of productive sectors such as agriculture, which include benefit-sharing standards.

contribute to the mandate of the UN Special Rapporteur on Human Rights and the Environment.[346]

These research and knowledge-exchange engagements have facilitated the monitoring of actual, potential, and missed connections among all the various international processes addressing fair and equitable benefit-sharing. In addition, these engagements have contributed to the development of new international legal materials, such as the UN Special Rapporteur John Knox's 2017 report on human rights and biodiversity and the 2018 UN Framework Principles on Human Rights and the Environment (notably Principle 15), or ongoing negotiations under the Nagoya Protocol[347] and the WHO.[348] In other words, this kind of legal research has been involved in 'persuasive adaptation' and therefore contributed to the progressive development of global law.[349] This provides both deep insights into the relevant international law-making processes, but also a specific (and potentially biased) perspective of the author, on which self-reflection will be offered in the following chapters. Such self-reflection will focus on the role of legal interpretation to support equity and environmental justice, as discussed in the next subsection.

4.4 Equity and Environmental Justice

The connection between equity and justice is a continuous and unresolved question for lawyers,[350] including global layers and global environmental lawyers. And yet there seems to be little systematic discussion linking the legal debate on the role of equity in international law and the growing, multi-disciplinary scholarship on global justice,[351] and in the case of benefit-sharing in particular, with environmental justice.[352]

Environmental justice is often defined in legal scholarship, at first instance, as the fair distribution of environmental burdens and benefits between States, as well as within States,[353] taking into account conditions of scarcity and inequality.[354] Fair and

[346] International expert consultation on human rights and biodiversity organized in cooperation with the UN Environment Programme (UNEP) by UN Special Rapporteur on Environment and Human Rights David Boyd (2019, Geneva, Switzerland); and International expert consultation on human rights and biodiversity organized in cooperation with the UN Environment Programme (UNEP), by UN Special Rapporteur on Environment and Human Rights John Knox (2016, Geneva, Switzerland).

[347] E Morgera, S Switzer, and M Geelhoed, Study for the European Commission on 'Possible Ways to Address Digital Sequence Information – Legal and Policy Aspects' (December 2019). The main recommendations from this study were then adopted as CBD COP Decision 15/9 (2022).

[348] E Morgera, 'Critical Considerations vis-à-vis the Possible Outcomes for Fair and Equitable Sharing of Pathogens, Genetic Sequences and Benefits under a Pandemic Instrument' in P Villarreal et al., *Averting a Collision Course? Beyond the Pandemic Instrument and the International Health Regulations*, discussion papers prepared for the event held on 26 April 2023 at the Geneva Graduate Institute, 16–22.

[349] Walker (n. 294), at 10.

[350] Rossi (n. 131).

[351] Walker cautioned about the 'gulf between global law and global justice and profound difficulties involved in closing the gap' (Walker (n. 305), at 166). However, see S Ratner, *The Thin Justice of International Law: A Moral Reckoning of the Law of Nations* (Oxford University Press, 2015).

[352] For a discussion of different understandings of justice and benefit-sharing in the context of the Nagoya Protocol, see Morgera (n. 296), at 113.

[353] Based on the discussion in A Nollkaemper, 'Sovereignty and Environmental Justice in International Law' in Ebbeson and Okowa (n. 13), 25, at 54.

[354] D Shelton, 'Describing the Elephant: International Justice and Environmental Law' in Ebbeson and Okowa (n. 13), at 58–59.

equitable benefit-sharing is therefore one way to *frame* environmental justice, by singling out the advantages (the positive outcomes or implications) of tackling global environmental challenges so as to help motivate participation by different stakeholders.[355] At the same time, however, it has been noted that there is confusion around how benefit-sharing itself is understood in terms of diverse forms of justice.[356] This may be because during relevant negotiations, attention was focused on *how* to deliver justice, rather than on explicitly discussing *what conception of* justice was being pursued in the first place.[357] The main argument put forward here is that benefit-sharing often conflates different dimensions of justice—recognition, commutative justice, distributive justice, and procedural justice. Such conflation may appear problematic as, while it remains implicit, it does not facilitate a systematic analysis of the relative weight that may have been attributed to one conception of justice rather than another.[358]

As much still remains to be understood in the relatively recent debate on environmental justice from a legal perspective,[359] this section will unpack different dimensions of justice related to benefit-sharing and evaluate relationships and tensions among them with a view to paving the way for a more methodical dialogue about the potential contribution of this legal concept to environmental justice in the following chapters. The starting point is the synthesis of the justice literature offered by environmental justice scholars who argue in favour of a pluralist notion of justice based on the complementarity and inter-connectedness of multiple conceptions of justice.[360] In particular, attention will focus on the need to better understand the interactions between distributive justice, recognition, procedural justice, and a composite notion of 'contextual justice'.[361]

Distributive justice has taken the majority of the attention.[362] Distributive justice focuses on the fair allocation of various social resources and detriments.[363] It delves into the preconditions, principles, and qualifications, addressing who the qualifying participants are in a world of scarce resources characterized by significant wealth

[355] G Laurie et al., 'Tackling Community Concerns about Commercialisation and Genetic Research: A Modest Interdisciplinary Proposal', paper presented at Scientific Advancements in Medicine: Legal and Ethical Issues, University of Birmingham, 2005, at 4.

[356] McCool (n. 329), at 3.

[357] KRM Suiseeya, 'Negotiating the Nagoya Protocol: Indigenous Demands for Justice' (2014) 14 Global Environmental Politics 102.

[358] Morgera (n. 296).

[359] J Ebbeson, 'Introduction: Dimensions of Justice in Environmental Law' in Ebbeson and Okowa (n. 13), at 35; R Falk, 'The Second Cycle of Ecological Urgency: An Environmental Justice Perspective', in Ebbeson and Okowa (n. 13), at 42; and generally Michelot (n. 139).

[360] See, e.g., D Schlosberg, *Defining Environmental Justice: Theories, Movements and Nature* (Oxford University Press, 2007); M McDermott, S Mahanty, and K Schreckenberg, 'Examining Equity: A Multidimensional Framework for Assessing Equity in Payments for Ecosystem Services' (2013) 33 Environmental Science and Policy 416; and U Pascual et al., 'Social Equity Matters in Payments for Ecosystem Services' (2014) 64 Bioscience 1027.

[361] McDermott, Mahanty, and Schreckenberg (n. 360), at 419.

[362] Which has also been the case in relation to the CBD: S Vermeylen and G Walker, 'Environmental Justice, Values and Biological Diversity: The San and Hoodia Benefit-Sharing Agreement' in JA Carmin and J Agyeman (eds), *Environmental Inequalities Beyond Borders: Local Perspectives on Global Injustices* (Cambridge University Press, 2011) 105, at 107–108.

[363] This refers to the debate incited by J Rawls, *A Theory of Justice* (Oxford University Press, 1971). See the discussion in Schlosberg (n. 360), at 11–29.

inequalities.[364] This theoretical effort, however, has been increasingly challenged by the notion of justice as recognition. Recognition has highlighted the social, cultural, symbolic, and institutional causes underlying instances of unjust distribution that relate to the diffuse reality of domination and oppression (patterns of non-recognition and disrespect of certain groups, stereotypical public and cultural representations of these groups, denial of their rights and denigration of their ways of life).[365] Both with regard to distribution and recognition, procedural justice is also factored-in or implied: due process and fair procedures with fair opportunities for all parties involved are largely seen as a precondition for social and institutional recognition and fair distribution.[366] In effect, justice theorists across the board ultimately emphasize the crucial role of participation for evaluating trade-offs between different concepts of justice and other principles in a specific context, in the absence of universal ethical grounds.[367]

Furthermore, the notion of 'contextual' justice has been proposed in the ecosystem services literature[368] to capture a combination of pre-existing social, economic, and political conditions that influence an actor's ability to enjoy all other (substantive and procedural) dimensions of justice. This notion arguably encompasses two sets of issues. On the one hand, it points to embedded power asymmetries, possibly also of a historical nature, that may not be captured by the dimension of justice as recognition. In these cases, it could be argued that corrective justice may be relevant, as it involves the restoration of equality among parties by recognizing that one party has suffered an injustice at the hands of another and establishing a direct correlation between the recognized injustice and its remedy.[369] In addition, contextual justice draws on theories of capabilities that see justice as the distribution of opportunities for individuals and groups to freely pursue their chosen way of life and well-being.[370] The notion of contextual justice has, furthermore, the merit of emphasizing the mutual influences among all the aforementioned notions of justice it underpins.[371]

Cognitive justice is also particularly relevant from a benefit-sharing perspective. It calls for the equal treatment of all forms of knowledge[372] and of all knowledge-holders

[364] D Schroeder and T Pogge, 'Justice and the Convention on Biological Diversity' (2009) 23 Ethics and International Affairs 267, at 274–275.

[365] This refers to the debate driven by M Young, *Justice and the Politics of Difference* (Princeton, 1990); N Fraser, *Justice Interruptus: Critical Reflections on the 'Postsocialist' Condition* (Abingdon, 1997); and A Honneth, *The Struggle for Recognition: The Moral Grammar of Social Conflicts* (Polity Press, 1995). See the discussion in Schlosberg (n. 360), at 13–20.

[366] Ebbeson (n. 359), at 12. For a discussion of how participatory justice emerges in other theories of justice, see Schlosberg (n. 360), at 25–29.

[367] As synthesized in McDermott, Mahanty, and Schreckenber (n. 360), at 419 and 424; see also the discussion of reflexivity and engagement in Schlosberg (n. 360), at 187–212.

[368] McDermott, Mahanty, and Schreckenber (n. 360), at 320.

[369] EJ Weinrib, 'Corrective Justice in a Nutshell' (2002) 52 University of Toronto Law Journal 349.

[370] This refers to the debate around MC Nussbaum and A Sen, *The Quality of Life* (Oxford University Press, 1993). See the discussion in Schlosberg (n. 360), at 29–34.

[371] See McDermott, Mahanty, and Schreckenber (n. 360), at 419; and the image in Pascual et al. (n. 360), at 1028.

[372] B Leibowitz, 'Cognitive Justice and the Higher Education Curriculum' (2017) 68 Journal of Education (University of KwaZulu-Natal) 93–112. See also J Chan-Tiberghien, 'Towards a 'Global Educational Justice' Research Paradigm: Cognitive Justice, Decolonizing Methodologies and Critical Pedagogy' (2004) 2 Globalisation, Societies and Education 191–213.

(Indigenous and local knowledge), but also the distinctive ways in which women and children, for instance, 'come to know, use, and care for the living world, are locally and culturally unique'.[373] Restorative justice involves facilitating remedies for environmental harm with a view to re-establishing the relationship between those that caused the harm and those that suffered negative impacts. It can also strive to prevent the long-lasting impacts of past injustices from continuing to affect people in the present—which may contribute to other forms of injustice—and from the same type of injustice recurring in the future.[374] Restorative justice highlights the need to move beyond merely preventing new injustices and acknowledging past ones.

Literature on benefit-sharing and justice,[375] in turn, has mainly made recourse to another notion of justice—commutative justice. This refers to an arrangement that is mutually beneficial to the specific parties involved in an exchange.[376] From that viewpoint, moreover, the need to reflect on the inter-connections among this and other dimensions of justice has been underlined with the aim of starting a debate on the relations between justice, equity, and international law on benefit-sharing.[377]

The underlying contribution of this body of literature lies in identifying the limitations of the law in pursuing multiple dimensions of justice by genuinely factoring-in the immense complexities of developing universal norms that are cognizant and apt to deal with local power dynamics and different cultural perspectives. Power and culture make the pursuit of justice in this context essentially a social process.[378] The need to connect environmental justice scholarship and environmental law research has also been recognized from a methodological perspective, so that legal research can be shaped in context by the needs of local communities.[379] At the very least this is necessary for avoiding oversimplification and for better understanding multiple perspectives.[380] In addition, particular attention should be paid to environmental justice scholarship from the Global South and its practice of standing in solidarity with community activities. As explained by Erwin and McGarry, this scholarship is rooted in an understanding of the relational nature of inequality and shaped by local and global structures. It recognises and explores plural understandings of justice as a means to imagine alternative futures for life on earth.[381] It draws attention to 'the

[373] K Erwin et al., 'Lalela uLwandle: An Experiment in Plural Governance Discussions' in R Boswell, D O'Kane, and J Hills (eds) *The Palgrave Handbook of Blue Heritage* (Palgrave Macmillan, 2022) 383.

[374] A Deplazes-Zemp, 'Challenges of Justice in the Context of Plant Genetic Resources' (2019) 10 Frontiers in Plant Science 1266.

[375] See, for instance, the special issue of Law Environment and Development Journal, 2013, entitled 'Fairness in Biodiversity Politics and the Law: Interrogating the Nagoya Protocol'.

[376] Schroeder (n. 28), at 205 and 207; McCool (n. 329), at 9; Vermeylen and Walker (n. 362), at 108–109 and 122; Schroeder and Pogge (n. 364); Stoll, 'Access to Genetic Resources and Benefit-Sharing: Underlying Concepts and the Idea of Justice', in Kamau and Winter (n. 15), at 3; and Stoll, 'ABS, Justice, Pools and the Nagoya Protocol', in Kamau and Winter (n. 264), at 305.

[377] McCool (n. 329), at 9; Schroeder and Pogge (n. 364); and JB Kleba, 'Fair Biodiversity Politics with and beyond Rawls' (2013) 9 Law Environment and Development Journal 221, at 223.

[378] Vermeylen and Walker (n. 362), at 109 and 122.

[379] J Holder and D McGillivray, 'Bringing Environmental Justice to the Centre of Environmental Law Research: Developing a Collective Case Study Methodology' in A Philippopoulos-Michalopoulos and V Brooks (eds), *Research Methods in Environmental Law: A Handbook* (Edward Elgar, 2017) 18.

[380] A Kotsakis, 'On the Relation between Scholarship and Action in Environmental Law: Methods, Theory, Change' in Philippopoulos-Michalopoulos and Brooks (n. 379), at 338.

[381] D McGarry, K Erwin, and E Morgera, 'What is Environmental Justice: Understandings from the Global South' One Ocean Hub info-sheet (2023).

histories they carry, [which] have been framed and defined mainly through Western ways of thinking and doing',[382] 'and are underlined by a perception that humans and other species of plants and animals are distinct and separate, on a universal scale'.[383] The transposition of these frameworks onto the Global South has resulted in further injustice.[384]

4.4.1 The Interpretation of Equity in International Law in the Context of Environmental Justice

What then is the role of an international lawyer in critically assessing and developing interpretations that need to take into account a plural and contextually located approach to the environment and justice? Connecting the debate on justice with the specific notion of equity in international law can help to identify weaknesses in international law with a full understanding of its potential. As a step in that direction, the 'commonly understood vocabulary' that has emerged from the brief discussion in the section above can be used to unpack different components of justice, identify any omissions, and tease out underlying assumptions[385] with regard to fair and equitable benefit-sharing under various areas of international law. The reflection on environmental justice scholarship provides fresh thinking on the well-established literature on equity in international law.

Equity is commonly considered as a general principle of international law[386] and therefore applicable even when it is not specifically invoked in the text of a certain treaty. It helps to address the inflexibilities of law when facing the specificities of individual cases.[387] Admittedly, the precise meaning and actual impact of equity in international law remains a matter of debate, but it seems useful to simplify theoretical questions to a practical consideration: equity is recognized as 'part and parcel of legal reasoning', whose logical necessity resides in a 'shared approach to a general need of a strictly legal nature'.[388] This pragmatic view serves to underline two key characteristics of equity in international law. First, as mentioned above, it serves to provide new perspectives on legal problems to the benefit of all States, not just to the advantage of—and sometimes to the disadvantage of—powerful States.[389] Second, equity is found *in* or derived from applicable international law, not outside it.[390] In other words, non-legal elements of justice (or subjective notions of justice)[391] cannot enter explicitly

[382] L Álvarez and B Coolsaet, 'Decolonizing Environmental Justice Studies: a Latin American Perspective' (2020) 31 Capitalism Nature Socialism 50–69.

[383] T Morton, *Ecology without nature: Rethinking environmental aesthetics* (Harvard University Press, 2009).

[384] S Vermeylen, 'Environmental Justice and Epistemic Violence' (2019) 24 The International Journal of Justice and Sustainability 89.

[385] That was also the purpose of the framework proposed by McDermott, Mahanty, and Schreckenber (n. 360), at 417.

[386] See, e.g., ICJ, *North Sea Continental Shelf* cases (n. 230), at 3, para. 85; and Thirlway (n. 230), at 78.

[387] See, e.g., M Akehurst, 'Equity and General Principles of Law' (1976) 25 International and Comparative Law Quarterly 801.

[388] Thirlway (n. 230), at 99 and 104.

[389] Burke (n. 40), at 250–251.

[390] Thirlway (n. 230), at 106; and ICJ, *North Sea Continental Shelf* cases (n. 230), para. 88.

[391] The understanding of equity as decisions to be taken *ex aequo et bono* (that is, 'in good conscience' on the basis of elements external to the law) subject to the explicit consent of the parties involved in light of ICJ Statute, Art. 38(2). See M Kotzur, 'Ex Aequo et Bono', in Wolfrum (n. 122).

legal reasoning.[392] For this reason, the following chapters will attempt to identify interpretative hooks for discussing different notions of justice in a treaty or soft law instrument, so that concrete understandings of justice can be deducted from existing international law, notably on human rights.

Against this background, the traditional classification of the functions of equity in international law will be interrogated as fairness discourse. Three functions are conventionally ascribed to equity.[393] First, equity operates *infra legem* (or within the law), when it affects the interpretation of existing rules particularly where these leave a margin of discretion to authorities. Second, it operates *praeter legem* (or beyond the law), when it creatively fills gaps in the law. And third, exceptionally, it operates *contra legem* (or against the law), when it serves to correct or derogate from applicable law,[394] and possibly also to modernize law in the light of changed circumstances.[395] The distinction is easier in theory than in practice. This is partly because legal scholarship on equity remains limited and partly because, for the most part, the academic debate has conceived of equity from an adjudication perspective.[396] Even within the latter perspective, distinguishing between these functions is not straightforward because they 'merge into one another to some extent'.[397] In addition, an extensive understanding of legal interpretation could cover all functions of equity, downplaying more its more creative uses for the progressive development of international law. Nonetheless, engaging with this distinction may be helpful in order to be more alert to the slightest nuance along the continuum between the interpretation, integration, correction, and making of rules of international law as they progressively develop.[398]

In the case of benefit-sharing,[399] there is very little international adjudication, except in the area of Indigenous peoples' territories and natural resources. On the other hand, there is increasing State practice in the form of international (hard or soft) law-making.[400] Benefit-sharing, therefore, provides an ideal case study to revisit the traditional discussion on the functions of equity, with a view to applying it to international treaty-making and soft law-making, against the background of the ongoing debate on the fragmentation or unity of international law (i.e. the debate on whether the proliferation of increasingly specialized international regimes could create conflicts between international norms).[401]

[392] ICJ, *Frontier Dispute (Burkina Faso/Republic of Mali)*, Judgment, 22 December 1986, ICJ Reports, 1986, 554; N Aräjarvi, 'The Lines Begin to Blur? *Opinio Iuris* and the Moralization of Customary International Law', EUI Working Paper 2011; and Thirlway (n. 230), at 86.

[393] ICJ, *North Sea Continental Shelf* cases (n. 230), para. 88; and ICJ, *Frontier Dispute* (n. 392), para. 28.

[394] See, e.g., Francioni (n. 137); and D Shelton, 'Equity', in D Bodansky, J Brunnée, and E Hey (eds), *The Oxford Handbook of International Environmental Law* (Oxford University Press, 2007), at 640.

[395] Francioni (n. 136), para. 29.

[396] Burke (n. 40), at 253.

[397] Akehurst (n. 387), at 802 and 810.

[398] Francioni (n. 136), para. 21.

[399] The exception is represented by *Saramaka* (n. 18); and *Endorois* (n. 24).

[400] See the mind maps produced by the BENELEX project, available at: https://www.strath.ac.uk/research/strathclydecentreenvironmentallawgovernance/benelex/researchoutputs/mindmaps/, accessed 28 July 2023.

[401] See International Law Commission (ILC), *Fragmentation of International Law: Difficulties arising from the Diversification and Expansion of International Law*, UN Doc A/CN.4/L.682 (2006); and PM Dupuy, 'L'unité de l'ordre juridique international: cours général de droit international public' (2002) 297

The following chapters will examine whether, in its different framings, benefit-sharing serves to operationalize equity within, beyond, or even against the law,[402] and questions these functions in light of different notions of justice.[403] What extent may multiple notions of justice be pursued simultaneously in international law through benefit-sharing? This question helps unveil systematically implicit legal design choices in relation to the pursuit of justice through international law-making. But it may also help identify interpretations of international legal instruments that can contribute to negotiating concrete understandings of justice on a case-by-case basis (through implementation or adjudication). This concept can enable the re-examination of the functions of equity in the realm of international law. In particular, it offers a fairly unexplored avenue to better understand the interactions between intra-generational equity—a relatively recent and yet to be resolved concept in international law[404]—and inter-generational equity.[405] The original normative claims made by the author in the following chapters are backed by mutually supportive interpretations with international human rights law that respond to specific issues identified from an environmental justice perspective.

5. Structure of this Book

Taking treaty law as a basis, this chapter has delineated a concept that could facilitate research across a variety of international and transnational legal materials, while allowing for the appreciation of differences in the context of varying logics of different areas of international law. Fair and equitable benefit-sharing has thus been conceptualized as a more profound form of cooperation—the concerted and dialogic process aimed at building partnerships in co-identifying and allocating economic, socio-cultural, and environmental benefits among State and non-State actors, with an emphasis on the vulnerable. Even in the context of bilateral exchanges, fair and equitable benefit-sharing encompasses multiple streams of benefits of local and global relevance, as it aims to benefit a wider group than those actively or directly engaged in bioprospecting, natural resource management, environmental protection, or use of knowledge where a heightened and cosmopolitan form of cooperation is sought.

The first two chapters will focus on fair and equitable benefit-sharing among States. Chapter 1 will apply the lenses of incomplete theorized agreement, global law, and

RCADI 9; and M Andenas and E Bjorge (eds), *A Farewell to Fragmentation: Reassertion and Convergence in International Law* (Cambridge University Press, 2015).

402 The question had already been posed by Francioni (n. 136), para. 28.

403 See, in this regard, ILC (n. 401), para. 480: 'By making sure that the outcome is linked to the legal environment, and that adjoining rules are considered – perhaps applied, perhaps invalidated, perhaps momentarily set aside – any decision also articulates the legal-institutional environment in view of *substantive preferences, distributionary choices and political objectives*' (emphasis added).

404 Birnie, Boyle, and Redgwell (n. 143), at 123.

405 Some discussion can be found in ISA (n. 35), para. 5; K Baslar, *The Concept of the Common Heritage of Mankind in International Law* (Martinus Nijhoff, 1998), at 100; J Murillo, 'Common Concern of Humankind and Its Implications in International Environmental Law' (2008) 5 Macquarie Journal of International and Comparative Environmental Law 133, at 142.

environmental justice to the development and implementation challenges of benefit-sharing in international regimes concerned with access and management of genetic resources within and outside national jurisdiction, focusing on the Convention on Biological Diversity and its Nagoya Protocol, the International Plant Treaty, the WHO PIP Framework, the BBNJ Agreement, as well as ongoing negotiations on digital sequence information. Chapter 2 will analyse international regimes in which the sharing of scientific information, capacity building, and technology transfer has been identified as forms of benefit-sharing through the lens of the human right to science. It will focus on the BBNJ Agreement and the international climate change regime.

Chapters 3 and 4 will then turn to inter-State benefit-sharing. Chapter 3 will assess the degree of cross-fertilization between international environmental law and international human rights law on fair and equitable benefit-sharing in relation to the rights of Indigenous peoples over natural resources traditionally used by them. It will evaluate the relevance of State obligations on fair and equitable benefit-sharing, as well as prior environmental and socio-cultural assessments and consent processes in the context of the regulation of extractive activities, fisheries, nature conservation (such as the creation of protected areas), freshwater management, and climate change response measures when they are situated, or may have an impact, on lands traditionally used by Indigenous peoples and local communities. Chapter 4 will reflect on international legal materials on non-Indigenous local communities, focusing on small-scale fishers, and intra-community benefit-sharing. This chapter will further reflect on international benefit-sharing obligations related to the traditional knowledge of Indigenous peoples and local communities, focusing on the interface of inter- and intra-State benefit-sharing obligations under regimes on access to genetic resources (discussed in Chapter 1 exclusively from an inter-State benefit-sharing perspective).

Chapter 5 investigates transnational dimensions of fair and equitable benefit-sharing. It will analyse the role of international fair and equitable benefit-sharing standards as part of the concept of due diligence in the context of business responsibility to respect human rights, as another transnational dimension. The chapter will focus on private sector-driven extractives and conservation in or near lands traditionally used by Indigenous peoples and local communities (discussed in Chapter 3 from an inter-State perspective). This will provide an opportunity to discuss the role of (domestic) private law on contracts and private international law in the context of transnational benefit-sharing agreements, as well as the role of public international law in the protection of foreign investment.

The Conclusions will reflect on the status of fair and equitable benefit-sharing in international law, considering limited and qualified treaty bases, the debated relevance of authoritative interpretations, as well as arguments already put forward in specialist literature. The chapter will develop an argument about fair and equitable benefit-sharing being a general principle of international law as a sub-set of the general principle of equity. The chapter will consider its implications for the exercise of States' discretionary powers in the absence of a treaty basis on benefit-sharing and for international organizations, with a view to further clarifying the potential contribution of fair and equitable benefit-sharing to frame the international duty to cooperate in the context of sustainable development.

1
Inter-State Benefit-Sharing from Access to Genetic Resources

1. Introduction

The global regime on access to genetic resources and fair and equitable benefit-sharing (ABS) is complex, evolving, and incompletely theorized. It relies on multiple global environmental law phenomena, including bilateral and standardized contracts, and seeks to address numerous environmental justice dimensions. This chapter will mainly analyse the current state of development and implementation challenges of benefit-sharing under the Nagoya Protocol on Access to Genetic Resources and the Fair and Equitable Sharing of Benefits Arising from Their Utilization[1] under the Convention on Biological Diversity (CBD).[2]

To reflect on the limitations of bilateral approaches to inter-State benefit-sharing from genetic resources under the CBD, the chapter will then engage in a comparison of the multilateral benefit-sharing approaches under the International Treaty on Plant Genetic Resources for Food and Agriculture (ITPGRFA),[3] the World Health Organization's Pandemic Influenza Preparedness Framework,[4] and the Agreement on marine biodiversity of areas beyond national jurisdiction (BBNJ).[5]

Each regime addresses historical, current, and emerging justice issues through different global law configurations. Reflecting on shared challenges, including with regard to digital sequence information, the chapter will suggest an evolutive, mutually supportive interpretation of existing benefit-sharing obligations in each regime based on the need to engage in deeper inter-State cooperation on the underlying global benefits expected to arise from international ABS instruments. The chapter will put forward a normative argument about the need to move away from predominantly transactional interpretations and applications of international ABS regimes, towards interpretations of equity that support effectiveness in the prevention of further global biodiversity loss and its negative impacts on the full enjoyment of human rights.

[1] Nagoya Protocol Additional to the Convention on Biological Diversity 1992, on Access to Genetic Resources and the Fair and Equitable Sharing of Benefits from their Utilization (Nagoya, 29 October 2010, in force 12 October 2014).

[2] Convention on Biological Diversity (CBD) (Rio de Janeiro, 5 June 1992, in force 29 December 1993).

[3] International Treaty on Plant Genetic Resources for Food and Agriculture (ITPGRFA) (Rome, 3 November 2001, in force 29 June 2004).

[4] The WHO Pandemic Influenza Preparedness Framework for the sharing of influenza viruses and access to vaccines and other benefits (effective 24 May 2011) WHO DOC WHA64.5.

[5] Agreement under the United Nations Convention on the Law of the Sea on the Conservation and Sustainable Use of Marine Biological Diversity of Areas beyond National Jurisdiction (New York, 19 June 2023, A/CONF.232/2023/4, not yet in force).

Fair and Equitable Benefit-Sharing in International Law. Elisa Morgera, Oxford University Press.
DOI: 10.1093/oso/9780198862130.003.0002

2. Justice Dimensions and the Need for International Cooperation on Genetic Resources

International regimes on access and benefit-sharing from genetic resources generally regulate transnational bioprospecting—the search for plants and animals that are found in one State, or in marine areas beyond national jurisdiction, and from which commercially valuable compounds are obtained in another State or only in few States that are technologically and financially advanced to gain access to areas beyond national jurisdiction. These regimes seek to balance a variety of equity concerns: first, equity between those States where most of the world's biodiversity is found (which are often developing countries) and States (often developed countries) where research and commercial development of genetic resources take place. Second, they address equity within States with regard to Indigenous peoples and local communities that hold traditional knowledge that can be used to identify potentially useful properties of a genetic resource (which is discussed in more depth in Chapter 4). And third, they consider the realization of potential global benefits in terms of sustainable development (such as innovation in the food, medicine, and renewable energy sectors), as well as contributions to the conservation of biodiversity and its sustainable use. Beyond bio-based innovation, bioprospecting contributes to further advancing our fundamental understanding of biodiversity—the diversity of life forms on the planet—and its importance for human well-being now and in the future.

Addressing these equity issues one by one, different environmental justice dimensions become apparent. Recognition issues arise for those countries that host more than 70 per cent of the world's biodiversity (mega-diverse countries such as Australia, Brazil, China, Colombia, the Democratic Republic of the Congo, Ecuador, India, Indonesia, Madagascar, Malaysia, Mexico, Papua New Guinea, Peru, the Philippines, South Africa, the United States of America and Venezuela).[6] Among these mega-diverse countries, however, capabilities vary: tropical developing countries' technological capacities to research and develop genetic resources held by them is limited,[7] which also implies unequal access to information on the scientific and technological value and the commercial potential of genetic resources among developed and developing countries.[8] In turn, this results in unequal access to resources and knowledge (including legal expertise and assistance) needed to negotiate ABS transactions.[9] All

[6] The UNEP World Conservation Monitoring Centre identified these countries as megadiverse in 2000; and megadiversity is determined on the basis of the 'total number of species in a country and the degree of endemism at the species level and at higher taxonomic levels': E Morgera, E Tsioumani, and M Buck, *Unraveling the Nagoya Protocol: Commentary on the Protocol on Access and Benefit-sharing to the Convention on Biological Diversity* (Martinus Nijhoff, 2014), at 7–8.

[7] S Oberthür and K Rosendal, 'Global Governance of Genetic Resources: Background and Analytical Framework' in S Oberthür and K Rosendal (eds), *Global Governance of Genetic Resources: Access and Benefit Sharing After the Nagoya Protocol* (Routledge, 2013), 1.

[8] PT Stoll, 'ABS, Justice, Pools and the Nagoya Protocol', in E Kamau and G Winter (eds), *Common Pools of Genetic Resources: Equity and Innovation in International Biodiversity Law* (Routledge, 2013), 305, at 309; PT Stoll, 'Access to Genetic Resources and Benefit-Sharing: Underlying Concepts and the Idea of Justice', in E Kamau and G Winter (eds), *Genetic Resources, Traditional Knowledge and the Law: Solutions for Access and Benefit Sharing* (Earthscan, 2009), 3, at 12.

[9] J Cariño et al., *Nagoya Protocol on Access to Genetic Resources and the Fair and Equitable Sharing of Benefits Arising from Their Utilization: Background and Analysis* (The Berne Declaration, Bread for the

these elements translate into unequal bargaining powers between States.[10] Justice as recognition here, therefore, serves to acknowledge the global contributions of mega-diverse countries as ecosystem stewards and suppliers of unique genetic materials needed to advance scientific knowledge and environmental protection for the benefit of all humanity.

Issues of restorative justice are also relevant. Colonialism allowed for the collection and appropriation of cultural and natural heritage into museums, zoological and botanical gardens, and other ex situ collections in colonizing countries.[11] While these countries have devoted financial and technical resources to protect and study these resources, including for the benefit of the global community, they have also accrued unacknowledged benefits in terms of enhanced capacities to use the knowledge arising from holding and managing these collections. In fact, the very organization and management of these collections is inherently geared towards the needs identified in Global North countries.[12]

The application of intellectual property rights (IPRs) to improved germplasm[13] has created further well-documented[14] injustices by restricting use of new products by countries in the Global South, while not supporting the enforcement of their claims to underlying biodiversity ownership in foreign jurisdictions where the IPR holders are based.[15] This issue has worsened due to the growth and increasing dominance of multinational corporations in the biotech sector[16] and the (mis)application of intellectual property rights over natural compounds.[17] While these issues have been included in the agenda of relevant international law-making processes (under the aegis of the World Trade Organization (WTO) and World Intellectual Property Organization (WIPO)), they do not seem to be nearing a solution in those forums. This impasse (which is combined with the lack of willingness to address IPR issues under international environmental law instruments on benefit-sharing) has led to a

World, Ecoropa, Tebtebba and Third World Network, 2013), at 5. On the North–South asymmetries and other conflicting objectives behind the ABS provisions of the CBD, see generally B De Jonge and N Louwaars, 'The Diversity of Principles Underlying the Concept of Benefit-sharing' in Kamau and Winter, *Common Pools* (n. 8).

[10] Stoll, 'ABS, Justice, Pools' (n. 8), at 309; and Stoll, 'Access to Genetic Resources and Benefit-sharing' (n. 8), at 12.

[11] Cariño et al. (n. 9), at 2. CBD Art. 2 defines 'ex situ conservation' as 'the conservation of components of biological diversity outside of their natural habitats'.

[12] S Laird and R Wynberg, 'Fact-finding and Scoping Study on Digital Sequence Information on Genetic Resources in the Context of the Convention on Biological Diversity and the Nagoya Protocol' UN Doc CBD/DSI/AHTEG/2018/13 (2018); E Morgera, S Switzer, M Geelhoed, 'Study for the European Commission on Possible Ways to Address Digital Sequence Information – Legal and Policy Aspects' (December 2019). Note that in this and other chapters, the terms 'Global South' and 'Global North' are used to emphasize the relevance of colonialism, colonial legacies, and current equity disparities between these countries on the basis of history, environmental justice, and other social sciences literature.

[13] M Petit et al., *Why Governments Can't Make Policy: The Case of Plant Genetic Resources in the International Arena* (International Potato Center, 2001), at 10 and 19.

[14] P Oldham, S Hall, and O Forero, 'Biological Diversity in the Patent System' (2013) 8 PLoS ONE e78737.

[15] See UK Commission on Intellectual Property Rights, *Integrating Intellectual Property Rights and Development* (Commission on Intellectual Property Rights, 2002), at 84.

[16] S Oberthür and K Rosendal, 'Conclusions' in Oberthür and Rosendal (n. 7) 241.

[17] See the discussion in Morgera, Tsioumani, and Buck (n. 6), at 9.

'contradictory policy context' that effectively undermines the realization of fairness and equity through benefit-sharing.[18]

The assumptions about the benefits of ABS have also contributed to distributive justice issues. ABS is expected to generate *economic* benefits (and thus provide an incentive) for biodiversity conservation in States that share the genetic resources over which they hold sovereign rights.[19] However, there is very little evidence on whether specific ABS deals have effectively provided economic benefits for mega-diverse countries in the Global South[20] or contributed to the CBD's other two objectives (conservation and sustainable use of biodiversity),[21] also due to difficulties in enforcement.[22]

Even leaving aside these serious questions of implementation, ABS instruments have raised concerns about the commodification of biodiversity (market-based conceptualizations of biodiversity conservation and sustainable use,[23] emphasis on the green economy,[24] and bio-based economies)[25] and the full appreciation of the multiple roles that biodiversity (including genetic diversity) plays in the provisions of essential benefits to humanity (ecosystem services). That said, understanding of ecosystem services (or of 'nature benefits to people', which is a label that distances itself from an economic framing of nature[26]) has become increasingly recognized under international law as essential for the protection of human rights to life, health, food, water,

[18] E Tsioumani, *Fair and Equitable in Agriculture: Reinventing Agrarian Justice* (Routledge, 2021), at 2.

[19] Oberthür and Rosendal, 'Conclusions' in Oberthür and Rosendal (n. 7), at 244–245.

[20] F Wolff, 'The Nagoya Protocol and the Diffusion of Economic Instruments for Ecosystem Services in International Environmental Governance' in Oberthür and Rosendal (n. 7), 134, at 135–139, 151, and 153 as part of a broader trend in incentive-based governance of biodiversity. See also R Pavoni, 'Channeling Investment into Biodiversity Conservation: ABS and PES Schemes' in PM Dupuy and JE Viñuales (eds), *Harnessing Foreign Investment to Promote Environmental Protection Incentives and Safeguards* (Cambridge University Press, 2013), 206; and CBD and UNEP-World Conservation Monitoring Centre (WCMC), 'Global Biodiversity Outlook' (Montreal and Cambridge, 2010), available at http://gbo3.cbd.int/, accessed 30 November 2013, at 19, where it is stated that 'There are few examples of the benefit arising from the commercial and other utilization of genetic resources being shared with the countries providing such resources'. See also Oberthür and Rosendal (n. 16), at 244–245, where it is argued that the assumption that ABS will 'quasi-automatically' create strong incentives for biodiversity conservation may be unrealistic.

[21] R Wynberg, 'Biopiracy: Crying Wolf or a Lever for Equity and Conservation?' (2023) 52 Research Policy 104674.

[22] See CBD Decision X/44 (2011), 'Incentive measures', para. 14.

[23] See, e.g., papers collected in the special issue of the Transnational Environmental Law published in October 2013, in particular the contribution by C Reid, 'Between Priceless and Worthless: Challenges in Using Market Mechanisms for Conserving Biodiversity' (2013) 2 Transnational Environmental Law 217, where the author draws attention to the challenges of 'defining the units that can be the subject of the economic or market devices', 'ensuring that such mechanisms do deliver conservation gains and establishing appropriate governance arrangements', as well as to 'ethical concerns' associated with the commodification of nature: ibid, 218.

[24] E Morgera and A Savaresi, 'A Conceptual and Legal Perspective on the Green Economy' (2013) 22 Review of European, Comparative and International Environmental Law 14.

[25] Organization for Economic Co-operation and Development (OECD), 'The Application of Biotechnology to Industrial Sustainability' (OECD, 2001), available at https://www.oecd-ilibrary.org/environment/the-application-of-biotechnology-to-industrial-sustainability_9789264195639-en, accessed 30 November 2013; and OECD, 'Towards the Development of OECD Best Practices for Assessing the Sustainability of Bio-based Products' (OECD, 2010), available at http://www.oecd.org/sti/biotech/45598236.pdf, accessed 30 November 2013.

[26] Note the shift of focus by IPBES from ecosystem services to 'nature's contributions to people', to acknowledge culture and Indigenous and local knowledge as pivotal in appreciating and understanding human-nature interactions. See S Díaz et al., 'Assessing Nature's Contributions to People' (2018) 359 Science 270; R Hill et al., 'Nature's Contributions to People: Weaving Plural Perspectives' (2021) 4 One Earth 910.

livelihoods, and cultures,[27] as well as the human right to a healthy environment.[28] In other words, from a human rights perspective, an emphasis on ecosystem services/nature's benefits to people points to the multiple values of biodiversity for human well-being and the interdependence of humans and other living organisms. From that perspective, it is possible to dispel the misconception that decisions on development options always set nature protection against human socio-economic development: rather, ecosystem services show that decisions in favour of nature are also in favour of basic human rights. A development decision should rather be assessed on the relative merits of immediate economic benefits to certain members of society involved in a development project versus the diffuse benefits to society as a whole (including the vulnerable) from conservation, potentially over a longer period of time.[29]

The tensions between specific economic values of biodiversity, its intrinsic value, and its interdependence with human well-being are already reflected in the ecosystem approach developed within the CBD framework. The CBD interpretation of the ecosystem approach has arguably attempted to reconcile economic valuation[30] with an increased focus on biodiversity's contribution to poverty eradication[31] and on the need for inclusion, particularly of the vulnerable, in decisions on biodiversity.[32] Divergent policy priorities of States within the international community are thus evident within benefit-sharing regimes, and this is reflected in the various tensions between international economic law and international human rights law that have a bearing on the implementation of inter-State benefit-sharing on the basis of incompletely theorized agreements.

It is partly because of these tensions that much remains to be fully theorized under treaties and international instruments on ABS from genetic resources: different States place varying priorities on different dimensions of justice and the role of international law in addressing them. In addition, earlier attempts at theorization in international law have rather muddled the water. Until the negotiation and entry into force of the CBD, an arguable[33] application of the concept of common heritage of [hu]mankind over biological resources had resulted in an almost free flow of genetic resources

[27] J Knox, 'Report of the Special Rapporteur on the Issue of Human Rights Obligations Relating to the Enjoyment of a Safe, Clean, Healthy and Sustainable Environment' UN Doc A/HRC/34/49 (2017).

[28] UNGA 'The Human Right to a Clean, Healthy and Sustainable Environment', UN Doc A/RES/76/300 (2022).

[29] E Morgera, 'Biodiversity as a Human Right and its Implications for the EU's External Action', Report to the European Parliament (2020), available at https://www.europarl.europa.eu/RegData/etudes/STUD/2020/603491/EXPO_STU(2020)603491_EN.pdf, accessed 26 June 2023.

[30] CBD Decision V/6 (2000), 'Ecosystem approach; and CBD Decision VII/11(2004), 'Ecosystem approach'.

[31] CBD Decision X/6 (2011), 'Integration of biodiversity into poverty eradication and development'; and CBD Decision XI/22 (2012), 'Biodiversity for poverty eradication and development'.

[32] For instance, CBD Decision X/4 (2011), 'Third edition of the Global Biodiversity Outlook: Implications for the Future Implementation of the Convention', paras 5(d) and (f), points to: enhancing the benefits from biodiversity to contribute to local livelihoods; empowering Indigenous and local communities; and ensuring their participation in decision-making processes to protect and encourage their customary sustainable use of biological resources.

[33] This understanding of common heritage should be compared to the common heritage regime, as provided for in Art. 140(2) of the United Nations Convention on the Law of the Sea (United Nations Convention on the Law of the Sea (UNCLOS) (Montego Bay, 10 December 1982, into force 16 November 1994; UNCLOS), which subjects resources that cannot be appropriated by any single State for exclusive sovereignty to an international managing and regulating institution. The aim is to provide benefits arising from the utilization of these resources to all States even if they are unable to participate in the actual process of

across boundaries.[34] Access to genetic resources in nature (in situ[35]) was considered free and unconditional, and the results of research on such resources were assumed to benefit future generations. This theorization was then abandoned under the CBD and the International Plant Treaty, which instead recognize that national sovereignty over natural resources extends to genetic resources,[36] thereby subjecting access to genetic resources to the prior informed consent of the State providing the resource.[37] After the CBD provided a paradigm shift in the theorization of ABS under international law, more specialized international instruments have furthered, to a certain extent, the development of the concept of benefit-sharing and relevant mechanisms. This is the case of the Nagoya Protocol under the CBD, the International Plant Treaty, the WHO instrument on pathogens, and the BBNJ Agreement, discussed below in turn.

Against this backdrop, international law can play different roles. First, it can foster the protection of the sovereign entitlement of one State to derive benefits from the use of its genetic resources that they ensure conservation of, once these resources are brought outside of its jurisdiction.[38] Second, it can support international cooperation for the realization of the international community's objective of ensuring fairness in transnational ABS relationships 'in recognition of the need to reduce enormous global asymmetries' among developed and developing States.[39] Third, international law can come into play to protect the underlying global benefits that may arise from specific ABS relationships.

Ultimately, it is international law that should provide a coherent approach to the interpretation and implementation of multiple international objectives that have been agreed upon under separate treaties, thereby giving content and advancing the theorization of fairness and equity for benefit-sharing purposes. In that connection, it is argued here that a mutually supportive interpretation of international biodiversity law and international human rights law should inform the understanding of international economic law and further law-making in the areas of international environmental, health, and ocean law in order to respond to the multiple justice dimensions identified. The challenges of current international ABS regimes will be discussed next.

extraction: see P Birnie, A Boyle, and C Redgwell, *International Law and the Environment*, 3rd edn (Oxford University Press, 2009), at 128–130 and 197.

[34] T Morten and T Young, *Beyond Access: Exploring Implementation of the Fair and Equitable Sharing Commitment in the CBD* (IUCN, 2007), at 1.

[35] CBD, Art. 2, defines 'in situ conditions' as 'conditions where genetic resources exist within ecosystems and natural habitats, and in the case of domesticated or cultivated species, in the surroundings where they have developed their distinctive properties'.

[36] See L Glowka, F Burhenne-Guilmin, and H Synge. *A Guide to the Convention on Biological Diversity* (IUCN, 1994), at 76; and E Tsioumani, 'International Treaty on Plant Genetic Resources for Food and Agriculture: Legal and Policy Questions from Adoption to Implementation' (2004) 15 Yearbook of International Environmental Law 119, at 122–124.

[37] CBD, Art. 15(5). See Morgera, Tsioumani, and Buck (n. 6), at 140–144.

[38] Stoll, 'ABS, Justice, Pools' (n. 8), at 309.

[39] B Dias, 'Preface' in E Morgera, M Buck, and E Tsioumani (eds), *The 2010 Nagoya Protocol on Access and Benefit-Sharing in Perspective: Implications for International Law and National Implementation* (Brill/Martinus Nijhoff, 2013) 1.

3. Nagoya Protocol

The Nagoya Protocol theorizes benefit-sharing as a matter of environmental sustainability,[40] linking it explicitly to other sustainable development issues[41] and justice.[42] The operational provisions of the Nagoya Protocol represent a significant expansion on the obligations of the CBD on access and benefit-sharing[43] in respect of genetic resources and traditional knowledge associated with those resources.[44] Specifically, the Protocol seeks to advance the third objective of the CBD[45] by detailing how to operationalize the provisions of CBD, Article 15,[46] which established in general terms that sovereignty over natural resources extends to a right to regulate access to genetic resources. It also stipulated that such access should be on mutually agreed terms (MAT) and with prior informed consent (PIC) (unless otherwise specified by the country concerned). This implies a bilateral ABS system between providers and users of genetic resources. These provisions are expanded upon in the Protocol and complemented by specific innovative obligations to support compliance with the domestic legislation of the party providing genetic resources, and contractual obligations reflected in MAT.[47]

In addition, the Protocol expands on the meaning of fair and equitable benefit-sharing, clarifying that benefits may be both monetary as well as non-monetary and providing an indicative list of both.[48] Ultimately, the Protocol requires States to introduce 'legislative, administrative or policy measures, as appropriate' to ensure the sharing of benefits upon MAT,[49] thereby calling for the creation of ABS regimes

[40] e.g. Nagoya Protocol, 7th preambular paragraph (which reads: 'Acknowledging the potential role of access and benefit-sharing to contribute to the conservation and sustainable use of biological diversity... and *environmental sustainability*' (emphasis added)) and 14th preambular paragraph (which reads: 'Recognizing the importance of genetic resources to ... biodiversity conservation and the mitigation of and adaptation to climate change'). See the discussion in Morgera, Tsioumani, and Buck (n. 6), at 54.

[41] e.g. Nagoya Protocol, 5th preambular paragraph (which reads: 'Recognizing the important contribution to *sustainable development* made by technology transfer and cooperation to build research and innovation capacities for adding value to genetic resources in developing countries') and 7th preambular paragraph (which reads: 'Acknowledging the potential role of access and benefit-sharing to contribute to ... *poverty eradication* ... thereby contributing to achieving the *Millennium Development Goals*' (emphasis added)). For a discussion, see Conclusions Morgera, Tsioumani, and Buck (n. 6), at 54.

[42] For a discussion predating the adoption of the Nagoya Protocol, see P Cullet, 'Environmental Justice in the Use, Knowledge and Exploitation of Genetic Resources' in J Ebbesson and P Okowa (eds), *Environmental Law and Justice in Context* (Cambridge University Press, 2009), 371; and P Stoll, 'Access to Genetic Resources (n. 8), 3. For a discussion after the conclusion of the negotiations of the Nagoya Protocol, see also P Stoll, 'ABS, Justice, Pools' (n. 8), at 305.

[43] Indeed, CBD, Art. 1 sets out that it is aimed, among other things, at the achievement of, 'the fair and equitable sharing of benefits arising out of the utilization of genetic resources, including by appropriate access to genetic resources and by appropriate transfer of relevant technologies, taking into account all rights over those resources and to technologies, and by appropriate funding'. See also CBD, Arts 8(j) and 15.

[44] See E Morgera, M Buck, and E Tsioumani, 'Introduction' in Morgera, Buck, and Tsioumani (n. 39), at 1–17.

[45] Nagoya Protocol, 2nd preambular recital, which reiterates the relevant wording of CBD, Art. 1.

[46] ibid, 4th and 12th preambular recital.

[47] See the discussion in Morgera, Tsioumani, and Buck (n. 6), at 139–169.

[48] Nagoya Protocol, Annex.

[49] ibid, Art. 5 (5)

through several paths of implementation and 'regime development', rather than actually *creating* an ABS regime per se.[50]

In that sense, the Nagoya Protocol is an incompletely theorized agreement as States could only agree on 'a highly abstract theory' about benefit-sharing from genetic resources (a bilateral approach to be specified in national law), but not necessarily on 'what it entails in particular cases'.[51] MATs provide further theorization of ABS, as a (often private-law) contract that is expected to clarify individual parties' specific rights and obligations, restrictions in the use of specific material throughout the user chain, as well as information sharing and monitoring duties.[52]

A further example of incomplete theorization can be found in the Nagoya Protocol provisions on other specialized ABS instruments. While it encapsulates agreement on the 'mid-level' principle that other ABS instruments can be considered 'specialized' ABS regimes, it lacks clarity on how the relationship plays out in particular circumstances.[53] On the one hand, it creates uncertainty. On the other hand, it arguably allows space for processes of mutual learning between States and the actors involved in this distinct space of ABS governance: for instance, on lessons learnt in the use of private contracts for the realization of fairness and equity,[54] or different methods to ensure the financial viability of international benefit-sharing mechanisms.[55]

The Nagoya Protocol is also an ideal case study of global environmental law.[56] The implementation of the Protocol entails complex and creative links between different areas of international law,[57] a dynamic web of provider and user countries' national laws and contractual arrangements between private parties feeding into a system of internationally recognized certificates,[58] based on the respect for the customary laws of local communities and Indigenous peoples at all these regulatory levels.[59] In this sense, the Protocol's approach to governance is *multi-level* rather than hierarchical, with possibilities existing for flexibility and learning through implementation domestically and internationally.[60] Such flexibility arguably provides room for *experimentation* with a number of provisions, such as that on model contract clauses,[61] allowing a range of actors to contribute to building legal understandings of their operation as

[50] T Young, 'An International Cooperation Perspective on the Implementation of the Nagoya Protocol' in Morgera, Buck, and Tsioumani (n. 39), 451, at 457 and 462.

[51] C Sunstein, 'Incompletely Theorized Agreements' (2005) 108 Harvard Law Review 1733, at 1739. See also C Sunstein, 'Incompletely Theorized Agreements in Constitutional Law', John M. Olin Law and Economics Working Paper No. 322 (2 D Series).

[52] Morgera, Tsioumani, and Buck (n. 6), at 167.

[53] For more on the different levels at which such agreements may be said to exist, see generally ibid.

[54] E Morgera and L Gillies, 'Realizing the Objectives of Public International Environmental Law through Private Contracts: The Need for a Dialogue with Private International Law Scholars?' in D French, V Ruiz Abou-Nigm, and K McCall Smith (eds), *Public and Private International Law: Strengthening Connections* (Hart 2018) 175.

[55] E Morgera, 'The Need for an International Legal Concept of Fair and Equitable Benefit-sharing' (2016) 27 European Journal of International Law 353.

[56] E Morgera, 'Global Environmental Law and Comparative Legal Methods' (2015) 24 Review of European Comparative and International Environmental Law 24.

[57] Morgera (n. 55).

[58] Nagoya Protocol, Art. 17(2–4).

[59] ibid, Art. 12(1).

[60] ibid.

[61] ibid, Art. 19.

well as their implementation. However, an acknowledged 'by-product' of flexibility is the challenge(s) this can pose to Parties involved in the Protocol's implementation.[62] The Protocol's flexible provisions have enabled a variety of legal approaches to implementation at different levels through creative connections between local, national, transnational, and international law. The Protocol's text itself specifically creates opportunities for horizontal[63] and bottom-up[64] regulatory cross-fertilization. The question that arises is therefore whether global law can contribute to advance the theorization of benefit-sharing and address the multiple dimensions of environmental justice that are relevant to bio-based innovation.

3.1 Justice Dimensions from an International Law Perspective

Academic literature has identified multiple dimensions of environmental justice concerning the Nagoya Protocol, but has rarely discussed them in a comprehensive manner.[65] A reading of the title of the Nagoya Protocol suffices to deduce that it aims to realize *commutative* justice: it suggests that benefits are shared in exchange for access to genetic resources. It might seem obvious that without access to genetic resources there would be no benefits to share. The Protocol is intended to regulate relations of exchange, and is premised on a bilateral relationship between a user and a provider country (through a notion of inter-State benefit-sharing).[66] However, the Preamble of the Protocol 'acknowledges the linkage' between access and benefit-sharing,[67] suggesting that the relationship between the two is more complicated than it first appears.

In effect a holistic reading of the Protocol indicates that there is more than a bilateral exchange at stake. Other provisions in the Protocol indicate the intention to incorporate the production of global public goods that benefit the whole international community into ABS transactions.[68] These include the contribution of benefit-sharing to the conservation and sustainable use of biodiversity,[69] but also the realization of sustainable development broadly conceived and contributions to food security, public health, and the fight against climate change.[70] According to a teleological

[62] See Morgera, Buck, and Tsioumani (n. 44), at 11.

[63] Nagoya Protocol, Art. 4(3), calling for paying due regard to 'useful and relevant ongoing work or practices under such international instruments and relevant international organizations'. For a discussion, see Morgera, Tsioumani, and Buck (n. 6), at 84–109.

[64] Nagoya Protocol, Art. 19–20 mandating the governing body of the Protocol to consider developments in model contractual clauses, codes of conduct, and guidelines. For a discussion, see Morgera, Tsioumani, and Buck (n. 6), at 293–300.

[65] This section is based on E Morgera 'Justice, Equity and Benefit-Sharing Under the Nagoya Protocol to the Convention on Biological Diversity' (2015) Italian Yearbook of International Law 113.

[66] This is particularly the case of Art. 6(3): see Morgera, Tsioumani, and Buck (n. 6), at 157–169. See the critique from a justice perspective of the bilateral approach of the Nagoya Protocol in De Jonge, 'Towards a Fair and Equitable ABS Regime: Is Nagoya Leading Us in the Right Direction?' (2013) 9 Law Environment and Development Journal 243.

[67] Nagoya Protocol, preambular recital 8 (unnumbered in the original). See Morgera, Tsioumani, and Buck (n. 6), at 387–389.

[68] E Morgera, 'Bilateralism at the Service of Community Interests? Non-Judicial Enforcement of Global Public Goods in the Context of Global Environmental Law' (2012) 27 European Journal of International Law 743.

[69] Which is enshrined in the objective of the Protocol (Art. 1).

[70] Nagoya Protocol, preambular recitals 7 and 14.

interpretation of the Protocol, therefore, the commutative justice pursued through benefit-sharing is one that at the same time foresees a bilateral exchange and an underlying global exchange. In that connection, justice in exchange serves to reward (and thereby recognize) the contributions of provider countries as ecosystem stewards and suppliers of unique materials needed to advance scientific knowledge and environmental protection for the benefit of all humanity.[71] Technology transfer is specifically seen as a means to acknowledge and reward the contribution of developing countries providing genetic resources.[72]

With regards to *distributive* justice, it has been argued that benefit-sharing is not only about granting access to valued goods, such as the products or profits derived from research and development of genetic resources,[73] but also the fulfilment of basic needs.[74] In effect, some of the non-monetary benefits listed in the Protocol could address basic needs within provider countries and relevant communities: contributions to the local economy, food and livelihoods security, and research directed towards priority needs, taking into account domestic uses of genetic resources in provider countries.[75] In addition, the Preamble makes reference to the potential of ABS transactions to contribute to global needs with regard to scientific progress and innovation, poverty reduction, food security, and public health, as well as the importance of technology transfer and cooperation for adding value to genetic resources in developing countries and building their research capacities,[76] which are potential global benefits.[77]

The operational provisions of the Protocol on special considerations are also relevant from a distributive justice perspective. Parties are to consider expeditious benefit-sharing towards those in 'need', in particular developing countries, in the context of health-related emergencies, and strike a balance between the Protocol's bilateral ABS architecture and the continuation of exchanges of genetic resources for food and agriculture with a view to ultimately contributing to food security.[78] Taken together, these are multiple elements of distributive justice, which concern both the countries and communities directly involved in an ABS deal, and in some cases much wider, if not global, constituencies. Admittedly, however, these obligations have been framed in a way that leaves a significant amount of discretion regarding their implementation.

[71] This is recognized in particular in Nagoya Protocol, Art. 8(a). See Morgera, Tsioumani, and Buck (n. 6), at 179–184.

[72] Nagoya Protocol, Art. 23; and Morgera, Tsioumani, and Buck (n. 6), at 314–321.

[73] This is notably the case of the monetary benefits listed in the Annex to the Nagoya Protocol, section 1 such as payment of royalties or joint ventures, but also of non-monetary benefits such as the sharing of research and development results, and access to scientific information relevant to the conservation and sustainable use of biodiversity: Nagoya Protocol, Annex, 2(a) and (k).

[74] D Schroeder and T Pogge, 'Justice and the Convention on Biological Diversity' (2009) 23 Ethics and International Affairs 267, at 277.

[75] Nagoya Protocol, Annex 2(l), (o), and (m).

[76] ibid, preambular recitals 5, 7, and 14.

[77] For a sceptic reading of this language in the Protocol from a distributive justice perspective, see generally JB Kleba, 'Fair Biodiversity Politics with and beyond Rawls' (2013) 9 Law Environment and Development Journal 223.

[78] Nagoya Protocol, Art. 8(b–c). Morgera, Tsioumani, and Buck (n. 6), at 185–191; and M Wilke, 'A Trace of Distributive Justice in the Nagoya Protocol: Rules for Health Emergencies', contribution to workshop on 'Fairness and Bio-Knowledge', University of Warwick, Coventry, 16–17 June 2011.

All these substantive dimensions of justice compressed within the legal concept of benefit-sharing ultimately rely for their realization on *procedural* justice. In that regard, the provisions of the Protocol on prior informed consent appear significantly concerned with ensuring procedural fairness towards those seeking access to resources,[79] and have been considered 'thin' from a justice perspective.[80] The Nagoya Protocol appears to assume that procedural justice in determining the specific details of benefit-sharing among the parties to the exchange will permeate the establishment of mutually agreed terms.[81] The Protocol itself does not provide, however, any criteria in that regard either at the stage of the regulation of MAT negotiations in domestic ABS frameworks, their establishment, or their enforcement through international cooperation.[82] Much is thus left to contractual freedom, and it remains to be seen if and how State Parties to the Protocol will take the opportunity to limit private parties' freedom in this regard. The Protocol, though, requires Parties individually and collectively (through the Protocol's governing body) to explore model contractual clauses[83] and voluntary instruments,[84] as well as awareness-raising[85] and training activities,[86] that may provide a bottom-up source of inspiration for fair and equitable benefit-sharing contracts.

Even if this potentially participatory process for determining contextually fair contractual provisions can be seen as a promising way forward, particularly in light of the variety of sectors involved in ABS, procedural justice remains a particularly challenging goal when one considers the well-documented inequality in bargaining power that characterizes ABS relationships. These factors clearly point to the inter-linkages between procedural and contextual justice whose relevance in the Nagoya Protocol is discussed in the next section.

3.2 Missing the Contextual Justice Dimension?

Whether the Nagoya Protocol, and the legal concept of benefit-sharing enshrined in it, also comprises a dimension of *contextual* justice is a question that will be addressed by focusing on capabilities, corrective justice, and the need to address other structural causes of injustice, in turn.

With regard to capabilities, the Protocol provisions on capacity building,[87] funding,[88] and technology transfer[89] appear relevant. In particular, it should be

[79] Nagoya Protocol, Art. 6(3). See Morgera, Tsioumani, and Buck (n. 6), at 157–169.

[80] JB Kleba and D Rangnekar, 'Introduction' (2013) 9 Law Environment and Development Journal 102, at 103–104.

[81] Nagoya Protocol, Art. 5(1), (2), and (5), and preambular recital 10.

[82] The Nagoya Protocol provisions concerning MAT are invariably of a procedural character: Arts 5, 6(3)(g), 15, and 18. Some reference to substantive guarantees only transpires in the Protocol provision on supporting Indigenous and local communities in securing fairness and equity when negotiating MAT (Art. 12(3)(b)), and in a more diffident way on capacity building for developing countries (Art. 22(4)(b)), and specific reference to equity in voluntary terms (Art. 22(5)(b)).

[83] Nagoya Protocol, Art. 19.

[84] ibid, Art. 20.

[85] ibid, Art. 21.

[86] ibid, Arts 22(4)(c) and 22(5)(b).

[87] ibid, Art. 22, particularly 22(4)(b) and (5)(b), (i), and (j). See Morgera, Tsioumani, and Buck (n. 6), at 305–313. From a justice perspective, see Kleba (n. 77), at 235.

[88] Nagoya Protocol, Art. 25. Morgera, Tsioumani, and Buck (n. 6), at 325–332.

[89] Nagoya Protocol, Art. 23. Morgera, Tsioumani, and Buck (n. 6), at 314–321 and 325–332.

noted that the Protocol addresses capacity building in detail, linking it to implementation and compliance, the negotiation of MAT, the development and enforcement of domestic ABS frameworks, and the development of endogenous research capabilities.[90] In addition, the Protocol not only addresses this question at the inter-State level, but also specifically calls upon State Parties to facilitate the involvement of Indigenous peoples and local communities in capacity building cooperation[91] and support the self-identification of their capacity needs and priorities.[92] Vested interests, however, may emerge in practice when user countries act as providers of financial and technological assistance, as well as capacity building.[93] User countries providing such assistance could create conditions in provider countries that unduly favour the access side of the exchange, particularly when provider countries find themselves dependent on external support or are offered pre-packaged solutions that may not fit their particular circumstances.[94] It remains to be seen in future practice whether the involvement of multilateral bodies providing guidance[95] or channelling resources[96] may be able to balance procedural and contextual justice in this regard.

Corrective justice could also have played a role in the Nagoya Protocol, and benefit-sharing could have served as compensation for a historical asymmetry between provider and user countries. Colonization, mandatory assimilation, relocation policies, and globalization forces have resulted in the appropriation of genetic resources from traditional territories and the marginalization of Indigenous peoples and local communities and the erosion of their cultures, governance, and traditional knowledge systems.[97] During the negotiations of the Nagoya Protocol, the African Group and civil society argued that benefit-sharing under the Protocol should also have addressed historical situations, with a view to expanding the range of situations in which the benefit-sharing obligations of the Protocol would apply and addressing possible loopholes related to gene banks in developed countries' existing ex situ collections. For these reasons the negotiations on the temporal scope of the Protocol were particularly contentious.[98] In the end, most commentators agree that the Protocol does not apply to genetic resources acquired prior to the entry into force of the Convention.[99] But it

[90] Nagoya Protocol, Art. 22(4).

[91] ibid, Art. 22(1).

[92] ibid, Art. 22(3).

[93] E Morgera, 'The EU and Environmental Multilateralism: The Case of Access and Benefit-Sharing and the Need for a Good-Faith Test' (2014) 16 Cambridge Yearbook of European Legal Studies 109.

[94] Morgera, Tsioumani, and Buck (n. 6), at 313.

[95] See, for instance, the governing body of the Nagoya Protocol. See also the Strategic Framework for Capacity-Building and Development to Support the Effective Implementation of the Nagoya Protocol on Access and Benefit-Sharing in Decision NP-1/8 (2014), Annex.

[96] The Global Environment Facility. See the discussion in Morgera, Tsioumani, and Buck (n. 6), at 327–329.

[97] For a comprehensive account of the threats and challenges that Indigenous peoples face and the response of the international community, see UN Permanent Forum on Indigenous Issues, 'State of the World's Indigenous Peoples' (2009), available at http://www.un.org/esa/socdev/unpfii/documents/SOWIP/en/SOWIP_web.pdf, accessed 26 June 2023.

[98] Nagoya Protocol, Art. 3. Morgera, Tsioumani, and Buck (n. 6), at 77–80.

[99] The Nagoya Protocol reference to 'genetic resources within the scope of Art. 15 of the Convention' (Art. 3) presupposes the existence of a Party to the Convention, i.e. that the Convention has entered into

remains debatable whether benefit-sharing obligations arise under the Protocol for new or continuing uses of genetic resources and traditional knowledge acquired in the interim period between the entry into force of the CBD and that of the Protocol,[100] which could provide some corrective justice for more recent appropriations of genetic resources and traditional knowledge. Until that is clarified, by a decision of the Protocol governing body or its compliance mechanism for instance, the role of corrective justice under the Protocol remains an open question that is addressed in different ways in domestic implementing measures. The incomplete theorization of the Nagoya Protocol is therefore underpinned by different policy agendas and has led to differing interpretations and practices by Parties.

Furthermore, it could be asked whether the Nagoya Protocol also attempts to address other preconditions determining an uneven playing field in the ABS context. In this context certain systems created in other areas of international law could be seen as a determining factor in shaping unequal power relationships. As has already been noted by Schroeder and Pogge with regard to the CBD,[101] there is no attempt in the Protocol to trigger a reform of the global economic order concerning bio-based research, and consequently benefit-sharing under the Nagoya Protocol is seen as a 'very partial remedy'.[102] The most obvious example of this approach can be found in the minimalistic treatment of IPRs under the Protocol, although the role of IPRs in bio-based innovations is largely seen as unjust.[103] The Nagoya Protocol avoids almost all reference to IPRs. Instead, it could have provided an authoritative mandate for its Parties to adopt national measures that might deviate from the relevant law of the WTO and afford protection in the event of a possible WTO legal dispute.[104]

While benefit-sharing under the Nagoya Protocol is certainly only a partial response, it may still work as an interim solution having the potential to gradually erode structural conditions of injustice from the inside. Systematically applied in light of the interpretative opportunities identified in this section, benefit-sharing could trigger beneficial dynamics nurtured by positive, mutual interactions between justice in exchange and recognition, as well as distributive and procedural justice. At the inter-State level, provider countries could truly benefit from fair ABS relationships in the long term if they are recognized and rewarded for their global contributions to the conservation of genetic resources and gradually build their own biotech capacities through their bilateral collaborations with user countries, as well as contributing together with user countries to the realization of other global goals such as poverty reduction, health protection, and food security.

force. That being said, it cannot be ruled out that this discussion may be reopened in the context of Nagoya Protocol, Art. 10. Morgera, Tsioumani, and Buck (n. 6), at 201–202.

[100] Morgera, Tsioumani, and Buck (n. 6), at 77–80.
[101] Schroeder and Pogge (n. 74), at 280.
[102] ibid.
[103] The vast majority of countries in the international community argue for a revision of the WTO Agreement on Trade-Related Aspects of Intellectual Property Rights. In this regard, see Pavoni, 'The Nagoya Protocol and WTO Law' in Morgera, Tsioumani, and Buck (n. 6), at 185, and 209, note 117.
[104] Morgera, Tsioumani, and Buck (n. 6), at 212.

The necessary and appropriate conditions for this vision to materialize are yet to be fully identified, as are the opportunities and risks regarding the potential and actual global benefits that may arise from bilateral exchanges, or the identification (and risks of exclusion) of the beneficiaries of specific bilateral exchange. To that end, a better understanding of the instruments that international law offers is needed. In particular, it appears necessary to rely on general international law to fully appreciate the opportunities and limitations of the Nagoya Protocol with regard to justice. The following sections, therefore, explore the correspondence between different notions of justice and different understandings of the role of equity in international law by revisiting the traditional debate on the functions of equity in the context of the continuous sub-specialization of different international regimes, with a view to ensuring unity across different international sub-systems.

3.3 Benefit-Sharing as Equity *Infra Legem*

With regard to equity within the law, the framing of fair and equitable benefit-sharing as the objective of the Protocol[105] suggests that the intended function is indeed an interpretative one.[106] Therefore, beyond the specific benefit-sharing obligations that can be found in the Protocol,[107] benefit-sharing can serve to guide Parties in balancing different interests at stake with regard to the implementation and application of the Protocol's other flexible provisions, such as mandates for national access measures,[108] international cooperation on compliance with national ABS measures of other State Parties,[109] and financial and technological solidarity.[110] This can serve to identify reasonable and appropriate measures that genuinely contribute to realizing fair and equitable benefit-sharing.[111] In that connection, benefit-sharing serves to provide a benchmark for applying proportionality: the measures to be adopted at the national level need to be suitable and necessary to share benefits fairly and equitably—that is, to realize justice in exchange, as well as distributive and procedural justice as discussed above. So understood, benefit-sharing as equity *infra legem* sets material limits to States' margin of discretion and provides a benchmark to explore the suitability of domestic measures[112] in pursuing both bilateral and global benefits for the purposes of both commutative and distributive justice. This interpretation can serve to support beneficiaries' agency and the co-development of solutions with them.

More difficult, however, is to understand whether the interpretative function of benefit-sharing can cater to procedural justice. The Protocol fundamentally leaves the

[105] Nagoya Protocol, Art. 1; Morgera, Tsioumani, and Buck (n. 6), at 48–58.
[106] VCLT, Art. 31(1).
[107] Nagoya Protocol, Art. 5.
[108] ibid, Art. 6.
[109] ibid, Art. 15.
[110] ibid, Arts 23 and 25.
[111] Morgera, Tsioumani, and Buck (n. 6), at 377–381.
[112] R Kläger, *Fair and Equitable Treatment in International Investment Law* (Cambridge University Press, 2013), at 237.

details of the negotiations for the identification of benefits and modalities of sharing them to private, contractual negotiations (MAT). In Francioni's words:

> This solution ... leaves uncertain whether equity is to be understood as *infra legem*, ie operating in the context of applicable principles and rules of international law, including the rules on the treatment of aliens and the rules governing the status of international public goods, or outside the law as an autonomous and unstructured source of principles which are assumed to inspire contractual arrangements.[113]

In effect, not only does the Nagoya Protocol omit any substantive criteria to ensure the establishment of equitable MAT,[114] but on the procedural side, it does not provide any explicit mechanism to ensure fair negotiations of MAT.[115] Nonetheless, it could be argued that interpreting States' obligations under the Nagoya Protocol in light of the objective of fairly and equitably sharing benefits would imply State Parties' governments should also have an active role in ensuring procedural justice at the stage of private contractual negotiations. This could be achieved through control and monitoring of private parties as part of States' due diligence under international law,[116] particularly when international human rights law is relevant and applicable. The Protocol seems to explicitly point to less interventionist approaches in this regard, limited to encouragement,[117] which can imply the creation of specific incentives to achieve that objective, or at the very least the removal of obstacles or disincentives, including in other related areas of national law.[118] Nothing in the Protocol, however, prevents Parties from taking bolder approaches in ensuring procedural justice at the point at which MAT are established, and supportive arguments based on equity within the law and procedural justice could provide a strong basis to that end.

3.4 Benefit-Sharing as Equity *Praeter Legem*

Although the Nagoya Protocol is mainly focused on bilateral ABS relationships, it foresees the opportunity to develop inter-State benefit-sharing as a global mechanism too. In effect, Article 10 of the Protocol calls upon Parties to determine whether a gap exists in international law with regard to situations in which the utilization of genetic resources occurs in transboundary situations or in situations in which it is not

[113] F Francioni, 'Equity' in R Wolfrum (ed.), *The Max Planck Encyclopedia of Public International Law* (Oxford University Press, 2012), online edition available at http://www.mpepil.com, accessed 6 March 2024, para. 28.

[114] Nagoya Protocol, Art. 5(1)(2) and (5), and preambular recital 10. See M Tedvt, 'Beyond Nagoya: Towards a Legally Functional System of Access and Benefit-Sharing' in Oberthür and Rosendal (n. 7), 158.

[115] Morgera, Tsioumani, and Buck (n. 6), at 376.

[116] ibid, at 131–132, 167–169, and 283–292.

[117] As specifically mandated by Art. 9 of the Nagoya Protocol in relation to directing benefits towards conservation and sustainable use (Morgera, Tsioumani, and Buck (n. 6), at 192–196).

[118] A series of domestic laws will likely affect the effective functioning of domestic ABS frameworks, such as general environmental law, social-welfare law, property law, administrative law, commercial law, and contract law: Young (n. 50), at 462–463.

possible for a State to obtain or grant prior informed consent. Should Parties reach that conclusion, a global benefit-sharing mechanism is to be established to fill that gap for the purposes of pursuing equity to the benefit of the conservation and sustainable use of biodiversity globally.[119] This could be understood as an instance in which the Nagoya Protocol engages in equity beyond the law, operationalizing equity in its gap-filling function. The question of whether the Protocol should serve to share benefits from the use of genetic resources in ex situ collections is among the outstanding questions that Parties to the Nagoya Protocol are considering with a view to determining a possible gap.[120] Therefore, there is a chance in that connection to address certain questions related to the temporal scope of the Protocol, potentially allowing for a degree of corrective justice.

Equity beyond the law could also be relevant for the Nagoya Protocol provision on relationships with other agreements, and in particular with future specialized ABS instruments.[121] While the question is quite controversial,[122] as various international regimes outside of the CBD may wish to retain their independence,[123] there is scope to consider how new international instruments can fill a gap with more specialized approaches than are possible under the Protocol. In that connection, it has been recommended that a principled approached based on international objectives (such as those of the CBD); international goals (such as the Sustainable Development Goals); and general principles of international law, such as good faith, effectiveness, and legitimate expectations guide international consideration of whether a gap exists for more specialized ABS instruments to fill.[124]

3.5 Benefit-Sharing as Equity *Contra Legem*

The question as to whether benefit-sharing as framed in the Nagoya Protocol could also operationalize equity *contra legem* is a very difficult one, which currently can only be answered in a speculative manner. Nevertheless, it will be attempted here to engage with this function in order to return to the questions of contextual justice identified in the previous section, notably in the context of the relationship between the Protocol and other international regimes, particularly outside the area of international environmental law. With regard to law-making, the fact that the Protocol avoided offering a legal basis for exploiting the exceptions and flexibilities in international law on IPRs arguably suggests that using benefit-sharing as equity *contra legem* could have been

[119] De Jonge (n. 66), at 251–253.

[120] This question remains pending as of December 2022: Decision NP-4/10. For some background, see E Morgera, 'Study on experiences gained with the development and implementation of the Nagoya Protocol and other multilateral mechanisms and the potential relevance of ongoing work undertaken by other processes, including case studies' UN Doc UNEP/CBD/ABS/A10/EM/2016/1/2 (2015).

[121] Nagoya Protocol Art. 4(4).

[122] This also remains pending: Decision NP-4/11 (2022) Specialized international access and benefit-sharing instruments in the context of Art. 4, para. 4 of the Nagoya Protocol.

[123] This is particularly the case of the instruments developed under the WHO.

[124] E Morgera, S Switzer, and E Tsioumani, Study into criteria to identify a specialized international access and benefit-sharing instrument, and a possible process for its recognition UN Doc CBD/SBI/2/INF/17 (2018).

theoretically possible, but States were unable to agree on this matter. It was argued during the negotiations that the question was being addressed under a more competent law-making forum, namely the World Intellectual Property Organization.[125] However, as the fate of these negotiations remains quite uncertain at the time of writing, the foundations for enhanced mutual supportiveness between intellectual property rights and benefit-sharing could have been laid, at least for the interim, by the Nagoya Protocol.

Another hypothetical avenue for benefit-sharing to operationalize equity *contra legem* could be the relationship between the Protocol and international investment law. The latter could be invoked by a user that can claim to act as a foreign investor and allege a conflict between a provider country's ABS measures and the terms of an applicable bilateral investment treaty.[126] In fact, the text of the Nagoya Protocol on relationships with existing international agreements[127] seems to support equity *infra legem* rather *contra legem* in this context. Parties should avoid any principled approach in assessing and addressing the relationship of the Nagoya Protocol with other existing international agreements, focusing on a pragmatic, case-by-case approach to mutual supportiveness through interpretation based on systemic integration.[128] Nonetheless, in both IPRs and international investment law, it is possible that an international adjudicator in the future may rely on fair and equitable benefit-sharing, as developed in the Nagoya Protocol and interpreted in a mutually supportive fashion with relevant international human rights law, to derogate from provisions in other international economic treaties that are difficult to reconcile with ABS.

As the above analysis shows, concrete opportunities for an interpretation of the Nagoya Protocol inspired by a pluralistic notion of environmental justice exist—which may appear quite a provocative finding when seen in the light of the criticisms concerning the limitations of the Protocol[129] and of the negotiating dynamics that led to its adoption.[130] At the very least, engaging with environmental justice assists in revealing implicit legal design choices that limit the types of justice pursued in international law-making. It also serves to systematically unveil existing opportunities for interpreting international law that could contribute to achieving justice through

[125] Namely, the WIPO Intergovernmental Committee on Intellectual Property and Genetic Resources, Traditional Knowledge and Folklore: WIPO General Assembly, 'Matters Concerning Intellectual Property and Genetic Resources, Traditional Knowledge and Folklore', WIPO Doc WO/GA/26/6, 3 October 2000.

[126] J viñuales, *Foreign Investment and the Environment in International Law* (Cambridge University Press, 2012), at 205.

[127] Nagoya Protocol, Art. 4(1).

[128] Morgera, Tsioumani, and Buck (n. 6), at 86–88.

[129] During the closing plenary, a number of delegations including the African Group, the Central and Eastern European Group, Venezuela, and Bolivia made statements for the record to emphasize their doubts about the new instrument's quality: Report of the tenth meeting of the Conference of the Parties to the Convention on Biological Diversity, UN Doc UNEP/CBD/COP/10/27 (2011), paras 98–102. See also Singh Nijar, 'An Asian Developing Country View on the Implementation Challenges of the Nagoya Protocol', in Morgera, Buck, and Tsioumani (n. 39), 247.

[130] See, e.g., Oberthür and Rabitz, 'The Role of the European Union in the Nagoya Protocol Negotiations: Self-Interested Bridge Building' in Oberthür and Rosendal (n. 7), 79; and B Coolasaet and J Pitseys, 'Fair and Equitable Negotiations? African Influence and the International Access and Benefit-Sharing Regime' (2015) 15 Global Environmental Politics 38.

equitable principles that can be employed in negotiating concrete understandings of justice on a case-by-case basis.

4. Differences and Common Challenges in Other ABS Regimes

The governance of ABS has been conceptualized as a regime complex consisting of the Nagoya Protocol, the CBD, ABS instruments under the WHO, and the Food and Agriculture Organization's (FAO) International Plant Treaty.[131] It also includes the 2023 BBNJ Agreement. While this chapter will not analyse the other regimes to the same depth as the Nagoya Protocol, the following sections will reflect on a different approach to fair and equitable benefit-sharing taken under these instruments (notably the preference for multilateral mechanisms for inter-State benefit-sharing) and identify some common challenges, particularly with regard to digital sequence information.

4.1 International Plant Treaty

While the International Plant Treaty has as its objective, in harmony with the CBD, the conservation and sustainable use of plant genetic resources for food and agriculture (PGRFA), as well as the fair and equitable sharing of benefits arising from their use, it adopted a multilateral approach to benefit-sharing. This was considered more suited to the specific characteristics of agricultural biodiversity. Agricultural biodiversity is characterized by a very high and historically well-established interdependence across countries, which results in it being virtually impossible to identify countries of origin. In addition, agricultural biodiversity is characterized by the need to use plant genetic resources for food and agriculture for the purposes of their conservation—in other words, compared to other genetic resources, these genetic resources are lost if they are not used in agriculture.[132]

In this specific context, distributive justice issues have arisen because 'seed companies were using PGRFA without cost, but they were restricting access to the improved varieties, which ought to have been shared with farmers as a matter of reciprocity.[133] IPRs have thus negatively impacted on traditional and small-scale farming communities, eroding their control over genetic and natural resources, with knock-on effects on their socio-cultural and economic well-being.[134] Meanwhile, assumptions that technological improvement by seed companies, such as high-yielding crop varieties, benefit society at large have been largely disproven, as the vast majority of benefits are reaped by the same transnational corporations.[135] This also raises recognition

[131] S Oberthür and J Pozarowska, 'Managing Institutional Complexity and Fragmentation: The Nagoya Protocol and the Global Governance of Genetic Resources' (2013) 13 Global Environmental Politics 100, at 106.

[132] Tsioumani (n. 18), at 16.

[133] ibid, at 29. This intra-State benefit-sharing dimension is discussed in Chapter 4.

[134] ibid, at 29.

[135] ibid, at 26.

issues, as it undervalues the contributions of farmers and their knowledge in contrast to the innovation driven by the agri-business sector. Equally, it raises contextual justice issues: the underlying conditions for small-scale farmers to flourish are undermined by agri-business, making it more difficult, if not impossible, for small-scale farmers to contribute to international goals and produce local benefits.

This has led Elsa Tsioumani to reach two conclusions. On the one hand, fair and equitable benefit-sharing in the context of agricultural biodiversity had been devised as a 'development tool to reap part of the gains of biodiversity market, as well as an incentive for stewards of biodiversity . . . to reward them and enable their continued contribution to the conservation and sustainable use of biodiversity'.[136] On the other hand, benefit-sharing has not been secured by benefit-sharing guarantees under the IPR system. Instead, the latter, not only has not contributed to ensuring compliance with benefit-sharing, but it has supported the 'continuous expansion of patentable subject matter in view of breakthroughs of modern biotechnology, high corporate concentration in the agro-chemical sector' and bilateral trade and investment agreements[137]

Against this background, the analysis in this section of fair and equitable benefit-sharing under the International Plant Treaty is aimed at highlighting innovations in treaty design as a response to these equity issues, as well as continuous challenges and tensions. The latter explain the still incomplete theorization of benefit-sharing in this legal framework, even if it is nonetheless one of the most sophisticated in the international arena.

The International Plant Treaty establishes a multilateral system of access and benefit-sharing[138] with a view to facilitating access to, and exchange of, a specified list of crops[139] (such as rice, potatoes, and maize)[140] that are under the management and control of State Parties and in the public domain, as well as those held by a network of collections 'in trust for the benefit of the international community'.[141] The specified crops are held in a common pool of plant genetic resources for food and agriculture. The collection was identified using criteria related food security and interdependence.[142] This pooling of resources has been possible due to a pre-existing 'internationally coordinated network of centres' (CGIAR centres), that were brought under the aegis and international objectives of the International Plant Treaty in order to confirm their mandate to hold their collections 'in trust for the benefit of the international community'.[143] While in theory this pool of resources could support voluntary inclusion of collections by private companies, as well as Indigenous peoples and local

[136] ibid, at 39.
[137] ibid.
[138] ITPGRFA, Art. 11.
[139] ITPGRFA, Annex I.
[140] ITPGRFA, Governing Body Res 2/2006 (2006).
[141] Agreement with FAO to Place the International Agricultural Research Centres of the Consultative Group on International Agricultural Research In-Trust Collections of Plant Genetic Resources under the Auspices of FAO (1994); and CGIAR Principles on the Management of Intellectual Assets (2012): E Tsioumani, 'Beyond Access and Benefit-sharing: Lessons from the Law and Governance of Agricultural Biodiversity', Edinburgh School of Law Research Paper No. 2016/18 (SSRN, 2016), available at https://papers.ssrn.com/sol3/papers.cfm?abstract_id=2796658, accessed 26 June 2023.
[142] ITPGRFA, Art. 11(1) and Preamble.
[143] Tsioumani (n. 18), at 11–12.

communities, it basically includes crops listed in Annex I to the Treaty that are 'under the management and control of parties and in the public domain, as well as those under the CGIAR centres'.[144] The exchange of crops and forages under the multilateral system 'should solely serve for research, breeding and training for food and agriculture, and not for other uses',[145] which are, instead, covered by the Nagoya Protocol.[146]

4.1.1 Standard Material Transfer Agreement Versus MATs

From a global environmental law perspective, although multilateral benefit-sharing is often conceived as an inter-State mechanism, all existing multilateral benefit-sharing mechanisms ultimately rely on standard contractual clauses to reach non-State actors that will ultimately be those producing benefits.[147] The crops in the multilateral system are in fact exchanged according to the terms of the standard Material Transfer Agreement (SMTA), which is a standardized contract that was intergovernmentally negotiated and adopted by the Treaty's governing body.[148] As opposed to ad hoc private contractual negotiations under the Nagoya Protocol, here recourse is had to contractual clauses agreed among States for the realization of the Treaty objective of fair and equitable benefit-sharing. In other words, States, who are bound to achieve Treaty objectives, were responsible for devising contractual clauses, such as to ensure that a private law instrument could achieve a public international law objective.[149] A standardized contractual approach, in principle, allows for the withdrawal of intergovernmental consensus on certain conditions to achieve fairness and equity in the relationship with a private user, while making a clear and explicit connection with the public international law dimension of the underlying inter-State benefit-sharing obligations.[150] To that end, such a contract can make reference to treaty objectives and international provisions as terms of reference for the interpretation of the contract[151] to ensure uniform interpretation across jurisdictions where users may be based. To some extent, further theorization can occur when successive negotiations (of the

[144] ibid, at 17.

[145] ITPGRFA, Art. 12(3)(a). Tsioumani (n. 18), at 16.

[146] C Chiarolla, S Louafi, and M Schloen, 'An Analysis of the Relationship between the Nagoya Protocol and Instruments related to Genetic Resources for Food and Agriculture and Farmers' Rights' in Morgera, Buck, and Tsioumani (n. 39) 83.

[147] J Harrison, 'Who benefits from the exploitation of non-living resources on the seabed? Operationalizing the benefit-sharing provisions in the UN Convention on the Law of the Sea', BENELEX blog (July 2015); and E Morgera, 'Multilateral benefit-sharing: whither from here?', BENELEX blog (June 2016). All BENELEX blog posts cited in this chapter can be found at https://benelexblog.wordpress.com, last accessed 28 July 2023.

[148] ITPGRFA Governing Body Res 2/2006 (2006).

[149] First, this is done through an express choice of law clause in the SMTA, which refers to 'General Principles of Law, including the UNIDROIT Principles of International Commercial Contracts 2004, the *objectives and the relevant provisions of the Treaty* and, where necessary for interpretation, the decisions of the Governing Body': SMTA, Art. 7 (emphasis added). In addition, the SMTA excludes disputes in national courts in different jurisdictions, thereby maximizing the chances of applying the contractual clauses in a uniform manner. This is also aided by the role of the FAO as the third-party beneficiary acting in the interests of the providers.

[150] Morgera and Gillies (n. 54).

[151] C Chiarolla, 'Plant Patenting, Benefit Sharing and the Law Applicable to the Food and Agriculture Organisation Standard Material Transfer Agreement' (2008) 11 Journal of World Intellectual Property 1, observes that: 'The reference to "the objectives and the relevant provisions of the Treaty" (i.e. truly international standards) reflects the important public interest functions discharged by the SMTA.'

SMTA) have allowed Parties to further advance regime design through a global law approach.

These considerations are not only relevant by way of contrast with the ad hoc contractual approach of the Nagoya Protocol. They may also be relevant *de lege ferenda*, if the Parties to the Nagoya Protocol decide to internationally endorse model contractual clauses[152] whether generally or as a 'predetermination of enforceability' that would enable Parties to ensure their automatic recognition in domestic courts.[153] This development could lead to a re-universalising experience of what was delegated to the contractual level to realize international treaty objectives. Specifically, the Nagoya Protocol creates a best-endeavour obligation for all Parties to support the development, update, and use of model contractual clauses for MAT.[154] This obligation can be undertaken unilaterally by State Parties establishing 'default' or 'standard' MAT for specific categories of genetic resources under their jurisdiction or for specific cases.[155] Such default MAT would likely have to be accepted by a user upon applying for access to genetic resources and/or traditional knowledge, or could apply automatically unless different MAT are negotiated.[156] Parties could also implement this obligation collectively in the context of bilateral or regional ABS frameworks,[157] as well as at the multilateral level.

This obligation should be read in conjunction with the obligation for Parties to endeavour to support, as appropriate, the development by Indigenous peoples and local communities of model contractual clauses for benefit-sharing arising from the utilization of traditional knowledge associated with genetic resources.[158] On this basis, the Protocol's governing body is to periodically 'take stock' of the use of standardized contractual clauses,[159] seeking to tap into normative activities undertaken by various ABS stakeholders. These include the research community, the private sector, Indigenous peoples and local communities, and NGOs at the national (but also sub-national and transnational) levels as a bottom-up source of inspiration for multilateral discussions on ways to facilitate implementation of and compliance with the Protocol.[160]

4.1.2 Accruing Monetary Benefits

The benefits shared under the International Plant Treaty are both monetary[161] and non-monetary. The latter encompass information exchange, technology transfer, and facilitated access to Annex I resources.[162]

[152] Nagoya Protocol, Art. 19(2).
[153] Young (n. 50), at 493. Such endorsement could be undertaken on the basis of Nagoya Protocol, Art. 26(4)(f).
[154] Nagoya Protocol, Art. 19(1).
[155] Morgera, Tsioumani, and Buck (n. 6), at 144.
[156] See, for instance, the standard conditions that apply to bioprospecting activities with non-commercial purpose on Commonwealth territories in Australia: 'Permits for Non-Commercial Purposes', Government of Australia, https://www.dcceew.gov.au/science-research/australias-biological-resources/permits-–-accessing-biological-resourc-1, accessed 5 February 2024.
[157] See Morgera, Tsioumani, and Buck (n. 6), at 93.
[158] Nagoya Protocol, Art. 12(3)(c). See Morgera, Tsioumani, and Buck (n. 6), at 216.
[159] Nagoya Protocol, Art. 19(2).
[160] E Morgera, M Buck, and E Tsioumani, 'Introduction' in Morgera, Buck, and Tsioumani (n. 39), 10.
[161] Tsioumani (n. 18), at 17.
[162] ITPGRFA, Art. 13.

The SMTA provides a choice between two mandatory monetary benefit-sharing options: a default scheme, according to which the recipient will pay 1.1 per cent of gross sales to the Treaty's benefit-sharing fund in case of commercialization of new products incorporating material accessed from the multilateral system and if its availability to others is restricted; and an alternative formula whereby recipients pay 0.5 per cent of gross sales on all products of the species they accessed from the multilateral system, regardless of whether the products incorporate the material accessed or whether the new products are available without restriction.[163] Those that make their products available for further research and breeding without restriction, however, are exempted from mandatory payments, but can make voluntary payments.[164]

Elsa Tsioumani unveiled a fundamental paradox in this approach. In theory, monetary benefit-sharing in this context serves as a form of compensation for patenting products arising from the pool of genetic resources. At the same time, it serves as a disincentive to patenting, in order to favour 'continued unrestricted exchanges of genetic resources for research and breeding'.[165] In fact, access to plant genetic resources for food and agriculture through a multilateral system is considered a benefit in itself under the Treaty, since the exchange of these resources is indispensable for the continuation of agricultural research and food security.[166] However, at the same time, it is conceived as the 'central tool for revenue generation' both for the intra-State benefit-sharing objective of the Treaty (accruing monetary benefits that can be distributed to farmers as a recognition of their historic and continued contributions) and inter-State benefit-sharing in the form of food security.[167] In other words, these contradictions represent an unresolved tension between recognition and support for 'modern scientific methods of identifying and developing new varieties on the basis of materials in ex situ collections and farmers' traditional agro-ecological approaches'.[168]

In addition to these inherent contradictions in how the design of inter-State benefit-sharing has sought to address both distributive justice and recognition under the International Plant Treaty, this approach to monetary benefit-sharing has not proved viable in practice. Only voluntary monetary contributions have been provided under the SMTA; no benefit-sharing payments. There are several practical reasons for this that are specific to the sector: the long and unpredictable time between research and commercialized innovation; the incomplete coverage of the multilateral system, leading innovators to access most materials from private companies' collections or non-party entities (effectively creating a loophole in the system);[169] and treaty parties' failure to notify the Secretariat of their genetic resources included in the MLS, rendering them inaccessible to users due to lack of awareness.[170]

[163] See the ITPGRFA Standard Material Transfer Agreement, Arts 6(7) and 6(11).
[164] Tsioumani (n. 18), at 17.
[165] ibid, at 20.
[166] ITPGRFA, Art. 13.
[167] Tsioumani (n. 18), at 20 and 36.
[168] ibid, at 21.
[169] E Tsioumani, 'Why Technicalities Matter – On the International Treaty on Plant Genetic Resources for Food and Agriculture and the Seventh Session of its Governing Body', BENELEX blog (March 2018).
[170] Tsioumani (n. 18), at 20.

On the whole, notwithstanding the limited transaction costs associated with a standard contractual approach, as opposed to the ad hoc one under the Nagoya Protocol, the SMTA is only used to a limited extent and no monetary benefits have yet been accrued.[171] A process is currently underway under the International Plant Treaty to develop an upfront subscription system (in the form of fees for accessing materials in the multilateral system)[172] that may replace or complement the current payment obligations after commercialization. The proposed system is expected to further reduce transaction costs (as it would save the costs of tracking genetic resources until their commercialization) and increase legal certainty.[173] These negotiations are expected to amend the standard contractual clauses,[174] reflecting on lessons learnt in the implementation of the Treaty so far. This process aims to advance the theorization of benefit-sharing in this specific context.

These challenges in accruing monetary benefits under the International Plant Treaty—the most sophisticated international benefit-sharing mechanism to date—cast a shadow over the feasibility of monetary benefit-sharing under other less sophisticated regimes such as the Nagoya Protocol (which identifies monetary benefits as profits in the form of access fees, upfront or milestone payments, royalties, or licence fees).[175] They also provide lessons for other ABS regimes.[176]

4.1.3 Sharing Monetary and Non-Monetary Benefits

The International Plant Treaty foresees benefit-sharing with all State parties, specifically focusing on developing countries as beneficiaries of technology transfer, capacity building, and the allocation of commercial benefits.[177] The Treaty also ensures that benefits deriving from the use of plant genetic resources for food and agriculture flow directly and indirectly to farmers in all countries, particularly in developing countries, irrespective of whether they have contributed relevant genetic material to the multilateral system, according to internationally agreed upon eligibility and selection criteria.[178]

A global Benefit-Sharing Fund established under the Treaty channels monetary benefits (as discussed above, voluntary donations) to particular activities in developing countries with a view to assisting specific communities and partner research institutions in producing global benefits (in terms of conservation and sustainable use

[171] Tsioumani (n. 189).

[172] IT/GB-6/15/6 Add.1 and Rev.1 (2015).

[173] S Gagnon et al., 'Summary of the Sixth Session of the Governing Body of the International Treaty on Plant Genetic Resources for Food and Agriculture' (2015) 9(565) Earth Negotiations Bulletin 4.

[174] These negotiations were halted in 2019 and resumed in 2022: see E Tsioumani et al., 'Summary of the Ninth Session of the Governing Body of the International Treaty on Plant Genetic Resources for Food and Agriculture (19–24 September 2022)' (2022) 9(782) Earth Negotiations Bulletin 1, https://enb.iisd.org/sites/default/files/2022-09/enb09782e_0.pdf, accessed 5 February 2024.

[175] Nagoya Protocol, Annex, 1(a–e).

[176] E Morgera, 'Critical Considerations vis-à-vis the Possible Outcomes for Fair and Equitable Sharing of Pathogens, Genetic Sequences and Benefits under a Pandemic Instrument' in Pedro A. Villarreal et al., *Averting a Collision Course? Beyond the Pandemic Instrument and the International Health Regulations*, discussion papers prepared for the event held on 26 April 2023 at the Geneva Graduate Institute, 16–22.

[177] ITPGRFA, Art. 13(2)(b)(ii–iii), 13(2)(c), and 13(4).

[178] ITPGRFA, Art. 13(3) and Annexes 1–3 to the Funding Strategy in 2007; FAO, Report of the Governing Body of the International Treaty on Plant Genetic Resources for Food and Agriculture (2007).

of biodiversity) as well as community livelihoods.[179] Monetary benefits, once shared through the Benefit-Sharing Fund, lead, through funded projects, to the production of further non-monetary benefits, such as training and partnerships between breeders and farmers.[180]

The Benefit-Sharing Fund represents a response to distributive justice issues, namely the realization that the 'strong belief that benefits would flow to developing countries in the form of distribution of plant genetic resources and related information' did not materialize due to 'global inequities regarding the distribution of infrastructures, knowledge and skills, which are necessary to make use of an open system'.[181] In addition, the Fund takes into account certain aspects of contextual justice by seeking to respond to 'changing needs and demands in the face of climate change, giving priorities to farmers in developing countries'.[182]

Equity and fairness were addressed through specific eligibility and selection criteria to assess project proposals, which were adopted by the Treaty's governing body and applied by a panel of experts. This approach served to create links between international and local benefits, taking into account how local contributions affect and are impacted by the realization of the SDGs in relation to traditional knowledge holders. At the same time, however, the competitive nature of this project-based approach took insufficient account of the unequal capacities of different countries and actors[183] and therefore created issues at the intersection of capabilities and distributive justice. To address some of these concerns, the Treaty Secretariat organized a series of workshops to help applicants prepare proposals.[184] In addition, in 2021, a new Monitoring, Learning and Evaluation Framework was adopted for the Benefit-Sharing Fund, which included indicators and outcomes on '(l)ivelihoods improved for small-scale farmers in developing countries, and food security and sustainable agriculture promoted, through the conservation and sustainable use of plant genetic resources for food and agriculture'.[185] These developments provide additional examples of the iterative adaptation of an ABS regime.

Prioritizing and effectively supporting beneficiaries in an increasingly complex landscape of diverse actors and different (public and private) interests remains an issue under the Treaty. Agricultural research centres are expected to be 'instrumental in addressing the unequal capacities of countries and communities to benefit from the [Treaty] and genetic resource use in general, and thus bridging the capacity, fairness and equity gap in agriculture and agrobiodiversity conservation'.[186] These centres often act as intermediaries, holding projects from the Benefit-Sharing Fund, and they are expected to work with farmers in their implementation as well as sharing the outcomes of research, such as improved seed varieties, information and training, and

[179] https://www.fao.org/plant-treaty/areas-of-work/funding/en/, accessed 3 August 2023.
[180] Tsioumani (n. 18), at 19.
[181] ibid, at 11.
[182] ibid, at 18.
[183] S Louafi, 'Reflections on the Resource Allocation Strategy of the Benefit Sharing Fund' (Swiss Federal Office for Agriculture, 2013).
[184] Tsioumani (n. 18), at 22.
[185] IT/GB-9/SFC-4/21/Proceedings (2021), https://www.fao.org/3/cb7281en/cb7281en.pdf#page=25, accessed 7 August 2023.
[186] Tsioumani (n. 18), at 19.

collaboration in participatory breeding programmes.[187] As discussed in Chapters 2 and 4, establishing fair research partnerships is crucial for achieving fair and equitable benefit-sharing on both inter- and intra-State levels. It requires considering different dimensions of justice in the context of research as an integral component of ABS governance.

It also remains to be discussed how the recognition, protection, and integration of Indigenous and local knowledge occurs in these partnerships. In principle, this approach could serve to create links between international and local benefits, taking into account how local contributions affect and are impacted by the realization of the SDGs in relation to traditional knowledge holders. As discussed in Chapters 3 and 4, however, there are further complexities to take into account that relate to inter-State and transnational benefit-sharing.

4.2 Pandemic Influenza Preparedness Framework

Fair and equitable benefit-sharing has also arisen in the context of global health where the sharing of genetic resources for bio-medical research may be perceived as more remotely linked to environmental protection (although research on the biodiversity–human health nexus[188] clarified significant inherent connections). Similar Global North–Global South equity concerns arise in the environmental and health sectors. Under the WHO, one of the most sophisticated benefit-sharing approaches has been created for the sharing of pathogens, with a view to enhancing disease surveillance activities, diagnostic capacity, risk assessment, as well as the development of vaccines and treatments such as antivirals.[189] This is coupled with 'fair and equitable access to diagnostics, vaccines and treatments' under the Pandemic Influenza Preparedness (PIP) Framework, which was adopted by the World Health Assembly in the form of a resolution in 2011.[190]

The PIP Framework was motivated by the avian influenza (H5N1) outbreak in 2006[191] when an inequitable situation similar to the one explored in the context of agricultural biodiversity came to the fore: '(d)eveloping countries provided information and virus samples to the WHO-operated system; pharmaceutical companies in industrialized countries then obtained free access to such samples, exploited them, and patented the resulting products, which the developing countries could not afford.'[192] This relates to justice issues of distribution, as well as capabilities.

[187] ibid, at 21.

[188] WHO and CBD Secretariat, *State of Knowledge Review on Biodiversity and Health, Connecting Global Priorities: Biodiversity Human Health,* 2016, Summary and Key messages, available at https://www.cbd.int/health/doc/Summary-SOK-Final.pdf, accessed 26 June 2023.

[189] WHO, 'Implementation of the Nagoya Protocol and Pathogen Sharing: Public Health Implications – Study by the Secretariat', available at https://www.who.int/publications/m/item/implementation-of-the-nagoya-protocol-and-pathogen-sharing-public-health-implications, accessed 5 February 2024. This section builds on S Switzer, G Burci, and E Morgera, 'Biodiversity, Pathogen Sharing and International Law' in S Negri (ed.), *Environmental Health in International and European Law* (Edward Elgar, 2019) 271.

[190] World Health Assembly, ResDo WHA64.5 (2011) on Pandemic influenza preparedness: sharing of influenza viruses and access to vaccines and other benefits.

[191] See generally Wilke (n. 78) and Morgera, Buck, and Tsioumani (n. 39), at 102–105.

[192] ibid.

Against this background, the PIP Framework specifically aims to promote the 'objective of a fair, transparent, equitable, efficient, and effective system for, *on an equal footing*: (i) the sharing of H5N1 and other influenza viruses with human pandemic potential; and (ii) access to vaccines and sharing of other benefits, such as diagnostics and antivirals.'[193] Accordingly, under the PIP Framework, the sharing of influenza viruses[194] with human pandemic potential is balanced with access to vaccines and the sharing of other benefits. This arguably represents a form of commutative justice.

While the PIP Framework is itself a soft law instrument for multilateral benefit-sharing towards global health security, it is enshrined in the International Health Regulations,[195] which, in contrast, is a legally binding international instrument. The PIP Framework then relies—as in the case of the International Plant Treaty—upon *private* law contractual instruments (SMTAs) and a network of collaborating research centres. Member States are expected to share viruses through the Global Influenza Surveillance and Response System (GISRS),[196] which consists of institutions collaborating under WHO terms of reference through SMTA1.[197] Transfers taking place under SMTA1 do not attract benefit-sharing obligations, nor can recipients apply for intellectual property rights for materials exchanged under the SMTA1.[198]

On the other hand, viruses transferred to recipients outside the system are regulated by a different standard material transfer agreement negotiated and concluded by the WHO (SMTA2). Parties to an SMTA2 can seek intellectual property rights but must share benefits in the forms listed in an annex to the Agreement, including vaccines and antivirals in the event of a pandemic influenza outbreak.[199] The choice of benefits is agreed on a case-by-case basis. It has been argued that SMTA2 thus assists in 'enrolling the private sector into a normative commitment to global health preparedness and response',[200] and in achieving the equity envisaged during the negotiations of the PIP Framework.[201] The benefit-sharing options have been targeted to different groups: vaccine and antiviral manufacturers; manufacturers of other pandemic related products

[193] WHO, Pandemic Influenza Preparedness Framework for the Sharing of Influenza Viruses and Access to Vaccines and Other Benefits, WHA64.5, 24 May 2011, http://apps.who.int/iris/bitstream/10665/44796/1/9789241503082_eng.pdf, accessed 26 June 2023 (hereinafter PIP Framework) (emphasis added).

[194] To the exclusion of seasonal influenza viruses, though there have been discussions on whether to expand PIP Framework's scope accordingly. Samples of seasonal influenza are shared through the GISRS, which predates the formation of the PIP Framework. GISRS is coordinated by the Global Influenza Programme although there is now close collaboration with the Secretariat of the PIP Framework; see generally AJ Hay and JW McAuley, 'The WHO Global Influenza Surveillance and Response System (GISRS)—A Future Perspective' (2018) 12 Influenza and Other Respiratory Viruses 551.

[195] World Health Assembly, Revision of the International Health Regulations, WHA58.3, 23 May 2005 (hereinafter IHR (2005)).

[196] PIP Framework, 5.1.1; 'Member States, through their National Influenza Centres and Other authorized laboratories, should in a rapid, systematic and timely manner provide PIP biological materials from all cases of H5N1 and other influenza viruses with human pandemic potential, as feasible, to the WHO Collaborating Centre on Influenza or WHO H5 Reference Laboratory of the originating Member State's choice.'

[197] PIP Framework, Annex 1.

[198] ibid.

[199] ibid, Annex 2.

[200] On the enrolment of the private sector into the normative underpinnings of the IHR, see GÓ Cuinn and S Switzer, 'Ebola and the Airplane – Securing Mobility through Regime Interactions and Legal Adaptation' (2019) 32 Leiden Journal of International Law 71.

[201] L Gostin, *Global Health Law* (Harvard University Press, 2014).

such as diagnostics; and all other recipients including universities, biotech companies, and research institutions.[202] Vaccine and antiviral manufacturers must commit to at least two benefit-sharing options from a list of six, including a commitment to donate 10 per cent of real-time pandemic vaccine production in the event of a pandemic influenza outbreak,[203] as well as a commitment to reserve at least 10 per cent of real-time pandemic production to the WHO at affordable prices. Manufacturers of other products relevant to pandemic preparedness and response, such as manufacturers of products such as diagnostics, must choose one benefit-sharing options from a list of six, including a commitment to provide a certain number of diagnostic kits in the event of a pandemic, or to reserve for the WHO a certain number of diagnostic kits. All others should '*consider* providing benefits' from the range of options applicable to manufacturers, as well as technology transfer, the granting of sub-licences to the WHO, and capacity building.

So far the WHO has established a virtual stockpile of 420 million doses available to the organization,[204] which could be relied upon in the event of a pandemic.[205] An assessment of the fourteen SMTAs found that 'all companies selected the benefits that involved donations of products and reserving products for pandemics to be sold at affordable prices to WHO, rather than benefits involving granting licences to or ownership of intellectual property rights'.[206] However, in at least one publicly available SMTA2, an influenza pandemic was included among the instances in which the manufacturer would be indemnified for almost every foreseeable difficulty to uphold its contractual obligations.[207]

An additional, innovative form of benefit-sharing established under the PIP Framework is the annual mandatory 'partnership contribution',[208] which has significantly contributed to ensuring the financial viability of the PIP benefit-sharing framework, as opposed to the issues encountered under the International Plant Treaty. The PIP partnership contribution consists of financial contributions from vaccine, diagnostic, and pharmaceutical manufacturers who use GISRS. The partnership contribution funds pandemic preparedness and response. The sum due is equivalent to 50 per cent of the running costs of the GISRS which at present is approximately $28 million.[209] Each year the WHO issues a questionnaire to identify potential contributors such as

[202] WHO, 'SMTA-2', available at https://www.who.int/initiatives/pandemic-influenza-preparedness-framework/standard-material-transfer-agreement-2-(smta2), accessed 7 August 2023.

[203] PIP Framework, Annex 2.

[204] WHO, 'SMTA2 with vaccine & antiviral manufacturers', available at https://cdn.who.int/media/docs/default-source/pip-framework/smta2/smta2_cata_20221115.pdf?sfvrsn=5f74516c_1, accessed 7 August 2023.

[205] S Switzer et al., 'Compilation of lessons learnt from international funding mechanisms' UN Doc CBD/WGDSI/1/INF/1 (2023).

[206] A Rizk et al., 'Everybody Knows This Needs To Be Done, But Nobody Really Wants To Do It': Governing Pathogen- And Benefit-Sharing (PBS). Global Health Centre Working Paper No. 23 (2020), available at https://www.graduateinstitute.ch/library/publications-institute/everybody-knows-needs-be-done-nobody-really-wants-do-it-governing, last accessed 5 February 2024.

[207] M Rourke, 'The Pandemic Influenza Preparedness Framework as a 'specialized international access and benefit-sharing instrument' under the Nagoya Protocol (2021) 72 Northern Ireland Legal Quarterly 411, at 433; see also M Rourke, 'Access by Design, Benefits if Convenient: A Closer Look at the Pandemic Influenza Preparedness Framework's Standard Material Transfer Agreements' (2019) 97 Milbank Quarterly 91.

[208] PIP Framework, 6.14.3; WHO, Pandemic Influenza Preparedness Framework for the Sharing of Influenza Viruses and Access to Vaccines and Other Benefits, WHO Doc WHA64.5, 24 May 2011, Art. 6(14)(3).

[209] See https://www.healthpolicy-watch.org/who-report-shows-global-progress-on-influenza-preparedness-response/, accessed 26 June 2023.

companies and institutions that conduct research and development in the field of influenza, as well as all recipients of pandemic influenza preparedness biological material recorded in the Influenza Virus Traceability Mechanism database,[210] which serves as a confidence-building measure, to track transfers of biological material within the system.

The WHO developed a multilateral approach to sharing benefits and a benchmark for equity in relation to the distribution of benefits based on the principles of public health risk and needs.[211] On this basis, a prioritization of beneficiary countries is carried out by the WHO's regional officers. In this context, therefore, 'the most affected countries and those with limited access to needed vaccines will be the first to receive vaccines in time of emergencies, rather than those that shared the utilized specimen unless they also are experiencing health risks and needs'.[212] The WHO Director General oversees the distribution of benefits with the support of an advisory group (consisting of internationally recognized policy-makers, public health experts, and technical experts) that monitors implementation and provides recommendations on the application of the fairness and equity criteria.[213] This arguably offers an opportunity for iterative learning and further theorization of benefit-sharing, with criteria based on risks and needs addressing contextual justice, in particular capabilities.

On the whole, the PIP Framework is seen as a unique approach to ABS because of its clear identification of users, which makes the mandatory partnership contribution approach viable. In addition, it has been highlighted that its effectiveness has not yet been tested in pandemic times.[214] It remains to be seen how much can be replicable in the context of ongoing negotiations for a broader instrument on pandemic preparedness, prevention, response, and recovery.[215]

4.3 BBNJ Agreement

For almost twenty years,[216] negotiators at the UN in New York have been debating the need for a new international instrument[217] to ensure benefit-sharing from the use

[210] https://www.who.int/initiatives/global-influenza-surveillance-and-response-system/virus-sharing/ivtm, accessed 3 August 2023.

[211] PIP Framework, Art. 6(1).

[212] M Wilke, 'The World Health Organization's Pandemic Influenza Preparedness Framework as a Public Health Resources Pool' in Kamau and Winter, *Common Pools* (n. 8), 315, at 332.

[213] PIP Framework, Art. 7(1)–(2) and Annex 3, 2(1)(d).

[214] AR Hampton et al., '"Equity" in the Pandemic Treaty: The False Hope of "Access and Benefit-Sharing"' (2023) 72 International and Comparative Law Quarterly 909.

[215] For updates on the negotiations, see the Geneva Graduate Institute's website on 'The Governing Pandemics Initiative', available at https://www.graduateinstitute.ch/GoverningPandemics, accessed 29 July 2023).

[216] UN General Assembly (UNGA) Res 59/24 of 2005, para. 73, establishing an Ad Hoc Open-ended Informal Working Group to study issues relating to the conservation and sustainable use of marine biological diversity beyond areas of national jurisdiction. See the official documentation, available at https://www.un.org/depts/los/biodiversityworkinggroup/biodiversityworkinggroup.htm, accessed 5 February 2024 and Earth Negotiations Bulletin (ENB) reports, available at https://enb.iisd.org/negotiations/conservation-and-sustainable-use-marine-biological-diversity-beyond-areas-national, accessed 5 February 2024. See also A Broggiato et al., 'Fair and Equitable Sharing of Benefits from the Utilization of Marine Genetic Resources in Areas beyond National Jurisdiction: Bridging the Gaps between Science and Policy' (2014) 49 Marine Policy 176.

[217] While the mandate of the negotiations refers to an 'international legally binding instrument' (UNGA Res 72/249 of 2017), it was expected to take a treaty form and serve as an implementing agreement to

of marine genetic resources of areas beyond national jurisdiction. The genetic material of marine sponges, krill, corals, seaweeds, and bacteria in remote areas of the ocean possesses unique characteristics that may lead to significant innovations in the pharmaceutical, food, and renewables sectors, among others.[218] Negotiations were complicated by a fundamental divergence[219] among States as to whether the freedoms of the high seas, the common heritage regime of the Area, or a hybrid regime should apply to marine genetic resources under this new instrument.[220] The role of equity was also unclear and controversial throughout the negotiations: tellingly, the mandate of the BBNJ negotiations was silent on whether benefit-sharing was linked to equity and fairness.[221]

The key justice issues in relation to marine bioprospecting in areas beyond national jurisdiction relate to the fact that only a handful of countries, and very few companies within them,[222] have been able to file patents related to marine genetic resources,[223] while the vast majority of developing countries are not part of these bioprospecting initiatives and are greatly underrepresented in general marine taxonomic research.[224] There is still little evidence, however, of patents or products being specifically or exclusively based on marine genetic resources of areas beyond national jurisdiction, as opposed to resources of other marine

UNCLOS: E Morgera et al., 'Summary of the Fourth Session of the Preparatory Committee on Marine Biodiversity of Areas beyond National Jurisdiction' (2017) 25 ENB 5. All ENBs cited in this chapter are available at http://enb.iisd.org, accessed 5 February 2024.

218 P Oldham et al., *Valuing the Deep: Marine Genetic Resources in Areas Beyond National Jurisdiction* (Defra, 2014); and D Leary et al., 'Marine Genetic Resources: A Review of Scientific and Commercial Interest' (2009) 33 Marine Policy 183.

219 Report of the Preparatory Committee established by UNGA Res 69/292, UN Doc A/AC.287/2017/PC.4/2 (2017).

220 There is abundant research on the question of how to 'fit' marine genetic resources in the context of the different regimes beyond national jurisdiction established by the UN Convention on the Law of the Sea: e.g. D Tladi, 'Conservation and Sustainable Use of Marine Biodiversity in Areas beyond National Jurisdiction: Towards an Implementing Agreement' in R Rayfuse (ed.), *Research Handbook of International Marine Environmental Law* (Edward Elgar, 2017) 259; L de La Fayette, 'A New Regime for the Conservation and Sustainable Use of Marine Biodiversity and Genetic Resources Beyond the Limits of National Jurisdiction' (2009) 24 International Journal of Marine and Coastal Law 221; DK Leary, 'Bioprospecting and the Genetic Resources of Hydrothermal Vents on the High Seas: What is the Existing Legal Position, where are we Heading and what are our Options' (2004) 17 Macquarie Journal of International and Comparative Environmental Law 137; N Morris-Sharma, 'Marine Genetic Resources in Areas beyond National Jurisdiction: Issues with, in and outside of UNCLOS' (2017) 20 Max Planck Yearbook of United Nations Law 71; and D Tladi, 'Genetic Resources, Benefit-sharing and the Law of the Sea: The Need for Clarity' (2007) 13 Journal of International Maritime Law 183.

221 C Salpin, 'Marine Genetic Resources of Areas Beyond National Jurisdiction: Soul Searching and the Art of Balance' in E Morgera and K Kulovesi (eds), *Research Handbook on International Law and Natural Resources* (Edward Elgar, 2016) 411, at 428.

222 A 'single corporation registered 47% of all marine sequences including in gene patents, exceeding the combined share of 220 other companies (37%)': R Blasiak et al., 'Corporate Control and Global Governance of Marine Genetic Resources' (2018) Science Advances 2.

223 Only ten countries account for 90 per cent of patents related to marine genetic resources (the United States, Japan, certain EU countries, Switzerland, and Norway): S Arnaud-Haond, J Arrieta, and C Duarte, 'Marine Biodiversity and Gene Patents' (2011) 331 Science 1521.

224 A Broggiato et al., '*Mare Geneticum*: Balancing Governance of Marine Genetic Resources in International Waters' (2018) 33 International Journal of Marine and Coastal Law 3, at 15–16, referring to

areas.[225] This raises issues regarding capabilities as a precondition for achieving distributive justice.

Against this background, during the BBNJ negotiations, proposals generally focused on types and triggers of benefits. Benefit-sharing was linked to access, based on the idea that various pre-conditions could be set for access by different actors or thresholds, including requirements to provide capacity building and technology transfer for the analysis and use of marine genetic resources.[226] Among the possible conditions, one was identified as an upfront monetary contribution by upstream researchers (collections and academic research institutions[227]) into a global benefit-sharing fund as a mandatory advance payment, or as a voluntary payment to ensure exclusive access to certain marine genetic resources.[228] This was a similar proposal to the one discussed under the International Plant Treaty. Another (additional or alternative) option was for upstream researchers to ensure facilitated access to marine genetic resource samples and research findings on the basis of existing UNCLOS obligations on marine scientific research. The sharing of pre-cruise information and samples, and the publication of cruise reports, were considered to have the potential to minimize the need for re-sampling.[229] This was aimed at contributing to preventing environmental harm while expediting access to marine genetic resources and generally supporting marine scientific research cooperation 'through transparency and coordination at regional and global scales'.[230]

As the value of genetic resources is not clear at the time of access, payments by operators further down the research-and-development chain were also considered upon commercialization of products derived from marine genetic resources.[231] Options for benefit-sharing independent or separated from the notion of access have also been put forward in the literature.[232] Fundamentally, however, divergent views persisted in the negotiations on whether and how benefit-sharing should be equitable, whether

K Juniper, 'Use of Marine Genetic Resources' in M Banks, C Bissada, and PE Araghi (eds), *The First Global Integrated Marine Assessment World Ocean Assessment I* (UN, 2016), at 7–8, and IE Hendriks and CM Duarte, 'Allocation of Effort and Imbalances in Biodiversity Research' (2008) 360 Journal of Experimental Marine Biology and Ecology 15, at 17.

[225] Broggiato et al. (n. 224), at 12–13 and 23.

[226] ENB (n. 174).

[227] E Morgera and G Geelhoed, Consultancy report to the European Commission on the notion of 'utilization' under the Nagoya Protocol and the EU ABS Regulation for Upstream Actors (2016), available at http://ec.europa.eu/environment/nature/biodiversity/international/abs/pdf/ABS%20Final%20Report%20upstream%20users.pdf, accessed 26 June 2023.

[228] Broggiato et al. (n. 224), at 28–29.

[229] T Greiber, 'Common Pools for Marine Genetic Resources: A Possible Instrument for a Future Multilateral Agreement addressing Marine Biodiversity in Areas beyond National Jurisdiction' in Kamau and Winter, *Common Pools* (n. 8), 399, at 409; A Rogers et al., 'Marine Genetic Resources in Areas Beyond National Jurisdiction: Promoting Marine Scientific Research and Enabling Equitable Benefit-sharing' (2021) 8 Frontiers in Marine Science 1, at 8 and 12.

[230] Rogers et al. (n. 229), at 5 and 17.

[231] Broggiato et al. (n. 224); M Tvedt and A Jorem, 'Bioprospecting in the High Seas: Regulatory Options for Benefit Sharing' (2013) 16 Journal of World Intellectual Property 150, at 154.

[232] F Humphries et al., 'A Tiered Approach to the Marine Genetic Resources Governance Framework under the Proposed UNCLOS Agreement for Biodiversity beyond National Jurisdiction (BBNJ)' (2020) 122 Marine Policy 1.

monetary benefit-sharing should be required, and whether an international benefit-sharing mechanism would be needed.[233]

Eventually, the 2023 BBNJ Agreement [234] provided for a multilateral benefit-sharing regime. It aims to fairly and equitably share the benefits from 'activities with respect to marine genetic resources'; build the capacity of, particularly, developing countries to carry out activities on these resources; transfer technology; and generate knowledge, scientific understanding, and technological innovation as a 'fundamental contribution to the implementation of the Agreement'.[235] From the outset, therefore, the BBNJ Agreement considers not only distributive justice, but also capabilities and the ultimate global benefit of advancing knowledge creation for the benefit of environmental protection—this is in fact an essential element for the effectiveness of the whole Treaty.

In the absence of an established network of research centres that could be comparable to those brought under the aegis of the International Plant Treaty and the PIP Framework, the BBNJ Agreement requires that States notify an international clearinghouse prior to the collection of marine genetic resources in areas beyond national jurisdiction. The notification must include a plan for open and responsible data governance and later provide indications of the repository of marine genetic resources.[236] States are also to make available an aggregate report on access to an international Access and Benefit-Sharing Committee.[237] As part of this notification process, non-monetary benefit-sharing are implicitly foreseen in terms of 'benefits to all humankind', notably 'advancing scientific knowledge' and promoting conservation and sustainable use, 'taking in particular consideration the interests and needs of developing States'.[238] In addition, the notification of access includes an obligation to include 'opportunities for scientists of all States, in particular developing states, to be involved or associated with the project' and the 'extent to which it is considered that States that may need and request technical assistance, in particular developing States, should be able to participate or be represented in the project'.[239] The BBNJ Agreement, therefore, engages directly with capabilities and global dimensions of distributive justice.

The BBNJ Agreement provision on fair and equitable benefit-sharing covers both monetary and non-monetary benefits. On the latter, it includes access to samples and sample collections, and open access to findable, accessible, interoperable, and re-usable data 'in accordance with current international practice', as well as technology transfer, capacity building, and increased scientific and technical cooperation.[240]

[233] Revised draft text of an agreement under the United Nations Convention on the Law of the Sea on the conservation and sustainable use of marine biological diversity of areas beyond national jurisdiction, UN Doc A/CONF.232/2020/3 (2020), Annex, draft Art. 11.

[234] Agreement under the United Nations Convention on the Law of the Sea on the Conservation and Sustainable Use of Marine Biological Diversity of Areas beyond National Jurisdiction (New York, 19 June 2023, A/CONF.232/2023/4, not yet in force) (hereinafter, BBNJ Agreement).

[235] ibid, Art. 7(c).

[236] ibid, Art. 12(2)(j).

[237] ibid, Art. 12(7).

[238] ibid, Art. 11(6).

[239] ibid, Art. 12(2)(h)–(i).

[240] ibid, Art. 14(2)(c).

These are effectively left to bilateral deals on the basis of national legislation. On the other hand, monetary benefit-sharing is to be accrued into a multilateral fund on the basis of modalities related to the use of genetic resources yet to be determined by the Conference of the Parties (COP). Additionally, Parties are expected to contribute annually at a rate of 50 per cent of their assessed contributions to the budget adopted by the COP.[241] The BBNJ Agreement, therefore, has sought to address the question of financial viability of a multilateral benefit-sharing approach, while leaving the accruing of monetary benefits from the use of marine genetic resources to a future stage of negotiations.

While it may appear that leaving this part of the benefit-sharing mechanism open is a source of uncertainty, incomplete theorization here can be explained by the challenges experienced in the other international benefit-sharing regimes and the creation, instead, of a gradual, participatory, and iterative multilateral process. To that end, the BBNJ Agreement sets up an ABS Committee to develop guidelines for benefit-sharing and ensuring transparency, from the accruing of monetary benefits, to the functioning of both the clearinghouse and the fund.[242] In addition, the BBNJ Agreement specifically provides for learning through regime interactions, with the ABS Committee having the power to 'consult and facilitate exchanges of information with relevant legal instruments and frameworks'.[243] Furthermore, based on Parties' self-reporting obligations and information on the clearinghouse, the ABS Committee will prepare periodic aggregate reports on ABS that will feed into the COP's role to make recommendations on other forms of benefits,[244] and the general implementation of the ABS provisions, taking into account 'the national capabilities and circumstances of Parties'.[245]

In many ways, therefore, the BBNJ Agreement has been designed as a response to the ascertained limitations of pre-existing multilateral benefit-sharing instruments: as such, its design has specifically provided for an iterative learning approach to fair and equitable benefit-sharing.

4.4 Preliminary Considerations on Multilateral Benefit-Sharing

The development of multilateral benefit-sharing mechanisms has advanced the theorization of fair and equitable benefit-sharing by complementing treaty provisions with more detailed approaches to create and manage international funds and standardized private contracts. In particular, the standardized contractual approach connected to these multilateral benefit-sharing mechanisms has, in principle, gathered intergovernmental consensus on certain conditions to achieve fairness and equity in the relationship with a private user, while making a clear and explicit connection with the

[241] ibid, Art. 14(6).
[242] ibid, Art. 15(1).
[243] ibid, Art. 15(5).
[244] ibid, Art. 15(6).
[245] ibid, Art. 16(3).

public international law dimension of the benefit-sharing obligations under an international instrument.[246] Experiences under international treaties that set out multilateral benefit-sharing systems seem to indicate that the international community can collectively create private contracts that may limit risks in coherently pursuing a treaty objective related to equity. Questions remain, however, about how to effectively take into account beneficiaries' needs, values, and priorities in the application of standardized contracts so that a combination of benefits can be co-identified to best serve to lay the foundation for a fair partnership that supports beneficiaries' agency.[247]

That said, the Nagoya Protocol's bilateral approach (leaving discretion to individual parties as to whether and to what extent to regulate private contractual negotiations) has a greater potential for misuse and divergent approaches due to the documented power imbalances among likely parties. Not enough literature has engaged with the rationale underlying this trend or its potential advantages and pitfalls for the functioning and legitimacy of international cooperation. However, whether the contracts are left to bilateral negotiations or to intergovernmental multilateral standardization, the sheer technical complexity of the subject-matter makes it difficult to predict which contractual clauses can in practice contribute to achieving such a treaty objective. In informal sectors (open-access seeds) where attempts have been made to use contracts to proactively contribute to global goals, huge difficulties have been encountered in making these contracts justiciable.[248] Fear of potential intellectual property litigation (due to an uncertain outcome, costs, and protracted procedures) generally inhibits small-scale users from enforcing proactive contractual obligations.[249] Thus, even when standardized, contractual arrangements in practice disadvantage private parties with fewer means and less knowledge. The need to couple reliance on standard contractual clauses with the provision of appropriate capacity building and other support from States in a treaty can therefore be quite significant. In addition, reliance on private contracts and alternative dispute resolution techniques for the realization of international treaty objectives also raise challenges in balancing confidentiality and the necessary degree of transparency linked to the pursuance of a global objective.[250] Further consideration, through a dialogue among public and private international lawyers, would first of all require building a certain level of familiarity with (or interest in) highly technical international regimes such as those on ABS that may be difficult to achieve, particularly in those countries where legal capacity is a scarce resource from the outset. Equally, such a dialogue requires that public international lawyers engage with very detailed and complex questions of private international law that are quite unfamiliar to them, to get to critical underlying policy choices. Nevertheless, such a

[246] Morgera and Gillies (n. 54), at 175.

[247] ibid.

[248] E Tsioumani et al., 'Following the Open Source Trail Outside the Digital World: Open Source Applications in Agricultural Research and Development' (2016) 14 tripleC 145.

[249] ibid.

[250] These questions have arisen in the specific context of the International Seabed Authority, but could be relevant in other treaty settings. See ITLOS, 2011 Advisory Opinion of the Seabed Disputes Chamber of International Tribunal for the Law of the Sea on 'Responsibilities and Obligations of States Sponsoring Persons and Entities with Respect to Activities in the Area', para. 225.

dialogue is needed, as it is on the minute and complex details of these bodies of law that opportunities for realizing equitable outcomes depend in practice.

It should also be noted that while a multilateral approach to benefit-sharing, as opposed to a bilateral approach, moves away from a mere logic of exchange, there is still room for predominantly transactional interpretations to persist. This predominant frame seems to emerge as a source of continued ineffectiveness of international benefit-sharing regimes, as it inherently de-emphasizes the global benefits underlying specific benefit-sharing relationships, as well as the challenges for beneficiaries to exercise their agency in the context of power asymmetries. As a practical way forward, all the multilateral benefit-sharing approaches examined in this chapter have increasingly devised ways to facilitate and broker, and possibly also oversee and identify gaps or issues in an otherwise ad hoc flow of non-monetary benefits, such as information sharing, scientific cooperation, and capacity building activities.[251] Therefore, on the one hand, fair and equitable benefit-sharing in the ABS context has not yet been fully theorized as a concerted, iterative dialogue aimed at finding common understanding in identifying and apportioning benefits to lay the foundation for a partnership among different actors in the context of power asymmetries.[252] On the other hand, the main challenges that have emerged in the operationalization of these benefit-sharing mechanisms prove the need for such a concerted and iterative institutionalized multilateral dialogue as a deeper form of cosmopolitan cooperation that is necessary to realize relevant international objectives.[253] This is also true with regard to monetary benefit-sharing, as the key lesson learnt across multilateral benefit-sharing instruments is that monetary benefits are very difficult to accrue in practice. Reliance on non-monetary benefits and voluntary financial contributions has become necessary, in particular—as Elsa Tsioumani underscores—because of the challenges in linking monetary benefits to intellectual property rights with the paradoxical result of restricting the use of materials that may provide other benefits for humanity.[254]

On the whole, iterative learning through some form of multilateral oversight or reflection on actual impacts on fairness and equity, and responsive redesign of multilateral benefit-sharing, has emerged as an essential approach to better understand how to generate and share global and local benefits in the achievement of international objectives of environmental protection, global food security, and global health security. Building on these lessons learnt from experiences worldwide, the BBNJ Agreement has explicitly embedded elements of iterative adaptation and oversight in its treaty design.

[251] E Morgera, 'Study on Experiences Gained with the Development and Implementation of the Nagoya Protocol and Other Multilateral Mechanisms and the Potential Relevance of Ongoing Work Undertaken by Other Processes, Including Case Studies' UN Doc UNEP/CBD/ABS/A10/EM/2016/1/2 (2016). This point is also made by Broggiato et al. (n. 224), at 24.

[252] e.g. ECOSOC, Report of the high-level task force on the implementation of the right to development on its second meeting (UN Doc E/CN.4/2005/WG.18/TF/3, 2005), para. 82. For a discussion, see Morgera (n. 55), at 363–366.

[253] Morgera (n. 55), at 364.

[254] Tsioumnai (n. 18), at 116–117.

5. Digital Sequence Information

Another common challenge has emerged across bilateral and multilateral approaches to inter-State benefit-sharing—digital sequence information on genetic resources (DSI).[255] Digital sequence information is a growing practice: it 'is the product of sequencing technologies that have become faster, cheaper and more accurate in recent years ... and permeates every branch of the life sciences and modern biology today'.[256] It thus presents opportunities to create global knowledge through dynamic partnerships and increases the 'potential for generating high-value products, and thus monetary and non-monetary benefits, with the increasing use of synthetic biology technologies in the future'.[257] It also has the potential to contribute to conservation and sustainable use of biodiversity.

DSI fundamentally challenges some of the key assumptions of ABS. Advances in gene synthesis, for example, are likely to reduce the need for reliance on physical samples. Although current scientific practices predominantly use sequences to complement rather than substitute work on physical organisms,[258] rapid technological developments could enable further detachment from physical access in the future.[259] DSI, therefore, significantly complicates the identification of relevant actors and discerning the distinctions among them (which impacts on the setting of triggers for benefit-sharing obligations). In addition, even if information is eventually made available through open-access databases, it does not guarantee that all individuals in different countries would have the same capacity to retrieve and utilize relevant information. Nor is there any guarantee that scientists will include in these databases promising or valuable information. Furthermore, determining provenance, tracking utilization, and pinpointing when value is generated are particularly challenging when digital sequence information is concerned. A whole new host of questions on distributive justice, recognition, and capabilities arise.

In 2016, the CBD Conference of the Parties recognized, for the first time, the relevance of DSI and the potential issues it poses for the achievement of the CBD's three objectives.[260] The underlying Global North–South divergence of views saw, on the one hand, developing countries arguing that the growing trend in bio-based research of relying on digital information may ultimately render physical access to the genetic resources unnecessary, thereby making the premise of current benefit-sharing regimes obsolete. Even if research and development based on physical access and digital

[255] This terminology was introduced by CBD Decision XIII/16. The scientific community and other international processes use related terms, such as 'resources in silico' and '(genetic) sequence information/data'. For a thorough analysis of the challenges surrounding the 'DSI' terminology, see Laird and Wynberg (n. 12), Chapter 2. On terminology and scope, see also M Bagley and AK Rai, *The Nagoya Protocol and Synthetic Biology Research: A Look at the Potential Impacts* (Wilson Centre, 2013), at 20–21.

[256] Laird and Wynberg (n. 12), at 8.

[257] ibid, at vi.

[258] ibid, at 32.

[259] C Lawson and M Rourke, 'Open Access DNA, RNA and Amino Acid Sequences: The Consequences and Solutions for the International Regulation of Access and Benefit Sharing' (2016) 24 Journal of Law and Medicine 96, at 116 refers to one example under the PIP Framework where a vaccine was produced without access to a physical sample.

[260] CBD COP, 'Digital Sequence Information on Genetic Resources' (2016) CBD/COP/DEC/XIII/16, Preamble 1.

information continues to coexist in practice, the exchange of digital sequence information might evade international benefit-sharing requirements, frustrating the objective of relevant treaties. Developed countries, on the other hand, argued that the scope of existing benefit-sharing instruments would not cover information, but only genetic resources in their physical form.[261] Developing countries' counterargument was that through sequencing and genetic manipulation in laboratories, digital information 're-materializes' as genetic resources in every sense of the term.[262] Similar concerns arose under the International Plant Treaty,[263] the PIP Framework,[264] and during the BBNJ negotiations.[265]

Under the CBD and the Nagoya Protocol, DSI has eventually led to a re-evaluation of the relevance of a multilateral benefit-sharing approach. Conversely, under the International Plant Treaty it has been possible to address certain issues related to DSI in an indirect way. The BBNJ Agreement has explicitly included DSI within its scope and its benefit-sharing mechanism, whereas the WHO is considering addressing DSI under a new pandemic treaty that remains under negotiation at the time of writing.[266] However, within all these international frameworks, the governance of DSI remains an open question. The following sections will provide an analysis of the specific challenges and developments that DSI has brought about under specific international regimes, after a preliminary discussion of the multiple justice dimensions of the DSI debate that are relevant across these regimes.

5.1 Justice Dimensions of DSI

DSI can be seen as 'a resource for the global community' that has led to 'dynamic knowledge hubs and diffuse scientific collaborations'.[267] It has thus been emphasized that technologies related to DSI can serve multiple biodiversity conservation and sustainable use purposes. It can 'deepen knowledge about biodiversity including by

[261] E Tsioumani et al., 'UN Biodiversity Conference Highlights: 6 December 2016' (2016) 9(669) ENB 1.

[262] E Tsioumani et al., Summary of the Seventh Session of the Governing Body of the International Treaty on Plant Genetic Resources for Food and Agriculture: 30 October–3 November 2017, 9(691) ENB.

[263] Summary of the Eighth Session of the Governing Body of the International Treaty on Plant Genetic Resources for Food and Agriculture: 11–16 November 2019, Rome, Italy, 9(740) ENB.

[264] The Health Assembly agreed that the WHO secretariat should comprehensively analyse, in consultation with Member States and relevant stakeholders, the implications of amending the definition of PIP biological materials to include genetic sequence data (May 2017). WHO, 'Pandemic Influenza Preparedness Framework for the Sharing of Influenza Viruses and Access to Vaccines and Other Benefits' (2011) A64/VR/10 ('PIP Framework'). See https://www.who.int/groups/pip-framework-advisory-group/genetic-sequence-data, accessed 3 August 2023.

[265] 3rd Session of the Intergovernmental Conference (IGC) on the Conservation and Sustainable Use of Marine Biodiversity of Areas Beyond National Jurisdiction: 19–30 August 2019, UN Headquarters, New York, IISD Reporting Services, available at https://enb.iisd.org/oceans/bbnj/igc3/, accessed 26 June 2023.

[266] WHO, 'Approaches to Seasonal Influenza and Genetic Sequence Data under the PIP Framework' (December 2018): for updates on the negotiations, see https://inb.who.int, accessed 3 August 2023. Note also that parallel negotiations on the amendment of the International Health Regulation are ongoing at the time of writing, and could also address DSI: https://www.who.int/teams/ihr/working-group-on-amendments-to-the-international-health-regulations-%282005%29, accessed 3 August 2023.

[267] Laird and Wynberg (n. 12), at 9–11.

identifying and mitigating risks to threaten species, engaging ability to track illegal trade, identifying species and geographic origin of products, and assisting with biodiversity planning and conservation management'.[268] Furthermore, DSI can lead to products that can be used to control invasive alien species, reduce consumption of fossil fuels, and reduce pollution from manufacturing.[269] DSI can also help to prioritize conservation efforts in situ and ex situ, evaluating the effectiveness of in situ conservation, collecting information on genetic variation, understanding resilience and adaptability of populations with regard to environmental changes and climate change, and reducing the need to take samples from wild populations.[270] In many ways, DSI can contribute to addressing capability issues related to the realization of CBD objectives.

Risks in relying on DSI for the realization of the CBD objectives were discussed among CBD parties. It has been argued that undue reliance on DSI could undermine the resolve to conserve biodiversity in situ. It could negatively impact (economically and culturally) other knowledge producers such as traditional knowledge holders, and it may lead to modifying organisms that could become invasive, even within a single country.[271] There is also concern that deriving genetic information and recreating genes from DSI could undermine the control of Indigenous peoples and local communities of their physical genetic resources and associated traditional knowledge.[272]

In addition, several Global North–South equity issues were identified in a CBD scoping study led by Laird and Wynberg. First, there are often-ignored equity issues in relation to sequence databases. Most countries do not have the funds or the capacity to maintain comparable databases and the benefits from DSI (usually underestimated) accrue to the few countries hosting databases and their users.[273] Power imbalances have also been highlighted in a similar study for the International Plant Treaty, which found that database operators and scientists, notwithstanding open-access and open-source sharing ethos, are resistant to implementing tracking and generally agree to 'publishing and making accessible other "parts" or information whose money-making potential is more theoretical', while 'strategically patent[ing] research tools with clear commercial applications'.[274] Furthermore, the study indicated that researchers would not normally share 'developments with commercial potential, particularly where, for example, the research was funded by government entities interested in local or regional job creation, and in seeing clear economic benefits returning

[268] ibid, at 9.

[269] ibid, at 13 and 10.

[270] CBD Secretariat, Synthesis of views and information on the potential implications of the use of digital sequence information on genetic resources for the three objectives of the Convention and the objective of the Nagoya Protocol, UN Doc CBD/DSI/AHTEG/2018/1/2 (2018), at 9–10.

[271] ibid, at 7 and 13–14.

[272] S Switzer et al., 'What Does the 2022 UN Biodiversity Summit Outcome on Digital Sequence Information Mean for the Ocean and Ocean Research? (Part 2)', One Ocean Hub blog (2023), available at https://oneoceanhub.org/what-does-the-2022-un-biodiversity-summit-outcome-on-digital-sequence-information-mean-for-the-ocean-and-ocean-research-part-2/, accessed 26 June 2023.

[273] ibid, at 13.

[274] EW Welch et al., *Potential Implications of New Synthetic Biology and Genomic Research Trajectories on the International Treaty for Plant Genetic Resources for Food and Agriculture* (Secretariat of the International Treaty on PGRFA, 2017), at 16.

to taxpayers'.[275] Meanwhile, relevant technologies have increasingly blurred 'distinctions between different industrial sectors, and between academic, government and industry research, … as academic research institutions require generation of economic value and to that end seek intellectual property rights'.[276] This means that devising benefit-sharing that differentiates between upstream and downstream actors, non-commercial and commercial entities within the research and development (R&D) chain (particularly for monetary benefit-sharing purposes), may be based on inaccurate assumptions.[277]

DSI also creates several technical challenges for the operationalization of fair and equitable benefit-sharing. With regard to identifying the provenance of DSI, the CBD study indicates that publication of new genetic sequences in databases is increasingly accompanied by information on provenance and meta-data.[278] However, the identification of provenance can be difficult in practice. The 'sequences from the same species from the same habitat might differ due to natural mutations over short periods of time and sequences from different species and origins may be similar' and/or because 'digital sequences can no longer be recognizable as belonging to a particular source because they undergo several modifications'.[279] The International Plant Treaty study, in turn, indicated that the importance of provenance information varies, as 'researchers may be less likely to return to the original material over time', 'database owners, sequencing companies and others are neither keeping nor requesting information about the material source of digital sequence information', and patents do not necessarily request geographic origin information.[280] In addition, and 'the information may be hidden if a particular sequence could be obtained from more than one kind of organism'.[281]

The International Plant Treaty study also found that DSI undermines the approach to monitoring 'the transmission of the rights associated with the resources through subsequent exchanges', which in turn relies on the capacity to identify exchanges and track individual germplasm samples.[282] The study acknowledged that database access could be tracked.[283] One option is relying on block chain technology (the same technology used for the electronic currency BitCoin),[284] which could be combined with the creation of unique identifiers for the materials that were subject to notification. However, the International Plant Treaty study found that, on the one hand, 'even with

[275] ibid, at 21.
[276] ibid, at 9–11.
[277] For a similar conclusion, see also E Morgera and G Geelhoed, Consultancy report to the European Commission on the notion of 'utilization' under the Nagoya Protocol and the EU ABS Regulation for Upstream Actors (2016), available at http://ec.europa.eu/environment/nature/biodiversity/international/abs/pdf/ABS%20Final%20Report%20upstream%20users.pdf, accessed 26 June 2023.
[278] Laird and Wynberg (n. 12), at 12.
[279] ibid, at 15.
[280] Welch et al. (n. 274), at iv–v.
[281] ibid.
[282] ibid, at v and 24.
[283] ibid, at 13.
[284] Sequencing the world: *How to map the DNA of all known plants and animal species on Earth*, 23 January 2018, *The Economist*; F Perron-Welch, Blockchain Technology and Access and Benefit-sharing (August 2018), https://abs-canada.org/blockchain-technology-and-access-and-benefit-sharing/, accessed 3 August 2023.

such tracking, identifying uses of accessed data would not be intuitive due to (1) the myriad ways that partial sequence information can be combined, and (2) the fact that the same sequence or portion of a sequence may be present in multiple organisms'.[285] From a holistic environmental perspective, the energy footprint of block chain raises concerns. The technology relies on the computational power of each participant in the network. It has been estimated that BitCoin's energy consumption alone, and notably a process called 'proof-of-work' which gives the blockchain ledger security against tampering, is comparable to the annual energy consumption in Austria, 'which costs 3.628 billion USD annually' and exacerbates resource use and carbon emissions.[286] In addition, it is also predicted to require 'high up-front investment for the setup of the system and permanent infrastructure costs for the upkeep'.[287] Accordingly, the benefits generated by such an expensive system are likely to be outweighed quite significantly by its broader costs.[288]

With regard to value generation, it has been considered difficult to assess value and contributions, as new collaborations do not include bilateral agreements or direct interaction among researchers.[289] In addition, the practice of 'bulk studies' raises different benefit-sharing issues compared to discrete and unique sequences associated with a particular organism of interest: value is often found in the aggregate as part of larger collections of sequences within databases against which searches and analyses are run.[290] On the whole, the dematerialization of genetic resources has 'led to a multiplication of innovation trajectories, diffuse uses and means of combining sequences and parts'[291] that 'makes articulation of a specific monetary value of a sequence within an entire new product or process challenging'.[292] This raises issues related to distributive justice.

Ultimately, the justice dimensions of DSI revolve around fairness and equity in the underlying research practices and scientific cooperation. For instance, the International Plant Treaty study concluded that monitoring the use of DSI requires a mechanism and incentives 'to build norms of exchange across multiple users and uses',[293] potential in the facilitation of public access (both entry-level and advanced users) to synthetic biology technologies and tools for education, participation in scientific endeavours, and low-cost investment with a view to supporting social and institutional innovations as mechanisms for identifying and capturing collective benefits (information sharing, capacity building, and technology transfer).[294] The CBD study, in addition, referred to new research agreements ('protected commons') that serve to ensure recognition and attribution of material through a flexible and easy process and to involve research collaborations, which do not address monetary benefit-sharing.[295]

[285] Welch et al. (n. 274), at 13.
[286] F Rohden et al., *Combined Study on DSI in Public and Private Databases and DSI Traceability* (Convention on Biological Diversity, 2019), at 47.
[287] Ibid, at 50.
[288] Morgera, Switzer, and Geelhoed (n. 12), at 19–21.
[289] Laird and Wynberg (n. 12), at 14.
[290] ibid, at 15.
[291] Welch et al. (n. 274), at vi and 36.
[292] ibid, at iv and 38.
[293] ibid, at vi and 36.
[294] Laird and Wynberg (n. 12), at 13.
[295] ibid, at 43.

Instead, they contribute to the creation of a global web of collaborators contributing in iterative ways to a final product that is openly available for use, including research areas that receive less private sector attention, thereby addressing a situation where each participant is at the same time a provider and a user through reciprocal benefit-sharing.[296]

5.2 Reconsidering a Multilateral Approach under the CBD

For a significant amount of time, CBD parties' views diverged as to whether DSI would be even comprised within the subject-matter scope of the CBD, notably in light of the interpretation of the terms 'utilization of genetic resources'.[297] Arguments against inclusion focused on the dematerialized state of DSI and presume that the definitions under the CBD only apply to physical resources.[298] Arguments in favour of inclusion were based on the interpretation of the terms under the CBD as including both tangible and intangible components, 'i.e. the physical material as well as the actual or potential value it contains in the form of information'.[299] Some members of the scientific community expressed preference for exclusion due to the likelihood of ongoing unrestricted access to DSI.[300] However, provider-countries could still impose stricter restrictions on the generation and publication of DSI in their domestic legislation on access.[301]

As argued elsewhere,[302] an interpretative solution that is capable of fostering increased cooperation and multilateral learning should be favoured under general principles of international law, notably effectiveness and good faith.[303] These principles support interpretations that contribute to ensuring the full effect of a treaty, aligning with its objectives and purpose, rather than interpretations that might diminish the practical impact of its provisions.[304] In effect, benefits associated with a genetic

[296] ibid, at 47 and 37.

[297] See, e.g., CBD, Art. 1 and Nagoya Protocol, Art. 1. See also Regulation (EU) No. 511/2014 of the European Parliament and of the Council of 16 April 2014 on Compliance Measures for Users from the Nagoya Protocol on Access to Genetic Resources and the Fair and Equitable Sharing of Benefits Arising from Their Utilization in the Union [2014] OJ L 150/59, Preamble 17 and Art. 3(4) and (5).

[298] See notably Ad Hoc Technical Expert Group (AHTEG) on Digital Sequence Information on Genetic Resources, 'Synthesis of Views and Information on the Potential Implications of the Use of Digital Sequence Information on Genetic Resources for the Three Objectives of the Convention and the Objective of the Nagoya Protocol' UN Doc CBD/SBSTTA/22/INF/2 (2018), at 36.

[299] ibid, at 35.

[300] See, e.g., 'Submission by the League of European Research Universities (Leru). Digital Sequence Information = Nucleotide Sequence Data! But More Clarity Is Needed on Its Scope' (Secretariat to the CBD, 2019), available at https://www.cbd.int/abs/DSI-views/2019/LERU-DSI.pdf, accessed 26 June 2023.

[301] SJ Hiemstra et al., *Digital Sequence Information (DSI). Options and Impact of Regulating Access and Bennefit Sharing—Stakeholder Perspectives* (University of Wageningen, 2019), at 13. See also MA Bagley, *Digital DNA: The Nagoya Protocol, Intellectual Property Treaties, and Synthetic Biology* (Wilson Centre, 2015), at 7–8.

[302] Morgera, Switzer, and Geelhoed (n. 12).

[303] Secretariat to the Convention on Biological Diversity (prepared by E Morgera, S Switzer, and E Tsioumani), 'Study into the Criteria to Identify a Specialised Access and Benefit-Sharing Instrument, and a Possible Process for Its Recognition' UN Doc CBD/SBI/2/INF/17 (2018), at 14.

[304] M Fitzmaurice, 'The Law of Treaties' in Malcolm Nathan Shaw (ed.), *International Law* (Oxford University Press, 2008), at 832–838.

resource are often linked to the *information* held within a genetic resource in addition to the physical traits of the specific specimen. There is also the underlying effectiveness question of circumventing the third objective of the CBD on fair and equitable benefit-sharing altogether, as a consequence of changing scientific practices. In other words, what degree data and information can be used to generate benefits without access to the physical resource, which would mean that requirements that follow from international law could be avoided altogether when DSI is excluded from its scope. On the other hand, including DSI within the scope of the CBD can support maximizing the contribution of DSI to the CBD obligations on scientific research and cooperation that contribute to realizing the CBD's objectives of conservation and sustainable use.

Including DSI within the scope of the CBD and the Nagoya Protocol thus seems more in line with the aim of enhancing the 'protection or implementation of universal values, and in addition [ensuring that] international institutions are involved to monitor or steer the process'.[305] That interpretation, however, calls into question whether DSI can be adequately addressed through the bilateral benefit-sharing approach favoured under the CBD and its Nagoya Protocol,[306] due to the challenges in identifying the origin, tracking, and attributing value to DSI. It has been emphasized that 'the value of an individual sequence from a species may be very difficult to quantify'[307] because its value lies in its potential to be screened with other sequences to find connections between traits and functions.[308] In other words, the value lies in the amount of data analysed, rarely in a single accession.[309] The long 'cognitive and material distance' between a resource and a final product is a challenge for valuation[310] if only a very small percentage of a particular sequence is used or when the product of biotechnology has seen many transformations.[311] Questions have therefore arisen as to when benefit-sharing obligations cease to exist[312] and where those obligations arise along a complex chain of providers and users.

In the face of all these complexities and increasing political pressure to find a resolution as part of a post-2020 global biodiversity framework[313] that could provide a more credible response to the continuous and alarming global rates of biodiversity loss,[314] the 2022 Kumming-Montreal Global Biodiversity Framework includes a specific target (Target 13) calling for benefits arising from the use of genetic resources

[305] S Zappalà, 'Can Legality Trump Effectiveness in Today's International Law?' in Antonio Cassesse (ed.), *Realizing Utopia* (Oxford University Press, 2012) 105.

[306] E Morgera, E Tsioumani, and S Switzer, 'Study into the Criteria to Identify a Specialised Access and Benefit-sharing Instrument, and a Possible Process for its Recognition' UN Doc CBD/SBI/2/INF/17 (2018).

[307] Welch et al. (n. 274), at 37.

[308] ibid.

[309] S Aubry, 'The Future of Digital Sequence Information for Plant Genetic Resources for Food and Agriculture' (2019) 10 Frontiers in Plant Science 1, at 4.

[310] G Dutfield in D Scott and D Berry, *Genetic Resources in the Age of the Nagoya Protocol and Gene/Genome Synthesis* (University of Edinburgh, 2016), 23.

[311] Laird and Wynberg (n. 12), at 51.

[312] LN Slobodian et al., *The Traceability of MGRs and Genomic Tech/Synthetic Biology* (PharmaSea Milestones, 2017).

[313] E Tsioumani et al., 'Summary of the UN Biodiversity Conference: 7–19 December 2022' (2022) 9(796) Earth Negotiations Bulletin 17.

[314] S. Díaz et al., Summary for policymakers of the global assessment report on biodiversity and ecosystem services of the Intergovernmental Science-Policy Platform on Biodiversity and Ecosystem Services (2019).

and DSI to be increased significantly by 2030.[315] CBD Parties adopted the decision to establish a multilateral mechanism for benefit-sharing from the use of DSI, including a global fund, with a view to supporting conservation and sustainable use of biodiversity and also benefit Indigenous peoples and local communities.[316] The decision recognizes that while the benefits from the use of DSI should be shared fairly and equitably, the distribution of DSI and distinctive practices regarding its use require a distinctive solution for benefit-sharing. This solution includes the establishment of a 'fair, transparent, inclusive, participatory and time-bound process to develop and operationalise the mechanism',[317] which seems a particularly welcome clarification to emphasize the importance of a representative and iterative approach to fairness and equity, as well as the need to explore further the viability of benefit-sharing arrangements from DSI.

According to the decision, a multilateral approach for sharing the resulting benefits has the potential to meet the following criteria:

> (a) Be efficient, feasible and practical; (b) Generate more benefits, including both monetary and non-monetary, than costs; (c) Be effective; (d) Provide certainty and legal clarity for providers and users of digital sequence information on genetic resources; (e) Not hinder research and innovation; (f) Be consistent with open access to data; (g) Not be incompatible with international legal obligations; (h) Be mutually supportive of other access and benefit-sharing instruments; (i) Take into account the rights of indigenous peoples and local communities, including with respect to the traditional knowledge associated with genetic resources that they hold.[318]

An annex to the decision sets out a range of issues for further consideration, including governance of the scheme, triggering points for benefit-sharing, and the interface between ABS national systems and any multilateral mechanism. While it may appear that leaving this open to future negotiations can be a source of continued uncertainty, incomplete theorization of inter-State benefit-sharing under the CBD and the Nagoya Protocol has created the space to explore a possible move towards an iterative process for co-designing benefit-sharing modalities taking into account beneficiaries' agency and different dimensions of justice. To that end, however, participatory governance plays a crucial role[319] in effectively addressing procedural justice issues, as a precondition for engaging with contextual justice issues.

In addition, a global multilateral fund could provide an 'opportunity to leverage wider benefits for biodiversity, not only from the sectors benefiting from the use of DSI, but also from industries such as agriculture and forestry that continue to rely on

315 Kunming-Montreal Global Biodiversity Framework, CBD Decision XV/3 (2022).
316 CBD COP Decision XV/9 (2022).
317 ibid.
318 ibid, para. 9.
319 S Leonelli, *Philosophy of Open Science* (Cambridge University Press, 2023); S Leonelli and H Williamson, 'Introduction: Towards Responsible Plant Data Linkage' in H Williamson and S. Leonelli (eds), *Towards Responsible Plant Data Linkage* (Springer, 2023) 1; S Leonelli, Data Science in Times of Pan(dem)ic' (2021) 3 Harvard Data Science Review https://doi.org/10.1162/99608f92.fbb1bdd6, accessed 5 February 2024; S Leonelli, 'Data Governance is Key to Interpretation: Reconceptualising Data in Data Science' (2019) 1 Harvard Data Science Review https://doi.org/10.1162/99608f92.17405bb6, accessed 5 February 2024.

biodiversity, but with little support for its conservation'.[320] This, including the calls for a 'biodiversity tax' by extractive industries such as mining, oil, and gas, could yield benefits for biodiversity conservation—and for the local custodians of biodiversity—that far outweigh those secured from the use of DSI.[321] It could serve to take into account contextual justice issues that are often overlooked in transactional approaches to ABS. It could also serve to address restorative justice issues. Thus, incomplete theorization in this case can potentially help address evolving scientific practices and iteratively understanding capabilities at stake.

5.3 Taking the Issue from the Side under the International Plant Treaty

While proposals to address DSI have not yet found sufficient support under the Treaty,[322] some progress on this issue was, nonetheless, made through its Global Information System (GLIS)[323] without necessarily first agreeing on a definition of DSI or on its inclusion in the scope of a new instrument. Rather, the Treaty addresses the issue indirectly,[324] focusing on existing information sharing obligations, thereby promoting transparency in this field and having the potential to gradually build some form of multilateral governance of genetic resource-related information.

The 2015 vision and programme of work of the GLIS explicitly acknowledged the need to provide principles and tools to support the operation of existing information systems in accordance with the Treaty principles and rules and promote transparency on the rights and obligations of users for accessing, sharing, and using such information.[325] What is noteworthy about the GLIS is that a web-based entry point to information and knowledge is specifically aimed at strengthening the capacity for conserving, managing, and utilizing plant genetic resources for food and agriculture.[326] In other words, it is a combination of elements to actively pursue the sharing of scientific information by promoting and facilitating interoperability among existing systems while creating a mechanism to assess progress and monitor effectiveness of these enhanced and more coordinated information sharing opportunities.[327] The GLIS is not just an online repository of information, as is the case with the CBD or Nagoya Protocol clearinghouses.[328] It aims both to strengthen capacity for the conservation,

[320] Switzer et al. (n. 272).
[321] ibid.
[322] ibid.
[323] ITPGR, Art. 17.
[324] Note that progress on including digital sequence information is most likely to be achieved by the World Health Organization: the Health Assembly agreed that the WHO secretariat should comprehensively analyse, in consultation with Member States and relevant stakeholders, the implications of amending the definition of PIP biological materials to include genetic sequence data (May 2017).
[325] ITPGR Res 3/2015; see also http://www.fao.org/plant-treaty/areas-of-work/global-information-system/en/, accessed 26 June 2023.
[326] ITPGR, Arts 13(2)(a) and 17.
[327] ITPGR Res 3/2015 (IT/GB-6/15/Res 3).
[328] Morgera, Tsioumani, and Buck (n. 6), at 237–240.

management, and utilization of resources and to share benefits, paying special attention to the needs of developing countries.[329]

The GLIS Programme of Work foresees a comprehensive phased approach, covering not only the creation of a web-based platform, but also aiming to facilitate access to sources and associated information. It also aims to promote and facilitate interoperability and transparency on rights and obligations of users, to enhance opportunities for communication and international and multidisciplinary collaboration, and to provide for capacity development and technology transfer for the conservation, management, and use of resources. Furthermore, it seeks to create a mechanism to assess its own progress and monitor effectiveness.[330]

In that way, the GLIS governance structure can arguably support a concerted and iterative dialogue to co-identify and respond to needs and priorities of beneficiaries in effectively making use of, and contributing to the production of, DSI. This process aligns with the principled understanding of benefit-sharing discussed earlier. The GLIS can arguably focus efforts on the priorities of the vulnerable by supporting a focus on 'high-priority material'.[331] In addition, it provides institutional support for setting priorities, brokering scientific cooperation, capacity building, and technology-transfer opportunities. Although this indirect approach focuses only on non-monetary benefits, it can possibly help explore in the interim technological solutions to move towards monetary benefit-sharing.

Another interesting aspect of the GLIS is its reliance on existing information systems[332] with a view to minimizing the impact on current infrastructures and procedures and focusing on improving interoperability.[333] One means it employs is adding a digital object identifier (DOI) to identify a resource. DOIs are designed to coexist with other identifiers that often aim to serve particular communities and the achievement of specific objectives. The DOIs are therefore intended to be used for 'all purposes that are beyond the intended scope of existing identifiers, such as information sharing across different information systems and different communities'.[334]

The GLIS has been arguably devised to address specific barriers to fair and equitable benefit-sharing from DSI in the form of information sharing through the inter-linked development of a multilateral platform for targeted dialogue and iterative learning, by creating a mechanism at the multilateral level to undertake a series of inter-related tasks that identify and address shortcomings in bilateral ABS relations. Such tasks include: assessing progress and monitoring effectiveness of enhanced and coordinated

[329] ITPGRFA, Arts 13(2) and 17 and ITPGRFA Res 3/2015, Annex 1, para. 6; see also E Morgera, 'Fair and Equitable Benefit-Sharing in a New International Instrument on Marine Biodiversity: A Principled Approach Towards Partnership Building?' (2018) 5 Maritime Safety and Security Law Journal 48, at 76. On how these articles relate to GIS and the other workings of the multilateral system, see also C Ker et al., 'Building a Global Information System in Support of the International Treaty on Plant Genetic Resources for Food and Agriculture' in Halewood et al. (eds), *Crop Genetic Resources as a Global Commons: Challenges in International Governance and Law* (Routledge, 2013) 283.

[330] ITPGRFA Res 3/2015, 4–6 with detailed indicators on how these broader objectives can be achieved.

[331] ibid.

[332] ITPGRFA, Art. 17(1).

[333] The Governing Body to the ITPGRFA, 'The Vision and the Programme of Work of the Global Information System' IT/GB-6/15/Res 3 (2015), Annex I, para. 3.

[334] 'FAQS—the GLIS Portal and Digital Object Identifiers', available at http://www.fao.org/plant-treaty/areas-of-work/global-information-system/faq/en/, accessed 26 June 2023.

information sharing opportunities; providing institutional support to broker and oversee scientific cooperation and capacity building; and identifying any gaps or issues that could proactively be addressed at international level.[335] The GLIS potentially showcases a method for devising a partnership-building approach, enhancing opportunities for collaboration and assessing progress and monitoring effectiveness through feedback and periodic consultations.

The GLIS is still in its infancy, however, having predominantly focused on assigning DOIs across organizations,[336] and its progress has not been without controversy.[337] Nonetheless, the GLIS offers a valuable example of conceptualizing fair and equitable benefit-sharing as a governance process that needs inter-institutional, inter-sectoral and cross-scalar learning. In particular, the GLIS, focusing on opportunities and synergies within and between existing systems, holds the potential for an approach that is developed from direct dialogue with the scientific community. This can help minimize risks of negative and unforeseen impacts on scientific cooperation and innovation and maximize opportunities for biodiversity conservation and its contributions to multiple SDGs. Such an approach can demonstrate sustained commitment to understanding the actual causes of inequity through ongoing dialogue with affected communities, and aims to co-develop in a transparent and multilateral setting solutions to problems that often arise, but that may go unnoticed or underestimated in their cumulative/systemic impacts at the bilateral level.

5.4 Specifically Including DSI in the Scope of the BBNJ Agreement

The BBNJ Agreement is the first treaty in which ABS from DSI have been specifically provided for. One of its objectives is to share fairly and equitably benefits derived from DSI and strengthen capacities for engaging in activities related to DSI,[338] including information generated before its entry into force, unless a Party makes an exception.[339] Parties are then required to share the database in which DSI is being deposited, clarifying that they relate to areas beyond national jurisdiction, as well as sharing data management plans and their updates. Benefit-sharing obligations then extend to access to DSI 'in accordance with current international practice',[340] while modalities for monetary benefit-sharing from DSI will be decided by the COP at a later stage.[341] In this context, an incompletely theorized agreement allows further learning to unfold, potentially drawing from anticipated developments in other forums.

The BBNJ Agreement also allows for reasonable conditions to which access to DSI could be subject to, such as reasonable costs associated with database maintenance. It also provides opportunities for access on fair and most favourable terms, including

335 ibid, 58. ITPGRFA, Art. 17; GLIS terms of reference.
336 A Alercia et al., *Digital Object Identifiers for Food Crops. Descriptors and Guidelines of the Global Information System* (FAO, 2018).
337 On issues with regards to the DivSeek initiative, see briefly Morgera (n. 329), at 75.
338 BBNJ Agreement, Art. 9(a).
339 ibid, Art. 10(1).
340 ibid, Art. 14(3).
341 ibid, Art. 14(7).

concessional and preferential terms with researchers from developing countries.[342] As discussed above, current scientific research and collaboration practices, however, entail their own justice-related aspects, and it remains unclear how these will be tackled under the BBNJ Agreement. To some extent, the role of the ABS Committee, as mentioned earlier, could be also that of iteratively learning about the positive and negative impacts on different equity dimensions related to the DSI-relevant provisions of the BBNJ Agreement, and the co-development of responses to them. There are also other parts of the BBNJ Agreement, discussed in Chapter 2, that can contribute to this question.

6. Conclusions: Iterative Learning and Regime Interaction

Navigating the international ABS landscape, which includes a variety of international treaties, other international instruments, as well as private contracts, provides insights into common challenges to designing and implementing fair and equitable benefit-sharing from bio-based innovation in different, but linked, sectors such as environmental protection, agriculture, and health. Facilitating opportunities for interactions to promote learning, including through deliberation by multiple stakeholders,[343] is increasingly recognized within international law processes as a fundamental imperative in situations where a range of actors, and indeed regimes, are stakeholders to a particular issue. Deliberative strategies seem to be required within and across the international ABS regimes discussed in this chapter. In fact, understanding the multiple dimensions of justice, as well as the agency and evolving needs of beneficiaries in the context of the evolving research practices and other collaborative endeavours would benefit from an iterative and participatory learning process that can support further theorization of fair and equitable benefit-sharing in specific contexts.

As explored elsewhere by Switzer and other colleagues,[344] the shared challenges in effectiveness and in the realization of equity experienced across the multiple international ABS instruments discussed in this chapter also create opportunities for learning across regimes. This can be specifically supported by *managing* interactions between regimes, particularly by 'enabling interplay management', which focuses on sharing knowledge, communication, and understanding among regimes.[345] This is a point echoed in the International Law Commission's report on the fragmentation of international law, which noted that while international law offers the structure for coordination and cooperation, either between States or between regimes and

[342] ibid, Art. 14(4).

[343] MA Young., 'Fragmentation or Interaction: The WTO, Fisheries Subsidies, and International Law' (2009) 8 World Trade Review 477, at 479.

[344] Switzer et al. (n. 272).

[345] S Oberthür, 'Interplay Management: Enhancing Environmental Policy Integration Among International Institutions' (2009) 9 International Environmental Agreements: Politics, Law and Economics 371, at 387. O Schram Stokke, 'The Interplay of International Regimes: Putting Effectiveness Theory to Work' (2001) FNI Report 14/2001, https://www.fni.no/getfile.php/132044/Filer/Publikasjoner/FNI-R1401.pdf, accessed 26 June 2023, at 10.

institutions, it does not contain clear-cut rules to solve issues faced by global society, so '[d]eveloping these is a political task'.[346]

Regime interplay management can thus be considered a critical element in advancing the incomplete theorization of different inter-State benefit-sharing regimes. In effect, the BBNJ Agreement, the development of which has drawn on multiple lessons learnt across pre-existing international ABS regimes, includes a variety of explicit provisions on regime interaction.[347] To foster interaction between other international ABS regimes, a valuable suggestion to consider within each regime discussed in this chapter (and potential new ABS regimes, such as the proposed pandemic treaty) is the need to establish multilateral institutions for dialogue, priority-setting, and oversight to support global partnerships among State and non-State actors, including beneficiaries. Such institutions need to provide space and support to reflect, in an iterative manner, on the actual barriers to the realization of equity and fairness in benefit-sharing that arise over time and across different ABS regimes (including due to overlaps or interactions among these regimes). These institutions can then co-develop responses that support more integrated implementation of other international obligations within the same treaty and opportunities to realize multiple international objectives.

For these institutions to make a difference, it is essential that they engage with the power imbalances that persist despite, or are even further embedded by, benefit-sharing mechanisms. For instance, the assumption that publication of sequences in open-access databases already represents a significant form of non-monetary benefit-sharing as it allows anyone, including researchers in provider countries and the Global South, to use the information.[348] This argument does not take into account the limited capacity of different countries and different users to access and utilize the information contained in databases.[349] Similarly, power imbalances may also have an impact on the way actors can control their data once it has been publicly shared, or on the way research collaborations are structured and conducted. These multilateral institutions could thus provide a space for dialogue between the range of actors involved in DSI (database managers, biodiversity researchers, innovators) or negatively affected by the use of DSI, with a view to co-producing a more nuanced understanding of the different dimensions of justice at stake and a more effective response to beneficiaries' needs.

Through these institutions, participatory governance would entail reaching out to and including different communities engaged in using DSI, thereby responding more effectively to the needs of researchers and the conservation community through co-development of solutions. Evolving features of scientific endeavours have critical, but often overlooked, implications for legal distinctions between commercial and non-commercial research, for instance. Apart from purely taxonomic activity, empirical

[346] International Law Commission, Fragmentation of International Law: Difficulties arising from the Diversification and Expansion of International Law, UN Doc A/CN.4/L.682 (2006), para. 488.

[347] BBNJ Agreement, Arts 15(5), 22(3), 24(2), 26(2), 29(2)–(3), 47(6)(c), 50(4)(d), 51(4), and 55(4).

[348] CBD/SBSTTA/22/Inf/2 (n. 298), at 21.

[349] ibid, at 20. Note, however, that the recent CBD study on traceability does find that users of information in the main databases (INSDC databases) are distributed fairly homogenously throughout the world: F Rohden et al., *Combined Study on DSI in Public and Private Databases and Dsi Traceability* (Convention on Biological Diversity, 2019) 27.

analysis of scientific practices has found it extremely difficult to predict if and when genetic resources will be used for research and/or for research and development purposes. So the lines between non-commercial/commercial, basic/applied research are becoming increasingly blurred and even the existence of intellectual property rights may not be a sufficient basis for determining whether research is commercial or non-commercial.[350]

Determined efforts would be also required to ensure the meaningful and respectful inclusion of Indigenous and local knowledge in decision-making procedures. This involves integrating perspectives from scientists from across various locations and capacities, database managers, and experts from different sectors. These are also aspects that the BBNJ Agreement has started to address explicitly in its institutional provisions, as discussed above. It would thereby entail providing support to build the capacity of all participants to learn from Indigenous and local knowledge.[351]

On a very practical level, the proposed institutions would help assess on an ongoing basis the financial viability and functionality of an international ABS regime, working collaboratively with database operators and researchers—both in the Global North and the Global South. This is with a view to adapting the system in light of changing scientific practices and the different economics underpinning particular sectors. These institutions could be an essential complement to the multilateral funds that have been established to ensure financial viability of ABS (such as under the CBD/Nagoya Protocol on DSI, the International Plant Treaty, and the BBNJ Agreement). These funds could have multiple approaches, co-developed in phases due to the learning approach supported by the multilateral multifunctional platform. This in turn could adapt to the diverse economic structures of different sectors and (sub)sectors.

The proposed institutions could therefore serve to: collaboratively identify integrated responses to capacity and operational needs and their financial implications; identify and co-develop funding approaches that take into account the range of needs of relevant actors, including safeguarding 'open science'; co-develop and review the application of *criteria* for disbursement of funds by a range of stakeholders, so that benefit-sharing effectively contributes to the holistic realization of international treaty objectives and relevant SDGs. In addition, they could contribute to governance structures of funds to ensure equity; create opportunities for learning and iterative design to ensure that the fund actively responds to evolving beneficiaries' needs and scientific practices; and convene dialogues with stakeholders to keep abreast of scientific and technological developments' implications for benefit-sharing and the fund.[352]

More fundamentally, such multilateral institutions would provide a way to institutionalize, as part of more traditional treaty review processes, a new approach to international cooperation as a cosmopolitan space to learn on an ongoing basis how benefit-sharing approaches can work (and when and why they do not) for scientists in the Global South and the Global North, as well as the implications for biodiversity

[350] Switzer et al. (n. 272).

[351] e.g. K Erwin et al., 'Lalela uLwandle: An Experiment in Plural Governance Discussions' in R Bosewell, D O'Kane, and J Hills (eds), *The Palgrave Handbook of Blue Heritage* (Springer, 2022) 383; and M Strand et al., 'Reimagining Ocean Stewardship: Arts-based Methods to 'Hear" and "See" Indigenous and Local Knowledge in Ocean Management' (2022) 9 Frontiers in Marine Science 1.

[352] Switzer et al. (n. 272).

conservation and sustainable use, global health, and global food security. This enables addressing fairness and equity concerns from a human rights perspective[353] in order to balance competing rights and interests, avoid discrimination, and respond to the needs of the vulnerable, while preventing negative environmental and socio-economic consequences of scientific research. Aligning recent international clarifications of the inter-dependence of biodiversity and basic human rights[354] and the need to interpret and implement the SDGs in accordance with human rights law would be particularly interesting.[355] Understanding the role of these international cooperation clauses in relation to their role in protecting everyone's rights to food, health, and a healthy environment, as well as other civil, political, economic, social, and cultural rights would support systemic thinking of the different dimensions of justice within ABS across biodiversity, broader environmental (including climate change), agriculture, and health sectors in light of the alarming findings on the unprecedented rate of biodiversity loss and its wide-ranging implications for human well-being.[356]

[353] Morgera (n. 329), based on Special Rapporteur in the field of cultural rights, 'The Right to Enjoy the Benefits of Scientific Progress and Its Applications' UN Doc A/HRC/20/26 (2012), paras 65–69.

[354] UN Special Rapporteur on Human Rights and the Environment John Knox, Biodiversity and Human Rights, UN Doc A/HRC/34/49 (2017).

[355] OHCHR, 'Promotion and protection of human rights and the implementation of the 2030 Agenda for Sustainable Development' UN Doc A/HRC/RES/37/24 (2018) and the report of the UN High Commissioner for Human Rights and OHCHR on promotion and protection of all human rights, civil, political, economic, social and cultural rights: 'Right to access to justice under Art. 13 of the Convention on the Rights of Persons with Disabilities' UN Doc A/HRC/RES/37/25 (2017).

[356] The 2019 Global Assessment of Biodiversity and Ecosystems Services indicated that current negative trends in biodiversity and ecosystems will undermine progress towards 80 per cent of targets assessed within the Sustainable Development Goals (SDGs) related to poverty, hunger, health, water, cities, climate, oceans, and land: Sandra Díaz et al., 'Summary for Policymakers of the Global Assessment Report on Biodiversity and Ecosystem Services of the Intergovernmental Science-Policy Platform on Biodiversity and Ecosystem Services' (IPBES, 2019).

2

Inter-State Benefit-Sharing as Scientific and Technological Cooperation

1. Introduction

This chapter analyses international regimes in which the sharing of scientific information, capacity building, and technology transfer have been identified as forms of fair and equitable benefit-sharing. These are even less theorized than inter-State benefit-sharing from genetic resources discussed in the previous chapter: the content of the duty to cooperate in this connection, and the underlying partnership model, remain vague. This chapter reflects on relevant practice under international biodiversity law and law of the sea, with international benefit-sharing institutions increasingly playing a proactive and brokering role in developing and administering integrated approaches to scientific cooperation and information sharing and financial and technology solidarity. The chapter then focuses on the specific example of the 2023 international Agreement on marine biodiversity of areas beyond national jurisdiction (BBNJ Agreement).[1] The chapter finally considers the opportunity and limitations of framing existing financial, technological, and capacity-building obligations under the international climate change regime.

The objective of the chapter is to advance the theorization of fair and equitable benefit-sharing as a concerted, dialogic, and iterative process for identifying the technology, funding, or capacity to be transferred according to context-appropriate modalities and beneficiaries' preferences, thereby fully supporting beneficiaries' agency. To that end, the chapter advances an interpretation of fair and equitable benefit-sharing through the lens of the human right to science, with a view to moving towards models of mutual capacity building and technology co-development to take into account multiple dimensions of justice, as opposed to donor-dominated technology and capacity development processes. As discussed in the Introduction, the human right to science provided one of the earliest expressions of benefit-sharing in international human rights law and in fact in international law generally.

The chapter will explore the role of fair and equitable benefit-sharing in addressing procedural and distributive justice, as well as recognition and capabilities. Often attention in scientific and technological cooperation is focused on distributive issues, with the assumption that transfers will only be possible from the Global South to the Global North. Procedural justice issues may also arise from the perspective of the international institutions that are designed to support scientific and technological

[1] Agreement under the United Nations Convention on the Law of the Sea on the Conservation and Sustainable Use of Marine Biological Diversity of Areas beyond National Jurisdiction (New York, 19 June 2023, A/CONF.232/2023/4, not yet in force) (BBNJ Agreement).

Fair and Equitable Benefit-Sharing in International Law. Elisa Morgera, Oxford University Press. © Elisa Morgera 2024.
DOI: 10.1093/oso/9780198862130.003.0003

solidarity. But in fact, there are capability issues at stake, which need to inform the science and technology on which cooperation is fostered in order for it to be effectively helpful to beneficiary countries. Recognition is also relevant, as notwithstanding scientific and technological divides there are opportunities for mutual learning between countries in the Global North and Global South that are generally overlooked in this context. From a justice perspective, a normative argument will be developed that fair and equitable benefit-sharing as capacity building and technology should be interpreted as fostering co-production of knowledge for transformative governance.

Transformation is 'a fundamental, system-wide change that includes consideration of technological, economic and social factors, including in terms of paradigms, goals or values' and to '[o]bstacles to achieving transformative change, including unequal power relations, lack of transparency, vested interests, unequal distribution of the costs and benefits of actions, tendencies for short-term decision-making, the psychology of losses and gains, the logic of market-driven processes, the lack of policy coherence and inertia'.[2] Transformation has been called for by the Intergovernmental Panel on Climate Change (IPCC) and the Intergovernmental Science-Policy Panel on Biodiversity and Ecosystem Services (IPBES).[3] Transformative change was also called for in the 2030 Agenda for Sustainable Development[4] and by the 2022 UN Ocean Conference, which recognized the need for transformative change to 'halt and reverse the decline in the health of the ocean's ecosystems and biodiversity and to protecting and restoring its resilience and ecological integrity'.[5]

The key to transformative change is addressing inequalities, which also undermines the fair and equitable sharing of benefits arising from the use of biodiversity and its conservation.[6] Arguably, transformation presupposes a shift from 'the technocratic and regulatory fix of environmental problems to more fundamental and transformative changes in social-political processes and economic relations',[7] by rather 'preventing a shifting of the burden of response onto the vulnerable; paying attention to social differentiation, through the lens of non-discrimination; and addressing issues of power and legitimacy'.[8] In that connection, I have argued elsewhere that human rights can contribute to transformative change,[9] through these participatory

[2] IPBES, Initial scoping report for Deliverable 1 (c): A thematic assessment of the underlying causes of biodiversity loss and the determinants of transformative change and options for achieving the 2050 Vision for Biodiversity (2021) available at https://ipbes.net/sites/default/files/Initial_scoping_transformative_change_assessment_EN.pdf, accessed 27 June 2023.

[3] V Masson-Delmotte et al. (eds), Special Report on the impacts of global warming of 1.5°C above pre-industrial levels and related global greenhouse gas emission pathways, in the context of strengthening the global response to the threat of climate change, sustainable development, and efforts to eradicate poverty (IPCC, 2018); and IPBES, Global assessment report of the Intergovernmental Science-Policy Platform on Biodiversity and Ecosystem Services (IPBES secretariat, Germany, 2019).

[4] UNGA, Transforming our world: the 2030 Agenda for Sustainable Development, Resolution 70/1 (25 September 2015).

[5] UN Ocean Conference, *Our Ocean, Our Future, Our Responsibility: Political Declaration for 2022 UNOC*, available at sdgs.un.org/documents/political-declaration-2022-unoc-46675, 25 May 2022, accessed 7 February 2024.

[6] ibid.

[7] IJ Visseren-Hamakers and MTJ Kok, 'Introduction' in I Visseren-Hamakers and M Kok (eds), *Transforming Biodiversity Governance* (Cambridge University Press, 2022) 3.

[8] ibid.

[9] B Erinosho et al., 'Transformative Governance for Ocean Biodiversity' in Visseren-Hamakers and Kok (n. 7), 313, at 328.

processes, which 'focus ... on the rights-holder as [the] central concern in response to asymmetries and power imbalances'.[10]

The chapter will first introduce the human right to science, which is still not very widely studied under international human rights law. It will then proceed to apply that lens to the provisions of the UN Convention on the Law of the Sea,[11] and the BBNJ Agreement, to reflect on how to contribute to the realization of inter-connected Sustainable Development Goals (SDGs), as aptly summarized by SDG target 14a: 'Increase scientific knowledge, develop research capacity and transfer marine technology ... in order to improve ocean health and to enhance the contribution of marine biodiversity to the development of developing countries.'[12] The chapter will conclude by reflecting on the relevance of these findings for the international climate change regime, with a view to considering the opportunity and limitations of a benefit-sharing framing for climate-related financial, technological, and capacity-building obligations.

2. The Human Right to Science

The human right to science is seen as an autonomous right that is worthy of protection for its contribution to the continuous raising of the material and spiritual standards of living of all members of society, both for individual emancipation and collective economic and social progress.[13] As such, it contributes to the enjoyment of other human rights, such as the rights to food and health,[14] and is therefore significant for the realization of SDGs 2 (hunger) and 3 (health and well-being). In addition, the right to science contributes to '[protecting] and [enabling] each person to develop his or her capacities for education and learning, to form enduring relationships with others, to take equal part in political, social and cultural life and to work without fear of discrimination',[15] therefore playing a part in the implementation of SDGs 4 (education), 8 (decent work), and 10 (inequality).[16]

The human right to science is not a new right. It was proclaimed in the Universal Declaration of Human Rights[17] and has been enshrined in several treaties, including

[10] V Bellinkx et al., 'Addressing Climate Change through International Human Rights Law: From (Extra) Territoriality to Common Concern of Humankind' (2022) 11 Transnational Environmental Law 69.

[11] United Nations Convention on the Law of the Sea (UNCLOS) (Montego Bay, 10 December 1982, into force 16 November 1994).

[12] M Ntona and E Morgera, 'Connecting SDG 14 with the other Sustainable Development Goals through Marine Spatial Planning' (2018) 93 Marine Policy 295.

[13] A Plomer, *Patents, Human Rights and Access to Science* (Edward Elgar, 2015).

[14] W Schabas, 'Study of the Right to Enjoy the Benefits of Scientific and Technological Progress and its Applications' in Y Donders and V Volodin (eds), *Human Rights in Education, Science and Culture: Legal Developments and Challenges* (Ashgate Publishing, 2007); M Mancisidor, 'Is There such a Thing as a Human Right to Science in International Law?' (2015) 4 European Society of International Law 1; A Chapman, 'Towards an Understanding of the Right to Enjoy the Benefits of Scientific Progress and its Applications' (2009) 8 Journal of Human Rights 1.

[15] Plomer (n. 13).

[16] See also E Morgera and M Ntona, 'Linking Small-Scale Fisheries to International Obligations on Marine Technology Transfer' (2018) 93 Marine Policy 214.

[17] See Schabas (n. 14) on the broad consensus regarding the inclusion of the human right to science in the UNGA, Universal Declaration of Human Rights UN Doc A/810 (1948).

the International Covenant on Economic, Social and Cultural Rights (ICESCR).[18] It is legally binding but its scope and content had remained underdeveloped until recently. For this reason, there have been virtually no efforts to implement the obligations to promote, protect, and fulfil this right. Nonetheless, current efforts to clarify the content of the right to science provide useful insights for present purposes and indicate that international human rights bodies will devote increasing attention to States' conduct in this area.

In 2011, the UN Special Rapporteur in the field of cultural rights, Farida Shaheed, suggested that the right to science encompasses four distinct elements: the right to access the benefits of science by everyone without discrimination; the opportunity for all to contribute to scientific research; the obligation to protect all persons against negative consequences of scientific research or its applications on their food, health, security, and environment; and the obligation to ensure that priorities for scientific research focus on key issues for the most vulnerable.[19] These normative elements chime with the notion of 'inclusive innovation', namely 'explicitly includ[ing] those who have been excluded from the development mainstream ... and produc[ing] and deliver[ing] innovative solutions to the problems of the poorest and most marginalised communities'.[20]

The first element identified by Shaheed is fair and equitable benefit-sharing, although the terminology has varied in this area of international law. While the Universal Declaration made reference to '*sharing in* the benefits', successive treaty formulations differ on this specific point. In particular, the International Covenant makes reference to the 'right to *enjoy* benefits', while UN Special Rapporteur Shaheed referred 'to benefit', to 'enjoy benefits', 'to participate in the benefits', 'to share benefits', and to have 'access to benefits'. Legal scholarship on the right to science, however, has emphasized that 'sharing' benefits is a key conceptual element that underpins agency.[21] Even if not everyone can play an active part in scientific advancements, everyone should indisputably be able to participate in the benefits derived from it.[22] This interpretation is aligned with the interpretation that benefit-sharing conveys the idea of the active participation in the co-identification of benefits and sharing modalities among those actors that are directly involved in scientific and technological development and those that are not, and across different worldviews.[23] The added value of benefit-sharing is

[18] International Covenant on Economic, Social and Cultural Rights (opened for signature 16 December 1966, entered into force 3 January 1976) 6 ILM 360 (ICESCR) Art. 15. See also Charter of the Organization of American States (opened for signature 30 April 1948, entered into force December 13, 1951) 119 UNTS 3, Art. 38; American Declaration on the Rights and Duties of Man (adopted 2 May 1948) OAS Res XXX, Art. XIII; Additional Protocol to the American Convention on Human Rights in the Area of Economic, Social and Cultural Rights (opened for signature 17 November 1988, entered into force 16 November 1999) 28 ILM 156, Art. 14; Arab Charter on Human Rights (adopted 23 May 2004), reprinted in International Human Rights Reports 893 (2005), Art. 42.

[19] UNGA, Report of the Special Rapporteur in the field of cultural rights Shaheed: the right to enjoy the benefits of scientific progress and its applications, UN Doc A/HRC/20/26 (2012), paras 1, 25, and 30–43.

[20] R Blasiak et al., *The Ocean Genome: Conservation and the Fair, Equitable and Sustainable Use of Marine Genetic Resources* (World Resources Institute, 2020), at 2637.

[21] Mancisidor (n. 14) argues that the understanding of the wording used in the Declaration should contribute to the interpretation of the different wording in the Covenant in full.

[22] Chapman (n. 14), at 5–6.

[23] E Morgera, 'Fair and Equitable Benefit-sharing at the Crossroads of the Human Right to Science and International Biodiversity Law' (2015) 4 Laws 803, at 803–831.

thus to foster deeper international cooperation, based on the recognition of power and capacity imbalances and of the need for a partnership across power divides, as opposed to a one-off form of collaboration related to matters of common concern of humankind.[24]

The other dimensions of the human right to science, as outlined by Rapporteur Shaheed, serve to address power dynamics that are affected or engendered by science and technology and are not explicitly addressed under international biodiversity law or the law of the sea. The benefit-sharing process could thus serve to critically assess whether information sharing, capacity building, and marine technology transfer lead to non-discriminatory results, prioritize the needs of the vulnerable, and factor in the need to protect against negative consequences of scientific research. In that way, the benefit-sharing process can prevent dependency on external, ready-made solutions that may not fit particular circumstances, or may allow for the exertion of undue influence by donor countries.[25] The human right to science, therefore, emphasizes key substantive considerations (e.g. non-discrimination, priority benefiting the vulnerable, and the prevention of environmental harm) that should inform international environmental law and law of the sea provisions on scientific cooperation, as well as capacity building and technology transfer, with a view to grounding science co-production.

As I have argued elsewhere, all four dimensions of the right to science can provide opportunities for cross-fertilization with the conceptualization of fair and equitable benefit-sharing in the context of international biodiversity law. A key argument in this respect is that the concept of 'sharing' benefits, as developed under international biodiversity law, can serve to interpret the right to science in its dimension of access to the benefits of science as a tool for cross-cultural inclusion and empowerment of different actors. The other dimensions of the right to science, in turn, appear helpful in interpreting fair and equitable benefit-sharing under international biodiversity law and identifying guarantees to protect the vulnerable. In either case, contrasting the conceptual elements of the right to science and of fair and equitable benefit-sharing serves to bring into the spotlight problematic legal issues that deserve further reflection.[26]

In 2020, the UN Committee on Economic, Social and Cultural Rights elaborated a General Comment to further clarify the content of the human right to science, emphasizing that 'the development of science in the service of peace and human rights should be prioritized by States over other uses'.[27] The Committee elucidated that the human right to science applies to natural as well as social sciences, and to pure as well as applied research.[28] Core obligations include ensuring access to those applications of scientific progress that are critical to the enjoyment of the right to health and other

[24] E Morgera, 'The Need for an International Legal Concept of Fair and Equitable Benefit-sharing' (2016) 27 European Journal of International Law 353, at 365.

[25] E Morgera, E Tsioumani, and M Buck, *Unraveling the Nagoya Protocol: A Commentary on the Nagoya Protocol on Access and Benefit-sharing to the Convention on Biological Diversity* (Brill, 2014), at 313 and 331.

[26] Morgera (n. 24), at 374.

[27] Committee on Economic, Social and Cultural Rights, General Comment No. 25 (2020) on science and economic, social and cultural rights (Arts 15(1)(b), (2), (3), and (4) of the International Covenant on Economic, Social and Cultural Rights, UN Doc E/C.12/GC/25 (2020), para. 6).

[28] ibid.

economic, social, and cultural rights. Another core obligation is prioritizing allocation of public resources to research in areas where there is the greatest need for scientific progress in health, food, and other basic needs related to economic, social, and cultural rights, and the well-being of the population, especially with regard to vulnerable and marginalized groups.[29]

In addition, the General Comment explicitly stated that the human right to science also applies to inter-State relations, so that the 'collective benefits of knowledge should be shared globally'.[30] The duty to cooperate internationally towards the fulfilment of all economic, social, and cultural rights[31] results in States' obligation to recognize the benefits from international scientific cooperation and to take steps through diplomatic and foreign relations to promote an enabling global environment for the advancement of science and the enjoyment of the benefits of its applications.[32] This, in turn, entails, as to take into account 'deep international disparities among countries in science and technology'.[33] So States engaged in international law-making processes are to promote collaboration between scientific communities of developed and developing countries to meet the needs of all countries and facilitating their progress, while respecting national regulations.[34] From the perspective of international human rights law, multilateral agreements should enable developing countries to build their capacity to participate in generating and sharing scientific knowledge and benefiting from its applications, as States acting on the international stage 'cannot ignore their human rights obligations'.[35]

In light of these obligations, a priority appears to be for States to, first of all, identify collectively the greatest need for progress in science to support basic economic, social, and cultural rights, as well as our evolving understanding of the ecosystem services and human rights dependent on them.

On the whole, compared to other human rights, the human right to science focuses on the agency of developing countries in co-identifying benefits and more equitable modalities for international scientific cooperation for the protection and full realization of other human rights (and multiple SDGs), with an emphasis on the vulnerable. Thus, the human right to science can be used to support the mutually supportive interpretation or progressive development of international environmental law in order to support 'effective, equitable, democratically legitimate and accountable processes and outcomes in relation to the application of science and technology'.[36]

It must be acknowledged, however, that there continues to be scepticism and criticism that recourse to human rights is inherently anthropocentric and detracts from focusing on ecosystem integrity. It is argued here, however, that growing scientific

[29] ibid, para. 52.
[30] AM Hubert, 'The Human Right to Science and Its Relationship to International Environmental Law' (2020) 31 European Journal of International Law 625. See also J Peel, 'The "Rights" Way to Democratize the Science–Policy Interface in International Environmental Law? A Reply to Anna-Maria Hubert' (2020) 31 European Journal of International Law 657.
[31] ICESCR, Art. 2; and Arts 55 and 56 of the Charter of the United Nations (1945) 1 UNTS XVI.
[32] ICESCR, Art. 15(4).
[33] UN Doc E/C.12/GC/25, para. 79.
[34] ibid.
[35] ibid.
[36] Hubert (n. 30), at 625.

understanding of the inter-dependencies of human well-being and biodiversity reveals a potentially undue concern about anthropocentricity: humans are part and parcel of ecosystems, as deeply as at the level of microbiota, for instance.[37] So as long as human rights are used to the benefit of that inter-dependency, ecosystems stand to benefit as much as humans. Considering these inter-dependencies creates opportunities for a more informed political debate that moves away from an expert-driven and technocratic approach focused on minimizing damage that is 'prevalent in international environmental law'[38] and speaks to the concerns about anthropocentrism. Instead, a broader understanding of the risks and benefits for both humans and nature can be supported by the consideration of the different dimensions of the right to science.[39]

Two areas can now be singled out as further exploring opportunities for cross-fertilization between the right to science and fair and equitable benefit-sharing under international environmental law and the law of the sea: information sharing and scientific cooperation; and technology transfer. A third area—the sharing of benefits arising from the use of the traditional knowledge of Indigenous peoples and local communities—will be discussed in Chapter 4.

2.1 Information Sharing and Scientific Cooperation as Benefit-Sharing

International environmental law and the law of the sea contribute to the realization of the human right to science through two forms of non-monetary benefit-sharing: the sharing of scientific information and scientific cooperation.

There are two general obligations under the Convention on Biological Diversity (CBD) that are related, but little-explored, namely CBD, Article 12(c) on research and training for 'Parties, taking into account the special needs of developing countries ... promote and cooperate in the use of scientific advances in biological diversity research in developing methods for conservation and sustainable use of biological resources'. In addition, CBD Article 17 on the exchange of information, calls on Parties to 'facilitate the exchange of information, from all publicly available sources, relevant to the conservation and sustainable use of biological diversity, taking into account the special needs of developing countries'. It adds that 'such exchange of information shall include exchange of results of technical, scientific and socio-economic research, as well as information on training and surveying programmes, specialized knowledge, indigenous and traditional knowledge as such and in combination with the technologies'.

Like the Nagoya Protocol, it includes among possible benefits the sharing of research and development results and admittance to databases.[40] Furthermore, it can

[37] World Health Organization and Secretariat of the Convention on Biological Diversity (WHO/CBD), *State of Knowledge Review on Biodiversity and Health, Connecting Global Priorities: Biodiversity Human Health*, 2016, Summary and Key messages https://www.cbd.int/health/doc/Summary-SOK-Final.pdf, accessed 26 June 2023.

[38] Hubert (n. 30), at 655.

[39] ibid, at 652.

[40] Nagoya Protocol, Annex, para. 2(a) and (e).

be expected that the possible development under the Nagoya Protocol of a global benefits-sharing mechanism[41] or the new process of digital sequence information (DSI) discussed in Chapter 1 could lead to the multilateral-level linking of public and private databases to facilitate the sharing of relevant scientific information dispersed across the globe.[42] Overall, this could contribute to the practical realization of the right to science in two dimensions: the sharing of research findings is a way to share benefits from science and to increase the chances for all to contribute to further scientific research. A key issue in this connection, however, concerns the distinction between obligations to share raw scientific data, whose contribution to the right to science rests on available capacity to use such data, as opposed to obligations to share analysis of data.[43]

The practice of information sharing as a form of benefit-sharing in international biodiversity law may be difficult to assess, as it is generally left to bilateral agreements among public and private parties.[44] The global mechanisms that were set in place to that end, such as the CBD clearinghouse,[45] have not led to remarkable results: the clearinghouse is considered 'underutilized' and 'developed rather haphazardly, without a clear mandate'.[46] It thus remains to be verified whether in practice the implementation of information sharing obligations under international biodiversity law can contribute to the realization of the right to science. Initiatives in addressing implementation challenges may, however, already provide useful lessons of potential relevance to the practical application of the right to science too. In addition, more proactive and institutionalized approaches to information sharing may be emerging under international biodiversity law.

Under the International Treaty on Plant Genetic Resources for Food and Agriculture (ITPGRFA), a Global Information System (discussed in Chapter 1) is specifically geared towards strengthening the capacity for the conservation, management, and utilization of plant genetic resources for food and agriculture.[47] For present purposes, it is worth highlighting that what is envisaged is a combination of elements to actively pursue not only the sharing of scientific information (by promoting and facilitating interoperability among existing systems and creating a mechanism to assess progress and monitor effectiveness), but also opportunities for all to contribute to

[41] ibid, Art. 10.

[42] T Dedeurwaerdere, A Broggiato, and D Manou, 'Global Scientific Research Commons under the Nagoya Protocol' in EC Kamau and G Winter (eds), *Common Pools of Genetic Resources: Equity and Innovation in International Biodiversity Law* (Routledge, 2014) 224, at 225–226.

[43] Note, for instance, Protocol to the Antarctic Treaty on Environmental Protection (Madrid, 4 October 1991, in force 14 January 1998) as amended by the 28th Antarctic Treaty Consultative Meeting on 14 June 2005, to include Annex VI on Liability Arising from Environmental Emergencies), Art. III.

[44] It is left to 'mutually agreed terms': CBD, Arts 15(7) and 19(2); Nagoya Protocol, Art. 5.

[45] CBD, Art. 18(3) and Cartagena Protocol, Art. 20. The ABS clearinghouse (Nagoya Protocol, Art. 14) is more concerned with sharing information about implementation, than about scientific information as such.

[46] T Young, 'An International Cooperation Perspective on the Implementation of the Nagoya Protocol' in E Morgera, M Buck, and E Tsioumani (eds), *The 2010 Nagoya Protocol on Access and Benefit-Sharing in Perspective: Implications for International Law and National Implementation* (Brill, 2013) 451, at 471; T Young 'Access to Information and the Biosafety Clearing-House' in M-C Cordonier Segger, F Perron-Welch, and C Frison (eds), *Legal Aspects of Implementing the Cartagena Protocol on Biosafety* (Cambridge University Press, 2013) 137.

[47] ITPGRFA, Arts 13(2)(a) and 17.

scientific research (by enhancing opportunities for collaboration and providing capacity development and technology transfer).[48]

Regarding scientific cooperation, the CBD provides for participation in biotechnological research.[49] The Nagoya Protocol includes, among possible benefits, collaboration, cooperation, and contribution in scientific research and development programmes; participation in product development; collaboration, cooperation, and contribution in education; and admittance to research facilities.[50] Similar to the observation about sharing scientific information above, however, it may be difficult to assess to what extent these obligations effectively contribute to the realization of the right to science, as they are generally left to bilateral agreements among public and private parties.

In addition, a specific provision of the Nagoya Protocol is devoted to research related to biodiversity conservation, including non-commercial research, through national law-making. It establishes a general obligation for State Parties to 'create conditions' favourable to research contributing to conservation and sustainable use when developing and implementing national frameworks.[51] It specifies that this should be implemented particularly when such research is carried out in developing countries. The provision appears to complement an often-forgotten CBD obligation for Parties to 'endeavor to develop and carry out scientific research based on genetic resources provided by other Parties with the full participation of, and where possible in, such Parties'.[52] The lessons learnt in the implementation of these provisions could contribute to understanding practical barriers to the realization of the right to science in relation to the opportunity for all to contribute to scientific research, in particular challenges in reaching those that need the most support to participate in scientific research.

The International Plant Treaty, instead, includes scientific cooperation among the benefits to be shared through its multilateral system.[53] Its Benefit-Sharing Fund finances activities that are designed to support farmers in developing countries in conserving crop diversity in their fields, also with a view to assisting farmers and breeders globally in adapting crops to changing needs and demands. In particular, it supports innovative partnerships between research centres, farmers, civil society, and public/private sector leaders at all levels, and projects with the potential to be scaled up across agro-ecological zones, ensuring best use of current scientific data.[54] As discussed in Chapter 1, the fund operates through a project-based approach.[55] This was criticized, however, for not adequately taking into account the unequal capacities of different

[48] ibid, Resolution 3/2015 (IT/GB-6/15/Res 3).
[49] CBD, Arts 1, 15(5), 16, and 19.
[50] Nagoya Protocol, Annex, para. 2(b)-(e).
[51] ibid, Art. 8(a).
[52] CBD, Art. 15(6).
[53] ITPGRFA, Art. 13(2)(c).
[54] https://www.fao.org/plant-treaty/areas-of-work/funding/en/, accessed 3 August 2023.
[55] The priorities, eligibility criteria, and operational procedures were adopted as Annexes 1–3 to the Funding Strategy in 2007. See Food and Agriculture Organization of the United Nations (FAO), Report of the Governing Body of the International Treaty on Plant Genetic Resources for Food and Agriculture (FAO, 2007).

actors to develop eligible project proposals.[56] This was remedied with a series of workshops to help applicants prepare proposals, which points to practical difficulties and concrete modalities under international biodiversity law to move towards a proactive and brokering role for international institutions in supporting scientific cooperation. These developments could contribute to the realization of the right to science as the opportunity for all to contribute to scientific research.

As opposed to general international obligations related to sharing scientific information and supporting scientific cooperation under other international environmental agreements, the framing of these obligations as fair and equitable benefit-sharing under international biodiversity law may arguably subject them to a concerted and dialogic process for co-identifying benefits and sharing modalities with beneficiaries. Such a process can arguably allow for the consideration of all four dimensions of the right to science, on the basis of a mutually supportive interpretation of benefit-sharing obligations and the right to science. The benefit-sharing process can thus serve to critically assess whether information sharing and scientific cooperation lead to non-discriminatory results, prioritize the needs of the vulnerable, and factor in the need to protect against negative consequences of scientific research from the perspective of beneficiary countries, not only donor countries.

2.2 Technology Transfer as Benefit-Sharing

In UN Special Rapporteur Shaheed's preliminary discussion of the content of the right to science, her reflections focused on the role of technology transfer as benefit-sharing,[57] making explicit reference to some international biodiversity treaties that prominently include technology transfer as a form of benefit-sharing.[58] Interestingly, however, Shaheed also hinted at technology transfer obligations under other multilateral environmental agreements, such as those on climate change, which are not framed as benefit-sharing.[59] A similar approach can also be found in the international process on a human right to international solidarity[60] and the long-standing efforts to clarify the controversial right to development.[61] All these efforts likely represent broad-based dissatisfaction with the low level of implementation of technological solidarity provisions. In light of the proposed conceptualization of fair and equitable benefit-sharing under international biodiversity law, it could be argued that the intuition behind this approach is to subject the interpretation and implementation of technology transfer obligations to a concerted and dialogic process for the identification of the type of

[56] S Louafi. *Reflections on the Resource Allocation Strategy of the Benefit Sharing Fund* (Swiss Federal Office for Agriculture, 2013).

[57] Chapman (n. 14), at 4 and 30.

[58] CBD, Arts 1 and 16; ITPGRFA, Art. 13(2)(b). Reference could also have been made to Nagoya Protocol, Art. 1 and Annex.

[59] Shaheed's report (n. 19), fn 76.

[60] Report of the Independent Expert on Human Rights and International Solidarity to the General Assembly, UN Doc A/68/176 (2013), para. 27(d).

[61] In its so-called 'third dimension': Report of the High-level Task Force on the Implementation of the Right to Development on its Sixth Session: Right to Development Criteria and Operational Sub-criteria UN Doc, A/HRC/15/WG.2/TF/2/Add.2 (2010), criteria 3(b)(i)–(ii).

technology to be transferred, the modalities of such transfer, and the beneficiaries, with a view to building fair and equitable partnerships.

With regard to the right to science, Shaheed pointed to an 'implied obligation for developing countries [to prioritize] the development, import and dissemination of simple and inexpensive technologies that can improve the life of marginalized populations rather than innovations that disproportionately favor educated and economically affluent individuals and regions'.[62] She then pointed to a 'corresponding obligation for industrialized countries to comply with their international legal obligations through provisions of direct aid, as well as development of international *collaborative* models of research and development for the benefit of developing countries and their populations'.[63] In addition, the need to take into account the preferences of intended beneficiaries and local contextual elements in assessing which technologies may be usefully and equitably shared was recommended by UN Special Rapporteur on the Right to Food Olivier De Schutter.[64] Furthermore, reference should be made to the need, at the time of the decision to transfer technology, to convey relevant information specifically to those who are going to manage its risks and/or be exposed to them (e.g. workers, civil society, and communities).[65]

While in principle framing technology transfer as fair and equitable benefit-sharing may contribute to address these concerns as part of a concerted and dialogic process of sharing, there is limited practice under international biodiversity law to assess whether this is indeed a distinct and viable approach to realize the right to science.[66] As with other forms of benefit-sharing, this is generally left to bilateral agreements among public and private parties. Nonetheless, an interesting example of bottom-up, pragmatic support for the realization of the sharing of scientific benefits and the opportunity to participate in scientific research may be found under the International Plant Treaty. A platform for the co-development and transfer of technologies has brought together a network of public and private institutions that collaborate in delivering a combination of information sharing, capacity building, and technology co-development and transfer with facilitated access to genetic material. The initiative is meant to complement the Benefit-Sharing Fund of the Treaty, by identifying real needs of targeted beneficiaries (e.g. small-scale farmers and their communities), assembling technology packages that could include training and other activities instrumental for fostering technology absorption capacity, as well as developing standardized conditions (such as humanitarian clauses).[67] While the platform was launched as a voluntary initiative of certain governments and stakeholders, it has gradually been integrated into the multilateral benefit-sharing structure of the Treaty.[68]

62 Shaheed's report (n. 19), para. 68.

63 ibid (emphasis added).

64 O De Schutter, 'The Right of Everyone to Enjoy the Benefits of Scientific Progress and the Right to Food: From Conflict to Complementarity' (2011) 33 Human Rights Quarterly 304, at 348.

65 S Jasanoff, 'The Bhopal Disaster and the Right to Know' (1988) 27 Social Science and Medicine 1113–1123.

66 e.g. CBD technology transfer work programme, Decision VII/29 (2004), paras 3.2.8 and 3.2.9.

67 FAO, Reports of Meetings on the Establishment of a Platform for the Co-development and Transfer of Technology (2013) FAO Doc IT/GB-5/13/Inf.16.

68 ITPGRFA, Resolution 4/2015 (2015) FAO Doc IT/GB-6/15/Res 4.

Similarly to the argument developed earlier in relation to scientific information sharing and cooperation, a mutually supportive interpretation of the right to science and technology transfer obligations framed as benefit-sharing could serve to integrate in a concerted and dialogic process for co-identifying the technology to be transferred and transfer modalities with beneficiaries a consideration of all four dimensions of the right to science. This can then aim to critically assess whether technology transfer leads to non-discriminatory results, prioritizes the needs of the vulnerable, and factors-in the need to protect against negative consequences from the perspective of beneficiary countries, rather than solely donor countries.

3. The Law of the Sea

The UN Convention on the Law of the Sea (UNCLOS)[69] contains the framework for international cooperation in the fields of marine science and technology transfer. UNCLOS commentators have mainly focused on the interactions between UNCLOS, the CBD, and the international regime on intellectual property rights (IPRs).[70] They emphasize the inherent tensions with IPRs' market-oriented underpinnings,[71] and IPRs have generally remained a controversial issue from the negotiations of these treaties to the present day.[72] This is not the only reason, however, for the widely acknowledged lack of implementation of international technology transfer obligations under UNCLOS.[73] Instead, developments related to fair and equitable benefit-sharing

[69] This section draws on Morgera and Ntona (n. 16).

[70] Agreement on Trade-Related Aspects of Intellectual Property Rights (TRIPS Agreement), 33 ILM 1197 (1994).

[71] See indicatively: CB Thompson, 'International Law of the Sea/Seed: Public Domain versus Private Commodity' (2004) 44 Natural Resources Journal 841–866; C Lawson and S Downing, 'It's Patently Absurd—Benefit Sharing Genetic Resources from the Sea under UNCLOS, the CBD and TRIPs' (2002) 5 Journal of International Wildlife Law and Policy 211–233; C Salpin and V Germani, 'Patenting of Research Results related to Genetic Resources from Areas beyond National Jurisdiction: The Crossroads of the Law of the Sea and Intellectual Property Law' (2007) 16 Review of European Community and International Environmental Law 12; A Bonfanti and S Trevisanut, 'TRIPs on the High Seas: Intellectual Property Rights on Marine Genetic Resources' (2011) 37 Brooklyn Journal of International Law 187; A Broggiato, 'Marine Genetic Resources Beyond National Jurisdiction - Coordination and Harmonisation of Governance Regimes' (2011) 41 Environmental Policy and Law 35; A Broggiato et al., 'Fair and Equitable Sharing of Benefits from the Utilization of Marine Genetic Resources in Areas beyond National Jurisdiction: Bridging the Gaps between Science and Policy' (2014) 49 Marine Policy 176.

[72] In the case of UNCLOS, this conflict is particularly palpable in the negotiating history and subsequent amendment of Part XI on the Area. In this connection, see indicatively: M Herdegen, *Principles of International Economic Law* (Oxford University Press, 2016), at 71–72; SN Nandan, M Lodge, and S Rosenne, *The Development of the Regime for Deep Seabed Mining* (Kluwer Law, 2022), at 2–3. More recently, the issue of IPRs arose in the context of the negotiations towards new energy efficiency regulations for international shipping under the auspices of the International Maritime Organization (IMO). In this connection, see J Harrison, 'Recent Developments and Continuing Challenges in the Regulation of Greenhouse Gas Emissions from International Shipping' (2013) 27 Ocean Yearbook 359, at 373–375. With regard to the CBD, see: M Chandler, 'The Biodiversity Convention: Selected Issues of Interest to the International Lawyer' (1993) 4 Colorado Journal of International Environmental Law and Policy 141; UNCTAD, The Convention on Biological Diversity and the Nagoya Protocol: Intellectual Property Implications, A Handbook on the Interface between Global Access and Benefit Sharing Rules and Intellectual Property, UN Doc UNCTAD/DIAE/PCB/2014/ (2014).

[73] UNGA, Report on the work of the United Nations Open-ended Informal Consultative Process on Oceans and the Law of the Sea at its eleventh meeting, UN Doc A/65/164 (2010), paras 53 and 57–58.

from the use of genetic resources provide practical insights into how to implement technology transfer obligations on the basis of partnerships.[74]

Scholarship and international debates have also focused on the interplay between UNCLOS and the CBD with regard to marine genetic resources, but the CBD can provide generally accepted standards to specify UNCLOS obligations[75] including with regard to linking scientific and technical capacity building with the identification, conservation, and sustainable use of biodiversity.

The following sections will explore international obligations on technology transfer under UNCLOS, as well as the guidance provided by the Intergovernmental Oceanographic Commission's Criteria and Guidelines on the Transfer of Marine Technology (the IOC Criteria and Guidelines).[76] The IOC Criteria and Guidelines, albeit not legally binding, provide generally accepted guidance that helps detail UNCLOS obligations of international cooperation for technology transfer, by way of interpretation.[77]

3.1 The Duty to Cooperate

Efforts made prior to the adoption of UNCLOS with regard to marine technology transfer were marred by insufficient funding, poorly designed assistance programmes, and inadequate national commitment on the part of receiving States.[78] As a response, UNCLOS established a technology transfer regime based on the diffusion of scientific and technological expertise and the creation of a policy environment to facilitate technology transfer at the regional level. Marine technology is not defined under UNCLOS, but the definition provided under the IOC Criteria and Guidelines has now been included in the BBNJ Agreement.[79] Marine technology therefore includes 'information and data, provided in a user-friendly format, on marine sciences and related marine operations and services; manuals, guidelines, criteria, standards and reference materials; sampling and methodology equipment for in situ and laboratory observations, analysis and experimentation; computer and computer software, including models and modelling techniques;[80] and expertise, knowledge, skills, technical,

[74] Morgera (n. 24), at 353.

[75] UNCLOS, Art. 271 (note in this connection that all UNCLOS Parties are party to the CBD). The dividing line between legally binding and non-legally binding instruments in international law becomes unclear when non-legally binding instruments are used to interpret legally binding ones: see generally A Boyle and C Chinkin, *The Making of International Law* (Oxford University Press, 2009); D Shelton (ed.), *Commitment and Compliance: The Role of Non-binding Norms in the International Legal System* (Oxford University Press, 2003).

[76] Intergovernmental Oceanographic Commission (IOC), Criteria and Guidelines on the Transfer of Marine Technology, adopted at the XXII Session of the General Assembly of the IOC, 2003 (hereinafter, the IOC Criteria and Guidelines).

[77] 'The Future We Want' and Agenda 2030 called for States to take into account the IOC Criteria and Guidelines with a view to, inter alia, enhancing the contribution of marine biodiversity to the development of developing States: UNGA, The Future We Want, UN Doc A/RES/66/288 (27 July 2012), para. 160; SDG 14.a.

[78] W Wooster, 'Some Implications of Ocean Research' (1977) 4 Ocean Development and International Law 39.

[79] BBNJ Agreement, Art. 1(10).

[80] Examples include food web and multi-species distribution models as well as habitat suitability models, which can be used to determine suitable catch levels as well as to identify areas that are important for

scientific and legal know-how and analytical methods related to marine conservation and sustainable use of marine biological diversity'.[81] This is understood to encompass the 'instruments, equipment, vessels, processes and methodologies required to produce and use knowledge to improve the study and understanding of the nature and resources of the ocean and coastal areas'.[82]

The central tenet is States' duty to cooperate,[83] either directly or through competent international organizations, with a view to promoting the development and transfer of marine science and technology on fair and reasonable terms and conditions.[84] This has been interpreted as a 'framework' commitment requiring the conclusion of several implementing arrangements to be effective,[85] on the understanding that this obligations is 'not formulated in terms of strict legal obligations'[86] and therefore 'too general to allow one to determine how it can be enforced against those who do not comply with it'.[87] This reading is compounded by the fact that UNCLOS does not create or call for the development of a cohesive administrative system to facilitate implementation.[88]

A different interpretation is favoured here, one that is based on good faith towards the objective and purpose of UNCLOS.[89] As other commentators have emphasized, cooperation 'is action',[90] so UNCLOS Parties are required to enter into negotiations 'with a view to transforming a provision worded in general terms into specific units of obligation for the purpose of implementation susceptible of being monitored and, where necessary, subjected to dispute settlement procedures'.[91] Other scholars have

biodiversity and/or ecosystem services, in line with an ecosystem-based approach to fisheries management. See also AJ Kenny et al., 'Delivering Sustainable Fisheries through Adoption of a Risk-based Framework as Part of an Ecosystem Approach to Fisheries Management' (2017) 93 Marine Policy 232.

[81] BBNJ Art 1(10); following closely Intergovernmental Oceanographic Commission (IOC), Criteria and Guidelines on the Transfer of Marine Technology, adopted at the XXII Session of the General Assembly of the IOC, 2003 (hereinafter, the IOC Criteria and Guidelines), para. A(2).

[82] IOC Criteria and Guidelines, para. A(2).

[83] UNCLOS, Arts 270 and 278. See also United Nations Agreement for the Implementation of the Provisions of the United Nations Convention on the Law of the Sea of 10 December 1982 relating to the Conservation and Management of Straddling Fish Stocks and Highly Migratory Fish Stocks (New York, 4 August 1995, in force 11 December 2001) (UNFSA), Art. 25(2).

[84] UNCLOS, Art. 266(1). See also UNFSA, Art. 25. The emphasis on international cooperation is further reinforced by the wording of the majority of the provisions of UNCLOS, Part XIV, which tends to weaken the element of obligation. Commentators have noted that there is a clear tendency for the UN General Assembly and other bodies dealing with the problem of technology transfer to developing countries, to place the emphasis more on international cooperation than on formal obligation: MH Nordquist et al., University of Virginia, Center for Oceans Law and Policy, *United Nations Convention on the Law of the Sea, 1982: A Commentary* (Martinus Nijhoff, 1985) 694.

[85] M Pinto, 'Transfer of Technology under the UN Convention on the Law of the Sea' (1986) 6 Ocean Yearbook Online 241, at 265; Nordquist et al. (n. 84), at 57 et seq, 59, 60, 95–96, and 668.

[86] BA Boczek, *The Transfer of Marine Technology to Developing Nations in International Law* (Law of the Sea Institute, University of Hawaii 1982), at 47.

[87] P Vigni, 'Antarctic Bioprospecting: Is it Compatible with the Value of Antarctica as a Natural Reserve?' in F Francioni and T Scovazzi (eds), *Biotechnology and International Law* (Hart, 2006) 129.

[88] C Alberts, 'Technology Transfer and its Role in International Environmental Law: A Structural Dilemma' (1992) 7 Harvard Journal of Law & Technology 63, at 68–69.

[89] Vienna Convention on the Law of the Treaties (VCLT) (Vienna, 23 May 1969, in force 27 January 1980), Art. 31(1).

[90] M Pinto, 'The Duty of Co-operation and the United Nations Convention on the Law of the Sea' in A Bos and H Siblesz (eds), *Realism in Law-Making: Essays on International Law in Honour of Willem Riphagen* (Martinus Nijhoff, 1986) 145.

[91] ibid.

also pointed to the idea that underpins these provisions as that of equality of capacity for rights and obligations between technologically advanced States and developing States, in accordance with the principle of cooperation in international law as enshrined in the UN Charter.[92] Similarly, it is argued here that the CBD obligations,[93] and the interpretative guidance provided by the decisions adopted under it, as well as the IOC Guidelines, provide further supplementary modalities that serve to detail UNCLOS obligations. CBD decisions, in particular, do so by way of interpretation in terms that have been negotiated and agreed upon by consensus[94] by all UNCLOS Parties in their capacity as CBD Parties.

Interestingly, the provisions of UNCLOS on the protection and preservation of the marine environment reiterate the obligation to provide scientific and technical assistance to developing States, including in the form of supplying them with the necessary equipment and enhancing their endogenous capacity to manufacture it.[95] These obligations have been interpreted as requiring developed States to 'either directly transfer publicly held environmentally sound technologies or finance the licensing of privately held technologies'.[96] States must therefore endeavour to foster favourable economic and legal conditions for the transfer of marine technology for the benefit of all parties concerned on an equitable basis,[97] and to promote the development of the marine scientific and technological capacity of States which may need and request technical assistance.[98] At the very least, States should remove legal barriers in this connection.

In addition, States must promote the acquisition, evaluation, and dissemination of marine technological knowledge; facilitate access to relevant information and data; promote the development of appropriate marine technology and of the infrastructure necessary to facilitate its transfer; encourage the development of human resources through training and education of nationals of developing States; and promote international cooperation at all levels, particularly at the regional, subregional, and bilateral levels.[99] The latter two objectives may be pursued through programmes of technical cooperation, particularly with developing States; the exchange of scientists and of technological and other experts; and the promotion of joint ventures and other forms of bilateral and multilateral cooperation.[100] Furthermore, States are required to

[92] P Payoyo, *Cries of the Sea: World Inequality, Sustainable Development and the Common Heritage of Humanity* (Martinus Nijhoff, 1997), at 102.

[93] VCLT, Art. 31(3)(c). On the CBD as a source of relevant and applicable rules of international law for the purposes of interpreting other treaties, see Morgera (n. 24), at 361–362.

[94] On the international law-making effect of consensus, in that 'this way of securing widespread support for a legal text *per se* legitimizes and promotes consistent State practice' see: Boyle and Chinkin (n. 75), at 260.

[95] UNCLOS, Art. 202(a).

[96] The UN General Assembly has also noted that current debates about technology transfer and the environment within the context of the World Trade Organization (WTO) raise the question of whether this is just another intellectual property and technology transfer debate, or whether environmentally sound technologies present distinctive challenges: UNGA, Options for a facilitation mechanism that promotes the development, transfer and dissemination of clean and environmentally sound technologies, UN Doc A/67/348) (31 August 2012) para. 44.

[97] UNCLOS, Art. 266(3).

[98] ibid, Art. 266(2).

[99] ibid, Art. 268. See also UNFSA, Art. 1.

[100] UNCLOS, Art. 269. Joint ventures are further explored in H Campbell and A Hand, 'Joint Ventures and Technology Transfer: The Solomon Islands Pole-and-line Fishery' (1998) 57 Journal of Development Economics 421; G Verhoosel, 'Beyond the Unsustainable Rhetoric of Sustainable Development: Transferring

promote the establishment of new, or the strengthening of existing, national marine scientific and technological research centres, particularly in developing coastal States, with a view to providing advanced training facilities and necessary equipment, skills, and know-how, as well as technical experts.[101] Moreover, nationals of other States fishing in the Exclusive Economic Zone (EEZ) must comply with the laws and regulations of the coastal State relating to requirements for the training of personnel and the transfer of fisheries technology, including with a view to enhancing the coastal State's capability to undertake fisheries research.[102]

The elaboration of coordinated bilateral, regional, or multilateral programmes, either directly by States or through competent international organizations, is crucial for the development of generally accepted guidelines, criteria, and standards for technology transfer.[103] The IOC Criteria and Guidelines promote capacity building through international cooperation,[104] with a view to enabling all parties to benefit from developments in ocean research, and in particular those activities that aim at stimulating the social and economic contexts in developing States on an equitable basis.[105] The IOC Criteria and Guidelines focus on the development of special financial and scientific schemes to facilitate marine technology transfer at the national, regional, or subregional levels; the transfer of marine technology free of charge or at a reduced rate for the benefit of the recipient State; the taking into account of the needs and interests of developing and land-locked States, as well as of other legitimate interests, including the interests of holders, suppliers, and recipients of marine technology; and the importance of the transfer of environmentally sustainable technologies. The IOC Criteria and Guidelines thus offer important insights from a capabilities perspective.

The CBD also requires Parties to establish and maintain programmes for scientific and technical education and training with respect to the identification, conservation, and sustainable use of biodiversity, taking into account the needs of developing States.[106] States are further expected to promote and encourage research that contributes to these objectives, and to cooperate in the use of relevant scientific advances to develop methods for conserving and sustainably using biological resources.[107] Considering socio-economic development and poverty eradication priorities of developing States,[108] the CBD calls upon Parties to take full account of the specific needs and unique circumstances of least developed countries (LDCs) with regard to technology transfer,[109] with special focus on the development and strengthening of national capabilities by means of human resources development and institution

Environmentally Sound Technologies' (1998) 11 Georgetown International Environmental Law Review 49, at 58–60.

[101] UNCLOS, Art. 275.
[102] ibid, Art. 62(4)(j).
[103] ibid, Arts 271–272.
[104] IOC, Criteria and Guidelines, para. A(1).
[105] ibid, para. B.
[106] <IBT >CBD, Art. 12(1).
[107] ibid, Art. 12(2) and (3).
[108] ibid, preambular para. 19.
[109] ibid, Art. 20(5).

building.[110] CBD Parties must also promote cooperation in the training of personnel and the exchange of experts for the purposes of developing and using technologies that contribute to the objectives of the Convention. Indigenous and traditional technologies are specifically referred to.[111] In addition, the CBD explicitly cautions that any technology transferred needs to be 'relevant to the conservation and sustainable use of biological diversity ... and ... not cause significant damage to the environment.'[112]

3.2 Multilateral Information Sharing

Notwithstanding the complementarity of multiple international legal instruments and guidance, the open-ended nature of the underlying international obligations has resulted in an ad hoc approach to implementation that makes it difficult to keep tabs on progress regarding the effective transfer of technology,[113] or equitable access to research results and data.[114] This arises from the lack of coordination between researching States, research institutions, private partners, and regional organizations.[115]

A barrier often mentioned by technologically advanced States is that research in, and development of, ocean technology is mainly undertaken by private corporations, particularly transnational corporations using their own resources.[116] Private companies are beyond the reach of governments 'under a free-enterprise system that does not allow to compel action by autonomous commercial entities'[117] whose technologies are available for purchase or protected from unauthorised use either by law or the maintenance of strict secrecy.[118] UNCLOS hints at this, by calling on States to have 'due regard' for the rights and duties of holders, suppliers, and recipients of marine technology,[119] which has been criticised for its weak formulation.[120] This raises distributive justice considerations.

110 ibid, Art. 18(2).

111 ibid, Art. 18(4).

112 ibid, Art. 16(1).

113 See the discussions on these points in the BBNJ PrepCom: e.g. Earth Negotiations Bulletin (ENB), Summary and analysis of the Third Session (2017) 25, available at: http://enb.iisd.org/download/pdf/enb25129e.pdf, accessed 17 July 2017, at 9–10.

114 C Salpin, V Onwuasoanya, and M Bourrel, 'Swaddling, Marine Scientific Research in Pacific Small Island Developing States' (2016) 95 Marine Policy 363, at 363.

115 On the increasing fragmentation of the international system of capacity-building mechanisms for technology and sustainable development, including within the UN system, see UNGA, Options for a facilitation mechanism that promotes the development, transfer and dissemination of clean and environmentally sound technologies, UN Doc A/67/348 (31 August 2012), paras 27 and 55 et seq.

116 C Gopalakrishnan, 'Transnational Corporations and Ocean Technology Transfer: New Economic Zones are Being Developed by Public/Private Partnerships but Deep Sea Miners Balk on Royalties' (1989) 48 American Journal of Economics and Sociology 373, at 375.

117 Morgera and Ntona (n. 16).

118 Pinto (n. 85), at 267.

119 UNCLOS, Art. 267.

120 J van Dyke and D Teichmann, 'Transfer of Seabed Mining Technology: A Stumbling Block to U.S. Ratification of the Law of the Sea Convention?' (1984) 13 Ocean Development and International Law 427, at 434. However, Nordquist et al. note that, unlike most of the provisions of Part XIV, Art. 267 is cast in the language of obligation, albeit flexible: Nordquist et al. (n. 84), at 682.

Multi-stakeholder partnerships,[121] as highlighted in the IOC Criteria and Guidelines,[122] can provide a starting point for inclusion of private companies, including regarding collaborative intellectual property systems and licensing (e.g. open source and general public licences),[123] albeit they have also been severely criticized.[124] The CBD calls upon Parties to promote the establishment of joint ventures and research programmes,[125] and to promote cooperation in the training of personnel and the exchange of experts for the purposes of developing and using technologies that contribute to the objectives of the Convention, including indigenous and traditional technologies.[126]

What is of interest here is whether partnerships can go beyond a mode of governance that is expected to loosely complement government efforts to implement relevant international obligations and commitments. Rather can partnerships seek to realize the ideal of global partnership enshrined in the 1992 Rio Declaration on Environment and Development,[127] both in terms of a 'new level of cooperation' between developed and developing States,[128] and a form of cosmopolitan cooperation[129] that is inspired by a vision of public trusteeship?[130] The latter approach could provide value by ensuring needs-based and integrated implementation of capacity-building and technological support obligations,[131] thereby realizing the guiding principle of UNCLOS and the IOC Criteria and Guidelines that the transfer of marine technology must always be conducted on 'fair and reasonable terms and conditions'.[132] This approach could also 'enable all parties concerned to benefit on an equitable basis from developments in marine science-related activities, particularly those aiming at stimulating the social and economic contexts in developing countries'.[133]

3.3 Scientific Cooperation for Environmental Protection

Even if Part XII of UNCLOS does not say so explicitly, scientific expertise, methods, and information are necessary to implement the obligations on the protection of the marine environment, notably in light of the precautionary principle. This can be seen

[121] I Zapatrina, 'Sustainable Development Goals for Developing Economies and Public-Private Partnership' (2016) 11 European Procurement & Public Private Partnership Law Review 39.

[122] IOC Criteria and Guidelines, para. B(d).

[123] ibid.

[124] C Streck, 'The World Summit on Sustainable Development: Partnerships as New Tools in Environmental Governance' (2003) 13 Yearbook of International Environmental Law 63.

[125] CBD, Art. 18(5).

[126] CBD, Art. 18(4).

[127] Rio Declaration on Environment and Development UN Doc A/CNF.151/26 (1992), Preamble, and Principles 7 and 27.

[128] PM Dupuy, 'The Philosophy of the Rio Declaration' in J Viñuales (ed.), *The Rio Declaration on Environment and Development: A Commentary* (Oxford University Press, 2015), 69, at 71 and 84.

[129] ibid, at 72, 85, and 89.

[130] P Sand, 'Principle 27: Cooperation in a Spirit of Global Partnership' in Viñuales (n. 128), 617. Sand refers to the ITPGRFA as a concrete example.

[131] ENB, Summary and analysis of the Third Session (2017) 25(121); ENB, Summary and analysis of the Third Session (2017) 25(124).

[132] UNCLOS, Art. 266(1); IOC Criteria and Guidelines, para. B(b).

[133] IOC Criteria and Guidelines, para. B.

as an integral part of due diligence obligations[134] to continuously predict, monitor, and respond to risks to the marine environment through exchange of information and establishing appropriate scientific criteria for rules on marine pollution.[135] Relying on the results of environmental impact assessments (EIAs) that are to be published or distributed through competent international organizations can also be considered part of this due diligence requirement,[136] and the deliberate withholding of monitoring results could amount to a material breach of UNCLOS.[137]

In addition, due diligence includes the duty to cooperate, and as part of that an obligation to integrate the efforts of scientists and remove obstacles to marine scientific research for mutual benefit,[138] ensuring that obligations to support marine scientific research are 'for the benefit of all'.[139] This is necessary to create opportunities for all to contribute to the establishment of scientific criteria to keep pace with scientific understanding of threats to the marine environment, and is essential for applying precautionary measures[140] with a view to identifying emerging threats.[141] The role of the BBNJ Agreement can thus be understood as supporting the creation of favourable conditions for marine scientific research, as required under UNCLOS, to further develop the obligation to cooperate through the conclusion of international agreements to '*integrate the efforts of scientists* in studying the essence of phenomena and processes occurring in the marine environment and the interrelations between them'.[142]

This would entail supporting 'dialogue and inter[action] among scientists' with a view to integrating their findings both for intra- and interdisciplinarity to better understand 'the role of the ocean in the life of the planet'.[143] While UNCLOS obligations of scientific cooperation, extending both to the conduct of marine scientific research and the analysis of information for ocean management, may appear quite open-ended, it has been argued that absolute inaction would be a violation of UNCLOS.[144] In effect, it can be further argued that the duty to cooperate would also be violated in the absence of active attempts to bring parties to the negotiating table, refusing invitations to negotiate, or not negotiating in good faith with a view to advancing cooperation.[145] Good faith, in particular, entails the need to show other countries individually and the international community as a whole respect for the reasonable interests and legitimate

[134] Hubert (n. 30), at 318, referring to International Tribunal for the Law of the Sea (ITLOS), *Responsibilities and Obligations of States sponsoring persons and entities with respect to activities in the Area*, Advisory Opinion of 1 February 2011 (Seabed Disputes Chamber), para. 113.

[135] UNCLOS, Arts 200, 201, and 204(1); J Harrison, *Saving the Oceans through Law* (Oxford University Press 2017), at 35; T Stephens, 'Article 201' in A Proelss (ed.), *United Nations Convention on the Law of the Sea: A Commentary* (Hart, 2017) 1345; E Blitza, 'Article 204' in Proelss (n. 135) 1363.

[136] UNCLOS, Art. 194; Harrison (n. 135), at 34; D Czybulka, 'Article 194' in Proelss (n. 135) 1303.

[137] UNCLOS, Art. 205; E Blitza, 'Article 205' in Proelss (n. 135) 1367.

[138] UNCLOS, Arts 242 and 243.

[139] AM Hubert, 'Marine Scientific Research and the Protection of the Seas and Oceans' in R Rayfuse (ed.), *Research Handbook on Marine Environmental Law* (Edward Elgar 2015) 313, at 320–321.

[140] UNCLOS, Art. 201.

[141] T Stephens, 'Article 200' in Proelss (n. 135) 1342.

[142] UNCLOS Art. 243 (emphasis added).

[143] ibid, Art. 243; see I Papanicolopulu, 'Article 243' in Proelss (n. 135) 1637.

[144] UNCLOS, Art. 242; see Papanicolopulu, 'Article 242' in Proelss (n. 135) 1631 and 1634.

[145] PCA, *Guyana v. Suriname*, Award, 17 September 2007, 2004-04, paras 476–477.

expectations of other States[146] in a predictable manner[147] so as to show trustworthiness and predictability. This can be demonstrated by relying on multilateral institutions to support the effective, objective, and even-handed promotion and protection of the international community's interests.[148] A 'genuine intention to achieve a positive result'[149] in this context, would also require treaty interpretation in good faith, that is avoiding unreasonably strict literal interpretations if they would allow a Party to obtain an unfair advantage, or exercise rights in a way that would be damaging to another Party,[150] to the detriment of the effectiveness of a treaty.[151]

These considerations have a bearing on UNCLOS obligations related to technology transfer. The 'key criterion' in UNCLOS technology transfer regime is enabling all parties concerned to benefit on an equitable basis from developments in marine scientific research, particularly those aimed at stimulating the social and economic development of developing countries with due regard to their capacity in marine sciences.[152] Obligations of scientific and technical assistance towards developing States are mandatary, but do not clarify the extent of States' discretion. This reflects broader reluctance by developed States to agree to stricter rules, even if this affects overall effectiveness of UNCLOS obligations to protect the marine environment.[153] These obligations, however, entail strengthening the autonomous scientific capacity in developing states[154] to reduce reliance on external assistance in the long term, including to conduct EIAs.[155]

Overall, the UNCLOS regime provides some elements for supporting ocean knowledge co-production, which is also called for by marine scientists,[156] but these elements are not fully developed and connected effectively with one another. In effect, there has been limited international law research on the UNCLOS regime on marine scientific research and capacity building,[157] UNCLOS rules on technology are seen as 'weak' and 'unclear'.[158] In addition, UNCLOS rules on capacity building are largely not implemented due to the '(still prevailing) lack of political will on the part of developed states',[159] and generally 'fall short … [of ensuring] continuous cooperation'.[160]

146 M Virally, 'Review Essay: Good Faith in Public International Law' (1983) 77 American Journal of International Law 130.

147 S Litvinoff, 'Good Faith' (1997) 71 Tulane Law Review 1645, at 1664.

148 B Simma, 'From Bilateralism to Community Interests in International Law' (1994) IV (250) Recueil des Cours 217, at 319.

149 *Delimitation of the Maritime Boundary in the Gulf of Maine Area (Canada v. United States)* (12 October 1984) ICJ Reports 246, para. 87; A Orakhelashvili, 'Treaty Interpretation: Effectiveness and Presumptions' in A Orakhelashvili (ed.), *The Interpretation of Acts and Rules in Public International Law* (Oxford University Press, 2008) 415; R Kolb, *Good Faith in International Law* (Hart, 2017) 43.

150 Orakhelashvili (n. 149), at 415.

151 M Fitzmaurice, 'The Law of Treaties' in M Shaw (ed.), *International Law* (6th edn, Oxford University Press, 2008) 810, at 832–838.

152 Y Tanaka, *The International Law of the Sea* (Cambridge University Press, 2012), at 350.

153 UNCLOS, Art. 202; J Harrison, 'Article 202' in Proelss (n. 135) 1349.

154 UNCLOS, Art. 244(2).

155 ibid, Art. 202; J Harrison (n. 153), at 1351.

156 A Rogers et al., 'Marine Genetic Resources in Areas Beyond National Jurisdiction: Promoting Marine Scientific Research and Enabling Equitable Benefit-sharing' (2021) 8 Frontiers in Marine Science 667274.

157 M Gorina-Ysern, 'Marine Scientific Research: Overview of Major Issues, Programmes and their Objectives' in HD Smith, JL Suarez de Vivero, and T Agardy (eds), *Routledge Handbook of Ocean Resources and Management* (Routledge, 2015) 127, at 129; K Bartenstein, 'Article 266' in Proelss (n. 135), 1766.

158 I Papanicolopulu, 'Article 278' in Proelss (n. 135), 1811.

159 Bartenstein (n. 157), at 1765.

160 K Bartenstein, 'Article 269' in Proelss (n. 135), 1788.

These rules therefore provide the legal basis for elaborating further regulations to clarify the extent of each State's discretion in this connection.[161] The BBNJ negotiations could thus be understood as the multilateral process that UNCLOS Parties engaged in to create common platforms and adequate financing for scientific research cooperation.[162] Equally, the negotiations should be understood as a process to expand on UNCLOS obligations to 'actively promote ... the *strengthening of the autonomous marine scientific research capabilities of developing States*',[163] to ensure that scientific cooperation effectively gives scientists from the Global South and traditional knowledge holders the opportunity to participate and benefit.[164]

Applying the lens of the human right to science here helps to bring into focus the need for more systematic consideration of the power issues that characterize marine scientific research and that prevent transformative governance. As social scientists have amply demonstrated, notwithstanding a culture of peer review and collaboration among scientists, in practice (natural and social) sciences may be marked by competitiveness, secrecy, and vested interests, and the need for interdisciplinarity may prevent the application of established disciplinary standards.[165] Exogenous power dynamics at play in science have also been increasingly revealed.[166] The impacts of neoliberalism on scientific research practices include the diminution of public funding, the narrowing of scientific agendas on the needs of commercial actors, and the intensification of intellectual property rights impeding the production and dissemination of scientific findings.[167] As a result, the selection and framing of research questions, and the selection and use of evidence,[168] have implications for other public policy objectives down the line such as inclusivity, responsiveness to societal needs,[169] and alignment with social practices and local meaning.[170]

This should not come as a complete surprise, as UNCLOS itself indicates that marine sciences are to be conducted in compliance with all relevant regulations,[171] which 'opens the door for the right to science to influence the interpretation of [this] regime'.[172] Clarifying that international obligations on marine scientific cooperation provide a vehicle for implementing human rights in turn serves to underscore their legally binding nature,[173] as questions have been raised in the BBNJ negotiations about

161 I Papanicolopulu, 'Article 244' in Proelss (n. 135), 1641.

162 ibid, at 1639.

163 UNCLOS, Art. 244(2) (emphasis added).

164 Papanicolopulu (n. 161), at 1631 and 1634.

165 S Jasanoff, 'Serviceable Truths: Science for Action in Law and Policy' (2015) 93 Texas Law Review 1723, at 1738–1740.

166 N Stehr, 'The Social and Political Control of Knowledge in Modern Society' (2003) 55 Science Journal 643; S Vermeylen, G Martin, and R Clift, 'Intellectual Property, Rights Systems and the Assemblage of Local Knowledge Systems' (2008) 15 International Journal of Cultural Property 201, at 210.

167 Special Issue on Science and Technology Studies and Neoliberal Science of (2010) 40 Social Studies of Science.

168 Jasanoff (n. 165), at 1742–1743.

169 S Jasanoff, 'Technologies of Humility: Citizen Participation in Governing Science' (2003) 41 Minerva 223.

170 S Jasanoff, 'A New Climate for Society' (2010) 27 Theory, Culture & Society 233.

171 UNCLOS, Art. 240(d).

172 Hubert (n. 30), at 647.

173 ibid, at 628.

whether or not a new agreement should include mandatory provisions on benefit-sharing, technology transfer, and capacity building.[174]

4. BBNJ Agreement

The focus on the human right to science helps to reveal that UNCLOS obligations related to scientific cooperation, capacity building, and technology transfer, which are often seen in purely inter-State terms, have human rights implications. Thus, while developed countries interpreted these obligation in terms of almost unfettered discretion, the degree of discretion is limited by the need to implement relevant international human rights law too.[175] In the particular context of the BBNJ Agreement, human rights implications should be connected to vulnerable communities in countries with strongest connectivity to areas beyond national jurisdiction (ABNJ).[176] As our scientific understanding of other inter-connections between ecosystem services in areas beyond national jurisdiction and human well-being on Earth progresses, we can also expect to identify human rights implications for other societies or vulnerable groups in different States.

Along these lines, this section will focus on the opportunities under the BBNJ Agreement to contribute to a more partnership-oriented approach to capacity building and technology transfer, with a view to enhancing the capacity of developing countries (particularly those that are most connected to ABNJ) to contribute to ocean science and participate in more integrated and inclusive decision making on BBNJ by fostering co-production of ocean knowledge and transformative governance.

This section will explore the extent to which the BBNJ Agreement has framed international cooperation obligations as the co-production of ocean knowledge. After revealing the science-related underpinnings of the topics under negotiation, the section will explore how and to what extent the different dimensions of the human right to science can help address power dynamics in ocean knowledge production with a view to clarifying legal and policy questions around the multilateral governance of BBNJ. The section will then focus on capacity building and technology transfer, emphasizing their inter-linkages with other areas of the BBNJ Agreement—area-based management tools (ABMTs) and EIAs—in order to shed light on the institutional architecture needed for more coherent, sustainable, and equitable approaches to international cooperation for the conservation and sustainable use of BBNJ through inclusive co-production of ocean science across scales.[177]

[174] E Morgera and M Ntona, 'Seize the Moment: Towards Fairer Capacity Building and Marine Technology Transfer (2018) IIED policy brief, available at https://www.iied.org/17479iied, accessed 27 June 2023.

[175] For an initial discussion, see Morgera (n. 23), at 803.

[176] E Popova et al., 'So Far, Yet So Close: Ecological Connectivity between ABNJ and Territorial Waters' (2019) IIED Policy Brief, available at https://pubs.iied.org/17500iied, accessed 27 June 2023.

[177] In this context, 'scale' is understood as different levels of social organization, from local to global, with a view to understanding how knowledge on the effectiveness of natural resource management approaches can scale up and down: O Young, *Governing Complex Systems: Social Capital for the Anthropocene* (MIT Press, 2017), at 37. The term 'scales' also serves to allude to separate, but inter-related questions of knowledge and management of different levels of socio-ecological systems, from cells and microbiomes to ecoregions.

4.1 Why is Ocean Knowledge Co-production Central to the BBNJ Agreement?

Marine areas beyond national jurisdiction[178] (the high seas and the Area)[179] represent '4 billion years of evolution'[180] and 'contain 90% of the total biomass of the global ocean', encompassing a 'wide range of ecological processes and dynamics, from large-scale migrations by hundreds of species to low-productivity, highly stable deep-sea benthic ecosystems rich in biodiversity'.[181] But our understanding of these dynamics, and the ecological impacts of human activities on them, is incomplete, which in itself undermines current conservation and sustainable use efforts.[182]

As already discussed in the previous chapter, the most contentious topic in the BBNJ negotiations was benefit-sharing from marine genetic resources (MGRs), to the point that it was often seen as an obstacle to the conservation elements of the package. In effect, MGRs represent the most prominent exemplar of common equity challenges across marine scientific research: MGRs are the tip of the iceberg due to the evidence of inequalities that arise from intellectual property applications, whereby only ten countries in the world appear to be benefiting from deep-sea research.[183] But other aspects of deep-sea research are also in the hands of a small number of States. Only a restricted number of countries can afford the costs and risks of deep-sea research vessels and therefore can control who has access to that source of knowledge. The vast majority of developing countries are not part of deep-sea bioprospecting efforts and are also greatly underrepresented in marine taxonomic research.[184] In effect, 'field capacity at the most basic level of technical and scientific knowledge [of the ocean] is lacking' in most regions of the world[185] and 'despite centuries of hydrographic survey effort, we have more and better data to describe the surface of the Moon or Mars than for most of the Earth's seas'.[186] This gap is particularly felt in the Caribbean, Africa, and Oceania where nautical charts need to be urgently modernized and made compatible with satellite-based positioning systems, but the capacity to plan and implement a

[178] This section draws on E Morgera, 'The Relevance of the Human Right to Science for the Conservation and Sustainable Use of Marine Biodiversity of Areas Beyond National Jurisdiction: A New Legally Binding Instrument to Support Co-Production of Ocean Knowledge across Scales' in V De Lucia, L Nguyen, and A Oude Elferink (eds), *International Law and Marine Areas beyond National Jurisdiction: Reflections on Justice, Space, Knowledge and Power* (Brill, 2022) 242.

[179] UNCLOS, Parts VII and XI.

[180] Rogers et al. (n. 156), at 667274.

[181] G Crespo et al., 'Beyond Static Spatial Management: Scientific and Legal Considerations for Dynamic Management in the High Seas' (2020) 122 Marine Policy 104102, at 1–2.

[182] ibid.

[183] Only ten countries account for 90 per cent of patents related to MGRs (the United States, Japan, certain EU countries, Switzerland, and Norway): S Arnaud-Haond, J Arrieta and C Duarte, 'Marine Biodiversity and Gene Patents' (2011) 331 Science 1521.

[184] A Broggiato et al., '*Mare Geneticum*: Balancing Governance of Marine Genetic Resources in International Waters' (2018) 33 International Journal of Marine and Coastal Law 3, at 15–16, referring to K Juniper, 'Use of Marine Genetic Resources' in M Banks, C Bissada, and P Eghtesadi Araghi (eds), *The First Global Integrated Marine Assessment World Ocean Assessment I* (UN, 2016) 7–8 and I Hendriks and CM Duarte, 'Allocation of Effort and Imbalances in Biodiversity Research' (2008) 360 Journal of Experimental Marine Biology and Ecology 15, at 17.

[185] Gorina-Ysern (n. 157), at 127 and 128.

[186] R Wilson, 'Surveying the Sea' in H Smith, J Suarez de Vivero, and T Agardy (eds), *Routledge Handbook of Ocean Resources and Management* (Routledge, 2015) 462.

prioritized survey programme is lacking.[187] Meanwhile, nations with modern charts 'actively prevent the release of data',[188] and restrict marine scientists' access because of 'the link between obtaining improved knowledge of the ocean and [States'] growing interest in exploring offshore natural resources and technological advances that might be relevant to naval security'.[189]

In addition, growing Global North–South scientific collaborations are 'characterized by pharmaceutical or biotech companies working with established centres of excellence located in high-income countries'.[190] As a result of these, as well as the increasing reliance on sequencing technologies and bioinformatics, 'the capacity to undertake genomic research ... is inequitably distributed among countries'.[191] Thus a call has been made to urgently 'promote inclusive and responsible research and innovation that addresses equity differentials and fosters capacity and access to technology, while facilitating the realization of commitments to conserve and sustainably use the ocean's genetic diversity'.[192]

Knowledge of the deep-sea[193] is what allows for enhanced understanding of the need for, and effectiveness of, conservation and sustainable use approaches both in areas beyond national jurisdiction and in areas within national jurisdiction due to the ecological connectivity of the ocean that relies on currents and the movement of migratory species.[194] Understanding the 'ocean genome' (the whole of the genetic material present in all marine biodiversity, including both the genes and the information they encode) is essential for 'determining the abundance and resilience of biological resources', 'increas[ing] awareness of the pressures facing marine biodiversity' and 'informing the designation of [marine protected areas] as well as innovative approaches to conservation'.[195] But while our knowledge of the ocean genome is making strides, there is still a vast amount we do not know. For instance, the 'functions of some 90 percent of genetic sequences collected from viruses remain unknown'.[196] In that connection, it is also highlighted that '[a]cknowledging the potential commercial value of biodiversity'—which tended to dominate the BBNJ negotiations, as opposed to the benefits of MGRs for conservation knowledge —'may lead to better funding for biodiversity surveys that access a broad range of marine life and assess these for bioactivity, which may lead to improved biodiversity conservation measures'.[197]

So, States with limited oceanic knowledge are going to be necessarily less able to participate in decisions on EIAs, marine protected areas, and other ABMTs in areas beyond national jurisdiction, as well as less able to manage sustainably marine spaces

187 ibid, at 470.
188 ibid, at 475.
189 Hubert (n. 139), at 313 and 314.
190 Blasiak et al. (n. 20), at 26.
191 ibid, at 3.
192 ibid.
193 The deep seas encompass both benthic and pelagic systems deeper than 200m. These areas significantly overlap with the high seas and the deep-seabed that comprise the ABNJs under UNCLOS.
194 Popova et al. (n. 176); S Yadav and K Gjerde, 'The Ocean, Climate Change and Resilience: Making Ocean Areas beyond National Jurisdiction More Resilient to Climate Change and Other Anthropogenic Activities' (2020) Marine Policy 104184, at 4–5.
195 Blasiak et al. (n. 20), at 3.
196 ibid, at 8.
197 ibid, at 14.

within national jurisdiction if they are among those with the strongest connectivity to areas beyond national jurisdiction and the shortest timeframes for that connectivity.[198] In turn, it is down to these decisions on the creation of area-based and other management tools in ABNJ to 'safeguard genetic diversity at the ecosystem level'.[199] This highlights the epistemic justice and recognition issues underlying the BBNJ negotiations.

In addition, there are fundamental procedural justice questions related to competing uses that may be impacted by ABMTs and that may benefit and disadvantage different sectors and groups. Being able to influence the evidence base upon which these decisions will be taken is a significant power that rests on the ability to produce the best available science. The role of science is also crucial to support the assessments of cumulative and transboundary impacts on marine biodiversity. The sectors of scientific knowledge that will be relevant to that end has been clarified in the BBNJ Agreement, which makes explicit references to climate change, ocean acidification, and deoxygenation.[200] On the whole, the equity and capacity gap in deep-sea knowledge production affects the opportunities of countries in the Global South to influence the further development of the law of the sea: the link between ocean knowledge and law development is already recognised under the law of the sea.[201]

Scientific cooperation provides not only the means to improve the quality of marine scientific research, but also spreads opportunities for deep-sea research, including technology sharing and co-development across different countries, which enhances capacity for ocean management. The capacity gap for integrated ocean science and holistic ocean governance is particularly felt regarding the need to bring together environmental, social, and economic dimensions of different human activities across all ecosystem components both within and beyond national jurisdiction.[202] It is therefore to be welcomed that during the BBNJ negotiations, MGRs have been increasingly linked to the negotiations on capacity building and technology transfer,[203] focusing on the fundamental contribution of the study of MGRs of areas beyond national jurisdiction to 'increasing humankind's knowledge about nature'.[204]

Advancing basic knowledge about MGRs of areas beyond national jurisdiction more equitably, by genuinely partnering with scientists from the Global South and

198 Popova et al. (n. 176). For a discussion on ecological connectivity and references to 'adjacency' in the BBNJ Draft text, see J Mossop and C Schofield, 'Adjacency and Due Regard: The Role of Coastal States in the BBNJ Treaty' (2020) 122 Marine Policy 103877.

199 Blasiak et al. (n. 20).

200 Revised draft text of an agreement under the United Nations Convention on the Law of the Sea on the conservation and sustainable use of marine biological diversity of areas beyond national jurisdiction, UN Doc A/CONF.232/2020/3 (2020), Annex (BBNJ Draft text), draft Arts 1(6) and 14(e); Annex I (f) and Annex II, (a)(iv). Although see unbracketed text under General Approaches: 'approach that builds ecosystem resilience to the adverse effects of climate change and ocean acidification and restores ecosystem integrity': BBNJ Draft text, Art. 5(h).

201 UNCLOS, Art. 238; see also N Matz-Lück, 'Article 238' in Proelss (n. 135), 1609.

202 M Vierros and H Harden-Davies, 'Capacity Building and Technology Transfer for Improving Governance of Marine Areas both Beyond and Within National Jurisdiction' (2020) 122 Marine Policy 104158, at 1.

203 BBNJ Draft text (n. 200), Art. 42(f).

204 R Wolfrum, 'Concluding Remarks' (2009) 24 The International Journal of Marine and Coastal Law 343, at 346.

traditional knowledge holders, can support the co-production of knowledge on the interconnectivity of the ocean and its relevance for life and well-being on Earth, which is relevant to the realization of multiple SDGs across all the elements of the BBNJ Agreement.

4.2 The Advances of the BBNJ Agreement

Against this background, this section will assess the extent to which the BBNJ Agreement has clarified the scope, and limited the discretion, of developed States in implementing international obligations on marine scientific cooperation, capacity building, and technology transfer because of the inter-dependence of UNCLOS obligations to protect the marine environment. This analysis is enriched by the consideration of the human rights dimensions of ocean knowledge co-production, as well as the human rights implications of failed or limited efforts in advancing ocean knowledge production, and of the resulting ineffective conversation and unsustainable use of the ocean. The aim is to understand the extent to which the BBNJ Agreement has addressed the above-outlined injustices in ocean knowledge production and further theorized capacity and technology cooperation obligations as fair and equitable benefit-sharing that can contribute to ocean knowledge co-production for transformative governance,[205] in line with proposals coming from marine scientists from the Global North and South for 'inclusive innovation'.[206] Knowledge co-production can also support the engagement with another question about equity and benefits under the BBNJ Agreement: climate change and its 'impacts on both ocean circulation and the global distribution of species indicat[ing] that today's patterns of ecological connectivity will not remain static in time'.[207] In other words, it will be investigated how a broad notion of fair and equitable benefit-sharing aligns both with the ecosystem approach and the human right to science. This will help to clarify the content of the duty to cooperate under UNCLOS by recognizing power and capacity imbalances in current marine scientific research in areas beyond national jurisdiction and the need for genuine partnerships as opposed to one-off forms of collaboration.

The preamble to the BBNJ Agreement refers to fairness in the same terms as UNCLOS, mentioning 'the importance of contributing to the realization of a just and equitable international economic order which takes into account the interests and needs of humankind as a whole, and in particular the special interests and needs of developing States, whether coastal or landlocked'.[208] In addition, it refers to the desire to 'act as stewards of the ocean in areas beyond national jurisdiction on behalf of present and future generations, by protecting, caring for and ensuring responsible use of the marine environment, maintaining the integrity of the ocean ecosystems and conserving the inherent value of biodiversity of areas beyond national jurisdiction'.[209]

205 Visseren-Hamakers and Kok (n. 7).
206 Blasiak et al. (n. 20), at 37.
207 Popova et al. (n. 176).
208 BBNJ Agreement, preambular, para. 5.
209 ibid, preambular, para. 11.

These pre-existing references to equity and the novel reference to ocean and marine ecosystem stewardship in an inter-generational perspective provide helpful background to the objective of the Agreement to 'ensure the conservation and sustainable use of [BBNJ] *for the present and in the long term*, through effective implementation of the relevant provisions of the Convention and *further international cooperation and coordination*'.[210] This arguably hints at the inter- and intra-generational equity dimensions of the more advanced forms of international cooperation regulated and facilitated by the Agreement.

A broad understanding of fair and equitable benefit-sharing as part of the human right to science and the ecosystem approach can possibly be based on some of the 'general principles and approaches' that guide Parties in achieving the objectives of the Agreement, where reference is made to the 'principle of equity and the fair and equitable sharing of benefits' and the ecosystem approach.[211] The importance of ocean knowledge production is then captured under the specific objectives of the MGR-related part of the Agreement, whereby Parties 'shall be guided by ... the generation of knowledge, scientific understanding and technological innovation, including through the development and conduct of marine scientific research *as fundamental contributions* to the implementation of the agreement'.[212] It is also reiterated with regard to 'activities with respect to [MGRs]', which are 'for the benefit of all humanity, particularly for the benefit of advancing the scientific knowledge of humanity and promoting the conservation and sustainable use of marine biodiversity, taking into particular consideration the interests and needs of developing States'.[213]

As I have argued elsewhere,[214] an integrated approach to benefit-sharing from MGRs could foster deeper cooperation with existing UNCLOS obligations on scientific research, capacity building, technology transfer, and environmental protection. This serves to contribute to responsible and inclusive research and innovation as 'the low chance of commercial success from biodiscovery, combined with the long timeframe for potential financial returns, means that some of the most significant benefits are non-monetary, emerging from the research process itself rather than from commercial products'.[215] So the question is whether the BBNJ Agreement supports a more concerted, institutionalized multilateral approach to ensure responsiveness to the needs of beneficiaries and oversee the distribution of benefits across different regions and scales. Such an assessment should focus on the co-identification of real-world opportunities to increase the capacities in the Global South and among traditional knowledge holders to actively participate in transformative ocean conservation and management, in the light of a shared understanding of power imbalances.

[210] ibid, Art. 2 (emphasis added).

[211] ibid, Art. 7(d) and (f).

[212] ibid, Art. 9(c). The more general provision on international cooperation on marine scientific research is quite weak: 'Parties shall promote international cooperation in marine scientific research and in the development and transfer of marine technology consistent with the Convention in support of the objectives of this Agreement' (ibid, Art. 8(3)).

[213] ibid, Art. 11(6).

[214] E Morgera, 'Fair and Equitable Benefit-sharing in a New International Instrument on Marine Biodiversity: A Principled Approach towards Partnership Building?' (2018–19) 5 Maritime Safety and Security Law Journal 48. This proposal was supported by Blasiak et al. (n. 20), at 38–39.

[215] Blasiak et al. (n. 20), at 38.

In effect, the BBNJ Agreement provides for periodic review, every two years, of monetary benefit-sharing[216] and the development of guidelines ensuring transparency, fairness, and equity in the sharing of both monetary and non-monetary benefits.[217] This will be based on advice from experts nominated by Parties from different geographies who will form an Access and Benefit-sharing Committee. This committee will base its recommendations on Parties' reports and the consideration of 'national capabilities and circumstances'.[218]

Support for knowledge co-production can also arguably be found in the objectives of capacity building and technology, with mandatory language on 'inclusive, equitable and effective cooperation and participation', the development of 'marine scientific and technological capacity', and the need to 'increase, disseminate and share knowledge on the conservation and sustainable use of' BBNJ,[219] as well as to 'partnerships with and involving all relevant stakeholders, such as, as appropriate, the private sector'.[220]

An interpretation of capacity and technology solidarity provisions supporting beneficiaries' agency, as opposed to the passive enjoyment of benefits,[221] and therefore a shift away from unidirectional (likely top-down) or one-off flows of benefits, can be based on the references to 'needs and requests of developing States[222] and account of their 'national policies, priorities, plans and programmes'.[223] In more effective terms, the BBNJ Agreement calls for 'a country-driven, transparent, effective and iterative process that is participatory, cross-cutting and gender-responsive',[224] reiterating that this process 'shall be based on and be responsive to the needs and priorities of developing States'.[225] The reference to 'iterative' is particularly notable, as fairness and equity in benefit-sharing are found in an iterative dialogue (procedural dimension) to develop a common understanding of what different States may see as benefits (substantive dimension) arising from the conservation and sustainable use of BBNJ. This approach can support mutual learning, adaptive governance, and explicit engagement with power imbalances, which have been highlighted by scholars advocating for centring BBNJ governance on the resilience of socio-ecological systems[226] and the inclusion of traditional knowledge.[227]

In the BBNJ context, this dialogue can serve to develop a common understanding across the different views of equity and of benefits that have already been voiced in the negotiations. For instance, the United States and other developed States affirmed that research and development on MGRs of ABNJ is a highly costly and time-consuming endeavour with uncertain results, which, when successful, would benefit humanity

216 BBNJ Agreement, Art. 14(10).
217 ibid, Art. 15(1).
218 ibid, Art. 16(3).
219 ibid, Art. 40(d).
220 ibid, Art. 41(2).
221 Mancisidor (n. 14), at 1.
222 BBNJ Agreement, Art. 42(4).
223 ibid, Art. 42(2).
224 ibid, Art. 42(3).
225 ibid, Art. 42(2).
226 Yadav and Gjerde (n. 194), at 5–6.
227 M Vierros et al., 'Considering Indigenous Peoples and Local Communities in Governance of the Global Ocean Commons' (2018) 119 Marine Policy 104039, at 7.

in the form of scientific advancements contributing to global public health, food security, and environmental protection.[228] On the other hand, developing countries have argued that fair and equitable sharing opportunities to participate in scientific expeditions, follow-up research, as well as the development of technology and research findings could notably enhance their capacity to conduct marine scientific research and contribute to the protection of the marine environment and its sustainable use.[229]

This consequently opens the door for developing countries to co-identify the benefits and needs for transformative ocean governance through the integrated implementation of capacity building, technology transfer, scientific cooperation, and information sharing obligations, even if these obligations are all dependent on resources in donor countries, who for that reason tend to 'call the shots'.[230] This resonates with the need to take into account the preferences of intended beneficiaries and local contextual elements in assessing which technologies may be usefully and equitably shared, as was cautioned by UN Special Rapporteur on the Right to Food, De Schutter.[231] It can support States' compliance with their international human rights obligations in the joint setting of priorities and understanding of basic economic, social, and cultural rights,[232] taking into account ecological connectivity between areas within and beyond national jurisdiction, as well as our evolving understanding of the ecosystem services provided by BBNJ in the context of capacity building and technology transfer.

Admittedly, however, the BBNJ Agreement has not addressed the ongoing inequalities in relation to IPRs. Rather, it has relied on non-committal language on technology transfer such as 'fair and most favourable terms, including concessional and preferential terms, and in accordance with mutually agreed terms' and 'account of all rights over ... technologies ... and due regard for all legitimate interests, including the rights and duties of holders, suppliers and recipients of marine technology, and taking into particular consideration the interests and needs of developing states for the attainment of the objectives of the Agreement'.[233] In other words, BBNJ negotiators did not take the opportunity to include minimum standards specifically required to ensure the protection of relevant human rights[234] and also to ensure benefit-sharing, capacity building, and technology transfer in the context of intellectual property, in the light of application of the human right to science. This could have provided an important departure from the UNCLOS deference to intellectual property rights seen as the 'promise of profit secured by exclusive commercialization rights'.[235]

[228] E Morgera, 'Benefit-sharing in marine areas beyond national jurisdiction: where are we at? (Part I)' BENELEX blog (2014), available at https://benelexblog.wordpress.com/2014/05/23/benefit-sharing-in-marine-areas-beyond-national-jurisdiction-where-are-we-at-part-i/, accessed 26 July 2021.

[229] ibid.

[230] ENB (n. 113), at 121 and 124.

[231] De Schutter (n. 64), at 348.

[232] See references to 'food security and other socio-economic objectives, including the protection of cultural values' in BBNJ Agreement, Art. 17(d) in relation to area-based management tools.

[233] BBNJ Agreement, Art. 43(4).

[234] With regards, for instance, to protecting the rights of traditional knowledge holders (discussed in Chapter 4), see Inter-American Court of Human Rights, *Case of the Saramaka People v. Suriname*, Judgment of 28 November 2007 (Preliminary Objections, Merits, Reparations and Costs), para. 194.d; *Case of Kaliña and Lokono Peoples v. Suriname*, Judgment of 25 November 2015 (Merits, Reparations and Costs), para. 305(d); *Kichwa Indigenous Community of Sarayaku v. Ecuador*, Judgment 27 June 2012 (Merits and Reparations), paras 299–300.

[235] K Bartenstein, 'Article 267' in Proelss (n. 135), 1774.

4.3 BBNJ Institutions

Co-identification of benefits can support more effective delivery through multilateral facilitative and brokering arrangements to operationalize relevant duties of cooperation with a view to ensuring equitable distribution across different regions, monitoring of effectiveness, and learning from experience. The need for such an approach has already been demonstrated in other international processes, such as the International Seabed Authority and the International Maritime Organization.[236] A reference to international brokering can also be found in the BBNJ Agreement, where facilitation of needs self-assessment can be provided by the Capacity Building and Technology Transfer Committee and by the BBNJ clearinghouse.[237]

As discussed in the previous chapter, an institutionalized, multilateral approach is needed to iteratively learn about benefit-sharing through dialogue, priority-setting, and oversight, to integrate expertise from the bottom up and support the agency of beneficiaries (traditional knowledge holders and scientists from the Global South), with a view to ensuring transparency, continuous learning, and genuine partnership-building to identify and assess obstacles, and to propose enhancements, to distribution of benefits across regions and scales.[238] To that end, an appropriate multilateral institutional structure would collectively identify the greatest need for progress in ocean science to support basic economic, social, and cultural rights, taking into account ecological connectivity between areas within and beyond national jurisdiction, as well as our evolving understanding of the ecosystem services provided by BBNJ.

There are several institutions under the BBNJ Agreement that can contribute to iterative learning.[239] First, the Capacity Building and Technology Transfer Committee will advise the Conference of Parties on the types of capacity building and technology, to 'respond and adapt to the evolving needs of States, subregions and regions'.[240] This is particularly necessary as 'a full inventory of national marine science capacity is lacking, as is an inventory of ocean-related [capacity building and technology transfer efforts'.[241] It could focus initially on non-monetary benefits, with a view to exploring in the interim technological solutions to move towards monetary benefit-sharing. This can be achieved by systematically tackling the inter-operability of databases and other online tools, facilitating the sharing of effective capacities and technologies, and enhancing opportunities for collaboration to help ensure inclusive participation in relevant research efforts.[242] In addition, it will review the self-identification of needs and priorities by developing countries and review the support provided, including identifying 'gaps in meeting needs', and measure performance, including on 'output,

[236] Morgera and Ntona (n. 16).

[237] BBNJ Agreement, Art. 51.

[238] E Morgera, S Switzer, and M Geelhoed, 'Study for the European Commission on 'Possible Ways to Address Digital Sequence Information – Legal and Policy Aspects' (December 2019).

[239] For an overview of the institutional options explored in the BBNJ negotiations, see N Clark, 'Institutional Arrangements for the New BBNJ Agreement: Moving beyond Global, Regional, and Hybrid' (2020) 122 Marine Policy 104143.

[240] BBNJ Agreement, Art. 46(3).

[241] Vierros and Harden-Davies (n. 202), at 2.

[242] Morgera, Switzer, and Geelhoed (n. 238).

outcomes, progress and effectiveness ... as well as successes and challenges'.[243] It is regrettable, however, that no explicit reference has been made to perceived fairness in the context of this periodic review.

In addition, an independent Scientific and Technical Body has been established to act 'in the best interest of the Agreement' and represent 'multi-disciplinary expertise'.[244] The latter is particularly noteworthy, as there is a need to integrate social sciences, as highlighted by the UN Decade of Ocean Science, for 'transformative ocean science',[245] to support a science-based engagement with equity in scientific cooperation, including with traditional knowledge holders.[246] The role of that body is yet to be determined,[247] so it remains to be seen whether the Scientific and Technical Body will facilitate dialogue with expected beneficiaries, with a view to co-developing integrated responses across a range of actors and different communities of practices involved in ocean knowledge co-production. Will it be able to advance a shared understanding of changing scientific practices and foster understanding of the different economics underpinning particular sectors and their contributions to BBNJ conservation and sustainable use?[248] This would be particularly useful as there are two distinct committees, one on MGRs and one on capacity building and technology transfer.

Third, the BBNJ Agreement creates a new international clearinghouse, which is not just an online, open-access repository of information. Instead, it is a platform that could arguably support concerted and iterative dialogue to align with the priorities of beneficiaries in effectively making use of, and contributing to, the production of ocean science for the conservation and sustainable use of BBNJ. This could serve to implement the right to science in terms of setting priorities for the vulnerable, by supporting a focus on 'high-priority material' for instance,[249] and assessing issues leading to discriminatory results in the sharing of information, by monitoring effectiveness through feedback and periodic consultations. In addition, it could serve to provide institutional support for the brokering of scientific cooperation, capacity-building, and technology-transfer opportunities.[250] The BBNJ Agreement indeed clarifies that the clearinghouse will support brokering by collecting requests and opportunities for capacity building and technology transfer, and facilitating the matching process between them.[251] It will also support inter-operability with other online databases and information-exchange platforms[252] and generally facilitate international collaboration and cooperation, 'including scientific and technical cooperation and collaboration'.[253]

243 BBNJ Agreement, Art. 45(2)(d).

244 ibid, Art. 49(2).

245 Summary of the Implementation Plan of the UN Decade for Ocean Science for Sustainable Development 2021–2030 (2021), 11 and 13.

246 BBNJ Draft text (n. 200), Art. 49. This is also supported in the Implementation Plan of the UN Decade for Ocean Science (n. 245). Along similar lines, see F Humphries et al., 'A Tiered Approach to the Marine Genetic Resources Governance Framework under the Proposed UNCLOS Agreement for Biodiversity beyond National Jurisdiction (BBNJ)' (2020) 122 Marine Policy 103910, 11–12.

247 BBNJ Agreement, Art. 49(4).

248 Morgera, Switzer, and Geelhoed (n. 238).

249 ITPGRFA Res 3/2015.

250 Morgera (n. 24); Humphries et al. (n. 246), at 4; Rogers et al. (n. 156), at 18.

251 BBNJ Agreement, Art. 51(3)(a)(iv) and (b).

252 ibid, Art. 51(3)(c).

253 ibid, Art. 51(3)(f).

This is reminiscent of the International Plant Treaty's GLIS discussed earlier. A more institutionalized multilateral approach has in effect emerged as a necessary precondition for information sharing, not only to ensure responsiveness to needs and more equitable distribution across different regions, but also to contribute to a more systematic encouragement of positive cycles between capacity-building, scientific cooperation, and technology transfer.[254]

Finally, the BBNJ Conference of the Parties (COP) is quite an innovation from a law-of-the-sea perspective, although it has been a feature of international environmental treaties for more than three decades. The BBNJ COP will keep under review and evaluation the implementation of the Agreement and establish appropriate processes to promote coherence in efforts to conserve and sustainably use BBNJ,[255] including review periodically the 'adequacy, effectiveness and accessibility of financial resources under the financial mechanism of the Agreement, for the delivery of capacity building and technology transfer.[256] Potentially these are sufficiently broad powers for the BBNJ COP to promote an enabling global environment for the inclusive advancement of ocean science and the enjoyment of the benefits of its applications,[257] in the face of the current deep international disparities among countries in the realms of science and technology. Consequently, the BBNJ COP could support States in ensuring access to those applications of scientific progress that are critical to the enjoyment of the right to health and other economic, social, and cultural rights; prioritizing allocation of public resources to research in areas where there is the greatest need for scientific progress in health, food, and other basic needs related to economic, social, and cultural rights, and the well-being of the population, especially with regard to vulnerable and marginalized groups.[258] It remains to be seen the extent to which the BBNJ COP will provide sufficient support for a genuine multilateral dialogue and oversight on the multiple equity issues underlying all elements of the BBNJ package. To support the human right to science, this support intends to collectively identify the areas needing progress in ocean knowledge co-production that would serve to support basic economic, social, and cultural rights, taking into account ecological connectivity between areas within and beyond national jurisdiction, as well as our evolving understanding of the ecosystem services provided by BBNJ.[259] The aim is to build stronger partnerships for the advancement of knowledge, conservation, and sustainable use of marine biodiversity across current capacity disparities.

The BBNJ Agreement introduces another notable aspect that is relevant in terms of potential future engagement with human rights dimensions. It contains various

[254] E Morgera, Study on experiences gained with the development and implementation of the Nagoya Protocol and other multilateral mechanisms and the potential relevance of ongoing work undertaken by other processes, including case studies, UN Doc UNEP/CBD/ABS/A10/EM/2016/1/2 (2015); E Morgera, 'Multilateral benefit-sharing: Whither from here?', BENELEX blog (2016), available at https://benelexblog.wordpress.com/2016/06/20/multilateral-benefit-sharing-whither-from-here/, accessed 3 August 2023.

[255] BBNJ Agreement, Art. 47(6)(c).

[256] ibid, Art. 52(16).

[257] ICESCR, Art. 15(4).

[258] UN Doc E/C.12/GC/25, para. 52.

[259] Elisa Morgera et al., 'Addressing the Ocean-climate Nexus in the BBNJ Agreement: Strategic Environmental Assessments, Human Rights and Equity in Ocean Science' (2023) 38 International Journal of Marine and Coastal Law 447.

provisions on transparency, consultation, and public participation[260] that could engender a more human rights-cognizant dynamic in the implementation of the treaty.

4.4 Relevance of the Other Provisions in the BBNJ Agreement

To a great extent, addressing fairness and equity in ocean knowledge co-production requires engaging directly with developed States in their capacity as ocean research funders and discussing funding priorities and coordinated approaches, with a view to increasing the 'rigor, efficiency and effectiveness in a number of aspects of marine scientific research including on MGRs of ABNJ'.[261] This can serve to support long-term capacity building and technology transfer, as well as skills development (particularly for early-career researchers) across disciplines throughout knowledge co-production, including contributing to EIAs.[262] Funders would be best placed to ensure support for new collaborative approaches and learning across scales[263] towards ocean knowledge co-production and transformative governance.

The four dimensions of the human right to science can in fact clarify the interdependence of fair and equitable benefit-sharing as capacity building and technology transfer and the underlying obligations of scientific cooperation underpinning environmental impact assessments and area-based management tools (ABMTs) in the BBNJ Agreement, with a view to supporting ocean knowledge co-production. Existing inequities could be addressed through the BBNJ multilateral institutional approaches and rules to ensure that all States can equally share in the benefits from scientific advances that can support ABMTs and EIAs without discrimination; have an opportunity to contribute to scientific research; contribute to protect against negative consequences of scientific research or its applications on food, health, security, and the environment; and set priorities for scientific research that focus on key issues for the most vulnerable.

These connections provide opportunities for more integrated implementation of the BBNJ Agreement: both parts of the Agreement emphasize the importance of the capacity of developing countries.[264] Support should be provided for advancing research to test the potential outcomes of protecting genetic diversity in multiple connected marine protected areas.[265] More specific international obligations and standards[266] on EIAs and strategic environmental assessments, in turn, could support the integration of genetic biodiversity into the planning and decision-making of multiple sectors that may impact and benefit from the ocean genome.[267] Equally, EIAs should refer to

[260] BBNJ Agreement, Arts 16, 21, 32, and 48. See Yadav and Gjerde (n. 194), at 6, on the importance of participation for resilience.
[261] Rogers et al. (n. 156), at 18 and 20.
[262] ibid, at 15 and 18.
[263] Morgera and Ntona (n. 16), at 303.
[264] BBNJ Agreement, Art. 7(b) and 21bis(f).
[265] ibid, 31.
[266] BBNJ Draft text (n. 200), Art. 23(3) alt1.
[267] Blasiak et al. (n. 20), at 30.

relevant human rights considerations; these can be read in the references to 'associated impacts, such as economic, social cultural, and human health impacts'.[268]

A notable new opportunity is provided by the BBNJ Agreement provisions on strategic environmental assessments (SEAs), which were quite controversial during the negotiations,[269] even though CBD Parties have an obligation to carry out SEAs.[270] Strategic assessments would allow considering of potential impacts on human rights, as well as opportunities to contribute to the different dimensions of the right to science. This would respond to the need to ensure that networks of marine protected areas support sustainable use for essential services such as scientific areas for harvesting genes for product development by industry, or wilderness areas to protect pristine habitats that provide key ecosystem services for those actors.[271] The BBNJ Agreement has created a power for the COP that can be quite significant in terms of ocean knowledge co-production; to conduct SEAs for an area or region to 'collate and synthesize the best available information, assess current and potential future impacts and identify data gaps and research priorities'.[272] While the BBNJ Agreement only notes the relevance of SEA results for EIAs, the outcomes of COP-mandated SEAs, and possibly those led by Parties, are clearly also relevant for the provisions on capacity and technology solidarity. In fact, the planning of COP-mandated SEAs (and possibly that of State-led SEAs, with the due guarantees) could provide an ideal context for co-developing marine scientific cooperation, capacity, and technology co-development taking into account the needs and priorities of developing States.[273]

5. Another Example: The International Climate Change Regime

While fair and equitable benefit-sharing is not included in the international climate change treaties, some references to it have been made in international climate-related guidelines (mainly in relation to intra-State dimensions and possible co-benefits of local climate change responses),[274] as well as local and transnational arrangements to share climate-related project benefits.[275] Nevertheless, Kim Bouwer has speculated

[268] BBNJ Agreement, Arts 31(b) and 35.
[269] BBNJ Draft text (n 200), Arts 1(13), 21bis(c), and partial brackets in Art. 28.
[270] Harrison (n. 153), at 46; CBD, Art. 14(b).
[271] Blasiak et al. (n. 20), at 29.
[272] BBNJ, Art. 39(2).
[273] K McQuaid et al., 'The Need for Strategic Environmental Assessments and Regional Environmental Assessments in ABNJ for Ecologically Meaningful Management' (2022) One Ocean Hub policy brief, available at https://oneoceanhub.org/publications/policy-brief-the-need-for-strategic-environmental-assestements-and-regional-environmental-assessment-in-abnj-for-ecologically-meaningful-management/, accessed 27 June 2023; E Morgera et al. (n. 259).
[274] A Savaresi, 'The Emergence of Benefit-Sharing Under the Climate Regime: A Preliminary Exploration and Research Agenda' BENELEX Working Paper no. 3 (SSRN, 2014) available at https://papers.ssrn.com/sol3/papers.cfm?abstract_id=2524335, accessed 27 June 2023.
[275] K Bouwer, 'Possibilities for Justice and Equity in Human Rights and Climate Law: Benefit- Sharing in Climate Finance' (2021) 11 Climate Law 1, at 10–13; see, e.g., C Armeni, 'Participation in Environmental Decision-Making: Reflecting on Planning and Community Benefits for Major Wind Farms' (2016) 28 Journal of Environmental Law 415.

that fair and equitable benefit-sharing could be read into the references to equity in the international climate regime and add value to existing equity principles, in particular in the light of the growing connections between international climate change law and international human rights law,[276] with a view to allocating advantages generated by the responses to climate change in a fair and equitable manner.[277] Notably, scholarship has been highlighting how attention to justice issues in international climate debates currently focus on ethical responsibility and burden-sharing,[278] whereas engagement with benefit-sharing could allow other dimensions of justice, such as capabilities, to be addressed. These perspectives also prompt consideration that intellectual property rights are not the only or even the most predominant barriers to international co-operation, particularly in the case of technological transfer, as various other factors have the potential to support or undermine these processes: instead, deeper forms of cooperation could result in shared ownership of intellectual property.[279] As discussed above, the engagement with fair and equitable benefit-sharing under the human right to science was partly inspired by the need to make progress on technology solidarity under the international climate change regime.[280]

Nicola Sharman, for instance, has aptly argued that fair and equitable benefit-sharing could add value to the interpretation of the still controversial common but differentiated responsibilities principle under the international climate change regime. Benefit-sharing could help shift attention from a pure consideration of burden and cost towards a more holistic effort to also consider the global and local advantages of environmental protection, notably with regard to global co-benefits of climate change mitigation and sustainable development in the recipient State. Benefit-sharing could also foster recognition by developed countries of the 'benefits in wealth, infrastructure and other assets that they have derived from their own carbon-based development models to date, and which are no longer available to developing States'.[281]

In addition, scholars have reflected on the specific role of benefit-sharing in the context of the international climate change law obligations on technology transfer, with a view to better contributing to global distributive justice.[282] The argument builds on the need to further develop the set of principles for international cooperation and decision making on technology transfer by 'stressing the importance of dialogue, partnership building, and empowerment of developing States'.[283] Accordingly, Nicola Sharman highlighted the treaty obligations under the UN Framework Convention on Climate Change 'to take all practicable steps to promote, facilitate and finance'

[276] e.g. S Duyck, S Jodoin, and A Johl (eds), *Routledge Handbook of Human Rights and Climate Governance* (Routledge, 2018).

[277] A Savaresi and K Bouwer, 'Equity and Justice in Climate Change Law and Policy: A Role for Benefit-Sharing' in T Jafry (ed.), *Research Handbook on Climate Justice* (Routledge, 2018) 128.

[278] Bouwer (n. 275), at 3.

[279] K Bouwer, 'Insights for Climate Technology Transfer from International Environmental and Human Rights Law' (2018) 23 Journal of Intellectual Property Rights 7, at 16.

[280] Shaheed's report (n. 19).

[281] N Sharman, 'Inter-State Climate Technology Transfer under the UNFCCC: A Benefit-Sharing Approach' (2022) Review of European, Comparative and International Environmental Law 435, at 443.

[282] ibid.

[283] ibid, at 445.

technology development and transfer'[284] and 'strengthen cooperative action' and provide support to developing countries in the light of 'the importance of fully realizing technology development and transfer' under the Paris Agreement. These can arguably serve to fulfil the treaty's goals[285] and could be interpreted in ways that advance understanding of the needs and contextual conditions in developing countries, as well as opportunities for building their own capacity to innovate in climate mitigation in the future, with global benefits in terms of enhanced effectiveness in the implementation of the climate regime.[286]

Nicola Sharman has developed specific suggestions on how to operationalize these interpretations under the UNFCCC Technology Mechanism with a view to supporting more genuine 'collaborative approaches rather than unidirectional provision of resources' that are 'overly dominated by neoliberal viewpoints that favour market-based incentives'.[287] She suggested that the required technology needs assessments, designed to provide an analysis of best practice through participation, strategic stakeholder engagement, and multi-criteria analyses, could be undertaken as an iterative benefit-sharing process with their content periodically reviewed and outcomes systematically tracked.[288] These outcome assessments could then focus on (existing and missed) opportunities for transformative partnership, such as 'permanent collaborative forums for research and development [rather than] singular hardware transfer projects could have great potential to build innovation ecosystems', and on 'neglected areas, such as adaptation technologies'.[289] Overall, the process could provide more co-defined understandings of equity, more diversified implementation approaches, and more opportunities for transformative change through holistic interactions between technology transfer and capacity building.[290]

From an institutional and normative perspective, Sharman suggested that the Technology Mechanism (through its Technology Executive Committee) integrate benefit-sharing principles in its policy recommendations, guidance, briefs, dialogues, and workshops.[291] She also recommended that the COP serving as the meeting of the Parties to the Paris Agreement could, by decision, incorporate benefit-sharing principles into an amendment of the Technology Framework, as part of the five-yearly periodic assessments of the Technology Mechanism; and the Climate Technology Centre and Network, as the Technology Mechanism's operational arm, could further translate policy recommendations into its own work.[292]

Equally, researchers have been reflecting on the role of fair and equitable benefit-sharing within broader approaches to capacity building under the international climate change regime with more substantive emphasis on human rights and entitlement to benefits. In this context, benefit-sharing can support multilateral decision making

[284] United Nations Framework Convention on Climate Change (UNFCCC) (New York, 9 May 1992, in force 21 March 1994), Art. 4(5).
[285] Paris Agreement (Paris, 12 December 2015, in force 4 November 2016), Art. 10.
[286] Sharman (n. 281), at 443.
[287] ibid, at 440.
[288] ibid.
[289] ibid, at 442.
[290] ibid, at 445.
[291] ibid, at 445.
[292] ibid.

that is driven first and foremost by potential and current host countries' needs and priorities, rather than financial viability of projects, and expanded collaborative initiatives that support interactive learning.[293]

Kim Bouwer has called attention to the role of models of collaborative working towards technology innovation such as Climate Innovation Centres or Climate Relevant Innovation Builders, which are established in developing countries on a trial basis and aim to foster innovation and capacity building in that context, as a way to challenge the 'unilateral' conceptions of transfer as a 'handing over' of equipment and hardware.[294]

These approaches rely on ongoing relationships between 'donor' and 'receiver' parties, ensuring that both maintain presence in the research and development of significant technologies. In addition, these partnership-based processes facilitate the development of much of the true operational capacity required by the 'receiver' State for the optimal local operation of the technologies in the relevant State. Bouwer consequently argues that these centres can also accommodate South–South cooperation, as well as iterative monitoring effectiveness of supported interventions, and brokering opportunities for collaboration, that could follow the example of the International Plant Treaty platform for the co-development and transfer of technologies discussed above.[295]

Climate finance, the safeguarding policies and standards adopted by different treaty funds also include, or at least support, benefit-sharing at project level.[296] The Financial Mechanism and its operating entities could further develop their linkages with the Technology Mechanism, and integrate benefit-sharing principles into their relevant decision-making processes and policies, with a view also to supporting coherent application across the regime.[297]

Overall these approaches could then be combined with intra-State and transnational benefit-sharing dimensions, as part a partnership-based approach across scales (see the discussion in Chapter 5),[298] including a protective safeguard and a system of active engagement, supporting less powerful parties and ensuring continuing engagement on the uses and development of climate change technologies.[299]

6. Conclusions

Applying the lens of international human rights law, and in particular the human right to science, to international provisions on capacity and technological solidarity serves, first, to clarify that international scientific cooperation is not just a matter of the law

[293] Bouwer (n. 279), at 14.

[294] ibid, at 11.

[295] ibid, at 15.

[296] ibid, at 29–39.

[297] Sharman (n. 281), at 445.

[298] For a discussion on how the technology needs assessment process under the climate regime can go some way towards supporting needs-based achievement of climate technology transfer, see Bouwer (n. 279). The Technology Executive Committee (which conducts these assessments) does not make any reference to benefit-sharing, but we argue that the approach taken is compatible with the concept of benefit-sharing as an element of the right to science.

[299] Savaresi and Bouwer (n. 277), at 135.

of the sea and of international environmental law. This should not come as a complete surprise, as UNCLOS itself indicates that marine science is to be conducted in compliance with all relevant regulations,[300] which 'opens the door for the right to science to influence the interpretation of [this] regime'.[301] Clarifying that international obligations on scientific cooperation, capacity building, and technology transfer provide a vehicle for implementing human rights, in turn serves to highlight their legally binding nature,[302] as questions continue to arise in international negotiations about whether or not international environmental law and the law of the sea include mandatory provisions on scientific cooperation, technology transfer, and capacity building.[303] A mutually supportive interpretation of fair and equitable benefit-sharing at the crossroads of international biodiversity law and the human right to science helps to interpret international obligations on information sharing, technology, and scientific cooperation (beyond the specific realm of access to genetic resources and fair and equitable benefit-sharing (ABS), discussed in Chapter 1) and advance the theorization of benefit-sharing in other areas of international law, such as the law of the sea and international climate change law.

In the case of the law of the sea, these developments have now been arguably crystallized in the BBNJ Agreement. The human right to science has thus helped identify and address injustices and power imbalances in the production and use of ocean knowledge, that in turn prevent more effective efforts to conserve and sustainably use BBNJ. The human right to science further serves to clarify that these injustices are considered a matter of international human rights law, so States have specific obligations to prevent negative impacts on human rights arising from these power asymmetries in ocean science and management. This normative understanding provides the rationale and the content for enhanced international cooperation and more defined due diligence obligations to co-develop effective solutions for the conservation and sustainable use of BBNJ through inclusive ocean science. To a significant extent, the BBNJ Agreement has followed a broad conceptualization of fair and equitable benefit-sharing by developing clearer rules and an institutionalized approach to critically assess whether information sharing, capacity building, and marine technology transfer address equity issues in an iterative way, with the potential to avoid discriminatory results, prioritize the needs of the vulnerable, and factor in the need to protect against negative consequences of scientific research.

Furthermore, the BBNJ Agreement includes obligations that support the co-production of ocean science as a basis for truly joint governance based on shared concepts of scientific collaboration and increased capacities in the Global South and among traditional knowledge holders to actively participate in transformative ocean conservation and management across scales. While it is too early to say whether the BBNJ COP will identify collectively the greatest need for progress in ocean science to support basic economic, social, and cultural rights, taking into account ecological connectivity between areas within and beyond national jurisdictions, as well as our

300 UNCLOS, Art. 240(d).
301 Hubert (n. 30) 647.
302 ibid, 628.
303 e.g. BBNJ Agreement, Art. 41.

evolving understanding of the ecosystem services provided by BBNJ, it has certainly made progress in the theorization of fair and equitable benefit-sharing in the area of capacity building and technology solidarity. It provides relevant examples that could also be relevant in other areas of international law, such as the international climate change framework, briefly discussed in this chapter, and ongoing negotiations (at the time of writing) by the World Health Organization.[304]

[304] WHO pandemic treaty and revised regulations. See the authors' comments reported on in https://healthpolicy-watch.news/updated-international-health-regulations-more-important-than-pandemic-accord/ (April 2023), accessed 27 June 2023.

3
Intra-State Benefit-Sharing
State Obligations towards Indigenous Peoples

1. Introduction

This chapter focuses on intra-State benefit-sharing in relation to the human rights of Indigenous peoples connected to their territories and the natural resources traditionally used by them. These benefit-sharing obligations have emerged in the context of the regulation of extractive activities (forestry, fisheries, mining), nature conservation (such as the creation of protected areas), freshwater management, and climate change response measures in areas Indigenous peoples traditionally use or where these activities might impact them.

Intra-State benefit-sharing has been incompletely theorized in both international biodiversity law and human rights law. International human rights lawyers[1] have focused on the complex and still unsettled notion of free prior informed consent (FPIC)[2] and difficulties in obtaining meaningful and appropriate compensation for human rights violations arising from environmental harm caused by extractive activities.[3] Consequently, references to benefit-sharing in international human rights law have relied on 'universal standards'[4] developed under the Convention on Biological Diversity (CBD).[5] Consensus guidance adopted under the CBD, in turn, has clarified how to concretely apply benefit-sharing in the specialized context of natural resources and protected areas governance. Such guidance provides a pragmatic complement to the evolving interpretation of the human rights obligation of sharing benefits. CBD instruments, however, have not engaged explicitly with

[1] Benefit-sharing is not explicitly referred to in the UN Declaration on the Rights of Indigenous Peoples (UNDRIP: UNGA Res 61/295, 2007). Even international human rights lawyers specifically focusing on international biodiversity law do not address benefit-sharing: e.g. Ellen Desmet, *Indigenous Rights Entwined with Nature Conservation* (Intersentia, 2011).

[2] e.g. UN Expert Mechanism, Advice No. 4: Follow-up report on indigenous peoples and the right to participate in decision-making, with a focus on extractive industries, UN Doc A/HRC/21/55 (2012), paras 38(b), 39(h), and 43; M Århén, *Indigenous Peoples in the International Legal System* (Oxford University Press, 2016), at 217–218; and C Rodrîguez-Garavito, 'Ethnicity.gov: Global Governance, Indigenous Peoples, and the Right to Prior Consultation in Social Minefields' (2011) 18 Indiana Journal of Global Legal Studies 263.

[3] e.g. F Lenzerini (ed.), *Reparations for Indigenous Peoples: International and Comparative Perspectives* (Oxford University Press, 2008).

[4] A Fodella, 'Indigenous Peoples, the Environment, and International Jurisprudence' in N Boschiero, et al. (eds), *International Courts and the Development of International Law: Essays in Honour of Tullio Treves* (Springer, 2013), 360, develops this argument with regard to international human rights law, not international biodiversity law.

[5] Convention on Biological Diversity (CBD) (Rio de Janeiro, 5 June 1992, in force 29 December 1993).

Fair and Equitable Benefit-Sharing in International Law. Elisa Morgera, Oxford University Press.
DOI: 10.1093/oso/9780198862130.003.0004

human rights language, avoiding questions related to minimum standards of protection and justiciability.[6]

Nevertheless, mutually supportive interpretations of the two areas of international law can serve to clarify the scope, content, and status of relevant international benefit-sharing obligations. The chapter will thus identify potential paths for developing a supportive understanding of international biodiversity and human rights law. The goal is to move beyond a defensive approach that conceptualizes benefit-sharing as a mere procedural safeguard in the context of a pre-determined set of development options. Rather, a mutually supportive interpretation points towards a potentially transformative collaboration across different worldviews and knowledge systems, with a view to addressing multiple dimensions of justice.

Intra-State benefit-sharing is predominantly understood from the perspective of distributive and procedural justice in the management of natural resources governed by the State: who gets to decide ultimately on the use of natural resources and under what conditions of participation, justification, and recourse. Fundamentally, however, intra-State benefit-sharing also raises issues regarding the recognition of Indigenous peoples as self-identified and self-determined peoples, involving their customary laws, traditional tenure, knowledge systems, world views and conceptions of nature, well-being, and development. In addition, contextual justice issues concerning historical and ongoing dispossession, displacement, and discrimination of Indigenous peoples that affect all the underlying conditions under which a particular benefit-sharing obligation is applied are critical for any consideration of fairness and equity, but often overlooked.

2. Indigenous Peoples' Territories and Natural Resources

International biodiversity law and international human rights law have been increasingly cross-fertilizing[7] with regard to the rights of Indigenous peoples[8] over their territories and the natural resources traditionally used by them.[9] As a result, fair and equitable benefit-sharing from the utilization of these territories and natural resources is becoming increasingly significant as a safeguard against imposed developments or other negative effects on these territories, together with prior environmental and socio-cultural assessments and FPIC processes.

[6] E Morgera, 'Under the Radar: Fair and Equitable Benefit-Sharing and the Human Rights of Indigenous Peoples and Local Communities Related to Natural Resources' (2019) 23 International Journal of Human Rights 1098, at 1102.

[7] U Linderfalk, 'Cross-fertilization in International Law' (2015) 84 Nordic Journal of International Law 428, at 436–438.

[8] Indigenous peoples' right to natural resources is considered separate from their right to land; see, e.g., Final Report of the Special Rapporteur Erica-Irene Daes on Indigenous Peoples' Permanent Sovereignty over Natural Resources, UN Doc E/CN.4/Sub.2/2004/30 (2004), para. 39; and J Gilbert, 'The Right to Freely Dispose of Natural Resources: Utopia or Forgotten Right?' (2013) 31 Netherlands Quarterly of Human Rights 314, at 314.

[9] J Knox, Report of the Special Rapporteur on the issue of human rights obligations relating to the enjoyment of safe, clean, healthy and sustainable environment, UN Doc A/HRC/37/59 (2018) (hereinafter: 'Framework Principles'), Principle 15.

The application of benefit-sharing itself, however, raises new justice issues. It is often perceived as a threat to the human rights of Indigenous peoples and is associated with offering money or other economic advantages (e.g. employment) in exchange for obtaining consent,[10] which 'encourages a climate of disrespect towards Indigenous peoples'.[11] Benefit-sharing has resulted in 'attempts to undermine social cohesion of affected communities' through bribes to community leaders or selective negotiations tactics.[12] In particular, monetary benefit-sharing is known to 'destruct the social network' of Indigenous groups,[13] putting in place self-defeating or paternalistic mechanisms that are not responsive to communities' specific needs.[14] Furthermore, regional human rights bodies have had occasion to highlight situations where promised benefit-sharing were not delivered,[15] or benefit-sharing arrangements were originally in place but broke down and/or were weakened by ineffective State monitoring of outsiders' activities.[16]

All of these benefit-sharing practices, however, can be considered 'contrary to international standards' interpreted in good faith.[17] This chapter thus clarifies a good faith interpretation of benefit-sharing obligations from the utilization of Indigenous territories and natural resources. International human rights law has used benefit-sharing to support a number of specific human rights, thereby clarifying the minimum content of the international obligation of intra-State benefit-sharing owed to Indigenous peoples.

The chapter will then offer an interpretation of benefit-sharing that is significantly different to current widespread practices of benefit-sharing. This interpretation pieces together standards of international human rights and environmental law that have been identified by different bodies at different points in time, and therefore remain isolated from one another. On that basis, the proposed interpretation supports a role for benefit-sharing that is more conducive to, and intertwined with, FPIC. This interpretation can contribute to clarifying the limits of national sovereignty over national resources in light of international human rights of Indigenous peoples[18] and

10 Inter-American Court of Human Rights (IACtHR), *Case of Kichwa Indigenous Community of Sarayaku v. Ecuador*, Judgment of 27 June 2012 (Merits and Reparations), para. 194.

11 ibid, paras 193–194.

12 ibid, para. 186. J Gilbert and C Doyle, 'A New Dawn over the Land: Shedding Light on Collective Ownership and Consent' in S Allen and A Xanthaki (eds), *Reflections on the UN Declaration on the Rights of Indigenous Peoples* (Hart, 2011) 289.

13 N Gomez, 'Indigenous Peoples and Psychosocial Reparations: The Experience with Latin American Indigenous Communities' in Lenzerini (n. 3) 143, at 158.

14 G Citrioni and K Quintana Osuna, 'Reparations for Indigenous Peoples in the Case of the Inter-American Court of Human Rights' in Lenzerini (n. 3) 317, at 340 and 324.

15 African Commission on Human and Peoples' Rights (Afr. Comm.), *Centre for Minority Rights Development (Kenya) and Minority Rights Group International on behalf of Endorois Welfare Council v. Kenya* (4 February 2010) Case 276/2003, para. 274.

16 IACtHR, *Case of Kaliña and Lokono Peoples v. Suriname*, Judgment of 25 November 2015 (Merits, Reparations and Costs), paras 77–84 and 183.

17 *Kichwa* (n. 10), para. 186. Gilbert and Doyle (n. 12), at 289.

18 F Francioni, 'Natural Resources and Human Rights' in E Morgera and K Kulovesi (eds), *Research Handbook of International Law and Natural Resources* 66 (Edward Elgar, 2016) 66, in light of the International Covenant on Economic, Social and Cultural Rights (ICESCR), 16 December 1966, 993 UNTS 3, Arts 1(2) and 2(1).

international obligations on environmental protection.[19] In addition, the chapter explores potential paths for further developing a mutually supportive interpretation of benefit-sharing that sheds light on the extent to which international law can accommodate different worldviews of nature and development[20] embodied in Indigenous peoples' distinctive ways of life.[21] In other words, the proposed interpretation illuminates the potential of international benefit-sharing obligations to challenge mainstream conceptions of economic development and attempts to romanticize, ossify, or bottle Indigenous Peoples' worldviews into neo-liberal or neo-colonial agendas,[22] by taking into account multiple dimensions of justice.

The chapter will thus unveil further potential paths for developing a mutually supportive interpretation by strategically analysing the *interplay* of intra-State benefit-sharing obligations[23] with environmental assessments and consultation practices. This will serve to substantiate four inter-linked normative claims. Benefit-sharing has a substantive core linked to Indigenous peoples' choices and capabilities, as well as a procedural core linked to Indigenous peoples' agency as part of a concerted, culturally appropriate, and iterative dialogue with the State. Viewed in this light, benefit-sharing expands considerably the scope and approach of environmental assessments and consultation practices. It enables a shift away from a defensive approach that conceptualizes benefit-sharing as a mere procedural safeguard[24] towards a potentially transformative collaboration in light of Indigenous peoples' understandings of nature, well-being, and development. Intra-State benefit-sharing should then be distinguished from compensation, with which it is often conflated under international human rights law,[25] as it does not depend on a violation of a human right. Finally, the proposed interpretation of intra-State benefit-sharing has implications for understanding its status in international law.

[19] e.g. Francioni (n. 18); V Barral, 'National Sovereignty over Natural Resources: Environmental Challenges and Sustainable Development' in Morgera and Kulovesi (n. 18) 3; Århén (n. 2), at 55; and F Lenzerini, 'Sovereignty Revisited: International Law and Parallel Sovereignty of Indigenous Peoples' (2006) 42 Texas International Law Journal 155.

[20] A Barros, 'The Fetish Mechanism: A Post-Dogmatic Case Study of the Atacama Desert Peoples and the Extractive Industries' in C Lennox and D Short (eds), *Handbook of Indigenous Peoples' Rights* (Routledge, 2016) 223, at 231–232.

[21] G Pentassuglia, 'Towards a Jurisprudential Articulation of Indigenous Land Rights' (2011) 22(1) European Journal of International Law 165, at 176; D McGregor, 'Living Well with the Earth: Indigenous Rights and the Environment' in Lennox and Short (n. 20) 167, at 175; Desmet (n. 1), at 58 and 175; and Francioni (n. 18).

[22] E Reimerson, 'Between Nature and Culture: Exploring Space for Indigenous Agency in the Convention on Biological Diversity' (2013) 22 Environmental Politics 992; Y Uggla, 'What is This Thing Called 'Natural'? The Nature-culture Divide in Climate Change and Biodiversity Policy' (2009) 17 Journal of Political Ecology 79.

[23] E Morgera, 'The Need for an International Legal Concept of Fair and Equitable Benefit-sharing' (2016) 27 European Journal of International Law 353.

[24] UN Special Rapporteur on Indigenous Peoples' Human Rights James Anaya, Progress report on extractive industries, UN Doc A/HRC/21/47 (2012), paras 52 and 62.

[25] Making reference more consistently to 'ensur[ing] reasonable *benefit or compensation* for indigenous peoples impacted by natural resource exploitation': Office of the High Commission for Human Rights (OHCHR), Mapping Human Rights Obligations Relating to the Enjoyment of a Safe, Clean, Healthy and Sustainable Environment: Individual Report on the International Convention on the Elimination of Racial Discrimination (2013), at 16–18 (emphasis added).

3. The Extent of Cross-Fertilization

This section sheds light on the incomplete theorization of fair and equitable benefit-sharing under international human rights and biodiversity law, and the current degree of cross-fertilization between them. It also calls attention to the respective blind spots of these two areas of law, with a view to highlighting the need for furthering mutual supportiveness.

The present discussion should be, at the outset, framed in the broader context of the extensive international law scholarship on Indigenous peoples' human rights related to land and the more specific literature on the protection of their territories (the entirety of the environment in the areas inhabited or utilized by these communities)[26] as part of their right to preserve their culture.[27] In that context, the protection of Indigenous territories aims to ensure respect for cultural differences, including collective identities that are characterized by specific cultural and spiritual attachments to traditional geographic areas and utilization of natural resources that are essential for their social and cultural reproduction as a group.[28] Such protection would inherently extend to Indigenous peoples' ways of life, access to means of livelihoods, protection of cultural heritage, and would ultimately ensure their survival with its civil, political, as well as economic, social, and cultural dimensions.[29] This raises justice concerns of recognition, intertwined with distributive justice and participation.

A distinction should be drawn between natural resources that are essential to sustain Indigenous peoples' lives and those that are linked to broader opportunities for their economic development.[30] The former entails State obligations to take all possible measures to prevent negative impacts (including those arising from environmental degradation) on the right to life, including the protection of the right to food (hunger and malnutrition), and the right to health (ensuring good nutrition, increasing life expectancy, eliminating epidemics, supporting the practice of traditional medicine), all of which may have a bearing on the recognition of Indigenous Peoples' customary territorial rights.[31] On the latter, certain limited impacts on ways of life and on the right to religion (including spiritual attachments to territories due to traditional ceremonies or burial grounds) may be acceptable if they do not deprive Indigenous peoples of their essential needs. In addition, the decision has involved genuine participation of Indigenous peoples in assessing the reasonableness of these limitations, as well as due attention to the continued economic sustainability of their ways of life.[32] With specific

[26] ILO Convention concerning Indigenous and Tribal People in Independent Countries (Geneva, 27 June 1987, in force 5 September 1991), No.169, 28 ILM 1382, Art 15(2) (hereinafter 'ILO Convention No. 169'). The ILO Committee has clarified that the term 'lands' is to be understood as including the concept of territories so defined: L Swepston, 'New Step in the International Law on Indigenous and Tribal Peoples: ILO Convention No. 169 of 1989' (1990) 15 Oklahoma City University Law Review 677, at 698; and Desmet (n. 1), at 88.

[27] e.g. J Gilbert, *Indigenous Peoples' Land Rights under International Law: From Victims to Actors* (Brill, 2017).

[28] IACtHR, report of the situation of human rights in Ecuador, OAS Ser L/V/II.96 Doc 10revI, 115 (1997).

[29] Gilbert (n. 27), at 172–173.

[30] ibid, at 178, fn 34.

[31] ibid, at 179–184.

[32] ibid, at 90–197.

regard to cultural heritage, the notion that has emerged in international human rights jurisprudence is that of cultural integrity, which provides a holistic understanding of both the tangible and intangible cultural elements of the 'fluid and multidimensional relationship' of Indigenous peoples with their territories.[33] This raises issues of capabilities and recognition.

In addition, the present discussion should be placed in the context of the debate on the right to self-determination for Indigenous peoples, which is currently understood (albeit with continued controversy) as a right to enter into 'territorial negotiations with the State' (without entailing secession). This is with a view to organizing mutual relationships through dialogue, taking into account that Indigenous peoples have historically been excluded from equal opportunities to join other societal groups in determining mutually agreed and fair terms for their participation in public life.[34] This raises procedural and contextual justice issues. This process of dialogue is also necessary because States' self-determination during decolonization happened without considering the negative impacts of colonization on Indigenous territories. In fact, it perpetuated the injustices inflicted by colonial powers on Indigenous peoples.[35] Self-determination is thus understood as a procedural right that does not determine a particular outcome, but serves to build a more equitable and genuine relationship between Indigenous peoples and the State. Self-determination crucially includes dialogue and participation in decisions potentially affecting the use of Indigenous territories. This is with a view to protecting Indigenous peoples' rights to freely dispose of their natural resources and not to be deprived of their means of subsistence and culture with regard to the exercise of State's national sovereignty over natural resources in the guise of a common interest.[36] Against the unfair or non-transparent imposition of the majority's view on the use of Indigenous territories that deprives Indigenous peoples of their autonomy, control over natural resources through FPIC has become an essential and concrete (albeit not the only) manifestation of their right to self-determination.[37] Whether this manifestation truly realizes self-determination, however, depends on whether Indigenous peoples are faced with pre-determined options for their development,[38] and this is where fair and equitable benefit-sharing can play a crucial role in its interplay with consent.

3.1 The Perspective of International Human Rights Law

On the human rights side, the only treaty-based reference to benefit-sharing in relation to Indigenous and tribal peoples can be found in ILO Convention No. 169 Concerning Indigenous and Tribal People in Independent Countries. ILO Convention No. 169 recognizes Indigenous and tribal peoples' right to participate in the use, management,

[33] ibid, at 204–205; IACtHR, *Case of Moiwana Community v. Suriname*, Judgment of 15 June 2005 (Preliminary Objections, Merits, Reparations and Costs), paras 101–103.
[34] Gilbert (n. 27), at 228.
[35] ibid, at 220.
[36] ibid, at 231–233.
[37] ibid, at 240–242.
[38] ibid, at 243.

and conservation of natural resources pertaining to their lands. This encompasses a right to participate in the benefits arising from these activities 'wherever possible', even where the State retains ownership or other rights to these resources.[39] Benefit-sharing is linked with other obligations under ILO Convention No. 169: the assessment of social, spiritual, cultural, and environmental impacts of planned development activities, good-faith consultation through Indigenous peoples' representative institutions, and cooperation with Indigenous peoples in adopting environmental protection measures in their territories.[40] As a result of these inter-linked obligations, impact assessments serve as tools to gather the information necessary to carry out consultations and benefit-sharing negotiations with Indigenous peoples, including fostering cooperation with them in safeguarding the environment within their territories.

The right to participate, 'wherever possible', in the benefits arising from the use, management, and conservation of natural resources 'pertaining to [Indigenous and tribal peoples'] lands', even when the State retains the ownership or other rights to these resources,[41] was considered one of the 'most polemic' in the negotiating history of the ILO Convention and 'entirely new'.[42] It is probably for these reasons that the Convention does not determine the exact scope of the benefit-sharing obligation, allowing for considerable scope for discretion in its implementation. Such scope serves to accommodate diverse approaches within domestic legal systems regarding the recognition of Indigenous and tribal peoples, but also offers the flexibility for adjusting implementation on a case-by-case basis, considering the specific circumstances of Indigenous peoples in each situation.[43] At the very least, the benefit-sharing provision arguably obliges State Parties to demonstrate when and why it is not possible to share benefits with Indigenous peoples.[44]

In practice, the ILO Convention provision on benefit-sharing has led to profit-sharing from extractive activities.[45] This, however, represents one of the blind spots of international human rights law. As former UN Special Rapporteur on Indigenous Peoples' Rights James Anaya warned, 'benefit-sharing must go *beyond restrictive approaches based solely on financial payments* which, depending on the specific

[39] ILO Convention No. 169, Art. 15.

[40] ibid, Arts 7(3), 5–6, and 7(4).

[41] ibid, Art 15.

[42] Swepston (n. 26), at 703. The only other reference to benefit-sharing in human rights law is in the Universal Declaration on Human Rights: M Mancisidor, 'Is There Such a Thing as a Human Right to Science in International Law?' ESIL Reflections (7 April 2015), available at https://esil-sedi.eu/post_name-132/, accessed 7 February 2024. While ILO Convention No. 169 uses the verb 'to participate' in benefits, its interpretative materials refer to benefit-sharing: e.g. Observation of the Committee of Experts on the Application of Experts, adopted 2009, published 99th ILC session (2010), para. 11.

[43] ILO, Monitoring Indigenous and Tribal Peoples' Rights through ILO Conventions: A Compilation of ILO Supervisory Bodies' Comments 2009–2010, Observation (Norway), Canadian Environmental Assessment Research Council 2009/80th session (2009), 95; ILO, 'Indigenous and Tribal Peoples' Rights in Practice: A Guide to ILO Convention No 169' (2009), 107–108; and L Sargent, 'The Indigenous Peoples of Bolivia´s Amazon Basin Region and ILO Convention No. 169: Real Rights or Rhetoric?' (1998) 29 University of Miami Inter-American Law Review, 451, at 510.

[44] Swepston (n. 26), at 704–706.

[45] ILO, Report of the Committee Set Up to Examine the Representation Alleging Non-Observance by Ecuador of ILO Convention No. 169, ILO Doc GB.282/14/4 (2001), para. 44(3); Report of the Committee set up to Examine the Representation alleging non-observance by Ecuador of ILO Convention No. 169, ILO Doc GB.282/14/4 (2001), para. 44(3).

circumstances, may not be adequate for the communities receiving them'.[46] In particular, empirical evidence suggests that non-monetary benefits may exceed the importance of monetary benefits for communities' well-being.[47] Furthermore, monetary benefits have had documented negative (including divisive) effects on communities, and have been linked to the exercise of undue influence and bribery. Benefit-sharing thus needs to be understood in its interaction with other obligations under ILO Convention No 169: the assessments of social, spiritual, cultural, and environmental impacts of planned development activities;[48] good-faith consultation through Indigenous peoples' representative institutions;[49] and cooperation with Indigenous peoples in adopting environmental protection measures in their territories.[50] It is the combination of these obligations that may provide an opportunity to consider Indigenous peoples' holistic worldviews of their territories.[51]

The benefit-sharing provision of ILO Convention No. 169 has proven influential, even when not formally applicable, in the *Saramaka* case[52] and the subsequent 'solid line of case law'[53] of the Inter-American Court of Human Rights. Benefit-sharing has been considered a safeguard for Indigenous and tribal peoples' right to freely dispose of their natural resources as a means to determine their own social, cultural, and economic development, and enjoy their way of life.[54] As is well known, the *Saramaka* line of reasoning has had a visible impact on the African framework on human rights,[55] as well as on global human rights processes.[56] As a result of these jurisprudential

[46] UN Special Rapporteur Anaya, Report on the situation of human rights and fundamental freedoms of indigenous people, UN Doc A/HRC/15/37 (2010), para. 80.

[47] R Wynberg and M Hauck, 'People, Power and the Coast: Towards an Integrated, Just and Holistic Approach' in R Wynberg and M Hauck (eds), *Sharing Benefits from the Coast: Rights, Resources and Livelihoods* (UCT Press, 2014) 143, at 158.

[48] ILO Convention No. 169, Art. 7(3).

[49] Combined reading with ibid, Arts 5–6.

[50] Ibid, Art. 7(4).

[51] ibid, Art. 15(2); Swepston (n. 26), at 698; and Desmet (n. 1), at 88.

[52] IACtHR, *Case of the Saramaka People v. Suriname*, Judgment of 28 November 2007 (Preliminary Objections, Merits, Reparations and Costs).

[53] For a recount of this line of case law, see IACtHR, *Kaliña and Lokono Peoples v. Suriname* (n. 16), Joint Concurring Opinion of Humberto Antonio Sierra Porto and Eduardo Ferrer Mac-Gregor Poisot, paras 4–9. See also IACtHR, *The Environment and Human Rights (State obligations in relation to the environment in the context of the protection and guarantee of the rights to life and to personal integrity – interpretation and scope of Articles 4(1) and 5(1) of the American Convention on Human Rights)*, Advisory Opinion OC-23/17 of 15 November 2017, Series A No. 23, para. 162; IACtHR, *Case of the Indigenous Communities of the Lhaka Honhat Association (Our Land) v. Argentina*, Judgment of 6 February 2020 (Merits, Reparations and Costs), Series C No. 400, para. 174; and IACtHR, *Case of the Indigenous Communities of the Lhaka Honhat Association (Our Land) v. Argentina*, Judgment of 24 November 2020 (Interpretation of the Judgment on Merits, Reparations and Costs), Series C No. 420, para. 26.

[54] *Saramaka* (Merits) (n. 52), paras 93–95 on the basis also of the Inter-American Convention on Human Rights (San José, 22 November 1969, in force 18 July 1978) (hereinafter 'Inter-American Convention'), Art. 29(b). Reiterated in IACtHR, *Kaliña and Lokono* (n. 16), para. 124; see, e.g., Århén (n. 2), at 93.

[55] G Pentassuglia, 'Indigenous Groups and the Developing Jurisprudence of the African Commission on Human and Peoples' Rights: Some Reflections' (2010) 3 UCL Human Rights Review 150, at 158 with respect to the *Endorois* (n. 15) case. See also African Court on Human and Peoples' Rights, *African Commission of Human and Peoples' Rights v. The Republic of Kenya* App. No. 006/2012 (26 May 2017), para. 191.

[56] Independent Expert on Environment and Human Rights John Knox, Preliminary Report on the Issue of Human Rights Obligations Relating to the Enjoyment of a Safe, Clean, Healthy and Sustainable Environment, UN Doc A/HRC/22/43 (2012), para. 41 and Mapping Report, UN Doc A/HRC/25/53 (2013), para. 78; UN Special Rapporteur on the Right to Food Oliver de Schutter, Large-scale land acquisitions and leases: A set of minimum principles and measures to address the human rights challenge, UN Doc A/HRC/

developments, benefit-sharing has been repeatedly identified as one of three safeguards, together with prior impact assessment and FPIC, in the case of proposed extractives in or near Indigenous lands.

Equally, benefit-sharing has been considered as a safeguard in situations involving proposed conservation activities, such as the establishment of protected areas within Indigenous territories. In conservation efforts, benefit-sharing works alongside FPIC and Indigenous peoples' effective participation in managing and monitoring their traditional territories, including continued access and utilization practices that are compatible with environmental protection.[57] The concerns about unfair conservation and the need to share benefits 'including conservation financing' have also been echoed by UN Special Rapporteur on Human Rights and the Environment David Boyd, while recognizing the 'delivering [of] ecosystem benefits essential for all people and future generations'.[58] Issues of distributive justice, recognition and contextual justice are thus intertwined here.

These obligations are triggered when proposed activities could threaten Indigenous peoples' physical or cultural *survival*.[59] The Inter-American Court identified two situations in which cultural survival is at stake: either proposed development projects or conservation initiatives concern natural resources that are *traditionally used* by Indigenous and tribal peoples; or the extraction of natural resources (notably minerals) that are not traditionally used by Indigenous peoples is likely to affect other natural resources that are.[60] This is in line with ILO monitoring bodies' view that not only projects implemented in traditional territories, but also those having an impact on communities' life require a heightened level of protection.[61] The African Commission's approach, in comparison, is more progressive, as the former underscored the need to protect natural resources found on or under Indigenous territories, rather than only those resources the extraction of which may have a negative impact on the group indirectly.[62]

The *Saramaka* line of reasoning has notably influenced the African Commission on Human and Peoples' Rights, although the Commission did not make any reference

13/33/Add.2 (2009), paras 30–33; Special Rapporteur Anaya, A/HRC/21/47 (n. 24), paras 52 and 62; UN Expert Mechanism, Indigenous Peoples and Human Rights, Setting a Framework for Consultation, Benefit-Sharing and Dispute Resolution, UN Doc A/HRC/EMRIP/2009/5 (2008); and UN Expert Mechanism, Indigenous peoples and the right to participate in decision-making (n. 2), para. 40.

[57] See *Endorois* (n. 15) and *Kaliña and Lokono* (n. 16); and Special Rapporteur Anaya, UN Doc A/HRC/15/37 (n. 46). Add.1, paras 257–267 (2010); and Special Rapporteur Anaya, Report to the General Assembly, UN Doc A/71/229 (2016), which does not refer to benefit-sharing as such, but to partnership building (paras 74 and 80).

[58] UN Special Rapporteur on Human Rights and the Environment, D Boyd and S Keene, Policy Brief No. 1: Human rights-based approaches to conserving biodiversity: equitable, effective and imperative (August 2021), https://www.ohchr.org/sites/default/files/Documents/Issues/Environment/SREnvironment/policy-briefing-1.pdf, accessed 28 June 2023.

[59] *Saramaka* (Merits) (n. 52), paras 122–123; P Thornberry, *Indigenous Peoples and Human Rights* (Manchester University Press, 2002), at 282.

[60] *Saramaka* (Merits) (n. 52), paras 155–158.

[61] S Errico, 'The Controversial Issue of Natural Resources: Balancing States' Sovereignty with Indigenous Peoples' Rights' in Allen and Xanthaki (n. 12), 348.

[62] Pentassuglia (n. 55), at 160.

to relevant standards in international biodiversity law. Nonetheless, in the groundbreaking *Endorois* case, the African Commission applied the *Saramaka* safeguards by analogy even though ILO Convention No. 169 was not applicable and the country had withheld approval of UNDRIP.[63] The African Commission relied on benefit-sharing not only with regard to mining concession on traditional territories, but also to the creation of a wildlife reserve, ascertaining a violation of Indigenous peoples' right to natural resources in addition to the right to property.[64] This was in itself a significant step forward from the African Commission's approach in the *Ogoni* case. In that case, the Commission limited itself to recommending enhanced procedural guarantees and adequate compensation, including the clean-up of lands and rivers damaged by oil operations, for a violation of the right to natural resources, due to the lack of community involvement in decisions affecting community development.[65] In the *Endorois* case, instead, the Commission took a more proactive stance and recommended that the State return ancestral lands, ensure unrestricted access to traditionally used sites, pay royalties to the Endorois from ongoing economic activities on their land, and ensure that they benefit from employment opportunities within the reserve, with a view to contributing to the improvement of their well-being.[66] The latter two are benefit-sharing modalities. The Commission emphasized the need to empower Indigenous peoples as a result of developments (whether commercial endeavours or conservation efforts) on their territories.[67]

The *Ogiek* decision of the African Court on Human and Peoples' Rights confirmed that benefit-sharing is part of the right to natural resources under the African regional human rights framework,[68] based on the claim that Indigenous peoples have the 'leading role to play as guardians of local ecosystems'.[69] It is interesting to note the Court's rejection of the State argument that the traditional lifestyle of the community had changed so significantly that they should not be recognized as culturally distinctive.[70] Instead, the Court emphasized the enduring importance of unchanged 'values' and 'shared mentality', as well as the need for 'special protection due to the communities' vulnerability'. [71] It has been noted that the decision 'emphasized the

[63] ibid, at 158.

[64] African Charter on Human and Peoples' Rights (27 June 1981, in force 21 October 1986) 1520 UNTS 217, Arts 21 and 14.

[65] Namely, the provision of information on environmental risks and meaningful access to regulatory and decision-making bodies: African Commission on Human and Peoples' Rights, *Social and Economic Rights Action Center (SERAC) and Center for Economic and Social Rights (CESR) v. Nigeria* (27 May 2002) Case 155/96 (2001), at 15. This limited understanding appears closer to the criteria established by the Human Rights Committee mentioned in *Saramaka* (Merits) (n. 52).

[66] African Commission, *Endorois* (n. 15), paras 227–228 and recommendations para. 1(d). This finds resonance in the ILO Conference 87th Session 1999, Report III (Part 1a), 434; discussed in Thornberry (n. 59), at 335 on development projects in Indigenous lands promoting 'improvements of conditions of life'.

[67] Gilbert (n. 27), at 256.

[68] African Court on Human and People's Rights, *African Commission on Human and People's Rights v. Republic of Kenya* (*Ogiek* decision), Judgment (Reparations) App. No. 006/2012 (23 June 2022), para. 191.

[69] Minority Rights Group, 'Huge Victory for Kenya's Ogiek as African Court sets major precedent for indigenous peoples' land rights' (26 May 2017), available at http://minorityrights.org/2017/05/26/huge-victory-kenyas-ogiek-african-court-sets-major-precedent-indigenous-peoples-land-rights/, accessed 28 June 2023.

[70] *Ogiek* decision (n. 68), para. 175.

[71] ibid, para. 185.

intrinsic link between culture and land', explaining that the right to property also includes 'rights guaranteed by traditional custom and law to access to, and use of, land and other natural resources held under communal ownership'.[72]

This progress in regional case law regarding benefit-sharing has significantly influenced the work of global human rights initiatives. This is evident in the work of entities like the Committee on the Elimination of Racial Discrimination (CERD);[73] Special Rapporteurs on human rights and the environment,[74] food,[75] Indigenous peoples' rights,[76] and toxics;[77] the UN Permanent Forum on Indigenous Issues (UNPFII);[78] and the Expert Mechanism on the Rights of Indigenous Peoples.[79] These initiatives have all relied on CBD materials on occasion.[80] This corroborates the view that in the context of the cross-fertilization from one human rights body to another,[81] CBD materials are understood as 'universal standards'[82] that serve to substantiate a contextual and evolving interpretation of human rights treaties.

[72] R Roesch, 'The Ogiek Case of the African Court on Human and Peoples' Rights: Not So Much News After All?' (EJIL Talk!, 16 June 2017), available at https://www.ejiltalk.org/the-ogiek-case-of-the-african-court-on-human-and-peoples-rights-not-so-much-news-after-all/, accessed 28 June 2023.

[73] CERD, Concluding observations on the combined thirteenth to fifteenth periodic reports of Suriname, UN Doc CERD/C/SUR/CO/13–15 (2015), para. 26.

[74] Independent Expert on Environment and Human Rights John Knox, Preliminary Report on the Issue of Human Rights Obligations Relating to the Enjoyment of a Safe, Clean, Healthy and Sustainable Environment, UN Doc A/HRC/22/43 (2012), para. 41 and Mapping Report, UN Doc A/HRC/25/53 (2013), para. 78.

[75] UN Special Rapporteur on the Right to Food Oliver de Schutter, Large-scale land acquisitions and leases: A set of minimum principles and measures to address the human rights challenge, UN Doc A/HRC/13/33/Add.2 (2009), paras 30–33.

[76] Special Rapporteur Anaya, A/HRC/21/47 (n. 24), paras 52 and 62; Joint Press Release by UN Special Rapporteur on Indigenous Peoples' Rights Victoria Tauli-Corpuz, and Francisco Eguiguren, Rapporteur on the Rights of indigenous peoples of the Inter-American Commission on Human Rights, 'Indigenous Peoples' Rights to Effective Participation and to Self-determined Development' (10 August 2016); UN Expert Mechanism, Indigenous Peoples and Human Rights (n. 56).

[77] UN Special Rapporteur on the implications for human rights of the environmentally sound management and disposal of hazardous substances and wastes to the Human Rights Council, Report on Human Rights and Extractive Industries, UN Doc A/HRC/21/48 (2012), paras 36 and 69(h).

[78] UNPFII, Review of Developments pertaining to the Promotion and Protection of Human Rights and Fundamental Freedoms of Indigenous Peoples, UN Doc E/CN.4/Sub.2/AC.4/2001/2 (2001), para. 27.

[79] FPIC 'establishes the framework for all consultations relating to the acceptance of projects that affect indigenous peoples and any related negotiations pertaining to benefit-sharing and mitigation measures': UN Expert Mechanism, Indigenous peoples right to participate in decision-making (n. 2), para. 40.

[80] CBD, Art. 8(j) was referred to by UNPFII (n. 78), para. 15. The CBD Akwé: Kon Voluntary Guidelines (CBD Decision VII/16 (2004), Annex) were referred to as a pre-condition for benefit-sharing by CERD (n. 73); UN Special Rapporteur Anaya, A/HRC/15/37 (n. 46), para. 73, and by the Expert Mechanism, UN Doc A/HRC/15/35 (2010), para. 37. The CBD work programme on protected areas (CBD Decision VII/28, 2004) was referred to by the Expert Mechanism, UN Doc A/HRC/15/35 (ibid), para. 37.

[81] Although in the African and Inter-American context, specific treaty rules justify cross-fertilization: reliance on external sources is based on American Convention on Human Rights (San José, 22 November 1969, in force 18 July 1978), Art. 29(b) against restricting rights by virtue of another convention to which a party is a party; and on African Charter on Human and Peoples' Rights (Banjul, 27 June 1981, in force 21 October 1986). Art. 60 allowing the Commission to draw inspiration from international law on human and peoples' rights, other instruments adopted by the United Nations and by African countries in the field of Human and Peoples' Rights, as well as from the provisions of various instruments adopted within the Specialised Agencies of the United Nations of which the Parties to the Charter are members.

[82] Fodella (n. 4), at 360, develops this argument about international human rights law, not international biodiversity law.

3.2 Incompletely Theorized Aspects and Contributions under International Human Rights Law

Admittedly, universal and regional human rights jurisprudence have not developed a consistent legal argumentation regarding benefit-sharing, and interpretative guidance has gradually been formulated across various decisions and other international materials. Different international human rights initiatives have used varying terminology in relation to benefit-sharing,[83] although former UN Special Rapporteur on Indigenous Peoples' Rights James Anaya indicated that 'the only clear international standard applicable to benefit-sharing [in relation to extractives and Indigenous peoples] is that such sharing must be fair and equitable'.'[84]

At the time of the *Saramaka* case, the Inter-American Court argued that benefit-sharing was already recognized in 'the text of *several* international instruments'.[85] However, there were actually only a few 'tentative'[86] legal bases on benefit-sharing in international human rights law on which it could rely upon. The UNDRIP, for instance, does not include an explicit reference to benefit-sharing, which has been considered implicit in its provisions on the right to natural resources over time (after the *Saramaka* decision).[87] CERD[88] and the UN Special Rapporteur on Indigenous Peoples[89] occasionally mentioned benefit-sharing before *Saramaka*, but have equally focused more systematically on benefit-sharing after the decision. The Inter-American Court referred to previous observations of the Human Rights Committee (HRC), which conditioned the acceptability of measures affecting culturally significant

[83] There is no such qualification for benefit-sharing in the text of ILO Convention No. 169. The CERD, UNPFII, and the Inter-American Court of Human Rights have referred to 'reasonable' benefit-sharing: CERD, Concluding Observations on Ecuador, UN Doc A/58/18 (2003), para. 62 and 16; UNPFII, Report of the International Workshop on Methodologies regard Free, Prior Informed Consent and Indigenous Peoples, UN Doc E/C.19/2005/3 (2005), para. 46(i)(e); and *Saramaka* (Merits) (n. 52), para. 140 and *Endorois* (n. 15), paras 269 and 297. See also discussion in Gilbert (n. 27), at 276–282.

[84] Special Rapporteur Anaya, A/HRC/15/37 (n. 46), paras 67 and 76–78.

[85] *Saramaka* (Merits) (n. 52), para. 130 and fn 128; and para. 138 and fn 137.

[86] Pentassuglia (n. 21), at 169.

[87] UNDRIP, Art. 31; Special Rapporteur Anaya, A/HRC/15/37 (n. 46), paras 67 and 76–78; UNPFII, Review of World Bank operational policies, UN Doc E/C.19/2013/15 (2013), para. 27; OHCHR, Mapping Human Rights Obligations Relating to the Enjoyment of a Safe, Clean, Healthy and Sustainable Environment: Individual Report on the Rights of Indigenous Peoples, UN Doc A/HRC/25/53 (2013), paras 45–46.

[88] CERD, Consideration of Reports submitted by State Parties under Article 9 of the Convention, Concluding Observations on Ecuador, UN Doc CERD/C/62/CO/2 (2003), para. 16. Note that a benefit-sharing requirement does not feature in the CERD General Recommendation No. 23 on Indigenous Peoples, UN Doc A/52/18 (1997), Annex V, but references to profit-sharing from natural resource use were made by CERD: Consideration of Reports, Comments and Information Submitted by States Parties: Bolivia, UN Doc A/66/18 (2012), para. 43(7)(f); and Consideration of Reports, Comments and Information Submitted by States Parties: Bolivia, UN Doc A/56/18 (2001), para. 335. International Convention on the Elimination of All Forms of Racial Discrimination (New York, 7 March 1966, in force 4 January 1969), 660 UNTS 195.

[89] Referring to 'mutually acceptable benefit-sharing' as part of FPIC: Report of the Special Rapporteur on the situation of human rights and fundamental freedoms of indigenous peoples, Rodolfo Stavenhagen, UN Doc E/CN.4/2003/90 (2003), para. 66; which was reiterated in his Progress report on preparatory work for the study regarding best practices carried out to implement the recommendations contained in the annual reports of the Special Rapporteur, UN Doc E/CN.4/2006/78/Add.4 (2006), para. 11.

economic activities to communities 'continu[ing] to *benefit* from their traditional economy'.[90]

The limited legal bases on benefit-sharing under international human rights law may explain why the Inter-American Court,[91] CERD,[92] and other global human rights processes[93] have increasingly made reference to other standards developed under the CBD. This is notably the case in the CBD Akwé: Kon Guidelines on socio-cultural and environmental impact assessments, which include references to benefit-sharing.[94] Similar guidance on benefit-sharing is found in CBD decisions on protected areas.[95] However, it was only in the 2015 *Kaliña and Lokono* decision that the Inter-American Court was particularly explicit about the need for, and merits of, mutual supportiveness with consensus guidance adopted under the CBD.[96] On that occasion, the Court emphasized States' obligations to protect, in a manner compatible with their international environmental obligations, Indigenous peoples' rights.[97]

In support of this interpretation, it cited the expert opinion of then UN Special Rapporteur on the Rights of Indigenous Peoples Victoria Tauli-Corpuz, as follows:

> International environmental law and international human rights law should not be considered separate, but rather interrelated and complementary, bodies of law. Indeed, the States Parties to the Convention on Biological Diversity (CBD) have incorporated respect for the related international rights and obligations into their decision on protected areas in relation to indigenous peoples.... The CBD, and its *authorized interpretation by the Conference of the Parties*, defends fully the rights of the indigenous peoples in relation to the protected areas and requires that these are established and managed in full compliance with the State's international obligations. This permits the application of the whole range of the State's human rights obligations as defined by the American Convention on Human Rights and established in the UN Declaration. It is also the consensus reflected in the main international policy norms and best practice.... The [UN] Rapporteur has adhered to these same basic principles

[90] HRC, *Case of Apirana Mahuika et al. v. New Zealand*, UN Doc CCPR/C/70/D/547/1993 (2000), para. 9.5 (emphasis added); *Saramaka* (Merits) (n. 52), para. 130. The same standard can be found in HRC, *Case of Ángela Poma Poma v. Peru*, UN Doc CCPR/C/95/D/1457/2006 (2009), para. 7.6, which in other ways builds upon *Saramaka* (Merits) (n. 52): Pentassuglia (n. 21), at 184.

[91] IACtHR, *Case of the Saramaka People v. Suriname*, Judgment of 12 August 2008 (Interpretation of the Judgment on Preliminary Objections, Merits, Reparations and Costs), para. 41 and fn 23.

[92] Which appears confirmed in CERD, Concluding observations on the combined thirteenth to fifteenth periodic reports of Suriname UN Doc CERD/C/SUR/CO/13–15 (2015), para. 26.

[93] UNPFII, CERD, Special Rapporteur Anaya, and the UN Expert Mechanism (n. 80).

[94] CBD Akwé: Kon Guidelines (n. 80), paras 46 and 56.

[95] CBD Work programme on protected areas (n. 80), paras 2(1) and 2(1)(4) (while the latter refers to both benefit- and cost-sharing, the focus on benefit-sharing is clarified in CBD Decision IX/18 (2008), Preamble para. 5).

[96] CBD, Arts 8(j), 10, and 14: IACtHR, *Kaliña and Lokono* (n. 16), paras 173–174, 177–178, 181, and 214, making reference to the CBD, Addis Ababa Principles and Guidelines for the Sustainable Use of Biodiversity, CBD Decision VII/12 (2004), Annex II and the CBD work programme on protected areas (n. 80).

[97] IACtHR, *Kaliña and Lokono* (n. 16), paras 181 and 193.

affirmed by the Human Rights Committee and the Committee for the Elimination of Racial Discrimination.[98]

The Inter-American Court, therefore, appears to consider the consensus decisions adopted by CBD parties as interpretative tools not only for the purposes of the CBD itself, but also for a mutually supportive interpretation of relevant international human rights law. Accordingly, it relied on Articles 8(j) and 10(c) of the CBD addressing Indigenous peoples' traditional knowledge and their customary sustainable use of biological resources as well as the CBD programme of work on protected areas[99] to identify safeguards for establishing conservation measures on traditional lands. These safeguards comprise effective participation, access and use of their traditional territories, and benefit-sharing, provided that they are compatible with protection and sustainable use.[100] Furthermore, the Court found that the absence of explicit mechanisms that guarantee benefit-sharing from conservation measures is a violation of political rights, relying on the CBD obligation on environmental impact assessments.[101] This shows the inter-linkage between procedural and distributive justice.

The argument put forward here is that on the whole, international human rights has identified in significant detail the minimum level of protection afforded by benefit-sharing, although guidance on how to implement benefit-sharing obligations remains limited and quite abstract. International human rights initiatives have indicated that prior environmental and socio-cultural assessments (which include consideration of benefit-sharing options) should be prepared by an independent, technically qualified entity with the 'active participation of Indigenous communities concerned'.[102] In addition, these assessments must respect Indigenous traditions and cultures.[103] This is a key clarification to ensure that communities influence the terms of the debate, rather than participate in a process already framed around a predetermined set of development options. With this conception, these assessments are expected to contribute towards realizing Indigenous peoples' right to participate in public affairs.[104] In addition, human rights bodies have recommended establishing processes for recording Indigenous communities' views when they are unable to attend public meetings due to remoteness or poor health, including through means other than written forms.[105] Governments are further expected to provide adequate human, financial, technical, and legal resources to support Indigenous expertise, in proportion to the scale of the proposed development.[106] In addition, the Guidelines recommend involving

[98] ibid, para. 174 (emphasis added).
[99] ibid, paras 178, and 214 n. 247; CBD Decision VII/28 (2004).
[100] IACtHR, *Kaliña and Lokono* (n. 16), para. 181.
[101] ibid, para. 197 (relying on CBD, Art. 14).
[102] *Kichwa* (n. 10), para. 300; *Kaliña and Lokono* (n. 16), para. 214; CERD, Concluding Observations on Ecuador (n. 88), para. 26.
[103] *Saramaka* (Interpretation) (n. 91), para. 41; *Kichwa* (n. 10), para. 206; *Kaliña and Lokono* (n. 16), para. 215; also citing Principle 10 of the Rio Declaration on Environment and Development, UN Doc A/CONF.151/26 vol 1, Annex 1 (1992).
[104] *Kaliña and Lokono* (n. 16), paras 197 and 202–203.
[105] ibid, para. 17.
[106] ibid, paras 18, 64–66, and 70.

Indigenous communities in the financial auditing processes of the development to ensure that the resources invested are used effectively.[107]

Procedural safeguards have thus featured prominently in human rights case law. International human rights bodies have also highlighted the need for benefit-sharing agreements to be recorded formally[108] in a legally binding agreement embodying the conditions for granting FPIC in alignment with communities' worldviews, and the safeguards against the disregard of such consent after it is granted.[109] Benefit-sharing agreements are further expected to undergo third-party verification,[110] and be made subject to an ongoing review of their effectiveness, conducted jointly with Indigenous peoples.[111]

Regional human rights jurisprudence has also elaborated on the need for judicial protection. The Inter-American Court emphasized States' obligation to deploy effective means to safeguard rights through judicial organs, and provide the means to execute relevant decisions of public authorities and judgments.[112] Remedies offered by the State should provide a 'real possibility' for Indigenous and tribal peoples to defend their rights and exercise effective control over their territory.[113] This should include the recognition of legal standing to file administrative, judicial, or another type of action collectively, through their representatives, or individually, taking into account their customs and cultural characteristics. Reference is also made to guarantees of access to justice that are accessible, simple, and within reasonable timeframes; access to technical and legal assistance, ensuring the community members can be understood in legal proceedings and can understand them; and facilitation of physical access to administrative and judicial institutions in light of geographical distance, elevated costs, or other challenges.[114] Such measures are also expected to respect internal mechanisms for deciding disputes on Indigenous issues, as long as they are in harmony with human rights.[115]

Finally, justiciability rests on the obligation for States to enshrine international benefit-sharing obligations in national law to clarify that benefit-sharing is an entitlement, not a mere privilege. This implies that benefit-sharing obligations are irrevocable and part of a legally backed opportunity to effectively control natural resources without outside interference.[116] The Inter-American Court has regarded appropriate national legislation on benefit-sharing as a means to guarantee that similar incidents do not recur.[117]

107 ibid, para. 46.
108 ibid, para. 193.
109 UN Expert Mechanism, Indigenous peoples right to participate in decision-making (n. 2), para. 43; Special Rapporteur Anaya, A/HRC/15/37 (n. 46), para. 46.
110 UNPFII (n. 87), para. 29.
111 ILO, Observation (Norway) (n. 43).
112 *Kaliña and Lokono* (n. 16), paras 239–240.
113 ibid.
114 ibid, para. 251(3).
115 ibid, para. 251(5).
116 ibid, para. 134; referring to *Saramaka* (Merits) (n. 52), para. 115.
117 *Saramaka* (Merits) (n. 52), para. 194.d; *Kaliña and Lokono* (n. 16), para. 305(d); and *Kichwa* (n. 10) paras 299–300.

Integrating these procedural guarantees as essential conditions for benefit-sharing under the CBD would respond to some of the main shortcomings arising from the lack of explicit discussion of human rights standards under international biodiversity law—the incomplete theorization of benefit-sharing in that area will be discussed in the next section.

3.3 The Perspective of International Biodiversity Law

To an international environmental lawyer, the growing references in international human rights materials to the CBD may have appeared surprising, at least until 2017 (as discussed below). The CBD and its decisions have tended not to include human rights terminology.[118] Rather, CBD negotiations provide ample evidence of States' efforts to separate this regime from international human rights law, resulting in complex and heavily qualified language that may have human rights implications.[119] Clearly, some of the 196 CBD Parties are reluctant to indirectly incorporate international standards on Indigenous peoples from global or regional human rights regimes to which they are not signatories, into the CBD. This is especially apparent when they have emphasized constitutional limitations in implementing the UNDRIP.[120]

In addition, the linkage between benefit-sharing and natural resources under the Convention is not immediately obvious. The relevant treaty basis under the CBD is a qualified obligation to 'encourage' equitable benefit-sharing from the use of *traditional knowledge* of Indigenous peoples,[121] interpreted in combination with the obligation to protect Indigenous communities' customary sustainable use of biological resources.[122] The CBD benefit-sharing obligation is thus arguably triggered by the *ecosystem stewardship* of Indigenous peoples.[123] This, in turn, hinges on the intrinsic connection

[118] P Birnie, A Boyle, and C Redgwell, *International Law and the Environment* (Oxford University Press, 2009), at 626–628; D Shelton, 'Principle 22: Indigenous People and Sustainable Development' in J Viñuales (ed.), *The Rio Declaration on Environment and Development: A Commentary* (Oxford University Press, 2015) 541, at 543.

[119] Note, for instance, the continued opposition of some CBD parties to making unequivocal reference to the right to 'prior informed consent' of Indigenous peoples (e.g. CBD, Mo'otz Kuxtal voluntary guidelines for the development of mechanisms, legislation, or other appropriate initiatives to ensure the 'prior informed consent', 'free prior informed consent', or 'approval and involvement', depending on national circumstances, of Indigenous peoples and local communities for accessing their knowledge, innovations, and practices; the fair and equitable sharing of benefits arising from the use and application of such knowledge, innovations, and practices; and for reporting and preventing unauthorized access to such knowledge, innovations, and practices, CBD Decision XIII/18 (2016), para. 6).

[120] E Morgera, 'Against All Odds: The Contribution of the Convention on Biological Diversity to International Human Rights Law' in D Alland et al. (eds), *Unity and Diversity of International Law* (Martinus Nijhoff, 2014) 983. For a recent report of CBD Parties' views on importing international human rights law terminology with regard to Indigenous peoples, see E Tsioumani et al., 'Summary and Analysis of the UN Biodiversity Conference' (2016) 9(678) Earth Negotiations Bulletin (ENB) 12–13.

[121] CBD, Art 8(j). Other provisions in the Convention (notably Arts 1 and 15) focus instead on an inter-State notion of benefit-sharing in the specific context of bioprospecting, although in time they have also come to be understood in an intra-State perspective: E Morgera, E Tsioumani, and M Buck, *Unraveling the Nagoya Protocol: A Commentary of the Protocol on Access and Benefit-Sharing to the Convention on Biological Diversity* (Martinus Nijhoff, 2014), at 24–30.

[122] CBD, Art. 10(c).

[123] Principles of the Ecosystem Approach, Decision V/6 (2000), para. 9, and CBD Decision VII/11 (2004), Annex I, annotations to rationale to Principle 4. This appears to be reflected in the General Assembly,

between these communities' knowledge and their natural resources—in other words, the development and transmission of traditional knowledge *through* the management of traditionally used natural resources.[124] Such knowledge is thus embodied in *traditional lifestyles*[125] that are inextricably linked to natural resources, shared cultural identity, and customary rules.[126] This resonates with the understanding, under international human rights law, of the traditional use of natural resources as 'part of a way of life'.[127]

The reticence of certain CBD State Parties to engage explicitly in human rights issues has resulted in guidance that does not include minimum guarantees or explicit limits to State discretion. This is the most significant blind spot in international biodiversity law. CBD guidance does provide, on the other hand, more detailed, practical indications on how to implement benefit-sharing in the context of environmental governance, which fills a gap in international human rights law. CBD guidance focuses on pragmatic considerations underlying benefit-sharing to counterbalance short-term gains motivating ecosystem degradation, by protecting the stake in conservation for those communities that more closely interact with nature. Benefit-sharing is thus seen as a means to ensure compliance with environmental protection law.[128] It serves as an *incentive* for ecosystem stewards' positive contribution to humanity's well-being that derives from the ecosystem services they provide, maintain, or restore.[129] This can arguably be inferred from CBD Parties' consensus on the types of benefit to be shared. First, more elaborate options on monetary benefit-sharing are outlined under the CBD than in international human rights law. They include not only profit-sharing through trust funds, but also licences with preferential terms, job creation for communities (which finds resonance in the *Endorois* decision of the African Commission[130]), and payments for ecosystem services.[131]

In addition, CBD Parties have identified benefits that support Indigenous peoples' own economic activities, such as: fostering local enterprises, participating in others' enterprises and projects, offering direct investment opportunities, facilitating access to markets, and supporting the diversification of income-generating (economic)

Strategic Framework for the period 2012–2013 (UN Doc A/65/6/Rev.1), para. 11(24)(b) and for 2014–2015 (UN Doc A/67/6 (prog 11)), para. 11(16). See the discussion in E Morgera, 'Ecosystem and Precautionary Approach' in E Morgera and J Razzaque (eds), *Encyclopedia of Environmental Law: Biodiversity and Nature Protection Law* (Edward Elgar, 2017) 70.

[124] In the light of the placement of CBD, Art 8(j) in the context of *in situ conservation* (CBD, Art. 8). J Gibson, 'Community Rights to Culture: The UN Declaration on the Rights of Indigenous Peoples' in Allen and Xanthaki (n. 12) 434, at 434–435.

[125] On the basis of the wording of CBD, Art. 8(j): see the definition of traditional knowledge in CBD Akwé: Kon Guidelines (n. 80).

[126] See generally B Tobin, *Indigenous Peoples, Customary Law and Human Rights: Why Living Law Matters* (Routledge, 2014).

[127] Thornberry (n. 59), at 334 and 353.

[128] CBD Addis Ababa Guidelines (n. 96), rationale to Principle 4 and operational guideline to Principle 12.

[129] CBD, Principles of the Ecosystem Approach (n. 123), para. 9.

[130] *Endorois* (n. 15), para. 297.

[131] CBD Akwé: Kon Guidelines (n. 80), para. 46. See M Menton and A Bennett, 'PES: Payments for Ecosystem Services and Poverty Alleviation?' and I Porras and N Asquith, 'Scaling-up Conditional Transfers for Environmental Protection and Poverty Alleviation' in K Schreckenberg et al. (eds), *Ecosystem Services and Poverty Alleviation: Trade-offs and Governance* (Routledge, 2018) 189 and 204 respectively.

opportunities for small and medium-sized businesses.[132] Further types of benefits have been identified to *improve and consolidate* the conditions under which ecosystem stewards and traditional knowledge holders develop and maintain their knowledge and practices: information sharing, capacity building, scientific cooperation, or assistance in diversifying management capacities.[133] Benefits also include the legal recognition for community-based natural resource management and conservation,[134] the incorporation of traditional knowledge in environmental and socio-cultural impact assessments[135] and in natural resource management planning.[136] The rationale of the CBD benefit-sharing obligation can thus also be understood as *recognition* for past and present contributions of Indigenous peoples and local communities to global environmental objectives with a view to ensuring that their traditional practices continue in the future.[137]

Under the CBD, therefore, a variety of economic and non-economic benefits have been identified, amounting to a 'menu' that allows for a large margin of discretion in implementation. This contrasts with the general laconicism with regard to benefit-sharing modalities and emphasis on monetary approaches of international human rights law discussed earlier. Having a wider choice of benefits enables consideration of communities' needs, values, and priorities on a case-by-case basis, as required under international human rights law, on the basis of a more nuanced understanding of opportunities within environmental governance. Such a menu can provide an opportunity to address multiple dimensions of justice: distribution, participation, recognition, capabilities, and context.

Equally, however, the menu of benefits reveals the limitation of international biodiversity law: in the absence of specific procedural guarantees and indications of the minimum level of protection, benefit-sharing could be used to impose certain views of development upon Indigenous peoples and local communities that could endanger their cultural or physical survival. Therefore, the main blind spot within the CBD is the absence of procedural guarantees to ensure that benefit-sharing works towards its stated objectives. For instance, under the CBD, participation in decision-making is often seen as a potential benefit,[138] blurring the distinction between required

[132] CBD, Guidelines on Biodiversity and Tourism, Decision V/25 (2000), paras 22–23, and 43.

[133] CBD Principles of the Ecosystem Approach (n. 123), para. 9; CBD expanded work programme on forest biodiversity, Decision VI/22 (2002), at goal 5, objective 1, activities; CBD work programme on mountain biodiversity, CBD decision VII/27 (2004), Annex, para. 1.3.7; CBD Akwé: Kon Guidelines (n. 80), paras 40 and 46; Addis Ababa Guidelines (n. 96), rationale to Principle 4; CBD, Bonn Guidelines on Access to Genetic Resources and Fair and Equitable Sharing of the Benefits Arising out of Their Utilization, CBD Decision VI/24 (2002) Annex, para. 50.

[134] e.g. CBD Decision VI/22 (2002), para. 31 and programme element 1, Goal 4, objective 3; CBD Decision VII/27 (n. 133), paras 2.2.1–2.2.5.

[135] CBD Akwé: Kon Guidelines (n. 80), para. 56.

[136] Addis Ababa Guidelines (n. 96), operational guidelines to Principle 4; and CBD work programme on forest biodiversity, para. 34. See also Agenda 21, UN Doc A/CONF.151/26/Rev.1 vol 1 (1992), Annex II, para. 15(4)(g) and Johannesburg Plan of Implementation, UN Doc A/CONF.199/20 (2002), Res 2, para. 44(j).

[137] E Morgera, 'Justice, Equity and Benefit-Sharing Under the Nagoya Protocol to the Convention on Biological Diversity' (2015) 25 Italian Yearbook of International Law 113.

[138] The CBD work programme on protected areas (n. 80), paras 2(1)(3)–2(1)(5), for instance, links the goal of promoting equity and benefit-sharing with engaging communities in participatory planning and governance.

protection and matters open to negotiation based on the specific context. Additionally, international biodiversity law is non-committal regarding the need to develop national legislation on benefit-sharing, which is increasingly emphasized under international human rights law as a precondition for avoiding human rights violations.[139] In effect, it has been documented that Indigenous peoples' negotiating position in the context of contractual approaches to benefit-sharing is heavily impacted by weak national legal frameworks on their rights.[140]

4. Consolidating a Mutually Supportive Interpretation of Fair and Equitable Benefit-Sharing

One of the reasons for this emergent cross-fertilization may be that benefit-sharing is framed[141] differently under international human rights law and under the CBD, which may lead to conceptually different, but still potentially compatible, approaches in the two regimes. Under the CBD, legal developments on benefit-sharing have focused on *equity* considerations, out of concern for Indigenous peoples that devote their efforts to, and bear the risks of, conservation and sustainable use, while the larger society benefits from these efforts without shouldering the related costs.[142] These considerations are generally treated as underlying assumptions within international biodiversity law, rather than issues expressly addressed by it. International human rights lawyers, however, have been sceptical of perceived 'unrealistic expectations regarding the conservationist behaviour of Indigenous peoples [that] may have detrimental consequences for the recognition and respect of their rights'.[143] There have been criticisms about the opportunities under the CBD to condition the recognition or protection of the rights of Indigenous peoples to their compatibility with pre-set environmental sustainability criteria.[144] This approach neglects the crucial aspect of justice in recognizing diverse knowledge systems within this context.

The CBD arguably authorizes its Parties to depart from existing international human rights obligations in rare instances where their implementation might seriously damage or threaten biodiversity.[145] Even in these instances, however, it should be understood as an obligation for CBD Parties to negotiate an interpretation of the CBD and other international instruments that allows for a solution that supports both

[139] Note the reference to legislative, policy, or administrative measures in the Nagoya Protocol Additional to the Convention on Biological Diversity 1992, on Access to Genetic Resources and the Fair and Equitable Sharing of Benefits from their Utilization (Nagoya, 29 October 2010, in force 12 October 2014), Arts 5(2), 5(3), 5(5), 6(3), 13(2), 1591), 16(1). In this context, however, benefit-sharing is specifically related to bioprospecting.

[140] C O'Faircheallaigh and T Corbett, 'Indigenous Participation in Environmental Management of Mining Projects: The Role of Negotiated Agreements' (2015) 14 Journal of Environmental Law and Policy 629, at 635.

[141] Morgera (n. 23), at 356.

[142] CBD Principles of the Ecosystem Approach (n. 123), Principle 8.

[143] Desmet (n. 1), at 41.

[144] ibid, at 131–132.

[145] CBD, Art. 22(1).

the CBD and international human rights law.[146] The latter understanding has been supported by the most recent case law of the Inter-American Court[147] recognizing the 'right to dispose of natural resources should not be interpreted as a freedom to engage in unsustainable uses of the environment. Rather, this right must be understood in the context of common responsibilities for maintaining the health of our ecological systems'.[148] This is in recognition of Indigenous peoples being an 'important part of the solution'.[149] International human rights law has thus relied on the CBD as part of a wider normative framework that legitimizes the reconciliation of different interests protected internationally.[150]

These interpretations were summarized and consolidated in the 2017 report of the UN Special Rapporteur on Human Rights and the Environment John Knox,[151] which focused on biodiversity and ecosystem services.[152] For the first time, CBD obligations have been authoritatively assessed as a matter of international human rights law, based on the unequivocal understanding that the full enjoyment of everyone's human rights to life, health, food, and water depend on healthy ecosystems and their benefits to people.[153] In other words, the protection and realization of basic human rights depends on successful efforts to prevent biodiversity loss.[154] Not only did Special Rapporteur Knox made references to the well-understood role of biodiversity as a reservoir of infinite potential for the development of new medicinal and food

[146] E Morgera, 'Far Away, So Close: A Legal Analysis of the Increasing Interactions between the Convention on Biological Diversity and Climate Change Law' (2011) 2 Climate Law 85.

[147] *Kaliña and Lokono* (n. 16), paras 181 and 193.

[148] M Fitzmaurice, 'The Question of Indigenous Peoples' Rights: A Time for Reappraisal?' in D French (ed.), *Statehood and Self-Determination: Reconciling Tradition and Modernity in International Law* (Cambridge University Press, 2013) 361; Desmet (n. 1), at 186–187; and S Wiessner, 'The Cultural Rights of Indigenous Peoples: Achievements and Continuing Challenges' (2011) 22 European Journal of International Law 121.

[149] J Ife, *Human Rights from Below: Achieving Rights through Community Development* 151 (Cambridge University Press, 2010). See also the increasing references under the CBD to the 'contribution of the collective action of indigenous peoples and local communities': CBD Decision XIII/3 (2016), Strategic actions to enhance the implementation of the Strategic Plan for Biodiversity 2011–2020 and the achievement of the Aichi Biodiversity Targets, including with respect to mainstreaming and the integration of biodiversity within and across sectors, paras 15, 18(b), and 98 and Decision XIII/20 (2016), Resource mobilization, paras 18–21 and Annex ('Guiding principles on assessing the contribution of collective action by indigenous peoples and local communities').

[150] R Pavoni, 'Mutual Supportiveness as a Principle of Interpretation and Law-Making: A Watershed for the WTO-and-Competing-Regimes Debate?' (2010) 21 European Journal of International Law 649, at 665.

[151] Knox, Framework Principles (n. 9).

[152] Ecosystem services are the benefits people obtain from ecosystems, such as food, water, timber, and fibre; regulating services that affect climate, floods, diseases, wastes, and water quality; cultural services that provide recreational, aesthetic, and spiritual benefits; and supporting services such as soil formation, photosynthesis, and nutrient cycling. See Millenium Ecosystem Assessment, 'Living Beyond Our Means: Natural Assets and Human Wellbeing' (2005), available at https://www.millenniumassessment.org/en/index.html, accessed 7 February 2024. Note that from 2017, the Intergovernmental Platform on Biodiversity and Ecosystem Services (IPBES) started using the term 'nature's contributions to people' to refer to 'all the positive contributions or benefits, and occasionally negative contributions, losses or detriments, that people obtain from nature' and 'explicitly embracing concepts associated with other worldviews on human-nature relations and knowledge systems'. IPBES, *Implementation of the First Work Programme of the Platform*, Art. III, paras 8–9, IPBES-5/1 (2017); U Pascual et al., Valuing Nature's Contributions to People: The IPBES Approach (2017) 26–27 Current Opinion in Environmental Sustainability 7, at 15, 8–9.

[153] Report of the Special Rapporteur on the Issue of Human Rights and the Environment John Knox, UN Doc A/HRC/34/49 (2017), para. 5.

[154] ibid.

products, but he also discussed the often-undervalued importance of biodiversity for mental health.[155] He further highlighted more subtle relationships between human well-being and biodiversity, such as the relationship between healthy pollinators and global food security.[156]

This multifaceted recognition of the implications of biodiversity underpins the role of civil and political rights in the context of biodiversity conservation and sustainable use. Special Rapporteur Knox highlighted that States' efforts to increase and make available information on biodiversity, as well as to ensure public participation in relevant decision-making processes and access to justice in biodiversity-related matters, should be seen as international human rights obligations.[157] In particular, States need to make more of an effort to protect biodiversity defenders because those protecting endangered species, as highlighted by Special Rapporteur Knox, are doing so for the benefit of human rights.[158] These are the individuals and communities that raise awareness about the negative impacts on human rights of unsustainable decisions on the environment.[159] Environmental human rights defenders are increasingly the object of (often lethal) attacks by governments or private actors, as well as harassment, denigration, and side-lining.[160] They are increasingly recognized and studied as agents of change,[161] including for their role in preventing unsustainable and unjust utilization of the environment that may lead to conflict.[162] Environmental human rights defenders are entitled to all the rights and protections set out in the 1998 UN Declaration on the Right and Responsibility of Individuals, Groups and Organs of Society to Promote and Protect Universally Recognized Human Rights and Fundamental Freedoms.[163] States must ensure a safe and enabling environment for them to operate free from threats, harassment, intimidation, and violence. Protection also involves publicly recognizing defenders' contributions to society and ensuring that their work is not stigmatized.[164] Recognition and protection of Indigenous peoples who act as environmental human rights defenders is, indeed, a crucial matter of justice.

These clarifications are particularly significant for moving away from an understanding of the procedural dimensions of biodiversity conservation and sustainable

155 ibid, para. 12.

156 ibid, paras 11–20.

157 ibid, paras 27–32.

158 ibid, paras 31–32 and 68.

159 ibid.

160 Global Witness, 'Defending Tomorrow: The Climate Crisis and Threats Against Land and Environmental Defenders' (2020), available at https://www.globalwitness.org/en/campaigns/environmental-activists/defending-tomorrow, accessed 29 June 2023.

161 A Nah et al., 'A Research Agenda for the Protection of Human Rights Defenders' (2013) 5 Journal of Human Rights Practice 522.

162 A Scheidel et al., 'Environmental Conflicts and Defenders: A Global Overview' (2020) 63 Global Environmental Change 102104, 1.

163 UNGA, Declaration on Human Rights Defenders, Res 53/144 (1999).

164 M Sekaggya, 'Human Rights Defenders' UN Doc A/66/203 (2011); and M Forst, Situation of Human Rights Defenders, UN Doc A/71/281 (2016); Regional Agreement on Access to Information, Public Participation and Justice in Environmental Matters in Latin America and the Caribbean (adopted 4 March 2018, entered into force 22 April 2021), Art 9; and UNECE Decision VII/9 on a Rapid Response Mechanism to Deal with Cases Related to Article 3(8) of the Convention on Access to Information, Public Participation in Decision-making and Access to Justice in Environmental Matters, UN Doc ECE/MP.PP/2021/CRP.8 (2021).

use[165] as mere good governance.[166] These clarifications further assist in understanding international human rights law obligations as limitations on the discretion of CBD parties in interpretating and implementing otherwise open-ended treaty language,[167] which undermines procedural justice.

In addition, Special Rapporteur Knox clarified that there are substantive human rights law obligations that serve to clarify the limits of State discretion in pursuing the CBD objectives relating to biodiversity conservation and sustainable use.[168] This acknowledgment has two implications. At the domestic level, in authorizing any activity, either conservation or use, CBD parties are to ensure that no unjustified foreseeable infringements of human rights may arise from the decision.[169] This is based both on potential public interventions that may infringe biodiversity-dependent human rights and on States' obligation to prevent business entities from violating these rights.[170] In other words, implementing the CBD obligations in a mutually supportive way with international human rights law clarifies that States must develop laws and institutions that effectively 'regulate harm to biodiversity from private actors as well as government entities' in a way that is 'non-retrogressive and non-discriminatory'.[171] These are crucial indications about the minimum content of the international obligations contained in the CBD, which often remain neutral regarding specific means of implementation. This forms yet another layer of procedural justice.

At the multilateral level, Special Rapporteur Knox indicated that inter-State cooperation on biodiversity also has human rights implications.[172] This implies both that donor States' duties to support biodiversity efforts in developing countries are relevant to realize human rights dependent on biodiversity and that such support should not be carried out in a way that may lead to violations of other human rights.[173] While the latter issue has already been addressed to some extent by CBD parties, with an explicit reference to the relevant international human rights instruments,[174] the former issue remains a matter for further study.[175] In his Framework Principles on Human Rights and the Environment, Special Rapporteur Knox further clarified that the human rights implications of the international duty to cooperate also entail deeper forms of engagement under multilateral environmental agreements, as well as consideration of the linkages between international environmental law—including international biodiversity law and human rights in the context of international trade and investment agreements.[176]

[165] Knox (n. 153), para. 67.

[166] E Brown Weiss and A Sornarajah, 'Good Governance' in R Wolfrum (ed.), *Max Planck Encyclopedia of Public International Law* (Oxford University Press, 2010).

[167] L de Silva, 'Public Participation in Biodiversity Conservation' in Morgera and Razzaque (n. 123), 471.

[168] Knox (n. 153), para. 34.

[169] ibid.

[170] ibid, paras 33–34.

[171] ibid, para. 69.

[172] ibid, para. 36–48.

[173] ibid, para. 70.

[174] CBD Decision XII/3 (2014), Annex 3, para. 3(b)–(c); see Claudia Ituarte-Lima et al., Safeguards in Scaling-up Biodiversity Financing and Possible Guiding Principles, UN Doc UNEP/CBD/COP/11/INF/7 (2012); C Ituarte-Lima et al., *Biodiversity Financing and Safeguards* (Stockholm University, 2014).

[175] CBD Decision XII/3 (2012), para. 1.

[176] Knox, Framework Principles (n. 9), paras 36–39. See, e.g., E Morgera, 'The Promotion of Environmental Rights through the Bilateral Agreements of the European Union: Mapping the Field' in F

More specifically on benefit-sharing and Indigenous peoples, the 2018 Special Rapporteur's Framework Principles on Human Rights and the Environment contain a specific reference to benefit-sharing in Framework Principle 15. It refers to States' obligations to ensure that Indigenous peoples 'fairly and equitably share the benefits from activities relating to their lands, territories or resources'. Framework Principle 15 concerns the use of lands, territories, and resources that are traditionally owned, occupied, or used by Indigenous peoples, including those to which they have had access for their subsistence and traditional activities, even when they do not have formal recognition of property rights or delimitation and demarcation of boundaries.[177] These resources are linked to Indigenous peoples' traditional knowledge and genetic resources.[178] Framework Principle 15 entails a series of interconnected obligations to ensure Indigenous peoples' full and effective participation in decision-making on the entire spectrum of matters that impact their lives, including legislative or administrative measures that may affect them directly, programmes for the exploration, exploitation, or conservation of resources pertaining to their lands or territories, and proposals to alienate lands or territories or otherwise transfer their rights.[179] These obligations entail consulting with Indigenous peoples to obtain their FPIC before taking or approving any measures that may affect their lands, territories, or resources, on the basis of access to all relevant information in understandable and accessible forms[180] and prior assessments of the environmental and social impacts of proposed measures.[181] These assessments 'should be in accord with the guidelines adopted by the Conference of Parties to the Convention on Biological Diversity', notably the Akwé: Kon Voluntary Guidelines on environmental and socio-cultural assessments.[182] Furthermore, Framework Principle 15 refers to States' obligations to ensure that Indigenous peoples and members of traditional communities 'fairly and equitably share the benefits from activities relating to their lands, territories or resources'.[183] This obligation is, in turn, connected with the need to respect and protect Indigenous peoples' traditional knowledge and practices in relation to the conservation and sustainable use of their lands, territories, resources,[184] and the environment, including through States' assistance to Indigenous peoples' efforts to preserve the productive capacity of their lands, territories, and resources.[185]

Framework Principle 15 provides the most comprehensive list of benefit-sharing triggers in international human rights law.[186] Special Rapporteur Knox further clarified that benefit-sharing must be consistent with Indigenous peoples' and traditional

Lenzerini and AF Vrdoljak (eds), *International Law for Common Goods: Normative Perspectives on Human Rights, Culture and Nature* (Hart, 2014) 421.

177 Knox, Framework Principles (n. 9), para. 48.
178 ibid, para. 53.
179 ibid, para. 50.
180 Which is linked to Knox, Framework Principles 7 and 8 (n. 9). ibid, paras 11–12.
181 ibid, para. 20.
182 CBD Akwé: Kon Guidelines (n. 80); Knox, Framework Principles (n. 9), para. 43.
183 Knox, Framework Principles (n. 9), para. 18.
184 ibid, para. 52.
185 ibid.
186 Morgera (n. 23), at 372–378.

communities' own priorities.[187] He implicitly links it to the need for recognition of rights to the lands, territories, and resources that they have traditionally owned, occupied, or used, as well as due respect for the customs, traditions, and land tenure systems of the peoples or communities concerned, and effective remedies for violations of rights.[188] Special Rapporteur Knox substantiated benefit-sharing on the basis of the particular vulnerability of Indigenous peoples to environmental harm 'because of their close relationship with the natural ecosystems on their ancestral territories'.[189]

Overall, Principle 15 reflects the cross-fertilization between international human rights law and international biodiversity law fostered by the work of former UN Special Rapporteur on Indigenous Peoples' Rights James Anaya[190] and the seminal case law of the Inter-American Court on Human Rights,[191] discussed above. Both have relied on decisions adopted under the CBD.[192] The reflection of this case law into the UN Framework Principles corroborates the view expressed by the Inter-American Court that benefit-sharing obligations are also implicit in global human rights instruments,[193] and this interpretation is therefore relevant for other regions.[194]

These developments have then found reflection in the CBD post-2020 Global Biodiversity Framework, a consensus decision adopted by the 169 CBD Parties, which calls for respecting Indigenous peoples' and local communities' rights in relation to the target on participatory planning and management of land and sea use change, to bring the loss of areas of high biodiversity importance close to zero by 2030 (target 1).[195] The Framework also has as a goal to ensure and enable that by 2030 at least 30 per cent of terrestrial, inland water, and coastal and marine areas are effectively conserved and managed, recognizing Indigenous and traditional territories (target 2).[196] Both targets address distributive and contextual justice issues, together with recognition. The Framework also adds reference to Indigenous peoples' and local communities' rights and territories with regard to ensuring the full, equitable, inclusive, effective, and gender-responsive representation and participation in decision-making, and access to justice and information related to biodiversity (target 22).[197] The latter speaks directly to procedural justice.

[187] Knox, Framework Principles (n. 9), para. 53.

[188] ibid, paras 47–49 and 53. Framework Principle 10 makes clear what 'effective remedies' entail. ibid, para. 13.

[189] ibid, at 47.

[190] E Morgera, 'The Legacy of UN Special Rapporteur Anaya on Indigenous Peoples and Benefit-sharing', BENELEX blog (29 May 2014), available at https://benelexblog.wordpress.com/2014/05/29/the-legacy-of-un-special-rapporteur-anaya-on-indigenous-peoples-and-benefit-sharing/, accessed 28 June 2023.

[191] See, e.g., *Saramaka* (Merits) (n. 52).

[192] See ibid; Special Rapporteur on the Rights of Indigenous Peoples James Anaya, 'Measures Needed to Secure Indigenous and Tribal Peoples' Land and Related Rights in Suriname' UN Doc A/HRC/18/35/Add.7 (2011), paras 8–12.

[193] *Saramaka* (Merits) (n. 52) (referencing the International Covenant on Civil and Political Rights (ICCPR) (New York, 7 March 1966, in force 4 January 1969), Arts. 1 and 27, and the International Covenant on Economic, Social and Cultural Rights (ICESCR) (New York, 16 December 1966, in force 3 January 1976), Art. 1.

[194] Morgera (n. 6), at 1109.

[195] Kunming-Montreal Global Biodiversity Framework, CBD COP Decision XV/1 (2022).

[196] ibid.

[197] ibid.

5. Further Advancing a Mutually Supportive Interpretation of Fair and Equitable Benefit-Sharing

The full potential for a mutually supportive interpretation of fair and equitable benefit-sharing will now be explored by piecing together existing sources of authoritative interpretation that have not yet been drawn together by international human rights bodies, but are implicitly compatible. First, the proposed interpretation will seek to clarify the procedural and substantive dimensions (fairness and equity) of benefit-sharing. It will then proceed to discuss the interplay of benefit-sharing with impact assessments and FPIC, arguing that benefit-sharing is intertwined with consent as an ongoing partnership-building process and should be distinguished from compensation.

5.1 Procedural Dimensions

Under the CBD, what fairness and equity mean is left to be determined through successive (often contractual) negotiations of benefit-sharing agreements.[198] In effect, case-by-case negotiations may be required for a contextual operationalization of benefit-sharing under international biodiversity and human rights law, as they both refer (independently of each other) to 'mutually agreed' benefits.[199] Furthering a mutually supportive interpretation of fair and equitable benefit-sharing may thus also serve to set minimum parameters for fairness and equity under international biodiversity law by relying on international human rights law notions, such as due process, non-discrimination, and proportionality.[200]

Along these lines, it can be argued that reference to 'fair and equitable' serves to make explicit both procedural (fairness) and substantive (equity) dimensions of justice.[201] This argument can then find resonance in the reasoning of both international human rights and biodiversity sources (independently of each other) highlighting the need for benefit-sharing to be endogenously identified and culturally appropriate.[202] In particular, the Inter-American Court has expressed the view that effective and appropriate measures to secure the use and enjoyment of traditional territories must accord with Indigenous and tribal peoples' cultural identity,

198 F Francioni, 'Equity' in Wolfrum (n. 166), para. 25. See Chapter 1.

199 *Kaliña and Lokono* (n. 16), paras 227–229 and 159. See A Lucas, 'Participatory Rights and Strategic Litigation: Benefits Forcing and Endowment Protection in Canadian Natural Resource Development' in L Barrera-Hernandez et al. (eds), *Sharing the Costs and Benefits of Energy and Resource Activity* (Oxford University Press, 2016) 339, at 342–345.

200 PM Dupuy and J Viñuales, 'Human Rights and Investment Disciplines: Integration in Progress' in M Bungenberg et al. (eds), *International Investment Law: A Handbook* (Bloomsbury, 2015) 1739.

201 See generally T Franck, *Fairness in International Law and Institutions* (Clarendon Press, 1995), and reflections by R Klager, *Fair and Equitable Treatment in International Investment Law* (Cambridge University Press, 2013), at 141–152.

202 IACtHR, *Saramaka* (Interpretation) (n. 91), para 25; CBD, Refinement and Elaboration of the Ecosystem Approach, COP 5 Decision, V/6 (2000), paras 1(8) and 2(1); CBD, Tkarihwaié:ri Code of Ethical Conduct to Ensure Respect for the Cultural and Intellectual Heritage of Indigenous and Local Communities, CBD Decision X/42 (2010), para. 14.

economic and social characteristics, potential vulnerabilities, customary laws, and special relationship with the land.[203] The UN Expert Mechanism on Indigenous Peoples' Rights has confirmed that benefit-sharing is expected to accord with communities' own understanding of benefits.[204] The ILO monitoring bodies have emphasized that benefit-sharing should provide concrete expression of Indigenous peoples' agreement on the basis of their values, customs and preferences.[205] These references clearly point to the interactions of procedural and substantive dimensions of justice, and seem to exclude unidirectional and/or top-down flows of benefits that would be externally imposed and unlikely to satisfy the standard of cultural appropriateness. Emphasizing endogenous identification reinforces the view that benefit-sharing is about supporting community agency[206] and Indigenous peoples' right to self-determination.[207]

The argument put forward here is that sparse interpretative guidance in international biodiversity and human rights instruments seem to indicate that the procedural dimension of benefit-sharing is a concerted and dialogic process aimed at developing a genuine partnership between Indigenous peoples and other (generally more powerful) actors based on a common understanding across different worldviews of what economic and non-economic benefits are at stake and how they should be shared. This presupposes an understanding of benefit-sharing as an iterative process, rather than a one-off exercise, of good-faith engagement[208] providing 'elements of confidence-building conducive to consensus'.[209] Such an approach would provide an opportunity to create a shared development vision on the basis of respect for each parties' views and mutual openness to persuasion.[210] In addition, it needs to factor in Indigenous peoples' evolving perceptions and understanding of benefits over time.[211] To sum up, and as agreed upon under the CBD, respectful and enduring partnership building 'means a continual process of building mutually beneficial, ongoing arrangements … in order to build trust, good relations, mutual understanding, intercultural spaces, knowledge exchanges, and to create new knowledge and reconciliation'.[212] These are key considerations that can underpin the minimum procedural guarantees spelled out under international human rights law.

[203] *Kaliña and Lokono* (n. 16), para. 251(4).

[204] UN Expert Mechanism, Indigenous peoples' right to participate in decision-making (n. 2), para. 39(h); also Special Rapporteur Anaya, Report to the General Assembly, UN Doc A/67/301 (2012), para. 78.

[205] ILO, Observation (Norway) (n. 43), at 95.

[206] Morgera (n. 23), at 363–364 and Mancisidor (n. 42).

[207] *Saramaka* (Interpretation) (n. 91), paras 25 and 46; CBD, Refinement and Elaboration of the Ecosystem Approach (n. 202), paras 1(8), 2(1); CBD, Tkarihwaié:ri Code (n. 202), para. 14.

[208] Morgera (n. 23), at 363–364.

[209] Special Rapporteur Anaya, Report on the situation of human rights and fundamental freedoms of indigenous peoples, UN Doc A/HRC/12/34 (2009), para. 53; and Special Rapporteur Anaya, Study on Extractive Industries and Indigenous Peoples, UN Doc A/HRC/24/41 (2013), para. 88.

[210] N Craik, 'Process and Reconciliation: Integrating the Duty to Consult with Environmental Assessment' (2016) 52 Osgoode Hall Law Journal 1, at 42 and 48.

[211] P Keenan, 'Business, Human Rights, and Communities: The Problem of Community Contest in Development', Illinois Public Law Research Paper No. 14–18 (SSRN 2013), available at http://ssrn.com/abstract=2353493, accessed 28 June 2023.

[212] CBD, Mo'otz Kuxtal Guidelines (n. 119), para. 23(a) and 8.

5.2 Substantive Dimensions

International sources have avoided or refrained from clearly and explicitly explaining the substantive content of benefit-sharing. Sparse interpretative guidance can be pieced together, however, on the basis of legal theory on equity in international law, the interpretation of the right to development offered by the African Commission, and the menu of benefits identified under the CBD.

Legal theory has identified two substantive dimensions of equity in international law. First, no participant can make claims that automatically prevail over the claims made by other participants.[213] In the specific case of fair and equitable benefit-sharing, this means excluding an overriding presumption in favour of State sovereignty over natural resources.[214] This argument finds resonance in the references in international human rights materials to the need to establish a genuine *partnership* through benefit-sharing. Accordingly, notwithstanding different power imbalances, all parties should treat each other as equals.[215] This approach accommodates both State sovereignty over natural resources (and the interests of the entire population dependent on these natural resources) and the rights of Indigenous peoples to self-determination[216] regarding their land upon which their physical and cultural survival[217] depends.

The second substantive dimension of equity, according to theories of international law, is that inequalities in substantive outcomes are only justifiable if they provide advantages to all participants.[218] This argument can in turn be related to the references in human rights jurisprudence on benefit-sharing to the concept of *reasonableness*[219] with respect to the need to balance the protection of the traditional way of life of Indigenous peoples that is intimately intertwined with and dependent on natural resources.[220] Regional human rights jurisprudence has indicated that benefit-sharing from natural resource exploitation should align with

[213] Klager (n. 201), at 163.

[214] C Burke, *An Equitable Framework for Humanitarian Intervention* (Hart, 2014), at 250.

[215] e.g., Special Rapporteur Anaya, A/HRC/12/34 (n. 209), paras 51 and 53; UNDRIP prembular para. 15 (and H Quane, 'The UN Declaration on the Rights of Indigenous Peoples: New Directions for Self-Determination and Participatory Rights?' in Allen and Xanthaki (n. 12), at 259, 270, and 276–277); UN Expert Mechanism, Indigenous peoples' right to participate in decision-making (n. 2), Annex, para. 28; and Report of the High-level Task Force on the Implementation of the Right to Development on its Second Meeting, UN Doc E/CN.4/2005/WG.18/TF/3 (2005), para. 82.

[216] Fitzmaurice (n. 148), at 375; and Special Rapporteur Anaya, A/HRC/12/34 (n. 209), paras 53 and 43(b).

[217] *Saramaka* (Interpretation) (n. 91), para. 2.

[218] Klager (n. 201), at 145.

[219] O Corten, 'Reasonableness in International Law' in Wolfrum (n. 166). See also Reports of the Committee on Economic, Social and Cultural Rights for the Forty-Second and Forty-Third sessions, Consideration of reports of States parties: Cambodia, UN Doc E/C.12/2009/3 (2009), para. 193, and for the Forty-Second and Forty-Third sessions, Consideration of reports of States parties: Democratic Republic of Congo, UN Doc E/C.12/2009/3 (2009), para. 289; OHCHR, Mapping Human Rights Obligations Relating to the Enjoyment of a Safe, Clean, Healthy and Sustainable Environment: Individual Report on the International Covenant on Economic, Social and Cultural Rights (2013), para. 48; and 1993 Vienna Declaration and Programme on Action, UN Doc A/CONF.157/23 (1993), part I, para. 20.

[220] *Endorois* (n. 15), para. 15.

decisions made by Indigenous peoples based on their customs and traditions, while taking into account proportionality with regard to public interest, including environmental protection.[221]

In the case of conservation measures, in particular, the Inter-American Court indicated that it may be 'reasonable' for the State to retain supervision, access, and management of areas of general and strategic interest and for safety reasons.[222] The same concerns appear implicitly reflected in CBD guidance related to the respect of Indigenous peoples' customary laws and practices[223] and benefits in the form of co-management of natural resources.[224] According to Århén, however, the proportionality test should not be conceived merely according to the understanding of the majority of the population (often influenced by market value) but also in terms of the Indigenous understanding of its cultural and spiritual value, to avoid discrimination against different worldviews.[225]

These considerations will now be related to guidance on benefit-sharing provided by the African Commission. The *Endorois* decision is the only international material that focuses on the substantive dimensions of benefit-sharing in relation to the human right to development.[226] The Commission clarified the substantive core of benefit-sharing as a matter of *choice* and increased *capabilities*,[227] resulting in Indigenous and tribal peoples' improved well-being[228] and empowerment.[229] Arguably, Special Rapporteur Anaya shed light in a similar way on the substantive elements of benefit-sharing, when he referred to empowerment both in procedural and substantive terms.[230] This line of reasoning, grounded in international human rights law on racial discrimination,[231]

[221] IACtHR, *Comunidad Garífuna de Punta Piedra y sus miembros vs Honduras* (Preliminary Exceptions, Merits, Reparations and Costs), 8 October 2015, para. 215; *Kaliña and Lokono* (n. 16), para. 168.

[222] *Kaliña and Lokono* (n. 16), para. 191.

[223] Gibson (n. 124), at 450.

[224] CBD work programme on protected areas (n. 80), para. 19; Addis Ababa Guidelines (n. 96), practical Principle 12, operational guidelines.

[225] *Endorois* (n. 15), para. 212. Århén (n. 2), at 207–212.

[226] *Endorois* (n. 15), paras 294–298. The right to development is explicitly protected under the African Charter (Art. 22), and is understood as an expression of the right to self-determination of Indigenous and tribal peoples comprising a distinctive bundle of rights to participation, culture, and natural resources: see Pentassuglia (n. 55), at 157, and generally and C Doyle and J Gilbert, 'Indigenous Peoples and Globalization: From "Development Aggression" to "Self-Determined Development"' (2008/9) 7 European Yearbook of Minority Issues 219.

[227] *Endorois* (n. 15), para. 279. C Morel, 'From Theory to Practice: Holistic Strategies for Effective Advocacy' in Lennox and Short (n. 20) 355, at 359; S Coulthard, J McGregor, and C White, 'Multiple Dimensions of Wellbeing in Practice' in Schreckenberg et al. (n. 131), 243.

[228] J Castellino, 'Indigenous Rights and the Right to Development: Emerging Synergies or Collusion?' in Allen and Xanthaki (n. 12) 367, at 369. On well-being as the substantive aim of benefit-sharing, see also Report of the Special Rapporteur in the Field of Cultural Rights: The Right to Enjoy the Benefits of Scientific Progress and Its Applications UN Doc A/HRC/20/26 (2012), para. 22; and ILO Conference 87th Session 1999, Report III (Part 1a), para. 434.

[229] *Endorois* (n. 15), para. 283, as well as paras 127–129 and 135. See, however, the words of caution by Thornberry (n. 59), at 298 against the understanding of well-being in economic and spatial terms, rather than cultural terms.

[230] Special Rapporteur Anaya, A/HRC/24/41 (n. 209), paras 75 and 59.

[231] *Endorois* (n. 15), paras 294 and 296; CERD, General Recommendation No. 23: Indigenous Peoples UN Doc A/52/18 (1997), Annex V, para. 4; CERD Concluding Observations on Ecuador (n. 83).

holds relevance not only in its specific regional context but also to other regional[232] and international regimes.[233]

The African Commission, however, did not elaborate on how the substantive dimensions of benefit-sharing could be realized.[234] The argument put forward here is that choice and capabilities find resonance in the range of monetary and non-monetary benefits that have been identified under the CBD. Choice can be realized through those benefits that provide or enhance 'resource control'—the realization of communities' worldview of their resources.[235]

Control benefits can thus take the form of community-based management of natural resources and joint ventures when the skills or technology of external actors may be needed. Additionally, they can also encompass the incorporation of traditional knowledge in environmental and socio-cultural impact assessments, resource management plans, and under certain conditions, the allocation of employment opportunities in the natural resource sector to communities.

Capabilities, defined as the availability of opportunities for individuals and groups to freely pursue their chosen way of life and well-being,[236] are distinctly mirrored in the *support*-benefits identified under the CBD. These include support for the economic activities of Indigenous peoples through direct investment opportunities, access to markets, and diversification of income-generating (economic) opportunities, or capacity building and technical support. This proposed distinction highlights benefits fundamentally designed to protect or enhance Indigenous peoples' *control* over natural resources (and thereby enhancing choice). These two sets of benefits can thus support the realization of multiple dimensions of justice in relation to distribution, recognition, and capabilities, as well as contextual justice.

This menu of benefits could also serve to rectify past injustices, where benefits aim to offer *support* (thereby enhancing capabilities) for the exercise of effective control, a facet not explicitly discussed within the CBD. The argument proposed here suggests that both types of benefits are essential. On the one hand, support benefits are extremely significant in their own right to prevent further marginalization of Indigenous peoples' voices due to the intricate nature of environmental management processes in which their views and preferences are to be integrated.[237] For instance, communities may be legally recognized as having full management of an area, but not supported in complying with highly technical aspects of applicable legislation, such as plant health

[232] M Orellana, 'Saramaka People v Suriname Judgment' (2008) 102 American Journal of International Law 841, at 846. Although note the limited cross-fertilization between the Inter-American and European courts of human rights: see generally R Pavoni, 'Environmental Jurisprudence of the European and Inter-American Courts of Human Rights: Comparative Insights' in B Boer (ed.), *Environmental Law Dimensions of Human Rights* (Oxford University Press, 2015) 69, at 105.

[233] On the 'glocalization' of right to development, see R Stavenhagen, 'Making the Declaration on the Rights of Indigenous Peoples Work: The Challenge Ahead' in Allen and Xanthaki (n. 12) 147, at 152–153. See also Pentassuglia (n. 21), at 201.

[234] K Sing' Oei and J Shepherd, 'In Land We Trust': The Endorois' Communication and the Quest for Indigenous Peoples' Rights in Africa' (2010) 16 Buffalo Human Rights Law Review 57, at 108–109.

[235] For their own primary benefit, including in terms of environmental sustainability, albeit without excluding opportunities for benefits to others according to views of broader society: see generally Y Omorogbe, 'Resource Control and Benefit-sharing in Nigeria' in Barrera-Hernandez et al. (n. 199).

[236] e.g., see generally M Nussbaum and A Sen, *The Quality of Life* (Clarendon Press, 1993).

[237] Shelton (n. 118), at 554.

requirements.[238] On the other hand, the absence of an explicit discussion of this distinction within the CBD poses the risk that support benefits may be offered as an alternative, rather than as a complement, to control benefits: for instance, communities may be offered employment opportunities without being involved in the decision-making processes concerning a forestry project or protected area.[239] In addition, employment opportunities might be confined to low-salary, low-skilled positions, failing to align with the development priorities of Indigenous peoples or recognizing their knowledge, thereby contributing to injustices related to distribution, recognition, and capabilities.

A fully fledged mutually supportive interpretation should guide the identification of appropriate benefits in a particular context by recognizing the need for both control benefits and support benefits to advance communities' own development priorities[240] and ensuring the full realization of their human rights as a form of reasonable partnership. This is particularly important for ensuring that fair and equitable benefit-sharing responds to the different dimensions of environmental justice at stake. For instance, lithium mining is considered central for transitioning away from fossil fuel-based economies, serving as a key component in batteries for electric cars (amongst many other uses).[241] However, this raises a challenge in balancing the pursuit of a global public good (the move to a low-carbon society) with the imperative to uphold local environmental justice, particularly concerning the Indigenous peoples whose lands hold lithium reserves. These areas may be essential for local livelihoods and culture, and may already be under severe environmental threats. One of the main apprehensions relates to the possible contamination of their fresh water supply due to the amount of water used in lithium extraction, and possible mixing between fresh and saltwater systems within the basins.[242] However, the Indigenous peoples in the area may also be in need of employment and often basic services, making investments in economic ventures in the area attractive, giving rise to fractures within the community.[243]

5.3 Benefit-Sharing and Impact Assessment

International human rights processes have been quite consistent in establishing that prior comprehensive environmental and socio-cultural impact assessments be carried out as a safeguard for Indigenous and tribal peoples' rights over their natural resources. This section explores how a mutually supportive interpretation of international biodiversity and human rights standards can clarify the interplay between

[238] L Parks, *Benefit-sharing from the Bottom Up: Local Experiences of a Global Concept* (Routledge, 2020).

[239] Note the mixed picture arising in this regard from benefit-sharing as part of community-based wildlife management initiatives in Africa: F Nelson, 'Introduction' in F Nelson (ed.), *Community Rights, Conservation and Contested Lands: The Politics of Natural Resource Governance in Africa* (Earthscan, 2010), at 3, 4 and 11.

[240] Special Rapporteur on the human rights obligations related to environmentally sound management and disposal of hazardous substances and waste, Report, UN Doc A/HRC/21/48 (2012), paras 36 and 69(h).

[241] Parks (n. 238), at 45–49.

[242] MA Marazuela et al., 'Hydrodynamics of Salt Flat Basins: The Salar de Atacama Example' (2018) 651 Science of the Total Environment 668.

[243] P Marchegiani, E Morgera, and L Parks, 'Indigenous Peoples' Rights to Natural Resources in Argentina: The Challenges of Impact Assessment, Consent and Fair and Equitable Benefit-Sharing in Cases of Lithium Mining' (2020) 24 International Journal of Human Rights 224, at 229.

benefit-sharing and impact assessments. The proposed interpretation highlights opportunities to engender a proactive approach to the protection and realization of human rights by supporting the understanding of different worldviews. The proposed interpretation builds on a detailed interrogation of the CBD Akwé: Kon Guidelines. It is also informed by a consideration of well-known implementation challenges in the environmental field and of the status, justiciability, and minimum content of impact assessment obligations under general international law.

Impact assessments are generally understood as oriented towards *damage prevention* or *damage control*, including as a way to provide information necessary for Indigenous peoples to decide whether to provide FPIC or not.[244] For instance, the Inter-American Court has consistently indicated that these assessments should aim to ensure that approved levels of impact do not endanger the survival of Indigenous peoples' members. Indigenous peoples should be made aware of possible risks, including environmental and health risks, so that they can make informed decisions on whether to accept proposed developments voluntarily and with full knowledge.[245] A mutually supportive interpretation, instead, reveals the potential for early consideration of culturally appropriate and endogenously defined benefit-sharing options as part of impact assessment expands the scope and approach of the latter quite significantly. The CBD Akwé: Kon Guidelines specifically clarify that impact assessments should identify, in an integrated fashion—that is, at least potentially in accordance with holistic worldviews—environmental, economic, and socio-cultural benefits,[246] in addition to potential damage to ways of life, livelihoods, well-being, and traditional knowledge.[247] In supporting FPIC processes,[248] the CBD Akwé: Kon Guidelines require that consideration of benefit-sharing starts appreciably early on in the process—as early as the screening and scoping phases of assessments.[249] As a result, the Akwé: Kon Guidelines move away from a damage-control approach to also collaboratively identifying and understanding opportunities for positive impacts according to Indigenous peoples' and local communities' worldviews[250] to determine the scope of the assessment.

The Akwé: Kon Guidelines, furthermore, arguably move away from a technocratic exercise, calling for collaborative procedures and methodologies aimed at ensuring the full involvement of Indigenous peoples. As it has been poignantly remarked, the general effectiveness of environmental assessments 'as procedural measures generating environmentally sound and just outcomes in socio-ecological systems characterized by uncertainty and normative disagreement' remains 'an open question, notwithstanding over forty years of practice across the globe'.[251] In particular, while participation of potentially affected stakeholders is a widely accepted and essential

[244] N Craik, 'Biodiversity-inclusive Impact Assessment' in Morgera and Razzaque (n. 123), 431, argues that consideration of biodiversity concerns more generally expands the range of issues and values to be included in environmental assessments. See also C Doyle, *Indigenous Peoples, Title to Territory, Rights and Resources: The Transformative Role of Free, Prior and Informed Consent* (Routledge, 2015), at 94.

[245] *Saramaka* (Merits) (n. 52), para. 133; *Kichwa* (n. 10), para. 205; *Kaliña and Lokono* (n. 16), para. 214.

[246] CBD Akwé: Kon Guidelines (n. 80), para. 23.

[247] ibid, para. 36.

[248] ibid, paras 8(e) and 53.

[249] ibid, Foreword, para. 3, and 13–14.

[250] ibid, para. 37.

[251] See Craik (n. 244), at 443.

element of environmental assessment,[252] the actual suitability of this tool and of settled assessment practices in different countries to effectively and respectfully integrate traditional knowledge with 'scientific knowledge',[253] remains to be explored. In addition, evidence confirms that environmental impact assessments (EIAs) may not provide a culturally appropriate and open space for understanding the worldviews of Indigenous peoples, due to embedded tendencies in EIA practice to privilege mainstream views of development. This may explain Indigenous peoples' preference for Indigenous assessments that are fully based on Indigenous laws and legal traditions.[254]

Consequently, according to the Akwé: Kon Guidelines, the breadth of the assessment ranges from cultural elements such as belief systems, languages, and customs,[255] to systems of natural resource utilization; the maintenance of genetic diversity through Indigenous customary management; and the exercise of customary laws regarding land tenure and distribution of resources and benefits.[256] It also extends to food and health,[257] community well-being, vitality, and viability (employment levels and opportunities, welfare, education, and availability and standards of housing, infrastructure, services),[258] as well as transgenerational aspects, such as opportunities for elders to pass on their knowledge to youth.[259] Governments are also expected to take into account Indigenous peoples' rights over lands and waters traditionally occupied or used by them and associated biodiversity.[260]

The Akwé: Kon Guidelines further call for caution on the risks of elite capture[261] associated with benefit-sharing: they draw attention to the 'affected community and its people as a whole' so as to ensure that 'particular individuals or groups are not unjustly advantaged or disadvantaged to the detriment of the community as a result of the development'.[262] Overall, the range of considerations to be integrated in an otherwise technical, information-focused assessment exercise emerge as an essential precondition to realize the transformational potential of impact assessments to develop a shared development vision informed by communities' worldviews.[263] These considerations can help address justice dimensions related to distribution, recognition, capabilities, and context.

As Neil Craik has pointed out, the analysis of alternatives in environmental assessments is essential. Consideration of alternatives demonstrates that good faith decisions have been made with a genuine commitment to the environment not just at the stage of the final decision but also throughout the interim stages. It highlights the

[252] Rio Principles 10 and 22; International Law Commission, Draft Articles on the Prevention of Transboundary Harm from Hazardous Activities, UN Doc A/56/1 (2001), Ch 5.E, Art 13; Independent Expert Knox, Mapping Report (n. 56).

[253] S Vermeylen et al., 'Intellectual Property, Rights Systems and the Assemblage of Local Knowledge Systems' (2008) 15 International Journal of Cultural Property 201.

[254] N Schabus, 'Traditional Knowledge' in Morgera and Razzaque (n. 123), 264.

[255] CBD Akwé: Kon Guidelines (n. 80), para. 6(f).

[256] ibid, paras 24, 27–28, and 34.

[257] ibid, para. 42.

[258] ibid, para. 6(d).

[259] ibid, para. 49.

[260] ibid, para. 57.

[261] Keenan (n. 211).

[262] CBD Akwé: Kon Guidelines (n. 80), para. 51.

[263] On such a transformational potential of impact assessment, see generally Craik (n. 210).

significance of consultations in the absence of clear quantitative standards to assess the acceptability of impacts.[264] Authorities must demonstrate that, at the very least, mitigation measures correspond to the preferred alternatives put forward by Indigenous peoples. This extends to situations where it is an alternative *to* the project, rather than just alternative means of carrying out the proposed project. If a different alternative is chosen, authorities' justification also needs to take into account Indigenous peoples' views.[265]

The practical relevance of a mutually supportive interpretation of environmental assessment obligations rests not only on the broad intergovernmental support for the CBD Guidelines, but also on the lessons learnt in the environmental domain with regard to the transformative potential of environmental assessments and the challenges to its realization. Different national frameworks for environmental assessments may offer differing levels of support for protecting the rights of Indigenous peoples, as the balancing of different interests may depend on whether constitutional protection is afforded to Indigenous rights and/or to the general interest in environmental protection.[266] While the International Court of Justice left the determination of the precise requirements of an EIA to the State's discretion,[267] Neil Craik argued that at least two components of impact assessments are required by general international law—cumulative impact assessments and post-project monitoring.[268] Both can have an important role to play in the protection and realization of Indigenous peoples' natural resource-related rights,[269] in particular with regard to an iterative process of identification and sharing of benefits, as the understanding of impacts evolve. For instance, a benefit-sharing arrangement in the context of the cultivation of a unique variety of rice may initially focus on production sharing between the community that has been the custodian of this variety of rice and the lands where it is traditionally cultivated and a State-subsidized company that conducts agricultural activities to support aging or otherwise economically active members of the community. Over time, however, the community may realize that creating seed nurseries and avoiding the use of harmful chemicals, which might damage other traditional land practices, are equally significant for the partnership as production sharing.[270]

Empirical research has shown that EIAs are 'overwhelmingly' in the hands of private developments, with project proponents having control of the timeliness, extent, and framing of information.[271] This allows companies to maximize perceptions

[264] N Craik, H Gardner, and D McCarthy, 'Indigenous—Corporate Private Governance and Legitimacy: Lessons Learned from Impact and Benefit Agreements' (2017) 52 Resources Policy 379.

[265] ibid.

[266] See generally Craik, Gardner, and McCarthy (n. 264); and also Desmet (n. 1), at 186–187. Note, however, Birnie, Boyle, and Redgwell (n. 118), at 287.

[267] International Court of Justice (ICJ), *Pulp Mills on the River Uruguay (Argentina v. Uruguay)*, Judgment of 20 April 2010, para. 205.

[268] N Craik, 'Principle 17: Environmental Impact Assessment' in Viñuales (n. 118, 451, at 460.

[269] M Barelli, 'Free, Prior and Informed Consent in the Aftermath of the UN Declaration on the Rights of Indigenous Peoples: Developments and Challenges Ahead' (2012) 16 International Journal of Human Rights 1, at 15. See, e.g., HRC, *Jouni E. Länsman et al. V. Finland*, Communication No. 671/1995, UN Doc CCPR/C/58/D/671/199 (1996) 5, para. 10.7.

[270] Parks (n. 238), at 65–68.

[271] ibid.

of local benefits over risks, even though the risks might pose a far greater threat to traditional livelihoods compared to the economic benefits, such as new employment opportunities. Equally companies may or may not continue good-faith dialogue to update benefit-sharing agreements according to evolving needs.[272] This is further compounded by the absence of State authorities in reviewing EIAs (including in terms of prior baseline studies) or in overseeing benefit-sharing negotiations as 'neutral facilitators and guarantors of human rights'.[273]

Finally, the prevailing practice in project-level environmental assessments does not include consideration of relevant historical context[274] and Indigenous peoples' territorial claims, and is less likely to address long-term implications of resource development on their interests. Rather, international biodiversity law has recourse to strategic environmental assessments (SEAs), at the level of policies, plans, and programmes, to take into account cumulative impacts. Human rights bodies should therefore give consideration, in order to support the examination of communities' broader territorial and historical perspectives,[275] to States' obligations to carry out strategic environmental assessments. This is not a common requirement outside of Europe,[276] but they are required under the CBD.[277] Consensus-based CBD guidance on SEAs include stakeholder engagement and transparency, technical assessment, information sharing and discussion among stakeholders, and monitoring and evaluation after the policy or plan has been adopted.[278] Importantly, CBD guidance clarifies the 'biodiversity triggers for SEA',[279] making reference to 'direct drivers of change' with known impact on ecosystem services, and as 'indirect drivers of change' through policies, plans, and programmes. While requirements for SEAs have not yet been explicitly stated by international human rights bodies, the well-understood negative impacts of climate change on Indigenous peoples' human rights, as well as less understood or known historical dispossession and discrimination,[280] and the need to consider potential human rights implications beyond the strict scope of EIAs arguably justify the need to also consider the CBD requirements for SEAs as mutually supportive to international human rights law.[281] This would serve to address contextual and restorative justice.

[272] Marchegiani, Morgera, and Parks (n. 243), at 8–9.

[273] ibid, at 8.

[274] S Vermeylen, 'Benefit-sharing, Justice and the Global South' BENELEX blog (April 2016) available at https://benelexblog.wordpress.com/2016/04/28/benefit-sharing-justice-and-the-global-south/, accessed 29 June 2023.

[275] See generally Craik, Gardner, and McCarthy (n. 264).

[276] Craik (n. 244), at 437–438.

[277] CBD, Art 4.

[278] CBD Decision XI/23 (2012), Annex, Part II, 'Marine and Coastal Biodiversity: Revised Voluntary Guidelines for the Consideration of Biodiversity in Environmental Impact Assessments and Strategic Environmental Assessments in Marine and Coastal Areas', para. 14.

[279] ibid, para. 28.

[280] This can be particularly the case in relation to marine territories and resources: see D Wilson, 'European Colonisation, Law, and Indigenous Marine Dispossession: Historical Perspectives on the Construction and Entrenchment of Unequal Marine Governance' (2021) 20 Maritime Studies 387.

[281] Morgera (n. 6), at 1106. See also J Nakamura, D Diz, and E Morgera, 'International Legal Requirements for Environmental and Socio-Cultural Assessments for Large-Scale Industrial Fisheries' (2022) 31 Review of European, Comparative and International Environmental Law 1.

5.4 Benefit-Sharing and Free Prior Informed Consent

This section further develops a mutually supportive interpretation of benefit-sharing as intertwined with FPIC, rather than as a subsequent step to FPIC. The discussion serves to identify areas of overlap between FPIC and benefit-sharing as iterative dialogic processes that are aimed not only at the protection, but also at the realization of Indigenous peoples' human rights over natural resources. In other words, a more developed mutually supportive interpretation helps move away from conceptualizing FPIC and benefit-sharing merely as safeguards to viewing them as proactive tools for the full realization of Indigenous peoples' rights. In addition, this section explores the contribution of CBD materials to the elucidation of the procedural and substantive content of FPIC, and the contribution of international human rights law to the identification of additional guarantees required for FPIC and benefit-sharing. Ultimately, the discussion serves to clarify that lack of fair and equitable benefit-sharing can provide legitimate grounds to withhold or withdraw consent.

Although it is commonly considered a relatively recent international legal concept,[282] prior informed consent originated in Indigenous peoples' own legal traditions and relations with other communities.[283] In the context of international human rights processes, FPIC has been interpreted as entailing that consent should be given freely, without coercion, intimidation, or manipulation. States are to allow sufficient time for internal discussion within the community,[284] seeking FPIC whenever there is a possible impact on traditional life[285] at all stages of development projects or conservation initiatives (from inception to final authorization and implementation).[286] State obligations thus include creating channels for sustained, effective, and reliable dialogue with Indigenous peoples' representative institutions.[287]

Different States show varying degrees of recognition or commitment to FPIC.[288] Under the CBD, while the Akwé: Kon Guidelines refer to 'prior informed consent',[289] more recent instruments[290] refer to 'prior informed consent or approval and

[282] E.g. UN Expert Mechanism, Final report of the study on indigenous peoples and the right to participate in decision-making, UN Doc A/HRC/18/42 (2011), para. 63, criticized by Doyle (n. 244), at 5.

[283] See generally Doyle (n. 244).

[284] *Kichwa* (n. 10), para. 180.

[285] *Kaliña and Lokono* (n. 16), Joint Concurring Opinion of Judges Sierra Porto and Ferrer Mac-Gregor Poisot, paras 14; UNPFII, Report on the tenth session, UN Doc E/2011/43-E/C.19/2011/14 (2011), paras 34–38, particularly para. 34.

[286] *Kaliña and Lokono* (n. 16), Joint Concurring Opinion of Judges Sierra Porto and Ferrer Mac-Gregor Poisot, para. 14.

[287] *Kichwa* (n. 10), paras 166 and 177; *Endorois* (n. 15), para. 289; *Kaliña and Lokono* (n. 16), Joint Concurring Opinion of Antonio Sierra Porto and Mac-Gregor Poisot, para. 15.

[288] Gilbert and Doyle (n. 12), at 325.

[289] CBD Akwé: Kon Guidelines (n. 80) paras 29, 52–53, and 60) refer consistently only to 'prior informed consent'.

[290] Nagoya Protocol, Art 6(2), with 'approval and involvement' being found in the wording of CBD, Art 8(j); Bonn Guidelines (n. 133), para. 31; and CBD Decision V/16 (2000), para. 5. For an indication of the continued divergence of views on utilizing UNDRIP language in the context of the CBD, see C Benson et al., 'Summary of the Seventh Meeting of the Working Group on Article 8(j) (2011) 9(557) ENB 5–6; and B Antonich et al., 'Summary of the Eighth Meeting of the Working Group on Article 8(j) and 17th Meeting of the Subsidiary Body on Scientific, Technical and Technological Advice of the Convention on Biological Diversity' (2013) 9(611) ENB 4, at 6–7 and 20.

involvement' reflecting the reluctance by some CBD Parties to fully endorse the standards enshrined in the UNDRIP. According to proponent countries, the expression 'approval and involvement' was introduced to allow for a greater degree of flexibility in implementation at the national level,[291] in the light of different domestic legal arrangements concerning the relations between governments and Indigenous peoples within their territories.[292] It can be hypothesized that these differences mainly concern the ways and degree to which the FPIC process is determined and controlled by Indigenous peoples.[293] Several commentators have suggested that CBD Parties can consider the two expressions as having essentially the same meaning in practice,[294] that is *effectively* empowering communities to genuinely *influence* decisions that affect their interests,[295] not merely a right to be *involved* in such processes.[296]

In effect, the dividing line between the general principle of international law on effective consultation and FPIC obligations is not clear-cut. The Inter-American Court emphasized the need for 'special and differentiated' consultation processes when the interests of Indigenous and tribal peoples may be affected,[297] with the public interest test set at a higher threshold because their physical and cultural survival is at stake.[298] In other words, FPIC goes beyond a more general right to consultation with the public, as a matter of *intensity* of the duty.[299] FPIC should arguably guarantee a 'distinguishable voice' for Indigenous and tribal peoples within a pluralistic and democratic society, with a view to supporting the realization of their right to decide their own development priorities.[300]

A key question regards the need to ensure that consent is given by the legitimate representatives of the peoples or communities concerned. International human rights materials emphasize the need to take into account Indigenous peoples' 'self-chosen and autonomously managed'[301] decision-making mechanisms.[302] Nevertheless, FPIC

[291] G Burton, 'Implementation of the Nagoya Protocol in JUSCANZ Countries: The Unlikely Lot' in Morgera et al. (eds), *The 2010 Nagoya Protocol on Access and Benefit-Sharing in Perspective: Implications for International Law and Implementation Challenges* (Martinus Nijhoff, 2013) 295, at 318–319.

[292] 'Joint submission Grand Council of the Crees (Eeyou Istchee)', 133–136, and comments by A Savaresi, 'The International Human Rights Law Implications of the Nagoya Protocol' in Morgera et al. (n. 291) 53, at 69; Special Rapporteur Anaya, A/67/301 (n. 204), paras 58–59.

[293] Special Rapporteur Anaya, A/HRC/24/41 (n. 209), paras 26–36.

[294] E.g. G Singh Nijar, *The Nagoya Protocol on Access and Benefit-sharing: An Analysis* (CEBLAW, 2011); and Special Rapporteur Anaya, HRC/A/67/301 (n. 204), paras 92 and 61, where the Special Rapporteur specifically expresses the 'hopeful expectation' that the provisions of the Nagoya Protocol will be implemented 'in harmony with' the UNDRIP.

[295] Doyle (n. 244), at 154; Thornberry (n. 59), at 349.

[296] UN Expert Mechanism on the Rights of Indigenous Peoples, Advice No. 2, Indigenous peoples and the right to participate in decision-making' (2011), para. 1 (emphasis added); Århén (n. 2), at 141.

[297] *Kichwa* (n. 10), paras 165–166.

[298] *Endorois* (n. 15), para. 212. Compare with K Gover, 'Settler-State Political Theory, 'CANZUS' and the UN Declaration on the Rights of Indigenous Peoples' (2015) 26 European Journal of International Law 345, at 372.

[299] See contra, the argument that the right to consultation is procedural, whereas FPIC as a core element of the internal aspect of the right to self-determination is substantive (the right to effectively determine the material outcome of a decision-making process): see Århén (n. 2), at 135–138. The present author is rather persuaded that procedural and substantive dimensions are intertwined in consultation as well as in FPIC, impact assessment, and benefit-sharing.

[300] In light of ILO Convention No. 169, Art. 7(1): A Fuentes, 'Judicial Interpretation and Indigenous Peoples' Rights to Lands, Participation and Consultation. The Inter-American Court of Human Rights' Approach' (2015) 23 International Journal of Minority and Group Rights 39, at 74–76 and 79.

[301] Doyle (n. 244), at 16.

[302] ibid, at 154; Thornberry (n. 59), at 349.

'does not necessarily require unanimity and may be achieved even when individuals or groups within the community explicitly disagree'.[303] Accordingly, States are responsible for ensuring the genuine involvement of legitimate representatives of Indigenous peoples and the authenticity of consent in the context of customary institutions, taking into account that consent may be withdrawn at a later stage.[304] It should be cautioned, however, that traditional authorities and customary guardians of Indigenous knowledge might not always be the same individuals within communities, and may have different recognition from State authorities.[305] These questions of representation are even more complex in the context of multi-level governance, where various national authorities are related to different national and international environmental governance institutions.[306]

Consensus guidance under the CBD has provided further insights on the 'prior' and 'free' components of FPIC as a *continual* process building mutually beneficial, *ongoing* arrangements[307] that should be free from 'expectations or timelines that are externally imposed'.[308] This formulation provides an additional layer of protection to the western notion of consent as merely devoid of more obvious forms of pressure, such as coercion and intimidation. In fact, this formulation benefitted from Indigenous representatives' inputs into intergovernmental negotiations.[309] In addition, this formulation elaborates on the characterization of FPIC as a 'constant process of dialogue' advanced in the Inter-American context,[310] and resonates with the description of benefit-sharing as an interactive process. Because of these shared procedural characteristics and the substantive connection between the objectives of FPIC and a culturally appropriate and endogenously identified benefit-sharing, the two should be seen as intertwined, rather than successive elements of human rights related to natural resources.[311]

With regard to the 'informed' dimension of FPIC, international human rights bodies have also clarified that FPIC should be based on an understanding of the full range of issues and implications entailed by the activity or decision in question. As discussed above, the relationship between FPIC and impact assessments has been explored by human rights bodies with a view to providing Indigenous peoples with 'full and objective information about all aspects of the project that will affect them, including the impact of the project on their lives and environment'.[312] As highlighted with regard to the interface between impact assessment and benefit-sharing, the assessment needs to focus not only on negative impacts but also on positive ones, which have been

303 UNGA Res 17/4 (2011), para. 11.

304 ibid.

305 P Mbhata, 'Unravelling the Perpetuated Marginalization of Customary Livelihoods on the Coast by Plural and Multi-level Conservation Governance Systems' (2022) 143 Marine Policy 105143.

306 ibid.

307 CBD, Mo'otz Kuxtal guidelines (n. 119), para. 6.

308 ibid, para. 14.

309 See generally E Morgera, 'Dawn of a New Day? The Evolving Relationship between the Convention on Biological Diversity and International Human Rights Law' (2018) 54 Wake Forest Law Review 691.

310 *Kaliña and Lokono* (n. 16), Joint Concurring Opinion of Judges Sierra Porto and Ferrer Mac-Gregor Poisot.

311 CBD Mo'otz Kuxtal Guidelines (n 119), para. 23(a) and 8.

312 See *Saramaka* (Merits) (n. 52), para. 134; and Fodella (n. 4), at 356 and 360.

identified by Indigenous peoples according to their worldviews. Thus, the interplay between impact assessments and benefit-sharing emerges as an essential precondition for FPIC, not just a means to prevent unwanted development, but also to ensure that Indigenous peoples 'shape developments by and for themselves',[313] providing 'the foundations for the emergence of a new resource governance model' premised on the notion of partnership.[314]

In addition, international law provides limited guidance on when the will of States should not prevail over that of Indigenous and tribal peoples in case of disagreement.[315] The question is therefore, how to reconcile with self-determination that applies to other sections of State populations with self-determination of Indigenous peoples,[316] neither of which is absolute.[317] This ultimately amounts to the right of Indigenous peoples to say 'no', taking in account other human rights that might affect the larger population. To some extent, this can be explained by the need to address these questions in a specific context. However, it has led to the problematic question of whether FPIC provides an absolute veto power to right-holding communities.[318] Several international human rights bodies have excluded that FPIC needs agreement by Indigenous peoples in all circumstances, although consultations should be carried out in good faith and in a form appropriate to the circumstances with the objective of achieving agreement.[319] Every effort is expected to be made to build consensus on the part of all concerned in reaching an agreement (including on benefit-sharing) that is seen as legitimate by the community,[320] in line with customary legal traditions.[321] Particular difficulties arise in situations where ownership over natural resources is not clarified in domestic frameworks, or when consultations with communities in this regard are inconclusive. In addition, further complexities arise in relation to the lack of recognition of customary laws of Indigenous Peoples and their collective rights ('a common interest which the group—rather than any specific individual—is entitled to claim').[322] ILO Convention No. 169 calls upon States to respect the 'special importance for the cultures and spiritual values of the peoples concerned of their relationship with the lands or territories, or both as applicable, which they occupy or otherwise

[313] Doyle (n. 244), at 131.

[314] See generally Doyle (ibid) and V Tauli-Corpuz, 'The Concept of Indigenous Peoples' Self-Determined Development or Development with Identity and Culture: Challenges and Trajectories' UN Doc CLT/CPD/CPO/2008/IPS/02 (2008).

[315] Århén (n. 2), at 225.

[316] Gilbert and Doyle (n. 12), at 313–315 and Tauli-Corpuz (n. 314).

[317] Århén (n. 2), at 138.

[318] UN Expert Mechanism, Access to justice in the promotion and protection of the rights of indigenous people, UN Doc A/HRC/24/50 (2013), para. 23. Gilbert and Doyle (n. 12), at 316; Thornberry (n. 59), at 217 and 349; Doyle (n. 244), at 98–99; and M Barelli, 'Development Projects and Indigenous Peoples' Land: Defining the Scope of Free, Prior and Informed Consent' in Lennox and Short (n. 20) 69, at 75.

[319] *Endorois* (n. 15), para. 289; Anaya A/HRC/12/34 (n. 209), para. 46. On the lack of a unified approach to FPIC at the international level, see Barelli (n. 318), at 75.

[320] Special Rapporteur Anaya, A/HRC/12/34 (n. 209), para. 53.

[321] Which are considered premised on principles of good faith, justice, friendship, and solidarity, as a notion that affirms and protects the rights of both parties and clarifies their duties towards one another: Doyle (n. 244), at 41.

[322] OHCHR, ' Frequently Asked Questions on a Human Rights-Based Approach to Development Cooperation;' (UN, 2016), available at https://www.ohchr.org/sites/default/files/Documents/Publications/FAQen.pdf, accessed 29 June 2023.

use, and in particular the *collective* aspects of this relationship'.[323] The UNDRIP emphasizes that Indigenous Peoples' collective rights to live in freedom, peace, and security are vital to their existence, well-being, and integral development as distinct peoples.[324] It also indicates that all infringements of collective rights should be met with appropriate access to justice and effective remedies, giving due consideration to the customs, traditions, rules, and legal systems of the Indigenous peoples concerned and international human rights.[325] The Declaration is notable for clarifying that collective rights extend to lands and natural resources according to customary laws.[326] Its Preamble emphasizes that collective rights are 'indispensable for the existence, well-being and integral development as peoples' of Indigenous peoples.[327]

Despite their recognition in international law over the last twenty years, the recognition and protection of collective rights still faces many challenges, and international law does not provide sufficiently clear guidance to States on how to address them.[328] The recognition of Indigenous peoples' collective rights relies on the recognition of Indigenous peoples as distinctive human rights-holders at the national level in a way that is aligned with international law requirements and corresponds to the self-identification and self-determination of Indigenous peoples in specific national and sub-national contexts.[329] However, there may be national legal instruments recognizing collective rights of Indigenous peoples in indirect or implicit ways, which makes the assessment of whether such recognition is actually present, albeit partial, more complicated, particularly in the absence of reliable data on implementation and the effects of legislation in practice. Most notably, there are several instances in which collective rights are recognized, but not specifically as human rights of Indigenous peoples: rather, they may be recognized as collective rights of various communities and groups, including but not limited to Indigenous peoples.

On the basis of the interface between impact assessment, FPIC, and benefit-sharing in relation to Indigenous peoples' rights to natural resources, it is argued here that Indigenous and tribal peoples should be legitimately entitled to say 'no' to proposed extractive operations or the creation of protected areas in the following circumstances. First, if the proposed activity is likely to affect traditionally owned or used resources, or has the potential to negatively impact on traditionally used resources threatening the community's cultural and physical survival.[330] Second, if an early, genuine, and culturally appropriate identification and discussion of benefits according to Indigenous peoples' worldviews, customary laws, and collective rights has not been undertaken at all; or has not had any impact on the final outcome, in the absence of sufficient reasons to justify such an outcome. Without early and genuine discussion of benefit-sharing, the State would not be able to prove that the decision is 'consistent with the full range

[323] Art. 13(1) (emphasis added).
[324] UNDRIP, Preamble and Art. 1.
[325] UNDRIP, Art. 40.
[326] Gilbert and Doyle (n. 12), at 297.
[327] J Eichler, *Reconciling Indigenous Peoples' Individual* and *Collective Rights Participation, Prior Consultation* and *Self-Determination* in *Latin America* (Routledge, 2019), at 72–73.
[328] ibid.
[329] ibid, at 92.
[330] ibid, at 8. See also International Law Association (ILA), Report on the Rights of Indigenous Peoples (2010).

of applicable international norms',[331] when Indigenous peoples' culture, society, and way of life are at stake.[332]

5.5 Benefit-Sharing and Compensation

As discussed above, under the CBD benefit-sharing has been interpreted as a *reward* and *incentive* for the good management practices of Indigenous peoples that are responsible for the production and sustainable management of ecosystem functions.[333] Occasional references to Indigenous peoples' ecosystem stewardship can also be found in international human rights law materials.[334] Principally, however, under international human rights law, benefit-sharing has been conceptualized as a form of *compensation*.[335] This may be a consequence of the emphasis on damage prevention and control in impact assessments, and on financial payments in benefit-sharing agreements. Nevertheless, the Inter-American Court's reliance on benefit-sharing has been considered 'promising' in increasingly focusing on Indigenous peoples' preferences, being deployed in accordance with their modes of governance, and empowering victims, while being more efficient and less expensive in its non-monetary form.[336] This section discusses how a fully-fledged mutually supportive interpretation may serve to clarify that fair and equitable benefit-sharing from the use of Indigenous peoples' territories and natural resources differs from reparations from a legal perspective, despite any overlap in practice in supporting the realization of communities' worldviews. It also highlights practical difficulties in implementation.

There has not been jurisprudential clarification of the distinction between benefit-sharing and compensation as yet. The Inter-American Court explained the emergence of benefit-sharing as 'inherent to the right of compensation'[337] for the 'deprivation of the regular use of the enjoyment' of traditionally owned natural resources.[338] The African Commission adopted the same reasoning.[339] UN Special Rapporteur James Anaya stated that the duty to share benefits is '*independent of compensation measures*', although it 'responds *in part to the concept of fair compensation* for deprivation or limitation of the rights of the communities concerned, in particular their right of communal ownership of lands, territories and natural resources'.[340] The point

[331] J Anaya, *Indigenous Peoples in International Law* (Oxford University Press, 2004), at 155.

[332] Århén (n. 2), at 139.

[333] CBD, Principles of the ecosystem approach (n. 123), Operational Guidance 2, para. 9; CBD refinement and elaboration of the ecosystem approach (n. 202), para. 12.5.

[334] *Saramaka* (Merits) (n. 52), para. 144; *Endorois* (n. 15), paras 235 and 249; and *Kaliña and Lokono* (n. 16), paras 35–36.

[335] *Saramaka* (Merits) (n. 52), paras 138–140; *Kaliña and Lokono* (n. 16), para. 227; *Endorois* (n. 15), paras 298–299 and 295. J Pasqualucci, 'International Indigenous Land Rights: A Critique of the Jurisprudence of the Inter-American Court of Human Rights in Light of the United Nations Declaration on the Rights of Indigenous Peoples' (2009) 27 Wisconsin Journal of International Law 51, at 92.

[336] Gomez (n. 13), at 147–148.

[337] Inter-American Convention on Human Rights, Art. 21(2).

[338] *Saramaka* (Merits) (n. 52), paras 13 and 140; see also paras 143, 153, and 156 making reference to reasonable share of benefits.

[339] *Endorois* (n. 15), para. 295.

[340] Special Rapporteur Anaya, A/HRC/15/37 (n. 46), paras 67, 89, and 91; and A/HRC/24/41 (n. 209), para. 76 (emphasis added).

became even more unclear in a subsequent report. Anaya noted that 'direct financial benefits—beyond incidental benefits like jobs or corporate charity—should accrue to Indigenous peoples because of the *compensation* that is due to them for allowing access to their territories, for giving up alternatives for the future development of their territories, for suffering any adverse effects', as well as for the 'significant social capital they contribute under the totality of historical and contemporary circumstances'.[341] As discussed above, these elements are unlikely to be captured in impact assessments, but could be more systematically addressed in strategic environmental assessments.

The practice of the Inter-American Court also points to some overlap in terms of aims of compensation and benefit-sharing. Reparations for material and immaterial *damage* (with the former including environmental damage affecting Indigenous peoples' subsistence and spiritual connection with their territory)[342] may take the form of community development funds (as a form of collective reparation). These funds aim at contributing to enhancing the protection and development of Indigenous peoples' cultural identity and guaranteeing the control of their territories. They are further expected to contribute to Indigenous peoples' development in alignment with their life plans and to their present and future needs, or enhancing the social and economic condition of the community, including in terms of increasing the productivity of natural resources or restoring degraded ecosystems.[343] Community development funds can also be a form of benefit-sharing. Nevertheless, Anaya seems to suggest that benefit-sharing may make up for *broader, historical inequities* that have determined the situation in which the specific material and immaterial damage has arisen.[344] These observations may support an argument whereby benefit-sharing is understood as a proactive tool for the full realization of human rights connected to natural resources in light of Indigenous peoples' worldviews. Benefit-sharing can thus, arguably, be distinguished from compensation as it aims to provide gains beyond loss of control over resources and opportunities for income generation.[345] Benefit-sharing combines *new* opportunities of income generation and *continued*, or possibly enhanced or restored, control over the use of the lands and resources affected by the development,[346] in line with the argument regarding support- and control-benefits outlined earlier.

[341] Special Rapporteur Anaya, A/HRC/24/41 (n. 209), para. 76.

[342] Orellana (n. 232), at 845 and 847.

[343] *Saramaka* (Merits) (n. 52), paras 201–202; *Garífuna de Punta Piedra* (n. 221), paras 316 and 333; *Kaliña and Lokono* (n. 16), para. 272; IACtHR, *Comunidad Garífuna Triunfo de la Cruz y Sus Miembros vs Honduras* (Merits, Reparations and Costs), 8 October 2015, para. 296 and concurrent opinion of Judge Humberto Antonio Sierra Porto, para. 26. Note also the inclusion of benefit-sharing among forms of compensation in T Ankowiak, 'A Dark Side of Virtue: The Inter-American Court and Reparations for Indigenous Peoples' (2014) 25 Duke Journal of Comparative and International Law 1, at 5.

[344] Special Rapporteur Anaya, A/HRC/24/41 (n. 209), para. 76. Other bodies have not elaborated on the point: UNPFII (n. 78), para. 27; Ecuador (2001) ILO Doc GB.282/14/2, para. 44(c)(3), and Bolivia (1999) ILO Doc GB.272/8/1: GB.274/16/7 (1999), para. 40.

[345] F Lenzerini, 'Reparations for Indigenous Peoples in International and Comparative Law: An Introduction' in Lenzerini (n. 3) 3, at 13–14. See also D Shelton, 'Reparations for Indigenous Peoples: The Present Value of Past Wrongs' in Lenzerini (n. 3) 47, at 60–61 and 66–69.

[346] Morgera (n. 6), on the basis of Special Rapporteur Anaya, A/HRC/21/47 (n. 24), paras 68, 74, and 76 and A/HRC/24/41 (n. 209), para. 75.

Another argument discussed in the Inter-American context can, notwithstanding a certain teleological overlap,[347] serve as a foundation for distinguishing compensation from benefit-sharing. As the Inter-American Court asserted, the creation of a community development fund as compensation for material and immaterial damage is 'additional to any other benefit present and future that communities are owed in relation to the general obligations of development of the State'.[348] The Inter-American Court contrasted the secondary obligation of compensation, deriving from and commensurate to a violation of human rights, and the State's general obligations to realize Indigenous peoples' right to the protection of the environment, the productivity of their territories and natural resources,[349] and the enhancement of their quality of life.[350] It is argued here that a similar distinction can apply to fair and equitable benefit-sharing as an inherent component of certain human rights: it is therefore part of a *general and permanent obligation* to protect and realize human rights connected to natural resources, which is *independent* of any violation of these rights and related compensation.[351] Distinguishing benefit-sharing from compensation for material and immaterial damage[352] could thus detach the former from the need to establish a causal nexus between an ascertained human rights violation, and a damage arising from the violation.[353] This is particularly significant in light of the Inter-American Court's tendency to mitigate a State's financial burden in cases concerning Indigenous peoples, and its inadequate account of the difficulties of Indigenous and tribal peoples to document environmental and cultural harm.[354]

Admittedly, the Court's remarks about 'any other benefit present and future that communities are owed in relation to the general obligations of development of the State' may also refer to the State's obligations to realize the generally applicable civil and political, as well as economic, social, and cultural rights of the population at large. This raises the issue of distinguishing benefit-sharing as an inherent component of human rights connected to natural resources from the State's overall duty to uphold general human rights, which is hard to do in practice. In effect, it has been empirically observed that 'communities are losing out on any additional benefits that may otherwise have been provided through benefit-sharing'[355] when the State has not delivered basic

[347] See the discussion on the potential for reparations to aim at restorative justice and be forward-looking (and controversy around that notion) in Shelton (n. 345), at 72. See also Gomez (n. 13), at 147–148.

[348] *Garífuna Triunfo de la Cruz* (n. 343), para. 295; *Garífuna de Punta Piedra* (n. 221), 332; *Kaliña and Lokono* (n. 16), para. 295.

[349] In light of UNDRIP, Art 29(1): *Garífuna de Punta Piedra* (n. 221), para. 333. Note, however, that the distinction between primary duties to fulfil general human rights and the secondary duty to provide reparation for violations of Indigenous and tribal peoples' rights connected to natural resources has not yet been fully established: Gomez (n. 13), at 149.

[350] Such as ILO Convention No. 169, Art 2.2.b: 'promoting the full realization of the social, economic and cultural rights of these peoples with respect for their social and cultural identity, their customs and traditions and their institutions': *Garífuna Triunfo de la Cruz* (n. 343), concurrent opinion of Judge Humberto Antonio Sierra Porto, paras 30–31.

[351] This interpretation appears to be supported by ILA (n. 330), at 42–43 with regard to UNDRIP, Art. 32(2) and opportunities offered by Indigenous lands to develop economic projects.

[352] Orellana (n. 232), at 845 and 847.

[353] And generally 'restricts damage to provable, proximate losses to avoid excessive recovery', although it includes some flexibility in the name of proportionality and equity: Shelton (n. 345), at 60.

[354] Ankowiak (n. 343), at 5.

[355] R Wynberg and M. Hauck (eds), *Sharing Benefits from the Coast: Rights, Resources and Livelihoods* (UCT Press, 2014) 158.

services to these Indigenous peoples. For instance, when a community consented to laying fibre optics in its traditional territory, it obtained as benefit-sharing the overdue issuance of IDs for its members, and free internet for the community school, but not for all community households. In other words, private developers used their knowledge of communities' needs to their advantage in benefit-sharing negotiations.[356] This example serves to reiterate the importance of thinking strategically about the interface of benefit-sharing with assessments and FPIC, as prior assessments could scope more broadly and proactively possible benefits in accordance with Indigenous peoples' worldviews. It also reinforces the argument made earlier regarding the importance of strategic environmental assessments to factor in historical and systemic issues that affect the understanding of benefits beyond decisions made solely at the level of individual projects. Issues of contextual justice, therefore, need to be researched, before engaging with questions of distributive justice through benefit-sharing.

6. Moving from Safeguarding to Fully Realizing Indigenous Peoples' Human Rights through Benefit-Sharing

At present, the emergence of fair and equitable benefit-sharing obligations in relation to the rights of Indigenous and tribal peoples over territories and natural resources is largely supported by authoritative interpretations, rather than unequivocal treaty provisions. In addition, the evolutionary interpretation of international human rights law is not yet firmly based on systematic and coherent reliance on international biodiversity law. Even after the clarifications provided by the UN Framework Principles on Human Rights and the Environment, there remains significant scope for scholars to assess the level of State support, particularly where key interpretative questions may not have been clearly and coherently addressed in universal, regional, and domestic processes. Nevertheless, as Special Rapporteur John Knox argued, at the very least growing 'coherence in the interpretation by binding human rights tribunals and authoritative human rights bodies' crystallizes 'best practices' that serve to 'facilitate the implementation' of existing international obligations.[357] This provides 'strong evidence of the converging trends towards greater uniformity and certainty in the understanding'.[358]

Within international biodiversity law, the legal nature of relevant CBD provisions has been openly contested.[359] In addition, the qualifications in the CBD guidance represent disagreement among CBD Parties as to whether certain interpretations are

[356] Marchegiani, Morgera, and Parks (n. 243), at 233.

[357] Knox, Framework Principles (n. 9), paras 7–8.

[358] To use the terminology employed by Knox (ibid), paras 7–9. See generally, C Buckley, A Donald, and P Leach (eds), *Towards Convergence in International Human Rights Law: Approaches of Regional and International Systems* (Brill, 2016).

[359] See generally S Harrop and D Pritchard, 'A Hard Instrument Goes Soft: The Implications of the Convention on Biological Diversity's Current Trajectory' (2011) 21 Global Environmental Change 474; and *Construction of a Road in Costa Rica Along the San Juan River (Nicaragua v. Costa Rica)* (*Road Case*) (Judgment) 16 December 2015, para. 164, which focused on CBD, Art. 14 on environmental assessments that has provided the basis for interpretative developments related to benefit-sharing in international biodiversity and human rights law, as discussed above.

reflecting existing or emerging international law, based also on the fact that each individual Party to the CBD may not have formally accepted the same underlying international human rights norms. This area of disagreement is confirmed in the wording of the 2022 Global Biodiversity Framework, where reference to 'human rights' as such is missing. Instead, CBD Parties have committed to ensuring that 'any sustainable use, where appropriate in [protected] areas, is fully consistent with conservation outcomes, recognizing and respecting the *rights of [I]ndigenous peoples and local communities, including over their traditional territories*'.[360]

At the very least, guidance adopted as consensus decisions under the CBD should also be considered a crystallization of 'best practices' that serve to 'facilitate the implementation' of existing international obligations. It thus becomes increasingly difficult for a State to defend an approach that goes against an internationally recognized best practice, particularly when it has actively engaged in intergovernmental negotiations and eventually consented to the distillation of these best practices.[361] Against this backdrop, a mutually supportive interpretation of international human rights and biodiversity law may support an original reflection on the legal status of an international benefit-sharing obligation at the intersection of these two areas. This section aims to shed new light on this matter by reflecting on the legal bases for benefit-sharing in international human rights law and the interplay of benefit-sharing with consent and impact assessment.

Benefit-sharing obligations have been associated with a variety of inter-linked human rights, such as Indigenous peoples' right to freely dispose of their natural resources.[362] This right is connected to their right to freely determine and enjoy their own social, cultural, and economic development, as well as the right to enjoy their way of life, which is closely associated with the use of resources[363] upon which their cultural identity depends.[364] The Inter-American Court substantiated these rights on the basis of its well-known evolutive understanding of the right to property,[365] in connection with the right to self-determination under common Article 1 of the two Covenants,[366] and the right to culture under Article 27 of the International Covenant on Civil and Political Rights.[367] For its part, the African Commission focused, in addressing benefit-sharing, on the right to development, which is explicitly provided for under the African Charter, but it argued that its interpretation also built on the Inter-American Court

[360] CBD Decision XV/4 (2022), para. 6.

[361] Morgera (n. 309), at 119.

[362] *Comunidad Garífuna Triunfo de la Cruz* (n. 343), para. 167. This interpretation is now enshrined in American Declaration on the Rights of Indigenous Peoples (2016), Art XXIX. See also *Endorois* (n. 15), paras 120–124.

[363] *Saramaka* (Merits) (n. 52), paras 93–95 on the basis also of Inter-American Convention, Art. 29(b). Reiterated in *Kaliña and Lokono* (n. 16), para. 124. For a succinct discussion of previous case law, see, e.g., Århén (n. 2), at 93.

[364] *Kaliña and Lokono* (n. 16), paras 181 and 193.

[365] American Convention on Human Rights (adopted 22 November 1969, in force 18 July 1978), Art. 21. *Saramaka* (Merits) (n. 52), paras 115 and 120; based on IACtHR, *Case of the Mayagna (Sumo) Awas Tingni Community v. Nicaragua*, Judgment (31 August 2001).

[366] See generally Anaya (n. 331), at 104–106 and 129–131; and Århén (n. 2).

[367] HRC, *Lubicon Lake Band v. Canada*, Comm No 167/1984 (26 March 1990) UN Doc Supp No 40 (A/45/40) and *Ángela Poma Poma v. Peru* (n. 90). This approach has been confirmed by the ICJ, *Navigational and Related Rights (Nicaragua v. Costa Rica)* (Judgment) 13 July 2009, ICJ Reports 213.

and CERD jurisprudence.[368] In effect, successive Inter-American Court cases following the Saramaka jurisprudence, have elaborated upon the notion of development as part of the need to ensure the physical and cultural survival of Indigenous peoples by protecting their right to natural resources.[369] In addition, the Inter-American Court equated explicit mechanisms that guarantee effective benefit-sharing with political rights.[370] Overall, benefit-sharing has emerged as part of an evolving understanding of 'overlapping and multi-layered international human rights grounded on the centrality of natural resources for the identity and recognition of Indigenous and tribal peoples'.[371]

As Special Rapporteur James Anaya indicated, benefit-sharing is thus not a new human right, but rather it is connected to existing rights,[372] in accordance with the argument that benefit-sharing is implicit in Indigenous peoples' human rights to natural resources under the UNDRIP, mentioned earlier. This view pre-empts the need to prove the emergence of new international obligations beyond those that have already been identified under several global and regional human rights treaties. The idea that benefit-sharing is an inherent component of existing human rights connected to natural resources, furthermore, allows a shift away from considering benefit-sharing as a mere safeguard, only coming into play for the protection of rights (in other words, a defensive tool). Instead, it supports the view that benefit-sharing also has the potential to support the realization of these rights (serving as a proactive tool).

7. Conclusions

Fair and equitable benefit-sharing has gradually emerged as an inherent component of Indigenous peoples' human rights connected to traditional territories and natural resources in its interplay with impact assessment and FPIC. This represents a growing area of cross-fertilization between international human rights and biodiversity law, even if the latter has avoided human rights language until 2022. While benefit-sharing is incompletely theorized under each area of international law, this analysis has pointed to further opportunities for a fully-fledged mutually supportive interpretation of benefit-sharing. Human rights standards can help identify the minimum content of States' benefit-sharing obligations, notably in relation to necessary procedural guarantees that tend to remain unspecified in international biodiversity law. This is a significant contribution in limiting State discretion in the choice of

[368] *Endorois* (n. 15), paras 294 and 296. As to the former, the African Commission presumably referred to *Saramaka* (Merits) (n. 52), paras 93–95, and *Saramaka* (Interpretation) (n. 91), para. 46. CERD, General Recommendation No. 23: Indigenous Peoples, UN Doc A/52/18 (1997), Annex V, para. 4; CERD, Concluding Observations on Ecuador, UN Doc A/58/18 (2003), para. 62.

[369] *Comunidad Garífuna Triunfo de la Cruz* (n. 343), para. 102; *Comunidad Garífuna de Punta Piedra* (n. 221), para. 167.

[370] *Kaliña and Lokono* (n. 16), para. 197, relying on CBD art 14 and Rio Principle 17.

[371] G Pentassuglia, 'Ethnocultural Diversity and Human Rights: Legal Categories, Claims, and the Hybridity of Group Protection' (2015) 6 Yearbook of Polar Law, 251, at 293, 276–277, 294, and 317; *Saramaka* (Merits) (n. 52), paras 25–27; *Endorois* (n. 15) para. 151; *Ogiek* (n. 68), para. 191.

[372] At the beginning of his mandate, UN Special Rapporteur on Indigenous Peoples' Rights James Anaya hypothesized that benefit-sharing could be a right in itself: A/HRC/15/37 (n. 46), paras 67 and 76–78, but his more definitive argument focused on benefit-sharing as a safeguard ancillary to existing rights: A/HRC/21/47 (n. 24), paras 52 and 62.

means of implementation under the CBD and enhancing justiciability. In addition, understanding benefit-sharing as an inherent component of specific international human rights helps illuminate its substantive content and status in international law. International biodiversity law, in turn, provides specific guidelines on how to implement human rights standards within the complex landscape of environmental regulations, thereby emphasizing the potentially proactive purpose of impact assessments, FPIC, and benefit-sharing to support the full realization of Indigenous peoples' rights, rather than just their protection.

Exploring the full potential for a mutually supportive interpretation has led to a series of further normative arguments to advance the theorization of inter-State benefit-sharing. First, benefit-sharing has both a procedural dimension (Indigenous peoples' agency in the context of a concerned and iterative dialogue aimed at understanding and accommodating different worldviews) and a substantive one (the enhancement of Indigenous peoples' choice and capabilities). To realize the latter, both benefits protecting or enhancing Indigenous peoples' *control* over natural resources, and benefits providing *support* for the exercise of effective control are needed. Second, the interplay between benefit-sharing, impact assessment, and FPIC highlights opportunities to move away from a technocratic, damage-control approach to natural resource development. It opens the way towards shifting to collaboratively identifying and understanding opportunities for positive impacts according to Indigenous peoples' worldviews, in addition to potential negative impacts. This necessitates reconsidering both the scope and methodological approach of existing impact assessments at the national level. In addition, the consideration of alternatives and justification of the final outcome need to evidence how assessments differed from merely providing a predetermined set of development options to Indigenous peoples. Different dimensions of justice could therefore be taken into account through this interpretation: distribution, participation, recognition, capabilities, and context.

With regard to FPIC, the interplay with benefit-sharing serves to identify circumstances under which Indigenous peoples would be legitimately entitled to say 'no' to proposed extractive operations or the creation of protected areas affecting their territories and traditionally owned or used resources, or having the potential to negatively impact on traditionally used resources threatening the Indigenous peoples' cultural and physical survival. Such circumstances include the lack of an early, genuine, and culturally appropriate identification and discussion of benefits according to Indigenous peoples' worldviews; or the lack of any impact for Indigenous peoples on the final outcome of benefit-sharing discussions, without sufficient reasons to justify such an outcome.

Furthermore, benefit-sharing should be distinguished from compensation, as the latter represents a secondary obligation deriving from and commensurate to a violation of the right to natural resources. On the other hand, benefit-sharing should be seen as an integral component of the *general and permanent obligation* that is *independent* of any violation of their rights and related compensation. These considerations also have implications for business due diligence to respect natural resource-related human rights and for States' obligations to ensure business due diligence through domestic law-making, enforcement, and access to justice, including oversight of contractual and international investment agreements (as discussed in Chapter 5).

4
Intra-State and Transnational Benefit-Sharing with Local Knowledge Holders

1. Introduction

This chapter will continue to clarify State obligations to fairly and equitably share benefits with certain sectors of society beyond Indigenous peoples. It will thus reflect on the outer limits of the concept of beneficiaries of intra-State benefit-sharing, analysing the reference to local communities under the Convention on Biological Diversity (CBD),[1] farmers under the International Plant Treaty,[2] legitimate tenure right holders and small-scale fishing communities under voluntary guidelines adopted by the Committee on Food Security,[3] and peasants under a UN Declaration adopted in 2019.[4] This chapter will also reflect on international legal materials on intra-community benefit-sharing, focusing on women's human rights.

On the whole, intra-State benefit-sharing with non-Indigenous communities and intra-community benefit-sharing are the most incompletely theorized manifestations in international law. These international law developments closely follow the safeguards for the protection of Indigenous peoples' human rights discussed in Chapter 3, with a view to supporting a similar partnership model across different worldviews. It remains a matter of debate whether the developments related to Indigenous peoples' human rights are an apt and appropriate basis to further theorize intra-State and intra-community benefit-sharing.

This chapter will also discuss transnational dimensions of benefit-sharing related to the traditional knowledge of Indigenous peoples and local communities, focusing on the interface of inter- and intra-State benefit-sharing obligations under regimes on access to genetic resources and in the context of scientific cooperation, information sharing, and technology (already discussed in Chapters 1 and 2 exclusively from an inter-State benefit-sharing perspective). Following an assessment of the progressive development of international law in these areas, the chapter will reflect on potential paths for further development on the basis

[1] Convention on Biological Diversity (CBD) (Rio de Janeiro, 5 June 1992, in force 29 December 1993).

[2] International Treaty on Plant Genetic Resources for Food and Agriculture (ITPGRFA) (Rome, 3 November 2001, in force 29 June 2004).

[3] Voluntary Guidelines on the Responsible Governance of Tenure of Land, Fisheries and Forests in the Context of National Food Security (VGGT Guidelines) UN Doc CL 144/9 (C 2013/20) (2012), Appendix D; and Voluntary Guidelines for Securing Sustainable Small-scale fisheries in the context of food security and poverty eradication (SSF Guidelines) (adopted at the 31st Session of the Committee on Fisheries, 9–13 June 2014), at 18.

[4] UN Human Rights Council, 'United Nations Declaration on the Rights of Peasants and Other People Working in Rural Areas', Res 39/12 (2018) (adopted by thirty-three votes to three—Australia, Hungary, and the UK; eleven abstentions); and UNGA Res 73/165 (2019) (hereinafter, UNDROP or 'the Declaration').

Fair and Equitable Benefit-Sharing in International Law. Elisa Morgera, Oxford University Press. © Elisa Morgera 2024.
DOI: 10.1093/oso/9780198862130.003.0005

of a mutually supportive interpretation with procedural human rights, natural resource-related substantive rights, and the human right to science.

All these phenomena of fair and equitable benefit-sharing are particularly relevant from an environmental justice perspective of recognition—recognition of different categories of beneficiaries and recognition of different knowledge systems grounded in socio-economic diversity and ecosystem stewardship. On the back of recognition, other dimensions of justice become prominent, including distribution, participation, and capabilities: discrimination and prejudice against these beneficiaries translates into their exclusion from environmental decision-making processes that have an impact on their human rights to livelihoods, food, and culture, and misses out on the opportunity to integrate their contributions to sustainable development to the benefit of everyone's human right to a healthy environment.

2. Intra-State Benefit-Sharing: Local Communities, Peasants, and Small-Scale Fishers

The following subsections will analyse references to intra-State benefit-sharing in treaty language and soft law with regard to other sectors of society beyond Indigenous peoples.[5] They will focus on the varying terminology and interpretative uncertainties in international environmental law and international human rights law on the beneficiaries of international benefit-sharing obligations, and indicate where more clarity has been reached on relevant State obligations.

2.1 Beneficiaries and Justice Dimensions

Under the CBD, local communities are arguably singled out because of their ecosystem stewardship,[6] which hinges on the intrinsic connection between these communities' knowledge and the natural resources they traditionally own, occupy, and/or use—in other words, the development and transmission of traditional knowledge *through* the management of traditionally used natural resources.[7] Such knowledge

[5] e.g. CBD, Art. 8(j) and 10(c); UN Special Rapporteur De Schutter, Interim Report, UN Doc A/67/268 (2012), para. 39; UN-REDD Programme, 'Guidelines on Free, Prior and Informed Consent' (2013), at 11–12; and Roundtable on Sustainable Biofuels, Principles and Criteria (2012): see E Morgera, E Tsioumani, and M Buck, *Unraveling the Nagoya Protocol: Commentary on the Protocol on Access and Benefit-sharing to the Convention on Biological Diversity* (Brill, 2014), at 40; and L Cotula and K Tienhaara, 'Reconfiguring Investment Contracts to Promote Sustainable Development' (2013) 2011–2012 Yearbook of International Law on Investment and Policy 281, at 301 and 303.

[6] Principles of the Ecosystem Approach, CBD Decision V/6 (2000), para. 9, and CBD Decision VII/11 (2004), Annex I, annotations to rationale to Principle 4. See the discussion in E Morgera, 'Ecosystem and Precautionary Approach' in E Morgera and J Razzaque (eds), *Encyclopedia of Environmental Law: Biodiversity and Nature Protection Law* (Edward Elgar, 2017) 70.

[7] In the light of the placement of CBD, Art. 8(j) in the context of *in situ conservation* (CBD, Art. 8). J Gibson, 'Community Rights to Culture: The UN Declaration on the Rights of Indigenous Peoples' in S Allen and A Xanthaki (eds), *Reflections on the UN Declaration on the Rights of Indigenous Peoples* (Hart, 2011) 434, at 434.

is thus embodied in *traditional lifestyles*[8] that are inextricably linked to natural resources, shared cultural identity, and customary rules.[9] These are the same bases on which Indigenous peoples are addressed under the CBD,[10] as discussed in Chapter 3. The distinction remains controversial, notwithstanding a specific international process to shed light on it.

In 2010, CBD Parties identified the need to better characterize local communities and convened an expert group of local community representatives to identify their common characteristics, to better distinguish them from Indigenous peoples.[11] In the resulting decision, CBD Parties were encouraged to consider the expert group's report as a 'potentially useful input to promoting full and effective participation by local communities in the work of the Convention'.[12] The decision also acknowledged the characteristics of local communities, which were listed in the report as potentially useful guidance within the mandate of the Convention.[13] The list included the following characteristics that can be considered shared with or comparable to those of Indigenous peoples discussed in Chapter 3:

- self-identification;
- lifestyles linked to traditions associated with natural cycles (symbiotic relationships or dependence), the use of and dependence on biological resources and linked to the sustainable use of nature and biodiversity;
- occupation of a definable territory traditionally occupied and/or used, permanently or periodically, which is important for the maintenance of social, cultural, and economic aspects of the community;
- traditions (often referring to common history, culture, language, rituals, symbols, and customs) that are dynamic and may evolve;
- social cohesion and willingness to be represented as a local community;
- traditional knowledge transmitted across generations, including orally;
- technology, knowledge, innovations, and practices associated with the sustainable use and conservation of biological resources;
- performance and maintenance of economic activities traditionally, including for subsistence, sustainable development, and/or survival;
- bio-cultural heritage;
- spiritual and cultural values of biodiversity and territories;
- culture, including traditional cultural expressions captured through local languages, common interest, and values;
- incorporation of biodiversity into traditional place names;

[8] On the basis of the wording of CBD, Art. 8(j): see the definition of traditional knowledge in Akwé: Kon Guidelines, CBD Decision VII/16C (2004), Annex.

[9] See generally B Tobin, *Indigenous Peoples, Customary Law and Human Rights: Why Living Law Matters* (Routledge, 2014).

[10] P Thornberry, *Indigenous Peoples and Human Rights* (Manchester University Press, 2002), at 334 and 353.

[11] CBD Decision X/43 (2010), Multi-Year Programme of Work on the Implementation of Article 8(j) and Related Provisions of the Convention on Biological Diversity, para. 21.

[12] CBD Decision XI/14 B (2021), para. 18.

[13] ibid, para. 19.

- foods and food preparation systems and traditional medicines that are closely connected to biodiversity;
- practice of traditional occupations and livelihoods;
- extended family, clan, or tribal structures.[14]

Some of the characteristics relate more explicitly to customary laws, notably:

- self-regulation through a set of social rules (e.g. that regulate land conflicts/sharing of benefits) and own traditional forms of organization and institutions;
- expression of customary and/or collective rights;
- shared common property over land and natural resources; and
- traditional right holders to natural resources.[15]

And some characteristics relate to the relationship of these communities with broader society and policy processes:

- little or no prior contact with other sectors of society resulting in distinctness or desire to remain distinct;
- marginalization from modern geopolitical systems and structures; and
- vulnerability to outsiders and little concept of intellectual property rights (IPRs).[16]

It remains difficult, in principle and in practice, to distinguish local communities from Indigenous peoples on the basis of these characteristics. The Post-2020 Global Biodiversity Framework reiterates previously agreed language for both categories under the CBD on: the full and effective participation and effective contributions, at all levels of government, for local communities;[17] and respect and full effect for the rights of local communities in the implementation of the Framework, including customary uses.[18] In addition, the Global Biodiversity Framework underscores the important roles and contributions of local communities as custodians of biodiversity and as partners in its conservation, restoration, and sustainable use; and respect and documentation of their knowledge associated with biodiversity, innovations, worldviews, values, and practices with their free, prior, and informed consent (FPIC).[19] FPIC was discussed as the central safeguard for Indigenous Peoples' human rights in Chapter 3. Not only does it remain subject to different interpretations and acceptance as an international standard by different CBD Parties with regard to Indigenous peoples, but it

[14] Report of the Expert Group Meeting of Local Community Representatives within the Context of Article 8(j) and Related Provisions of the Convention on Biological Diversity, UN Doc UNEP/CBD/WG8J/7/8/Add.1 (2011).

[15] ibid.

[16] ibid.

[17] CBD Decision XV/4 (2022), para. 4 and Targets 19(f) and 21.

[18] ibid, para. 6 and Targets 1, 3, 5, 9, and 22.

[19] ibid, paras 7(a) and 22(a), and Goal C. Note ibid, fn 7, which reads: 'In this framework, free, prior and informed consent refers to the tripartite terminology of "prior and informed consent" or "free, prior and informed consent" or "approval and involvement".'

also remains controversial whether the same or a comparable standard applies to non-Indigenous communities.

Under the International Plant Treaty, reference is made to farmers' rights with regard to the protection of their traditional knowledge, the right to equitably participate in sharing benefits arising from the utilization of plant genetic resources for food and agriculture, and the right to participate in decision-making at the national level on related matters.[20] Elsa Tsioumani clarified that the emergence of farmers' rights can be understood as 'a reaction to the asymmetry between farmers as donors of germplasm in the form of traditional seeds and the producers of commercial varieties that ultimately rely on such germplasm'.[21] This is due to three factors: the lack of a 'system of compensation, reward or incentive' for farmers; the need for protection against the restrictions in use associated with IPRs that would adversely affect farmers' practices; and the need for support for farmers to 'continue ... in their contribution to the conservation and development of agricultural biodiversity and food security globally' 'as a crucial tool for conservation'.[22]

Other international soft-law instruments appear to have expanded the meaning of beneficiaries to include 'tenure right holders' (i.e. those having a formal or informal right to access land and other natural resources for the realization of their human right to an adequate standard of living and well-being).[23] The 2012 UN Voluntary Guidelines on the Responsible Governance of Tenure of Land, Fisheries and Forests in the Context of National Food Security (VGGT)[24] call for States to ensure responsible governance of tenure because land, fisheries, and forests are central for the realization of human rights.[25] The VGGT call for the recognition and respect of all legitimate tenure rights, referring to both Indigenous and other communities with customary tenure systems, including vulnerable groups, and women's rights. They apply to the governance of 'all forms of tenure, including public, private, communal, *collective*, indigenous and customary'.[26] They further note that where 'there are publicly-owned land, fisheries and forests that are *collectively* used and managed (in some national contexts referred to as *commons*), States should, where applicable, recognize and protect such lands, resources and their related systems of collective use and management, including in processes of allocation by the State'.[27] Considerations of tenure have also been linked to the notion of local communities under the CBD. The CBD Parties have emphasized the need to take into account the VGGT Guidelines in the

[20] ITPGRFA, Art. 9(2). For a discussion, see E Tsioumani, 'Beyond Access and Benefit-sharing: Lessons from the Law and Governance of Agricultural Biodiversity' (2018) Journal of World Intellectual Property 1. Note that farmers' rights were first introduced in the International Undertaking on Plant Genetic Resources as an Agreed Interpretation of the Undertaking, adopted by FAO Res 4/89, which acknowledged that 'farmers, especially those in developing countries, should benefit fully from the improved and increased use of the natural resources they have preserved': E Tsioumani, *Fair and Equitable Benefit-sharing in Agriculture: Reinventing Agrarian Justice* (Routledge, 2021), at 72.

[21] Tsioumani, *Fair and Equitable Benefit-sharing* (n. 20), at 72.

[22] ibid.

[23] VGGT (n. 3), para. 8(6).

[24] ibid.

[25] ibid, para. 4(1).

[26] ibid, para. 2(4).

[27] ibid, para. 8(3).

application of the Convention,[28] and so have the Parties to the UN Convention on Desertification.[29]

Under the VGGT, beneficiaries include families such as those seeking home gardens, women, informal settlement residents, pastoralists, historically disadvantaged groups, marginalized groups, youth, gatherers, and small-scale food producers, but also Indigenous peoples.[30] Tsioumani identified two rationales for the identification of these beneficiaries: the merit of 'smallholder farmers and agricultural producers in general, in the pursuit of public-interest objectives including food security, agricultural productivity and rural livelihoods', which should be taken into account in the allocation of land concessions; and the vulnerability of the rural poor or the landless, including women, which should be taken into account in land allocation processes.[31]

The Food and Agriculture Organization (FAO) Guidelines on Small-Scale Fisheries (SSF) built on the VGGT, while responding to the need for a specific focus on the challenges faced by small-scale fishing communities.[32] While there is no universally agreed definition, the SSF Guidelines note that small-scale fishers and fish workers are often 'self-employed and engaged in directly providing food for their household and communities as well as working in commercial fishing, processing and marketing'.[33] Furthermore, the SSF Guidelines do not limit the understanding of SSF actors to those solely engaged in fishing operations and related activities, but rather include 'fishers, fish workers, their communities, traditional and customary authorities, and related professional organizations and [civil society organizations]'.[34] The SSF Guidelines then note that 'States should, as applicable, recognize and safeguard publicly owned resources that are *collectively* used and managed, in particular by small-scale fishing communities'.[35]

Under international human rights law, a variety of groups have been recognized as benefiting from the protection of universally applicable human rights (such as those related to property, subsistence, and culture),[36] which may be negatively affected by interferences with these communities' customary relations with land and natural resources.[37] Under the Framework Principles on Human Rights and the Environment, UN Special Rapporteur on Human Rights and the Environment John Knox referred to 'traditional communities' based on their comparable vulnerability to Indigenous peoples due to a similarly close relationship with territories and direct dependence 'on nature for their material needs and cultural life' without them self-identifying

[28] CBD Decision XII/5 (2014), Section 2(b).

[29] UN Convention to Combat Desertification in Countries Experiencing Serious Drought and/or Desertification, Particularly in Africa (Paris, 14 October 1994, in force 26 December 1996); 'New and Emerging Issues: Land Tenure', UN Doc ICCD/COP(14)/20 (2019); Tsioumani, *Fair and Equitable Benefit-sharing* (n. 20), at 61.

[30] VGGT (n. 3), para. 15(5).

[31] Tsioumani, *Fair and Equitable Benefit-sharing* (n. 20), at 54.

[32] SSF Guidelines (n. 3), para. 5(1).

[33] ibid, preface, para. 4.

[34] ibid, preface, para. 2(3).

[35] ibid, para. 5(6).

[36] A Bessa, 'Traditional Local Communities in International Law' (PhD dissertation, European University Institute, 2013).

[37] O De Schutter, 'The Emerging Human Right to Land' (2010) 12 International Community Law Review 303, at 319 and 324–325.

as Indigenous peoples.[38] In other words, they are emerging 'rights of ecologically concerned non-indigenous local communities'.[39] Framework Principle 3 on non-discrimination sheds further light on this issue. Benefit-sharing is hinted at as an 'additional measure to protect those who are most vulnerable to, or at particular risk from, environmental harm'.[40] This is with a view to complementing effective measures against the underlying conditions that cause or help to perpetuate discrimination, such as those measures that have disproportionately severe effects on communities that rely on ecosystems (such as mining and logging concessions) or historical or persistent prejudice against groups of individuals, which can be reinforced by environmental harm.[41]

In turn, the term 'peasant' has been reclaimed[42] under the 2019 UN Declaration on the Rights of Peasants and Other People Working in Rural Areas (UNDROP), including by the social movements that contributed to its adoption.[43] This is based on 'three main assumptions', namely:

> Peasants have a special relationship with the land, water and natural resources on which they depend for their livelihoods; they provide a unique contribution to economic development, biodiversity conservation and improvement as well as realization of the right to food and food security at the local, national and global levels; [and] they suffer disproportionately from poverty, hunger, malnutrition and the consequences of environmental degradation.[44]

Under the UNDROP,[45] the definition of a peasant includes a person who engages in 'artisanal or small- scale agriculture, crop planting, livestock raising, pastoralism, fishing, forestry, hunting or gathering, and handicrafts related to agriculture or a related occupation in a rural area artisanal or small-scale fishing and related handicrafts in rural areas ... for subsistence and/or for the market'.[46] This definition is broad enough to encompass people involved in multiple activities, including related preparatory works and cultural practices (e.g. net making and mending, boat maintenance in the context of small-scale fisheries) conducted by peasants.[47] The Declaration also applies to hired

38 Report of the Special Rapporteur on the issue of human rights obligations relating to the enjoyment of a safe, clean, healthy and sustainable environment' (Framework Principles on Human Rights and the Environment), UN Doc A/HRC/37/59 (2018), para. 48.

39 S Seck, 'Transnational Corporations and Extractive Industries' in S Alam et al. (eds), *International Environmental Law and the Global South* (Cambridge University Press, 2015) 380, at 392. See also C Doyle and J Gilbert, 'Indigenous Peoples and Globalization: From "Development Aggression" to "Self-Determined Development"' (2008–2009) 7 European Yearbook of Minority Issues 219.

40 Framework Principles on Human Rights and the Environment (n. 38), para. 9.

41 ibid.

42 M Edelman, 'Defining Peasants in the UNDROP' in M Albarese et al. (eds), *The United Nations Declaration on Peasants' Rights* (Routledge, 2022) 19.

43 L Cotula, 'The Right to Land' in Albarese et al. (n. 42) 91.

44 M Albarese et al., 'Introduction' in Albarese et al. (n. 42), 1, at 3.

45 E Morgera and J Nakamura, 'Shedding a Light on the Human Rights of Small-scale Fishers: complementarities and contrasts between the UNDROP and the Small-Scale Fisheries Guidelines' in Albarese et al. (n. 42), 62.

46 UNDROP, Art. 1(1).

47 See S Jentoft and A Eide (eds), *Poverty Mosaics: Realities and Prospects in Small-Scale Fisheries* (Springer, 2011).

workers, and broadly encompasses professional small-scale fishers along the supply and value-chain. For instance, the Declaration extends to all migrant and seasonal workers on aquaculture farms,[48] who may have an alternative occupation as small-scale fishers.[49] In addition, the UNDROP sets out two parameters for understanding the concept of 'peasants': (i) reliance on family labour or other non-monetized way of organizing labour, and (ii) special dependency on and attachment to the land.[50]

The choice of the term 'peasant' under the UNDROP also serves to capture the multiple grounds of discrimination experienced by these communities, such as expropriation of land, forced evictions and displacement, gender discrimination, the absence of agrarian reform and rural development policies, the lack of minimum wage and social protection, and the repression and criminalization of movements protecting their rights.[51] These persisting discriminatory treatments have hindered the ability of peasants, including small-scale fishers and fish workers, to have their voice heard, defend their human rights and tenure rights, and secure sustainable use of natural resources that they depend on.[52] They have also precluded the appreciation and recognition of peasants' present and future contributions to development, conserving and improving biodiversity, which constitute the basis of food production throughout the world.[53]

The UNDROP points towards the need to address systemic and engrained sources of discrimination, the multiple dimensions of poverty, and the underlying need to support the voice and vision of peasants, including their control over natural resources, as part of the protection, respect, and full realization of their human rights.[54] The notion of socio-economic diversity explains why the UNDROP highlights the explicit link between peasants' right to adequate standards of living and 'concrete, productive dimensions' and 'real-life factors'.[55] These include having the right to facilitated access to means of production, production, and processing, as well as technical assistance, credit, and insurance, which are necessary to gain access to local, national, and regional markets at prices that guarantee them a decent income and livelihood.[56]

The Declaration emphasized the need to protect the collective, as well as individual, human rights of peasants, with a view to safeguarding their distinctive socio-economic and cultural practices, and their solidarity approaches and transmission of knowledge,

[48] UNDROP, Art. 1(3).

[49] The migratory move of small-scale fishers also happens for reasons other than fishing, often constituting a way of life. See IN Wanyonyi et al., 'Artisanal Fisher Migration Patterns in Coastal East Africa' (2016) 119 Ocean & Coastal Management 93.

[50] UNDROP, Art. 1(1) reads: 'For the purposes of the present Declaration, a peasant is any person who engages or who seeks to engage alone, or in association with others or as a community, in small-scale agricultural production for subsistence and/or for the market, and who relies significantly, though not necessarily exclusively, on family or household labour and other non-monetized ways of organizing labour, and who has a special dependency on and attachment to the land.'

[51] E Riedel, G Giacca, and C Golay, 'The Development of Economic, Social, and Cultural Rights in International Law', in E Riedel, G Giacca, and G Golay (eds), *Economic, Social and Cultural Rights in International Law: Contemporary Issues and Challenges* (Oxford University Press, 2014) 3, at 8.

[52] UNDROP, Preamble.

[53] ibid.

[54] Cotula (n. 43).

[55] L Cotula, 'Between Hope and Critique: Human Rights, Social Justice and Re-imagining International Law from the Bottom Up' (2020) 48 Georgia Journal of International and Comparative Law 475, at 510.

[56] UNDROP, Art. 16.

while protecting them from large-scale developments.[57] The emerging argument here is that the main distinction from the international protection of Indigenous peoples is: protecting self-determination on the basis of indigeneity (ethnic ancestry) leads to demands for 'restoration of original entitlements and redress of past injustices deriving from colonialism'.[58] In turn, the human rights of peasants refer to the respect and protection of socio-economic diversity based on an ecological culture (including natural commons and ecological knowledge) that is negatively affected by the inequitable distribution of national resources.[59] The latter, however, also affects Indigenous peoples in current contexts.

2.2 Security of Tenure

The protection of tenure cuts across all the international law developments discussed above, and provides a key entry point to understand non-Indigenous communities' distinctive knowledge systems and experiences of discrimination. Tenure represents intertwined justice dimensions of recognition of current and historic ecosystem stewardship, and distribution in terms of access to territories, natural resources, and capabilities.[60] As Tsioumani emphasized:

> A crucial question concerning implementation of benefit-sharing from land use is its relationship with actual access to the resource; the benefit to be shared is often the land itself or the right to use it. Examination of benefit-sharing is thus inextricably linked to redistribution efforts for land or agrarian reform in view of chronic inequality in land distribution in many countries, complex interactions between formal tenure systems and customary arrangements around the globe and the fundamental question of who has decision-making authority, and thus control over land allocation and use. Control of rights to land has historically been an instrument of oppression and colonization, giving birth to social movements demanding land redistribution as a means towards social justice, and the right to control the type of development undertaken. [61]

Tsioumani also highlighted that the rights of local communities are a recent innovation in international law, and are connected to 'participatory rights, as well as to livelihoods, food security and rural development considerations'.[62] In contrast to intra-State benefit-sharing in the context of bio-based innovation (specifically agricultural research and development), international instruments specifically related to land governance 'are less binding, references to benefit-sharing less explicit

[57] A Bessa and J Gilbert, 'Indigenous Peoples and Traditional Local Communities in the UNDROP' in Albarese et al. (n. 42), 32, at 35.

[58] ibid, at 37.

[59] ibid.

[60] See, for instance, the case of the pastoralists on the island of Ikaria in Greece discussed by Tsioumani, *Fair and Equitable Benefit-sharing* (n. 20), at 85, 96, and 110–112.

[61] Tsioumani, *Fair and Equitable Benefit-sharing* (n. 20), at 113.

[62] ibid, at 62.

and benefit-sharing systems less developed'.[63] Tsioumani thus distinguishes the area in which benefit-sharing is applied, considering that whereas genetic resources are largely seen as renewables, land is not because its 'loss and degradation are not recoverable within a human lifespan'.[64] As a result, 'benefit-sharing is inextricably linked to redistribution efforts for land or agrarian reform' in the latter case,[65] and is primarily regulated by national law, although international norms play an increasing role in relation to human rights and environmental protection, as well as foreign investment.[66] She indicates that, in this context, fair and equitable benefit-sharing not only relates to the (re)distributive outcome but also to 'enabling conditions', which in addition to secure tenure also entail 'access to seeds, as well assistance in the organization of co-operatives and local seed banks, legal recognition of customary agricultural practices, training and access to markets'.[67]

Tsioumani also identified a series of justice-related challenges for small-scale farmers and arguably also other local communities: land and natural resource grabbing; insecure market access; inability to benefit from markets due to infrastructure barriers to access; lack of access to information and financial services; inability to obtain certification, or comply with export and food safety standards; limited support from the public sector; insufficient or tokenistic recognition of contributions to sustainable development, food security, and nutrition; and generally a lack of an enabling legal and policy environment.[68]

The VGGT provide guidance both on the protection of legitimate tenure rights and on mechanisms for transparency, participation, and accountability in decision-making regarding land allocation. Respect for legitimate tenure rights is considered a general principle of responsible tenure governance under the VGGT. It is reflected in several provisions, including on safeguards, ownership and control of public lands, customary tenure systems, investments, restitution, and expropriation.[69] Especially in the context of investments, the VGGT require responsible investments to safeguard against dispossession of legitimate tenure right holders and environmental damage, and provide safeguards to protect legitimate tenure rights, human rights, livelihoods, food security, and the environment from risks that could arise from large-scale transactions in tenure rights.[70] Such safeguards, according to the VGGT, could include ceilings on permissible land transactions, promotion of production, and investment models that do not result in the large-scale transfer of tenure rights to investors and partnerships with local tenure right holders. States should also consider conducting prior independent assessments on the potential positive and negative impacts of investments based on large-scale transactions of tenure rights, ensuring systematic and impartial identification of tenure rights.[71]

63 ibid, at 51.
64 ibid, at 52.
65 ibid.
66 ibid, at 53.
67 ibid.
68 ibid, at 55.
69 VGGT (n. 3), Arts 3(a), 7–9, 12, 14, and 16.
70 ibid, Arts 12(4) and (6).
71 ibid, Art. 12(10); see Tsioumani, *Fair and Equitable Benefit-sharing* (n. 20), at 105–106.

UNDROP indicates that States 'shall take appropriate measures to provide legal recognition for land tenure rights, including customary land tenure rights not currently protected by law, recognizing the existence of different models and systems, as well as 'recogniz[ing] and protect[ing] the natural commons and their related systems of collective use and management'.[72] The Declaration also refers to a series of peasants' collective rights, such as the right to not be arbitrarily or unlawfully deprived of their lands; return to their land of which they were arbitrarily or unlawfully deprived, individually and/or *collectively*, in association with others or as a community. In cases of natural disasters and/or armed conflict, peasants' collective rights also include access to the natural resources used in their activities and necessary for the enjoyment of adequate living conditions, whenever possible, or to receive just, fair, and lawful compensation when their return is not possible.[73] In addition, peasants' collective rights include the right to have an adequate standard of living for themselves and their families, and facilitated access to the means of production necessary to achieve them, including production tools, technical assistance, credit, insurance and other financial services. Furthermore, their collective rights include the right to engage freely in association with others or as a community in traditional ways of farming, fishing, livestock rearing, and forestry and to develop community-based commercialization systems.[74]

States are to ensure that peasants enjoy physical and economic access at all times to sufficient and adequate food that is produced and consumed sustainably and equitably, respecting their cultures, and preserving access to food for future generations. States are also to ensure a physically and mentally fulfilling and dignified life for peasants, individually and/or collectively, responding to their needs.[75]

Addressing distributive justice, the UNDROP provides for the facilitation of equitable access through redistributive reform.[76] The Declaration thus contains an express obligation to give *priority* to peasants in the allocation of public lands, fisheries, and forests, in line with the immediate relationship it establishes between land (including fishing grounds, as discussed below) and the attainment of an adequate standard of living.[77] In addition, under the UNDROP, the 'right to land' establishes a more immediate relationship between the *control* of agricultural and pastoral lands, as well as fishing grounds and the attainment of an adequate standard of living.[78] This arguably provides 'a more explicit normative foundation for redistributive agrarian reforms'.[79] In comparison, the SSF Guidelines call for the appropriate granting of *preferential access* to land, fishery resources, and to fish in waters under national jurisdiction, as well as 'exclusive zones for small-scale fisheries', and 'co-management'.[80]

72 UNDROP, Art. 17(3).
73 ibid, Art. 17(5).
74 ibid, Art. 16(1).
75 ibid, Art. 15(2).
76 SSF Guidelines (n. 3), para. 5.4; UNDROP, Art. 17.6.
77 Cotula (n. 55), at 508–513.
78 ibid, at 508–513, which refers more generally to the notion of terrestrial land.
79 ibid, at 509.
80 SSF Guidelines (n. 3), paras 5(1), 5(3)–(5), 5(7), and 5(15).

With regard to recognition of ecosystem stewardship, the Declaration's provision on the right to have access to, sustainably use, and manage 'land and the water bodies, fisheries, pastures and forests therein'[81] serves to bring attention to the various habitats in which peasants may conduct activities. In the case of small-scale fishers, for instance, these habitats are not only limited to fishing grounds, but also alternative or complementary livelihoods on land during closed seasons, closed areas, or in the event of disasters and crisis where fishing is not possible. The UNDROP also recalls the CBD's duty to conserve and sustainably use biodiversity, connecting it with the need 'to promote and protect the full enjoyment of the rights of peasants and other people working in rural areas'.[82] Such environmental standards are reflected in the SSF Guidelines through the ecosystem approach to fisheries.[83] The latter entails both involving small-scale fishers in sustainably managing fishery resources for the benefit of habitat, biodiversity, and ecosystem well-being, and ensuring that small-scale fishers can benefit from fishery resources maintained by healthy ecosystems.[84]

So what is the legal significance of the UNDROP and SSF Guidelines vis-à-vis the treaty provisions on intra-State benefit-sharing under the CBD and International Plant Treaty? On UNDROP, it has been argued that those States that voted in favour of the Declaration would be bound to respect it as part of their underlying obligations under the UN Charter to 'protect human dignity, eliminate all forms of discrimination, promote the right to self-determination and progressively eliminate material obstacles that hinder economic, social and cultural development'.[85] And its interpretative value under other international human rights treaties can be confirmed by relevant international human rights bodies.[86] In that connection, it has also been argued that in the light of the international human rights law principle *pro personae*, the UNDROP should be taken into account in the interpretation of more general international human rights treaties as it is more beneficial to specific human rights holders (in other words, as the 'most advanced interpretation of peasants and rural workers' human rights').[87] For that reason, it should prevail over more general treaties.[88] The legal arguments based on the UN Charter are applicable also to the understanding of the legal value of the VGGT and the SSF Guidelines in contributing to a mutually supportive interpretation of international biodiversity law and international human rights law.

[81] UNDROP, Art. 17(1).

[82] ibid, Art. 20.1.

[83] Morgera and Nakamura (n. 45), at 69 and 71.

[84] See FAO, *The Ecosystem Approach to Fisheries* (FAO Technical Guidelines for Responsible Fisheries No. 4, Suppl 2, FAO 2003) 112. See also the definition of 'ecosystem' under the CBD, Art. 2: 'a dynamic complex of plant, animal and micro-organism communities and their non-living environment interacting as a functional unit' and of an ecosystem approach in CBD Decisions V/6 and VII/11 (n. 6): 'a strategy for the integrated management of land, water and living resources that promotes conservation and sustainable use in an equitable way'. See also Morgera (n. 6), at 70.

[85] F Francioni, 'The Peasants' Declaration: State Obligations and Justiciability' in Albarese et al. (n. 42), 4, at 10.

[86] ibid, at 12.

[87] N Posenato, 'The UNDROP and the Case Law of the Inter-American Human Rights System' in Albarese et al. (n. 42), 237, at 243.

[88] ibid.

2.3 Comparative Reflections on Benefit-Sharing

All international instruments on non-Indigenous communities include references to benefit-sharing, but these have different formulations and areas of focus. The International Plant Treaty focuses on facilitated access to plant genetic resources for food and agriculture, the exchange of information, access to and transfer of technology, capacity building, and the sharing of monetary and other benefits arising from commercialization with farmers,[89] as discussed in Chapter 1. Tsioumani understands this approach to intra-State benefit-sharing as 'arising from the *past and present* contribution of farmers to the utilization of genetic resources for research and development purposes, and the possible commercialization of the resulting varieties or products'.[90] The International Plant Treaty is also oriented towards rewarding smallholder farmers as *users* and *stewards* of agricultural biodiversity on farm, the benefits of which flow to humanity at large as global public goods, with benefits that 'enable farmers' *continued* contribution to the stewardship of the resources in the *future*'.[91] This can be seen as recognition of farmers' contributions to everyone's human right to a healthy environment.

Other provisions in the International Plant Treaty can be read as clarifying that benefit-sharing concerns parties' support to farmers' efforts in the conservation, exploration, collection, characterization, evaluation, and documentation of plant genetic resources for food and agriculture.[92] The same applies to rules on the development of legal and policy measures, including on promoting the expanded use of local and locally adapted crops, supporting the wider use of a diversity of varieties and species in on-farm management and reviewing regulations on variety release and seed distribution.[93]

The VGGT, in turn, call for the equitable distribution of benefits from State-owned land and the establishment of transparent, participatory, and accessible mechanisms for the allocation of tenure rights, thus linking benefit-sharing with broader social, economic, and environmental objectives.[94] They seek to improve governance of tenure 'for the benefit of all, with an emphasis on vulnerable and marginalized people'.[95] This links, in Tsioumani's view, land tenure governance with poverty alleviation and giving general priority to the vulnerable among possible beneficiaries.[96] Specifically, the VGGT call on States to 'strive to develop policies that promote equitable distribution of benefits from State-owned land, fisheries and forests';[97] consistency with broader social, economic, and environmental objectives; and due consideration of local communities that have traditionally used the land in the reallocation of tenure rights. In addition, ensuring that allocation of tenure rights does not threaten the livelihoods of

[89] ITPGRFA, Art. 13.
[90] Tsioumani, *Fair and Equitable Benefit-sharing* (n. 20), at 76–77 (emphasis in the original).
[91] ibid.
[92] ITPGRFA, Art. 5.
[93] ibid, Art. 6; Tsioumani, *Fair and Equitable Benefit-sharing* (n. 20), at 77.
[94] VGGT, Art. 8.
[95] ibid, Art. 1(1).
[96] Tsioumani, *Fair and Equitable Benefit-sharing* (n. 20), at 101.
[97] VGGT, Art. 8(6).

people by depriving them of their legitimate access to resources; development and implementation of participatory processes of tenure governance;[98] and support services, including technical assistance and access to credit and to markets.[99]

Both the UNDROP and the VGGT include references to intra-State benefit-sharing in relation to environmental impact assessment and consultations, similarly to the safeguards identified under the CBD and international human rights law discussed in Chapter 3. The UNDROP broadly requires environmental impact assessments prior to authorizing *any* exploitation affecting natural resources that peasants may hold or use,[100] whereas the SSF Guidelines limit this requirement to the implementation of large-scale projects.[101] In addition, it clarifies that peasants and other people working in rural areas have the right to 'active, free, effective, meaningful and informed participation' prior to the adoption of decisions that may affect them, also taking into account relevant instruments on Indigenous peoples.[102] The UNDROP requires good-faith consultation broadly, before carrying out natural resources exploitation, and participation in the preparation and implementation of food safety, labour, and environmental standards.[103] The SSF Guidelines, in turn, require consultation specifically prior to the implementation of large-scale projects; the adoption of policies and management measures related to migration of fishers and fish workers, international trade, climate change and disasters, inland and marine spatial planning; and the setting of research priorities.[104] Neither international instrument provides for the standard of FPIC, which is instead emphasized in the UNDRIP and the UN Framework Principles on Human Rights and the Environment.[105] The UNDROP provides for the need to respect Indigenous peoples' rights, which may be 'construed as diminish[ed], impair[ed] or nullif[ied]' on the basis of the Declaration.[106]

Furthermore, the UNDROP calls upon States to 'take measures to ensure that any exploitation affecting the natural resources that peasants traditionally hold or use is permitted based on ... modalities for the fair and equitable sharing of benefits of such exploitation'.[107] The SSF Guidelines, in turn, support the 'equitable distribution of the benefits yielded from responsible management of fisheries and ecosystems, rewarding small-scale fishers and fish workers, both men and women'.[108] The SSF Guidelines, therefore, explicitly link benefit-sharing with non-discrimination (based on gender, discussed below),[109] which is also a dimension recognized under the UN Framework Principles on Human Rights and the Environment.[110] In addition, the SSF Guidelines

[98] ibid, Arts 8(7) and 4(10); see Tsioumani, *Fair and Equitable Benefit-sharing* (n. 20), at 102.
[99] VGGT (n. 3), Art. 15(8).
[100] UNDROP, Art. 5(2) (emphasis added).
[101] SSF Guidelines (n. 3), para. 5(10).
[102] ibid, para. 3(1)(6); UNDROP, Art. 2(3).
[103] UNDROP, Arts 5(2)(b) and 10(2).
[104] SSF Guidelines (n. 3), paras 5(10), 6(10), 7(7), 7(9), 9(2), 9(6), and 11(9).
[105] Framework Principles on Human rights and the Environment (n. 38), Framework Principle 15.
[106] UNDROP, Art. 28(1). Bessa and Gilbert (n. 57), at 34 and 41.
[107] UNDROP, Art. 5(2)(c).
[108] SSF Guidelines (n. 3), para. 5(1).
[109] ibid, para. 6(2).
[110] Framework Principles on Human Rights and the Environment (n. 38), Framework Principle 15, para. 9; E Morgera, 'A reflection on benefit-sharing as a Framework Principle on Human Rights and the Environment proposed by UN Special Rapporteur John Knox (Part I)' BENELEX blog (2018), available

note the cross-scale dimensions of benefit-sharing, by reference to the need to ensure that SSF communities benefit from wider economic developments at the local level (such as tourism)[111] and international trade.[112] The SSF Guidelines also offer a word of caution about evolving local contexts for benefit-sharing, noting that '[c]ustomary practices for the allocation and sharing of resource benefits in small-scale fisheries, which may have been in place for generations, have been changed as a result of non-participatory and often centralized fisheries management systems, rapid technology developments and demographic changes'.[113]

Tsioumani concludes that benefit-sharing with non-Indigenous communities comes into play in three different scenarios. First, as opportunities for meaningful participation and recognition of legitimate right holders in decision-making process that may affect their lives. Second, as safeguards for local land rights against arbitrary or unfair interference. And, third, as contractual arrangements for revenue-sharing and non-monetary benefit-sharing, such as infrastructure development. Benefit-sharing thus relates to both the enabling conditions related to communities' participation in the decision-making process and the substantive outcomes for non-Indigenous communities.[114]

The three key safeguards (impact assessments, consultation, and benefit-sharing), however, have all been criticized because they may arguably be 'consistent with the penetration of commercial forms of production' and 'operate in ways that are co-extensive with extractivist models'.[115] They are also perceived as implementing self-defeating or paternalistic mechanisms that fail to address communities' specific needs.[116] An application of these guarantees, however, that genuinely builds upon international human rights and biodiversity law[117] can arguably make space for different worldviews of nature and development[118] embodied in peasant communities' distinctive ways of life.[119] For instance, the SSF Guidelines' emphasis on the need for providing *support* for the exercise of small-scale fishing communities' rights can arguably contribute to the transformative application of the three safeguards when read

at https://benelexblog.wordpress.com/2018/04/08/a-reflection-on-benefit-sharing-as-a-framework-principle-on-human-rights-and-the-environment-proposed-by-un-special-rapporteur-john-knox-part-i/ accessed 29 June 2023.

111 SSF Guidelines (n. 3), para. 6(8).
112 ibid, paras 7(8) and 7(10).
113 ibid, at x.
114 Tsioumani, *Fair and Equitable Benefit-sharing* (n. 20), at 116.
115 Cotula (n. 55), at 514 and 520.
116 G Citrioni and KI Quintana Osuna, 'Reparations for Indigenous Peoples in the Case of the Inter-American Court of Human Rights' in F Lenzerini (ed.), *Reparation for Indigenous Peoples: Is International Law Ready to Ensure Redress for Historical Injustices?* (Oxford University Press, 2008), at 317–324 and 340.
117 E Morgera, 'Justice, Equity and Benefit-Sharing Under the Nagoya Protocol to the Convention on Biological Diversity' (2015) 24 Italian Yearbook of International Law 113.
118 A Barros, 'The Fetish Mechanism: A Post-Dogmatic Case Study of the Atacama Desert Peoples and the Extractive Industries' in C Lennox and D Short (eds), *Handbook of Indigenous Peoples' Rights* (Routledge, 2016), 223, at 231–232.
119 G Pentassuglia, 'Towards a Jurisprudential Articulation of Indigenous Land Rights' (2011) 22 European Journal of International Law 165–176; D McGregor, 'Living Well with the Earth: Indigenous Rights and the Environment' in Lennox and Short (n. 118), 167; E Desmet, *Indigenous Rights Entwined with Nature Conservation* (Intersentia, 2011), at 58–175.

together with the need to protect or enhance communities' *control* over natural resources, which is emphasized by the UNDROP.

The main normative argument explored here is that, interpreted together, the ecosystem-based approach framing the SSF Guidelines, the CBD, and the International Plant Treaty and the human rights-based approach that underpins the SSF Guidelines, the VGGT, and the UNDROP can shift the practice of impact assessments, consultation, and benefit-sharing away from a technocratic, damage-control approach, towards collaboratively identifying opportunities for creating positive impacts on non-Indigenous communities according to their views and distinctive knowledge systems, in addition to avoiding potential negative impacts.[120] Interpreted and applied in this way, these three safeguards can serve to challenge mainstream conceptions of economic development and tackle attempts to bottle non-Indigenous communities' worldviews into neo-liberal agendas.[121] To that end, impact assessments, consultation, and benefit-sharing need to genuinely support communities' *agency* through a concerned and iterative dialogue aimed at understanding and accommodating different worldviews with a view to enhancing communities' choice and capabilities.[122] That transformative potential can be supported by better understanding peasant communities' needs, values, knowledge systems, and priorities, as reflected in the UNDROP, as well as their ecosystem stewardship, as emphasized under the CBD and SSF Guidelines, so as to inform contextual and culturally appropriate implementation of international human rights law. These are, in essence, comparable normative arguments to those already explored in Chapter 3 towards the full realization of non-Indigenous communities' human rights to food, livelihoods, and culture, in recognition of their contributions to everyone's human right to a healthy environment.

3. Intra-Community Benefit-Sharing and Women's Human Rights

Rural women experience greater financial and resource constraints, lower levels of access to information, and less decision-making authority in their homes, communities, and countries.[123] In addition, women are particularly exposed to harm arising from environmental degradation, including climate change and biodiversity loss. Biodiversity loss places a disproportionate burden on rural women by increasing the time they spend obtaining water, fuel wood, and medicinal plants, thereby

[120] E Morgera, 'Under the Radar: Fair and Equitable Benefit-sharing and the Human Rights of Indigenous Peoples and Local Communities connected to Natural Resources' (2019) 23 International Journal of Human Rights 1098.

[121] E Reimerson, 'Between Nature and Culture: Exploring Space for Indigenous Agency in the Convention on Biological Diversity' (2013) Environmental Politics 22; Y Uggla, 'What is This Thing Called "Natural"? The Nature-culture Divide in Climate Change and Biodiversity Policy' (2009) Journal of Politics Ecology 17.

[122] Morgera (n. 117), at 14–16.

[123] United Nations Development Programme (UNDP), *Gender Equality in National Climate Action: Planning for Gender-Responsive Nationally Determined Contributions* (UNDP, 2016).

reducing the time they can spend on income-generating activities and education.[124] Entrenched and systemic discrimination can lead to gender-differentiated impacts of climate change with respect to health, food security, livelihoods, and human mobility, among other things.[125] In addition to distributive and procedural justice dimensions, the lack or limited legal recognition of women's ownership of natural resources, and the lack or limited access to supporting resources (such as capital, technology, and capacity-building opportunities), combined with limited recognition of women's role as ecosystem stewards, undermine women's decisions and actions that contribute to environmental protection and the realization of their human rights.[126]

The intersection of gender and the environment is particularly evident for Indigenous women and girls, as highlighted by the UN Committee on the Elimination of Discrimination against Women (CEDAW) in 2022.[127] This is because land and territories are an integral part of the lives, identity, views, well-being, livelihoods, cultures, and spirit of Indigenous women and girls. The limited recognition of women's ownership of their ancestral territories, and/or the absence of titles to their lands and legal protection of their traditions and heritage in many countries undermine and fuel disrespect for Indigenous women's rights by State and private actors.[128] This in turn leads to poverty, food and water scarcity, and barriers to accessing natural resources needed for women's and girls' survival, and can create unsafe conditions, contributing instances of gender-based violence. On the other hand, it is recognized that preventing and addressing gender discrimination benefits society as a whole, as women are significant agents of change.[129]

Gender equality is referred to in the UN Charter, which promotes the respect of human rights for all without distinctions based on gender,[130] as reiterated under the Universal Declaration of Human Rights.[131] The CEDAW considers that the failure of States to take adequate action to prevent, adapt to, and remediate serious instances of environmental harm affecting women and girls constitutes a form of discrimination and violence against them that needs to be promptly addressed.[132]

[124] Report of the UN Special Rapporteur, John Knox, on the issue of human rights obligations relating to the enjoyment of a safe, clean, healthy and sustainable environment, UN Doc A/HRC/37/59 (2018), para. 41(a).

[125] Committee on the Elimination of Discrimination against Women (CEDAW), General recommendation No. 37 on gender-related dimensions of disaster risk reduction in the context of climate change; and UN Doc A/HRC/41/26.

[126] Report of the UN Secretary-General's High-Level Panel on Women's Economic Empowerment, 'Leave No One Behind: Taking Action for Transformational Change on Women's Economic Empowerment', available at https://www.unscn.org/uploads/web/news/UNSG-HLP-WEE-2nd-Report-.pdf, accessed 29 June 2023.

[127] CEDAW, General recommendation No. 39 on the rights of Indigenous Women and Girls, UN Doc CEDAW/C/CG/39 (2022).

[128] OHCHR, Report on the Right to Land under the United Nations Declaration on the Rights of Indigenous Peoples: A Human Rights Focus Study of the Expert Mechanism on the Rights of Indigenous Peoples UN Doc A/HRC/45/38 (2020), paras 5–9.

[129] UN Special Rapporteur on Human Rights and the Environment David Boyd, Report on women, girls and the right to a clean, healthy and sustainable environment, UN Doc A/HRC/52/33 (2023).

[130] Charter of the United Nations (San Francisco, 26 June 1945, in force 24 October 1945), Art. 1.

[131] Universal Declaration of Human Rights (Paris, 10 December 2048), Art. 2.

[132] CEDAW, General recommendation No. 39 (n. 127).

Against this backdrop, references to intra-community benefit-sharing in international instruments on rural women's human rights are inconsistent. References to intra-community benefit-sharing arising from rural development can be found, for instance, under the Convention on the Elimination of All Forms of Discrimination against Women.[133] Here, benefit-sharing relates to women's rights in the ownership, acquisition, management, administration, enjoyment, and disposition of land,[134] and the prevention of non-discrimination in rural areas. These serve as entry points for ensuring the respect and full realization of women's rights regarding the conservation and use of biological and genetic resources,[135] particularly in the context of rural development (which is understood to comprise agricultural and water policies, forestry, livestock, fisheries, and aquaculture).

Furthermore, the CEDAW recommended ensuring that rural development projects (including actions for the conservation and sustainable use of biodiversity) are implemented only after conducting participatory gender and environmental impact assessments with full participation of rural women, obtaining rural women's FPIC, and ensuring benefit-sharing (for instance, in revenues generated by large-scale development projects[136]).

Incomplete theorization of benefit-sharing with regards to women and girls is, however, evident in CEDAW guidance, where no specific mention is made of benefit-sharing in relation to territories and natural resources. The 2022 recommendations on Indigenous women and girls include seeking Indigenous women and girls' FPIC before authorizing economic, development, extractive, and climate mitigation and adaptation projects on their lands and territories and affecting their natural resources.[137] The Committee also recommended acknowledging their contribution to food production, sovereignty, and sustainable development; protect ancestral forms of farming and sources of livelihood for Indigenous women; and ensure the meaningful participation of Indigenous women and girls in the design, adoption, and implementation of agrarian reform schemes and the management and control of natural resources.[138]

The CEDAW guidance, however, incorporates language on benefit-sharing with regard to women's knowledge. It recommends that States act with due diligence to prevent, investigate, punish transgressors, and provide reparations to victims in instances of unauthorized use or appropriation of the cultural knowledge and heritage of Indigenous women and girls without their FPIC and adequate benefit-sharing.[139] Similarly, there is a reference to ensuring that women have '*access to the benefits* of

[133] United Nations Convention on the Elimination of All Forms of Discrimination against Women (Copenhagen, 18 December 1979, in force 3 September 1981), 1979, Art. 14(2).

[134] ibid, Art. 16(1)(h).

[135] N Kenney and M Schroder, 'Gender Equality and Benefit Sharing: Exploring the Linkages in relation to Land and Genetic Resources', BENELEX blog (2016), available at https://benelexblog.wordpress.com/2016/12/05/GENDER-EQUALITY-AND-BENEFIT-SHARING-EXPLORING-THE-LINKAGES-IN-RELATION-TO-LAND-AND-GENETIC-RESOURCES/, accessed 29 June 2023; and V Jenkins, 'Gender and the Convention on Biological Diversity', in Morgera and Razzaque (n. 6) 331.

[136] CEDAW, Concluding observations on the seventh periodic report of Argentina, UN Doc CEDAW/C/ARG/CO/7 (2016).

[137] CEDAW, General recommendation No. 39 (n. 127), para. 61.

[138] ibid.

[139] ibid, para. 55(c).

scientific progress and technological innovation to be able to achieve food and water security and that they are compensated for their contributions and technical knowledge.'[140]

On the other hand, the 'key messages' developed jointly in 2021 by the Office of the United Nations High Commissioner for Human Rights, the United Nations Environment Programme, and UN Women, highlighted the main human rights obligations of States with respect to gender and the environment, including to 'ensure equal ownership of, access to, and *benefits from* resources for women and persons with diverse gender identities',[141] without providing further guidance. UN Special Rapporteur on Human Rights and the Environment David Boyd, in turn, recommended conserving, protecting, and restoring healthy biodiversity and ecosystems, while guaranteeing that women and girls '*share equally in the benefits* of using nature'.[142] Boyd used similar language in the context of recognizing and prioritizing the collective and individual needs and rights of women and girls in these communities in all climate actions and efforts to conserve, protect, restore, and sustainably use biodiversity.[143] The textual and conceptual framing of intra-community benefit-sharing in human rights sources is thus quite under-developed.

Under the CBD, intra-community benefit-sharing has emerged in Conference of the Parties' (COP) decisions. The CBD Akwé: Kon Voluntary Guidelines on socio-cultural and environmental impact assessments call for examining the potential impacts of a proposed development on women in the affected community with due regard to their role as providers of food and nurturers of family, community decision-makers, and heads of households, as well as custodians of biodiversity and holders of particular elements of (gender-specific) traditional knowledge, innovations, and practices.[144] In addition, the CBD Mo'otz Kuxtal Voluntary Guidelines indicate that benefit-sharing from the use of Indigenous and local knowledge should be fair and equitable within and among relevant groups, taking into account relevant community-level procedures, and appropriate gender and age/intergenerational considerations.[145]

Furthermore, the Nagoya Protocol on Access to Genetic Resources and the fair and equitable sharing of benefits arising from their utilization recognizes, in its Preamble, 'the vital role that women play in access and benefit-sharing and [. . .] the need for the full participation of women at all levels of policy-making and implementation for biodiversity conservation'. It further specifically provides for Parties to endeavour to support, as appropriate, the development by Indigenous and local women of community

[140] ibid, para. 59 (emphasis added).

[141] OHCHR, United Nations Environment Programme, and UN Women, Human Rights, The Environment and Gender Equality (undated), available at https://www.unwomen.org/sites/default/files/2022-06/Policy-paper-Human-rights-environment-gender-equality-en.pdf, accessed 29 June 2023.

[142] Boyd (n. 129), paras 61–86 (emphasis added).

[143] ibid. See also UN Special Rapporteur on Indigenous Peoples' Rights Jose Francisco Cali Tzay, Indigenous women and the development, application, preservation and transmission of scientific and technical knowledge, UN Doc A/HRC/51/28 (2022), paras 64, 78, and 107(g) recommending benefit-sharing from the use of Indigenous women's knowledge.

[144] CBD Decision VII/16 (2004), Annex, paras 52.

[145] CBD Decision XIII/18 (2006), Annex, para. 14.

protocols, minimum requirements for benefit-sharing, and model contractual clauses on the use of traditional knowledge associated with genetic resources.[146]

The CBD 2015–2020 Gender Plan of Action, which aimed to mainstream a gender perspective in implementing the Convention and promote gender equality in achieving the objectives of the Convention, only refers to benefit-sharing from genetic resources, in calling for '[a]pplying a human rights-based approach to advancing gender equality'.[147] The same gap can be found in the post-2020 Global Biodiversity Framework. The latter, however, starts to build a bridge with international human rights law on women's rights. It includes, as targets, to ensure the full, equitable, inclusive, effective, and gender-responsive representation and participation in decision-making, and access to justice and information related to biodiversity by women and girls.[148] It also calls for ensuring gender equality in the Framework implementation through a gender-responsive approach, whereby all women and girls have equal opportunities and capacities to contribute to the three objectives of the Convention. It then refers to recognizing their equal rights and access to land and natural resources and their full, equitable, meaningful, and informed participation and leadership at all levels of action, engagement, policy, and decision-making related to biodiversity.[149]

The normative argument proposed here is that guidance provided by the CEDAW, discussed earlier, is relevant in interpreting State obligations under the CBD and clarifying the legal significance of the guidance adopted by CBD Parties. The latter includes matters such as establishing gender-responsive enabling institutional, legal, and policy frameworks, that are adequately budgeted, on rural development, agriculture, water, forestry, livestock, fisheries, and aquaculture. It also extends to developing and implementing temporary special measures to enable rural women to benefit from the public distribution, lease, or use of land, water bodies, fisheries, forests, and from agrarian reform policies, rural investments, and management of natural resources in rural areas, giving priority to landless rural women in the allocation of public lands, fisheries, and forests.[150]

The three safeguards (impact assessments, consultation, and benefit-sharing) are also relevant to prevent and address gender discrimination in the context of reforms and resettlement schemes, according to the UNDROP.[151] These safeguards also pertain to the designing, planning, and implementation of management measures under to the SSF Guidelines,[152] which specifically note the role of benefit-sharing from the management of fisheries and ecosystems for *women* in small-scale fisheries.[153] These

[146] Nagoya Protocol Additional to the Convention on Biological Diversity 1992, on Access to Genetic Resources and the Fair and Equitable Sharing of Benefits from their Utilization (Nagoya, 29 October 2010, in force 12 October 2014), Art. 12.

[147] CBD, Gender Action Plan: CBD Decision XV/11 (2022), para. 2(c)–(d) and Objective 1.3.

[148] Kunming-Montreal Global Biodiversity Framework, CBD Decision XV/4 (2022), Target 22.

[149] ibid, Target 23.

[150] CEDAW, General recommendation No. 34 on the rights of rural women, UN Doc CEDAW/C/GC/34 (2016).

[151] UNDROP, Art. 4(2)(h).

[152] SSF Guidelines (n. 3), para. 5(15).

[153] ibid, para. 5(1) (emphasis added).

safeguards can also address other grounds for non-discrimination and ensure consideration of the human rights of children.[154]

As argued above, UNDROP and the SSF Guidelines help to develop a mutually supportive interpretation of the CBD and international human rights law. The UNDROP reiterates relevant provisions of the Convention on Discrimination against Women, which allowed a shift away from an emphasis on family farming, and includes clear provisions on non-discrimination on grounds of sex for economic and political participation.[155] But the UNDROP has been criticized for not including other critical gender dimensions: women's rights to inherit land, equal tenure rights in agrarian reform processes, women's rights to equality in marriage and in family relations, disproportionate burden of unpaid labour, and gender identity and sexual orientation as grounds of discrimination.[156] Gender experts have also emphasized the need to more explicitly highlight the links between the protection of women's dignified lives and the combined oppression of patriarchy and capitalism in the context of women's economic exploitation, the invisibility of their contribution, the limitation of their political participation, and their economic dependence on men, which reinforce the instances of violence against women.[157]

The SSF Guidelines call for preferential treatment of women—by providing services and implementing non-discrimination and other human rights—where it is required to ensure equitable benefits.[158] The SSF Guidelines indicate support for '*equitable distribution of the benefits* yielded from responsible management of fisheries and ecosystems, rewarding small-scale fishers and fish workers, both men and women'.[159] Capacity development is also required so that women in small-scale fisheries can adapt to and benefit equitably from global market trends and local conditions while minimizing any potential negative impacts.[160] States and other relevant parties should promote research into the working conditions, including those of migrant fishers and fish workers, along with aspects such as health, education, and decision-making in the context of gender relations, in order to inform strategies for ensuring equitable benefits for men and women in fisheries. Efforts to mainstream gender perspectives should involve the use of gender analysis in the design phase of policies, programmes, and projects for small-scale fisheries in order to design gender-sensitive interventions. Gender-sensitive indicators should be used to monitor and address gender inequalities and to capture the extent to which interventions have contributed towards social change.[161]

[154] Special Rapporteur on the issue of human rights obligations relating to the enjoyment of a safe, clean, healthy and sustainable environment John Knox, UN Doc A/HRC/37/58 (2018). See also the UN Committee on the Rights of the Children, General Comment No. 26 on children's rights and the environment with a special focus on climate change (2023).

[155] J Bourke Martignoni and P Claeys, 'No Food Sovereignty without Feminism? Negotiating Gender Equality in the UNDROP' in Albarese et al. (n. 42), 47, at 54.

[156] ibid, at 47–48.

[157] ibid, at 50.

[158] SSF Guidelines (n. 3), para. 6(2).

[159] ibid, para. 5(1) (emphasis added).

[160] ibid, para. 7(10).

[161] SSF Guidelines (n. 3), para. 11(10).

On the whole, intra-community benefit-sharing highlights intersectionality as underpinning different dimensions of justice that arise and intertwine both within and beyond communities. Much remains to be done to fully clarify the role of fair and equitable benefit-sharing in this context and ensure that mutually supportive interpretations at the crossroads of international environmental law and international human rights law effectively prevent discrimination and nurture transformative change. This involves fully recognizing and fostering learning from women's distinctive ecological knowledge and their special relationships nurturing both people and nature.[162]

4. Transnational Benefit-Sharing from the Use of Traditional Knowledge

Probably one of the most challenging aspects of international standards on fair and equitable benefit-sharing concerns the traditional knowledge of Indigenous peoples and local communities. It involves intra-State, intra-community, and transnational dimensions of fair and equitable benefit-sharing. The key justice issues are that existing international provisions on benefit-sharing from knowledge use need fundamentally to support respectful dialogue, mutual learning, and partnership building across different knowledge systems. However, they face two underlying challenges in ensuring that knowledge holders' views and voices are truly listened to, rather than merely creating platforms where different views are voiced without genuine attention or consideration. First, overcoming 'prejudicial stereotypes' about the authority and credibility of different knowledge holders, thereby challenging 'misconceptions' about their ability to make meaningful contributions.[163] Second, preventing any 'unfair distribution of conceptual resources needed for speakers to have a say', where knowledge holders require culturally appropriate and accessible resources to ensure they can meaningfully contribute. This also entails taking into account that audiences may be unaware of their own communicative practices and 'fail to give appropriate uptake to their attempts to communicate'.[164]

In his academic commentary on the human right to science (discussed in Chapter 2 with regard to inter-State benefit-sharing), Schabas highlighted the need to prohibit by law the use of traditional knowledge without sharing ownership, control, use, and benefits with traditional knowledge holders.[165] International human rights bodies focused on the human rights of Indigenous peoples have also identified, but not elaborated upon, the need to obtain the FPIC of,[166] and to share benefits with,[167] traditional

[162] ibid, at 59.

[163] D Lupin and L Townsend, 'The Right to Consultation is a Right to Be Heard' in D Lupin (ed.), *A Research Agenda for Human Rights and the Environment* (Edward Elgar, 2023) 103.

[164] ibid, at 107.

[165] WA Schabas, 'Study of the Right to Enjoy the Benefits of Scientific and Technological Progress and its Applications' in Y Donders and V Volodin (eds), *Human Rights in Education, Science and Culture: Legal Developments and Challenges* (Ashgate Publishing, 2007) 297, at 294.

[166] UN Committee on Economic, Social and Cultural Rights (CESCR), General Comment No. 21, UN Doc E/C.12/GC/21 (2009), para. 37.

[167] UN Permanent Forum on Indigenous Issues, Review of World Bank operational policies, UN Doc E/C.19/2013/15 (2013), para. 27; Expert Mechanism on the Rights of Indigenous Peoples, 'Promotion and

knowledge holders.[168] The UN Committee on Economic, Social and Cultural Rights clearly indicated that when negotiating international agreements, States should ensure that traditional knowledge is protected through an obligation to obtain FPIC when State or non-State actors conduct research and make decisions or create policies related to science that have an impact on Indigenous peoples, or when using their knowledge.[169]

On the whole, the human right to science focuses on the agency of traditional knowledge holders in co-identifying benefits and more equitable modalities for international scientific cooperation for the protection and full realization of other human rights, with an emphasis on the vulnerable.[170] A key challenge is to secure ongoing opportunities for Indigenous peoples' and other knowledge holders' to govern and steward traditional knowledge, in line with their customary laws and 'the web of relationships defining who may use it, when and how'.[171]

In effect, the justice dilemmas around the recognition and integration of traditional knowledge in environmental management are: whose knowledge (scientific, modern, or traditional) determines environmental sustainability approaches? How are the knowledge contributions of Indigenous peoples and local communities to sustainability assessed and taken into account in decision-making processes? Respectful and genuine integration of traditional knowledge can arguably be an essential step towards the realization of Indigenous peoples' self-determination, local communities' socio-cultural and economic preferences, and rural women's distinctive ecological knowledge and nurturing practices, as well as enriching environmental approaches for the benefit of society as a whole. International provisions on traditional knowledge are thus essential for effectively acknowledging knowledge holders and their contribution to sustainable development and environmental protection, and equally giving them a voice in decision-making processes that may affect their ways of life and livelihoods.[172]

International guidance emphasizes that respecting traditional knowledge requires valuing it equally with, and complementary to, scientific knowledge, in order to promote the full respect for the cultural and intellectual heritage of Indigenous peoples and local communities relevant to the conservation and sustainable use of

protection of the rights of indigenous peoples with respect to their cultural heritage' UN Doc A/HRC/EMRIP/2015/2 (2015).

[168] Unlike the Nagoya Protocol, neither the ILO Convention Concerning Indigenous and Tribal People in Independent Countries (Geneva, 27 June 1987, in force 5 September 1991) nor UN Declaration on the Rights of Indigenous Peoples (UNDRIP: UNGA Res 61/295, 2007), discussed in Chapter 3, link benefit-sharing and traditional knowledge. CESCR, General Comment No. 21 (n. 166), para. 37, refers to prior informed consent, but not benefit-sharing, with regard to traditional knowledge.

[169] CESCR, General Comment No. 25 on science and economic social and cultural rights (ICESCR, Art. 15(1)(b), (2), (3), and (4), UN Doc E/C.12/GC/25 (2020), para. 40.

[170] E Morgera, 'The Relevance of the Human Right to Science for the Conservation and Sustainable Use of Marine Biodiversity of Areas Beyond National Jurisdiction: A New Legally Binding Instrument to Support Co-Production of Ocean Knowledge across Scales' in V deLucia, L Nguyen, and AG Oude Elferink (eds), *International Law and Marine Areas beyond National Jurisdiction: Reflections on Justice, Space, Knowledge and Power* (Brill, 2022) 242.

[171] T Williams and P Hardison, 'Culture, Law, Risk and Governance: Contexts of Traditional Knowledge in Climate Change Adaptation' (2013) 120 Climatic Change 531, at 534.

[172] E Morgera, 'Fair and Equitable Benefit-sharing at the Crossroads of the Human Right to Science and International Biodiversity Law' (2015) 4 Laws 803.

biodiversity.[173] The actual impact on decision-making, however, depends on whether traditional knowledge holders have sufficient procedural access to the relevant decision-making processes.[174] In addition, even if traditional knowledge is recognized as a form of science, its integration in various decision-making processes may impose unfair burdens on traditional knowledge holders, constraining the further development of knowledge systems in light of changes in circumstances, including changes to traditional lifestyles within which traditional knowledge is rooted.[175] Furthermore, various risks need to be duly taken into account. Indigenous peoples and other knowledge holders may lose control of their knowledge once it is shared and becomes subject to laws other than their customary rules.[176] Additionally, the use of traditional knowledge may fail to reflect or protect the values of these Indigenous peoples and knowledge holders in research findings or management measures that are developed on the basis of traditional knowledge.[177]

The following subsections will discuss relevant international law materials on fair and equitable benefit-sharing from Indigenous and local knowledge, focusing, in turn, on developments related to land, fisheries, bio-based innovation, and international science-policy platforms.

4.1 Land-Based Knowledge

International environmental law treaties have recognized the relevance of traditional knowledge,[178] and some have made specific reference to the need to ensure FPIC and fairly and equitably share the benefits arising from the use of this knowledge with Indigenous peoples and local communities. However, this is not always the case, and it is also essential to see when treaty language actually excludes traditional knowledge. A good example can be found in the Paris Agreement, where the recognition of the significance of Indigenous and local knowledge for climate change adaptation[179] implicitly indicates that Parties do not consider traditional knowledge relevant for mitigation purposes.

The UN Convention to Combat Desertification (UNCCD) recognizes the value of local and traditional knowledge with regard to natural resource management, relying on uneven terminology.[180] The UNCCD promotes the exchange of Indigenous and

[173] CBD Tkarihwaié:ri Code of Ethical Conduct on Respect for the Cultural and Intellectual Heritage of Indigenous and Local Communities, CBD Decision X/42 (2010), Annex, Preamble.

[174] S Seth, 'Putting Knowledge in its Place: Science, Colonialism and the Postcolonial' (2009) 12 Postcolonial Studies 373.

[175] S Vermeylen, G Martin, and R Clift, 'Intellectual Property, Rights Systems and the Assemblage of Local Knowledge Systems' (2008) 15 International Journal of Cultural Property 201.

[176] Williams and Hardison (n. 171).

[177] ibid, at 539.

[178] D Shelton, 'Principle 22: Indigenous Peoples and Sustainable Development' in J Viñuales (ed.), The Rio Declaration on Environment and Development (Oxford University Press, 2015) 541.

[179] The Paris Agreement recognizes the role of 'traditional knowledge, knowledge of indigenous peoples and local knowledge systems' as a means to adapt to climate change (Paris Agreement (Paris, 12 December 2015, in force 4 November 2016), Art. 7.5).

[180] United Nations Convention to Combat Desertification (UNCCD) (Bonn, 17 June 1994, in force 26 December 1996), Arts 16–17; Tsioumani, *Fair and Equitable Benefit-sharing in Agriculture* (n. 20), at 61.

local knowledge 'with appropriate *return of the benefits* derived from it to the local populations concerned, on an equitable basis and on mutually agreed terms'.[181] It also calls for ensuring that knowledge owners directly benefit from any commercial utilization or technological development derived from its integration in research and development processes[182] and technology transfer.[183]

The CBD qualified obligation to promote the wider application of traditional knowledge with the approval and involvement of knowledge holders and encourage equitable benefit-sharing[184] from the use of this knowledge has been interpreted through a series of soft-law decisions to apply more broadly to communities' customary sustainable use of biological resources in accordance with traditional cultural practices that are compatible with conservation or sustainable use requirements.[185] These obligations have been subject to more detailed interpretation as part of the CBD ecosystem approach, which entails the integration of 'Western' and Indigenous and local knowledge,[186] equity, and appropriate representation of community interests in decision-making processes.[187] Further soft-law guidance adopted under the CBD emphasizes that to respect traditional knowledge requires valuing it equally with, and complementary to, scientific knowledge. This is in order to promote the full respect for the cultural and intellectual heritage of Indigenous peoples and local communities relevant to the conservation and sustainable use of biodiversity.[188] Questions have been raised, however, as to whether this guidance is based on a post-colonial connotation of 'modern' science in opposition to, or to the exclusion of, traditional knowledge,[189] and whether the representatives of Indigenous peoples and local communities have sufficient procedural access to the relevant decision-making processes.

The 2016 CBD Mo'otz Kuxtal Guidelines focus on consent and benefit-sharing from the use of traditional knowledge. These Guidelines have been intergovernmentally negotiated with significant contributions from Indigenous peoples' representatives and were adopted by consensus.[190] The Guidelines contain several elements that serve to explain what 'free' prior and informed consent means, which remains controversial in international biodiversity[191] and human rights

[181] UNCCD, Art. 16.
[182] ibid, Art. 17.
[183] ibid, Art. 18; see also Tsioumani, *Fair and Equitable Benefit-sharing in Agriculture* (n. 20), at 68.
[184] 'Subject to its national legislation' and 'as far as possible and as appropriate': CBD, Art. 8(j).
[185] CBD, Art. 10(c), which has then been reflected in all the thematic areas of the Convention's work: e.g. CBD revised work programme on inland water biodiversity, Decision VII/4 (2004) Annex, para. 9; CBD work programme on island biodiversity, Decision VIII/1 (2009) Annex, Target 9.2; and CBD work programme on drylands, Decision VIII/2 (2006), Target 9.2.
[186] CBD Decision V/6 (2002), Annex, Principle 11.
[187] CBD Decision VII/11 (2004), Annex I, para. 2.5.
[188] CBD Tkarihwaié:ri Code of Ethical Conduct (n. 173), Preamble.
[189] L Whitt, *Science, Colonialism and Indigenous Peoples* (Cambridge University Press, 2009); S Seth, 'Putting Knowledge in its Place: Science, Colonialism and the Postcolonial' (2009) 12 Postcolonial Studies 373.
[190] E Morgera, 'Towards International Guidelines on Prior Informed Consent and Fair and Equitable Benefit-sharing from the Use of Traditional Knowledge', BENELEX Blog (9 December 2015), available at https://benelexblog.wordpress.com/2015/12/09/towards-international-guidelines-on-prior-informed-consent-and-fair-and-equitable-benefit-sharing-from-the-use-of-traditional-knowledge/, accessed 29 June 2023.
[191] It should be noted that CBD Parties have differing views on adopting the term 'FPIC' in the title of the Mo'otz Kuxtal Voluntary Guidelines for the development of mechanisms, legislation or other appropriate

law.[192] Fundamentally, the Guidelines emphasize that FPIC is a '*continual* process of building mutually beneficial, *ongoing* arrangements between users and holders of traditional knowledge, in order to build trust, good relations, mutual understanding, intercultural spaces, knowledge exchanges, and to create new knowledge and reconciliation'.[193] This is key clarification highlights that consent or approval is an iterative process, not a one-off exercise, which 'should underpin and be an integral part of developing a relationship between users and providers of [traditional knowledge]'.[194] In line with this understanding, the Mo'otz Kuxtal Guidelines emphasize that benefit-sharing is also about iterative partnership building, rather than a top-down, one-off, or unilateral flow of benefits where Indigenous peoples are passive beneficiaries.[195] Furthermore, the Mo'otz Kuxtal Guidelines draw attention to the role of benefit-sharing in supporting cultural reproduction, by stating that 'benefit-sharing could include a way of recognizing and strengthening the contribution of [I]ndigenous peoples and local communities to the conservation and sustainable use of biological diversity, including by supporting the intergenerational transmission of [traditional knowledge]'.[196]

Although the CBD text itself does not distinguish between commercial and other utilization of traditional knowledge, other international instruments that intend to build on international biodiversity law have made this distinction.[197] A systematic reading of the Nagoya Protocol would highlight an international obligation to seek FPIC and share (arguably non-monetary) benefits arising from non-commercial research on traditional knowledge, including when the research is intended to contribute to the global goal of conserving biodiversity.[198] The extreme caution with which the issue of intra-State benefit-sharing from non-commercial research has been treated by CBD parties on other occasions, however, may imply that this is debatable. Such caution is particularly palpable in the CBD Tkarihwaié:ri Code of *Ethical* Conduct on Respect for the Cultural and Intellectual Heritage of Indigenous and

initiatives to ensure the 'prior and informed consent', 'free, prior and informed consent', or 'approval and involvement', depending on national circumstances, of Indigenous peoples and local communities for accessing their knowledge, innovations and practices, for fair and equitable sharing of benefits arising from the use of their knowledge, innovations and practices relevant for the conservation and sustainable use of biological diversity, and for reporting and preventing unlawful appropriation of traditional knowledge (CBD Decision XIII/18 (2016)) (hereinafter CBD Mo'otz Kuxtal Voluntary Guidelines).

[192] e.g. M Åhrén, *Indigenous Peoples in the International Legal System* (Oxford University Press, 2016), at 217–218; JC Morales (UN Expert Mechanism on the Rights of Indigenous Peoples), Follow-up Report on Indigenous Peoples and the Right to Participate in Decision-making, with a Focus on Extractive Industries, UN Doc A/HRC/21/55 (2012), paras 38(b), 39(h) and 43.

[193] CBD Mo'otz Kuxtal Voluntary Guidelines (n. 191), para. 8 (internal citations omitted) (emphasis added).

[194] ibid.

[195] ibid, para. 23(a). The need for partnership with Indigenous and local knowledge holders is also emphasized by C Yow Mulalap et al., 'Traditional Knowledge and the BBNJ Instrument' (2020) 122 Marine Policy 104103, 7.

[196] CBD Mo'otz Kuxtal Voluntary Guidelines (n. 191), para. 13.

[197] See, for instance, how international finance institutions have reflected international biodiversity law on this point in their standards: International Finance Corporation (IFC), Performance Standard 8 (2012), https://www.ifc.org/en/insights-reports/2012/ifc-performance-standards, last accessed 19 February 2024, para. 16.

[198] Nagoya Protocol, Art. 8(a), read with Art. 5 and Annex, and Arts 16–17.

Local Communities.[199] Traditional knowledge holders, in turn, may wish to be involved in scientific research, both because of the recognition of their contribution to scientific advancements and as a way to increase their influence in decision-making processes that rely on those scientific advancements.

Whether for commercial or non-commercial purposes, the use of traditional knowledge raises specific challenges with regard to the notion of FPIC and benefit-sharing, which have been addressed in CBD guidelines and can be related to different dimensions of the human right to science. With regard to the dimension of sharing benefits from scientific progress, CBD Parties agreed that Indigenous peoples and local communities should receive fair and equitable benefits for their contribution to activities by academic institutions and other potential stakeholders in research projects related to traditional knowledge associated with biodiversity that are proposed to take place on, or that are likely to impact on, sacred sites and lands and waters traditionally occupied or used by communities.[200]

In relation to the second component of the human right to science (opportunity for all to contribute to scientific research), the CBD Tkarihwaié:ri Code of Ethical Conduct highlights that Indigenous peoples and local communities should have the opportunity to actively participate in research that impacts them or that makes use of their knowledge. The Code does not go as far as indicating in that context whether traditional knowledge holders should also contribute to set priorities for scientific research with a focus on key issues for the most vulnerable (the fourth component of the right to science). However, it indicates that Indigenous peoples and local communities should decide their own research priorities and conduct their own research.[201]

Acknowledging a significant layer of complexity, the Tkarihwaié:ri Code also highlights the connection between the protection of traditional knowledge and communities' land tenure, continued access to natural resources, and relationship with the environment.[202] This is an aspect that has so far been overshadowed by the perception that intellectual property rights are the greatest threat to traditional knowledge. The linkage between fair and equitable benefit-sharing and land tenure as an essential precondition for the protection and preservation of traditional knowledge remains to be elicited in the context of growing international guidance on responsible agricultural investment,[203] discussed in Chapter 5, and international human rights and investment disputes concerning land,[204] discussed earlier.

Even if traditional knowledge is recognized as a form of science, however, such recognition risks bringing about an idealized understanding of it as fixed in time. This may impose unfair burdens on traditional knowledge holders, constraining the further development of their knowledge systems in light of changed circumstances,

[199] CBD Tkarihwaié:ri Code of Ethical Conduct (n. 173), paras 1 and 14, which indicate that the code is not intended to 'interpret the obligations of the CBD'.

[200] CBD Tkarihwaié:ri Code of Ethical Conduct (n. 173), para. 14.

[201] ibid, para. 25. See also CESCR, General Comment No. 21 (n. 166), paras 36 and 50(c).

[202] CBD Tkarihwaié:ri Code of Ethical Conduct (n. 173), paras 15 and 17–18.

[203] VGGT (n. 3), Art. 8.6; and Committee on Food Security, Principles for Responsible Investment in Agriculture and Food Systems (2014), para. 23, iv.

[204] L Cotula, 'Land: Property and Sovereignty in International Law' in E Morgera and K Kulovesi (eds), *Research Handbook on International Law and Natural Resources* (Edward Elgar, 2015), 137.

including changes to traditional lifestyles within which traditional knowledge is rooted.[205] In effect, several of the possible benefits to be shared under the CBD are aimed at allowing communities to continue to provide global benefits by preserving and protecting the *communal way of life* that develops and maintains traditional knowledge and ecosystem stewardship.[206] Non-monetary benefits to be shared to this end comprise the legal recognition of community-based natural resource management[207] and the incorporation of traditional knowledge in environmental impact assessments[208] and in natural resource management planning.[209] These can serve as ways for traditional knowledge holders to be formally recognized as partners in natural resource management.

Another key benefit specific to the agricultural sector is the continuation of traditional seed uses and exchanges,[210] which is considered essential for farmers to continue to significantly contribute to global food security.[211] In addition, though, non-monetary benefits comprise different forms of support to enable communities to navigate increasingly complex and ever-changing technical, policy, and legal landscapes (from global to local level) that affect their traditional way of life. Such benefits include scientific and technical information and knowledge, direct investment opportunities, facilitated access to markets, and support for the diversification of income-generating opportunities for small and medium-sized businesses.[212] It is difficult to assess, however, whether these provisions are making a difference in practice, in the absence of systematic reporting and assessment of compliance under the CBD. Nevertheless, these guidelines arguably provide a detailed interpretative basis upon which to raise issues regarding the protection of Indigenous peoples' and other communities' traditional knowledge under relevant international human rights monitoring processes.

What remains to be further clarified is the interaction between FPIC and fair and equitable benefit-sharing from the use of traditional knowledge so that Indigenous peoples and local communities can be fully recognized and rewarded as co-creators of knowledge essential for the realization of local, national and global public goals. In principle, intra-State benefit-sharing should be seen as an embodiment of the conditions for granting FPIC,[213] as well as of the safeguards against the disrespect of such

[205] Vermeylen, Martin, and Clift (n. 175), at 207.

[206] CBD Secretariat, 'How Tasks 7, 10 and 12 Could Best Contribute to Work under the Convention and to the Nagoya Protocol', UN Doc UNEP/CBD/WG8J/8/4/Rev.2 (2013), para. 23.

[207] CBD expanded work programme on forest biodiversity, CBD Decision VI/22 (2002), para. 31 and programme element 1; CBD work programme on protected areas, CBD Decision VII/28 (2004), paras 2(1)(3)–2(1)(5).

[208] CBD Akwé: Kon Guidelines (n. 8), para. 56.

[209] Addis Ababa Principles and Guidelines on the Sustainable Use of Biodiversity, CBD Decision VII/12 (2004), Annex II, operational guidelines to Principle 4; CBD expanded work programme on forest biodiversity, CBD Decision VI/22 (2002), para. 13.

[210] Nagoya Protocol, Art. 12(4); ITPGR, Art. 9(3).

[211] E Tsioumani, 'Exploring Fair and Equitable Benefit-Sharing from the Lab to the Land (Part I): Agricultural Research and Development in the Context of Conservation and the Sustainable Use of Agricultural Biodiversity' Edinburgh School of Law Research Paper No. 2014/44 (SSRN, 2014), available at http://papers.ssrn.com/sol3/papers.cfm?abstract_id=2524337, accessed 29 June 2023, at 36–37.

[212] Addis Ababa Principles and Guidelines (n. 209), rationale to Principle 4; and CBD Guidelines on Tourism and Biodiversity, CBD Decision V/25 (2000), paras 22–23 and 43.

[213] So benefit-sharing could contribute to culturally appropriate and effective consultations: UN Expert Mechanism, Follow-up Report (n. 192), para. 43.

consent after it is granted.[214] In practice, however, benefit-sharing may be offered in exchange for obtaining consent.[215] The normative argument is that a mutually supportive interpretation and application of the human right to science and international biodiversity law can serve to critically assess how and to what extent FPIC and fair and equitable benefit-sharing effectively ensure that Indigenous and local knowledge holders influence decision-making processes that are underpinned by the science and evidence base they have contributed to create.

4.2 Small-Scale Fishers' Knowledge

The importance of small-scale fishers' knowledge is recognized by the SSF Guidelines and the UNDROP.[216] The latter recalls the rights to culture, practices, and knowledge, including ways of life, methods of production, and technology.[217] It specifically emphasizes traditional ways of fishing and community-based commercialization systems.[218] It also highlights the rights to use and protect peasants' traditional medicines, and to maintain their health practices using plants, animals, and minerals for medicinal use.[219] Complementing the UNDROP with a focus on means of implementation, the SSF Guidelines include as one of their objectives 'to enhance public awareness and promote the advancement of knowledge on the culture, role, contribution and potential of small-scale fisheries, considering ancestral and traditional knowledge, and their related constraints and opportunities'.[220] The SSF Guidelines emphasize the need for technical and financial assistance to maintain, organize, exchange, and improve traditional knowledge of aquatic living resources and fishing techniques.[221]

The UNDROP distinctly highlights the use of traditional knowledge of peasants, including small-scale fishers, in the design and implementation of climate change adaptation and mitigation policies,[222] which is less explicit in the SSF Guidelines. The UNDROP affirms their rights in contributing through the 'use of practices and traditional knowledge' in such endeavours,[223] whilst the SSF Guidelines do not mention 'traditional knowledge' in the section devoted to disaster risks and climate change.[224]

[214] Benefit-sharing would thus provide concrete expression of the accord granted by Indigenous peoples on the basis of their own understandings and preferences: UN Special Rapporteur on Indigenous Peoples' Rights James Anaya, Study on Extractive Industries and Indigenous Peoples, UN Doc A/HRC/24/41 (2013), para. 43.

[215] Inter-American Court of Human Rights, *Kichwa Indigenous Community of Sarayaku v. Ecuador*, Judgment of 27 June 2012 (Merits and Reparations), para. 194.

[216] SSF Guidelines (n. 3), paras 3.(1)(2), 5(18), 11(4), and 11(7); UNDROP, Arts. 18(3), 19(1)(2), 20(2), and 26.

[217] UNDROP, Art. 26.

[218] ibid, Art. 16(1).

[219] ibid, Art. 23(2).

[220] SSF Guidelines (n. 3), para. 1(1)(f).

[221] ibid, paras 11(4) and 11(7).

[222] UNDROP, Art. 18(3) (emphasis added, to contrast with the limitation to adaptation under the Paris Agreement discussed above).

[223] ibid, Art. 18(3).

[224] SSF Guidelines (n. 3), Section 9.

The UNDROP rather calls for full effective consultation with fishing communities, including Indigenous peoples, men, and women in the development of policies and plans to address climate change in fisheries.[225] The SSF Guidelines highlight the need for support in addressing climate change, through measures that secure disaster preparedness, emergency response, relief, and rehabilitation, and the role of small-scale fishers in supporting energy efficiency in their sector.[226] They further call for transparent access to adaptation funds, facilities, and culturally appropriate technologies for climate change adaptation.[227]

The need for caution in engaging with traditional knowledge holders and the safeguards related to consultation and benefit-sharing with traditional knowledge holders is clearly recognized in both international human rights jurisprudence and international biodiversity law,[228] but is not explicitly recalled in the UNDROP or the SSF Guidelines.[229] Nevertheless, the relevance of these safeguards can be read into the UNDROP, based on the combined effect of its provisions on traditional knowledge and on the right of access to natural resources,[230] as the development and transmission of traditional knowledge are intrinsic to the land tenure (including fishing grounds) and customary governance of natural resources.[231]

Arguably in line with the requirements of consultation and benefit-sharing at the intersection of international human rights law and international biodiversity law,[232] the UNDROP points to the role of the State in encouraging 'equitable and participatory partnerships' with scientists.[233] This is an important point with regard to the interface between small-scale fishing (and other peasant) communities' traditional knowledge and technology transfer.[234] While there may be growing political awareness of the benefits that could arise from marine technology transfer to these communities, the same attention has not been paid to actual and potential risks. This is particularly true with regard to technologies that seek to enhance the cost-efficiency of natural resource development. For instance, empirical evidence indicates that small-scale fishing communities' own local technologies are more likely to meet local needs for food[235] and

[225] ibid, para. 9(2).
[226] ibid, paras 9(2)–(8).
[227] ibid, paras 9(7) and 9(9).
[228] Framework Principles on Human rights and the Environment (n. 38), Framework Principle 15. See E Morgera, 'The Need for an International Legal Concept of Fair and Equitable Benefit Sharing' (2016) 27 European Journal of International Law 353.
[229] Though it has been subject to FAO's technical scrutiny in later studies. See J Fischer et al. (eds), *Fishers' Knowledge and the Ecosystem Approach to Fisheries: Applications, Experiences and Lessons in Latin America* (FAO, 2015) 591.
[230] UNDROP, Art. 5.
[231] This has been recognized internationally, which is evident in examples such as the preamble of the Nagoya Protocol: 'the interrelationship between genetic resources and traditional knowledge, their inseparable nature for indigenous and local communities . . . ' See Nagoya Protocol on Access to Genetic Resources and the Fair and Equitable Sharing of Benefits arising from their Utilization to the Convention on Biological Diversity (adopted 29 October 2010, entered into force 12 October 2014).
[232] See generally Morgera (n. 172).
[233] UNDROP, Art. 25(3).
[234] E Morgera and M Ntona, 'Linking Small-Scale Fisheries to International Obligations on Marine Technology Transfer' (2018) 93 Marine Policy 295.
[235] DS Johnson, 'Category, Narrative, and Value in the Governance of Small-scale Fisheries' (2006) 30 Marine Policy 747.

be sensitive to the location in which they are applied, the relative abundance of fishery resources, and the complex, traditional resource use rights.[236] Partnerships between peasant communities and scientists could thus focus on examining and evaluating 'local-specific, small-scale technologies, coupled with community-oriented, participatory measures to protect the ecological integrity of the living [. . .] resources', with a view to facilitating 'technology blending' to take advantage, where appropriate, of the positive aspects of other technologies.[237]

Returning to the matter of whether the protection of traditional knowledge helps address tensions around the environmental sustainability of small-scale fisheries and other peasant activities, the UNDROP frames these issues in terms of the environmental *rights* of peasants,[238] their entitlements to the conservation and sustainable use of rural areas and biodiversity as part of the efforts to protect their traditional knowledge and their right to livelihoods.[239] The SSF Guidelines, in turn, spell out the environmental *duties* of small-scale fishing communities (e.g. utilize non-destructive fishing practices and energy-efficiency operations),[240] once again taking the States' viewpoint as implementers of international fisheries law and applying the human rights-based approach to sector-specific contexts.

What the UNDROP adds, in that connection, is highlighting the need to 'challenge ingrained prejudices about the "backwardness", or "modernity," of different systems of livelihoods and beliefs, and of different forms of natural resource use'.[241] As Lorenzo Cotula emphasized, these prejudices indeed 'underpin the structural discrimination that peasants and Indigenous peoples experience in many legal systems'.[242] Moreover, these prejudices are reflected in the mainstream approaches to environmental sustainability in the fisheries sector.[243] In addition, the UNDROP puts traditional knowledge and innovation on equal grounds to ensure the full enjoyment of peasants' human rights[244] especially in relation to climate change. Commentators have pointed to States' obligations to provide adequate training on climate change adaptation, and potentially mitigation,[245] as an opportunity to create a partnership with traditional knowledge holders in that context.[246]

[236] C Bailey, D Cycon, and M Morris, 'Fisheries Development in the Third World: The Role of International Agencies' (1986) 14 World Development 1269.

[237] J Kurien, 'Small-scale Fisheries in the Context of Globalisation' (1998) CDS working papers series 29.

[238] That is, the 'right to conservation and protection of the environment and the productive capacity of their lands, and of the resources that they use': UNDROP, Art. 18(1) (emphasis added). The UNDROP is limited in providing environmental duties, with the exception of the duty not to store and dispose of hazardous material, substance or waste on peasants' land. See Art. 18(4).

[239] ibid, Art. 20.

[240] SSF Guidelines, paras 5(14) and 9(8) (emphasis added).

[241] Cotula (n. 55), at 520.

[242] ibid.

[243] Morgera and Nakamura (n. 45).

[244] E Cristiani and G Strambi, 'Farming Models and Peasants' Rights' in Albarese et al. (n. 42) 177, at 183.

[245] UNDROP Art. 25; M Albarese and A Savaresi, 'The UNDROP and Climate Change' in Albarese et al. (n. 42), 165, at 166–167.

[246] Albarese and Savaresi (ibid), at 170.

4.3 Indigenous and Local Knowledge in Bio-Based Innovation

The CBD provisions on intra-State benefit-sharing have also been developed into a binding obligation under the Nagoya Protocol in relation to traditional knowledge 'associated with genetic resources' in the specific context of bio-based research and development.[247] Because of the political emphasis placed on biopiracy as the unlawful use of traditional knowledge for commercial innovation purposes, however, limited attention has so far been paid under international biodiversity law to FPIC and benefit-sharing from the non-commercial use of traditional knowledge, including in the context of pure research aimed at providing global benefits (such as advancing biodiversity and climate science).[248]

It could be argued that the innovative provisions of the Nagoya Protocol on benefit-sharing with Indigenous peoples and local communities[249] serve to recognize and reward these communities for sharing their traditional knowledge in ways that benefit humanity as a whole in terms of conservation and sustainable use of biodiversity.[250] In addition, the Protocol contains provisions embodying recognition, such as the acknowledgement of communities' worldview that genetic resources and traditional knowledge are interconnected,[251] despite being regulated separately under the Protocol. The latter seems to indicate conceptual and political difficulties in embodying Indigenous and local communities' understanding into the operative text of the treaty.

Some of the benefits listed in the Nagoya Protocol may further contribute to recognition, such as the joint ownership of intellectual property rights[252] and what is laconically termed 'social recognition'.[253] Furthermore, the Protocol contains an obligation for Parties to take into consideration communities' customary laws, protocols, and procedures,[254] and a qualified prohibition of restricting customary uses and exchanges of genetic resources among these communities.[255] This provision has been hailed as the first instance in international environmental law of inter-cultural legal pluralism,[256] but has also raised concerns about the 'magnitude of challenges for a

[247] Nagoya Protocol, Arts 5(5) and 7; ITPGR, Arts 9(2)(a) and 13(3). Morgera, Tsioumani, and Buck (n. 5), at 126–130; E Tsioumani, 'Exploring Fair and Equitable Benefit-Sharing from the Lab to the Land (Part I): Agricultural Research and Development in the Context of Conservation and the Sustainable Use of Agricultural Biodiversity' Edinburgh School of Law Research Paper No. 2014/44 (SSRN, 2014), available at http://papers.ssrn.com/sol3/papers.cfm?abstract_id=2524337, accessed 29 June 2023, at 34–39.

[248] Consider, for instance, Intergovernmental Panel on Climate Change, 'Climate Change 2007: Impacts, Adaptation and Vulnerability. Contribution of Working Group II to the Fourth Assessment Report of the Intergovernmental Panel on Climate Change' (2007), at 138 and 673 and UNESCO Declaration on Bioethics and Human Rights (2005), Art. 17.

[249] Nagoya Protocol, Arts 5(2), (4), and 7.

[250] This understanding derives from tracing the origins of these provisions in the Protocol back to CBD, Art. 8(j) and the CBD decisions on the ecosystem approach (CBD Decision V/6 (2000) and CBD Decision VII/11 (2004)). See the discussion in Morgera (n. 172), at 813.

[251] Nagoya Protocol, preambular recital 22.

[252] ibid, Annex, 1(j) and 2(q).

[253] ibid, Annex 2(p).

[254] ibid, Art. 12(1). See Morgera, Tsioumani, and Buck (n. 5), at 217–227.

[255] Nagoya Protocol, Art. 12(4). See Morgera, Tsioumani, and Buck (n. 5), at 227–228.

[256] K Bavikatte and DF Robinson, 'Towards a People's History of the Law: Biocultural Jurisprudence and the Nagoya Protocol on Access and Benefit Sharing' (2011) 7 Law Environment and Development 35, at 35.

cosmopolitan and intercultural legal order that does justice to the means of knowing of Indigenous peoples' on the basis of terms agreed in international law that 'pre-arranged and confined by hegemonic forms of scientific knowledge and policy visions'.[257] Therefore, in this specific regard international law cannot simply be 'imposed but must be negotiated, tested and modulated in response to the realities of differing worldviews, value systems and legal visions'.[258]

In many ways, the Nagoya Protocol frames benefit-sharing from traditional knowledge as *procedural* justice. Its provisions on prior informed consent appear significantly concerned with ensuring procedural justice towards those seeking access to resources,[259] and may be considered 'thin' from a justice perspective.[260] In addition, the language concerning the prior informed consent of Indigenous peoples and local communities is heavily qualified.[261] Nevertheless, these provisions are the first explicit treaty language in international law on the need for consent in relation to traditional knowledge and genetic resources.[262]

To ensure that these provisions are interpreted in a mutually supportive way with international human rights law, the substantive dimensions of FPIC clarified by international human rights jurisprudence should be respected: benefits shared with Indigenous peoples should be culturally appropriate and endogenously determined.[263] This understanding needs, therefore, to guide those seeking access to Indigenous peoples' genetic resources and traditional knowledge, by also seeking to understand their values, norms, and decision-making processes. It also entails that benefit-sharing in this context should be seen as integral to the need for better recognition and realization of communities' rights to the lands and natural resources traditionally used and occupied by them, while improving material conditions for their livelihoods and self-determination. In other words, the mutually supportive interpretation of intra-State benefit-sharing (drawing on the Nagoya Protocol preambular reference to the UN Declaration on the Rights of Indigenous Peoples[264]) can contribute to commutative and distributive justice, as well as to justice as recognition.

[257] JB Kleba and D Ragnekar, 'Introduction' (2013) 9 Law Environment and Development Journal 98, at 103–104, referring to S Vermeylen, 'The Nagoya Protocol and Customary Law: The Paradox of Narratives in the Law' (2013) 9 Law Environment and Development Journal 185, at 185. See also U Brand and A Vadrot, 'Epistemic Selectivities and the Valorisation of Nature: The Cases of the Nagoya Protocol and the Intergovernmental Science-Policy Platform for Biodiversity and Ecosystem Services' (2013) 9 Law Environment and Development Journal 204.

[258] B Tobin, 'Bridging the Nagoya Compliance Gap: The Fundamental Role of Customary Law in the Protection of Indigenous Peoples' Resources and Knowledge Rights' (2013) 9 Law Environment and Development Journal 144, at 162.

[259] Nagoya Protocol, Art. 6(3). See Morgera, Tsiouamani, and Buck (n. 5), at 157–169.

[260] Kleba and Ragnekar (n. 257), at 102.

[261] Nagoya Protocol, Arts 6(2) and 7. See Morgera, Tsioumani, and Buck (n. 5), at 145–156 and 170–174.

[262] UN Special Rapporteur on the Rights of Indigenous Peoples James Anaya considered the recognition of the right to prior informed consent over traditional knowledge as 'positive aspects' of the adoption of the Protocol: Human Rights Council, Follow-up Report (n. 192), para. 59.

[263] See Inter-American Court of Human Rights, *Case of the Saramaka People v. Suriname*, Judgment of 12 August 2008 (Interpretation of the Judgment on Preliminary Objections, Merits, Reparations and Costs), paras 25–27; Refinement and Elaboration of the Ecosystem Approach, CBD Decision VII/11 (2004), Annex, paras 1(8) and 2(1); and CBD Tkarihwaié:ri Code of Ethical Conduct (n. 173), para. 14.

[264] Nagoya Protocol, preambular recital 26; United Nations Declaration on the Rights of Indigenous Peoples, UNGA Res 61/295 (2007).

4.4 Indigenous and Local Knowledge at the International Science-Policy Interface

International environmental science-policy processes have increasingly engaged with Indigenous and local knowledge, giving rise to transnational dimensions of benefit-sharing in this context. The Intergovernmental Science-Policy Platform on Biodiversity and Ecosystem Services (IPBES)[265] has been developing approaches and participatory processes to integrate traditional knowledge into regional and thematic assessments of biodiversity and ecosystem services.[266] These approaches are based on the respect for Indigenous and local knowledge systems' validation procedures, as well as FPIC, benefit-sharing, and recognition of rights and attribution,[267] taking into account guidance adopted under the CBD.[268] However, the work of IPBES has also highlighted unresolved questions regarding how to empower traditional knowledge holders to contribute to global environmental assessment processes, and the lack of adequate finance and capacity-building mechanisms.[269] More empirical evidence is needed to ascertain whether and to what extent the integration of traditional knowledge in IPBES work is developing into a fair and equitable benefit-sharing practice that can support transformative change.

Along similar lines, the Paris Agreement Parties set up an Indigenous Peoples and Local Communities' Platform for the exchange of experiences and sharing of best practices on mitigation and adaptation for working with Indigenous and local knowledge, including the use of safeguards; information to strengthen linkages to knowledge, technologies, practices, and efforts to address climate change; and information on other processes beyond the United Nations Framework Convention on Climate Change (UNFCCC).[270] The Platform was expected to build capacity among Indigenous peoples and local communities to effectively engage in international climate change governance and facilitate the integration of diverse knowledge systems in climate change-related actions, programmes, and policies. This entails supporting national and regional efforts to build synergies between local and Indigenous knowledge and science to inform climate change decision-making, and facilitating cooperation to support local communities and Indigenous peoples to apply their traditional knowledge and practice to climate action.[271]

[265] C Chiarolla, and A Savaresi, 'Indigenous Challenges under IPBES: Embracing Indigenous Knowledge and Beyond' in M Hrabanski and D Pesche (eds), The Intergovernmental Platform on Biodiversity and Ecosystem Services (IPBES): Challenges, Knowledge and Actors (Earthscan, 2016). See also A Vadrot, *The Birth of a Science-Policy Interface for Biodiversity: The History of IPBES* (Routledge, 2017) 190.

[266] IPBES, Update on Deliverable 1(c) Indigenous and Local Knowledge Procedures and Approaches, IPBES/3/INF/2 (2014), Annex II.

[267] See also the Knowledge, Information and Data Plan and draft strategy in IPBES, Update on Deliverable 1(d) Data and Knowledge (2014) IPBES/3/INF/3, Annex I, para. 9.

[268] IPBES/1/INF/5, 3.

[269] IPBES Task Force on Indigenous and Local Knowledge Systems, 97; see the discussion in A Savaresi, 'Traditional Knowledge and Climate Change: A New Legal Frontier?' (2018) 9 Journal of Human Rights and the Environment 32.

[270] United Nations Framework Convention on Climate Change (UNFCCC) (New York, 9 May 1992, in force 21 March 1994). UNFCCC Decision 1/CP.21 (2016), 135–136; Decision 2/CP.23 (2018).

[271] A Savaresi, 'Benefit-sharing and traditional knowledge: recent developments and new frontiers in the climate regime', BENELEX blog (8 November 2017) **https://benelexblog.wordpress.com/2017/11/08/bene**

The Platform was also meant to embody the following principles: full and effective participation of Indigenous peoples; equal status of Indigenous peoples and Parties; self-selection of Indigenous peoples representatives in accordance with Indigenous peoples' own procedures; and adequate funding to support participation in the work of the Platform.[272] These principles are particularly important because previously, the climate regime's subsidiary bodies undertook action to collate existing traditional knowledge databases on adaptation,[273] but at that time Parties had not adopted specific guidance.[274]

While the Indigenous Peoples and Local Communities' Platform has evolved in a self-organized space within the international climate change framework for significant exchanges among Indigenous peoples and other knowledge holders, UN Special Rapporteur on Climate Change and Human Rights Ian Fry raised serious concern in 2022 about it 'not [being] an adequate substitute for meaningful and active participation in negotiations'.[275] Instead, Fry reported that Indigenous peoples have virtually no say in the negotiations or input into their outcomes 'apart from brief interventions in the opening plenary meetings'.[276]

In comparison, this section will focus on the integration of Indigenous and local knowledge in the 2023 Agreement on the Conservation and Sustainable Use of Marine Biological Diversity of Areas beyond National Jurisdiction (BBNJ),[277] as an example of a treaty where transnational dimensions of fair and equitable benefit-sharing are taken into account, implicitly and explicitly, through a series of provisions that concern both national-level action and participation in multilateral institutions and global processes. This is particularly interesting as initially in the BBNJ negotiations it was not clear whether Indigenous and local knowledge had any relevance or presence in relation to marine areas beyond national jurisdiction. Over time, however, traditional knowledge has been increasingly recognized as relevant in relation to: connectivity of species and marine processes across areas within and beyond national jurisdiction; traditional management practices that can provide models for areas beyond national jurisdiction; and (revived) traditional instrument-free navigation in areas within and beyond national jurisdiction, which may offer potential pathways for bioprospecting endeavours.[278] However, equity issues concerning epistemic justice and recognition have emerged regarding the inclusion of traditional knowledge in the notion of 'best

fit-sharing-and-traditional-knowledge-recent-developments-and-new-frontiers-in-the-climate-regime/, accessed 31 July 2023.

[272] ibid.

[273] UN Doc FCCC/SB/2015/2 (2015).

[274] UN Doc FCCC/TP/2013/11 (2013), at 8.

[275] UN Special Rapporteur on the promotion and protection of human rights in the context of climate change Ian Fry, 'Promotion and protection of human rights in the context of climate change mitigation, loss and damage and participation', UN Doc A/77/226 (2022), para. 80.

[276] ibid, para. 77.

[277] Agreement under the United Nations Convention on the Law of the Sea on the Conservation and Sustainable Use of Marine Biological Diversity of Areas beyond National Jurisdiction (New York, 19 June 2023, A/CONF.232/2023/4, not yet in force).

[278] M Vierros et al., 'Considering Indigenous Peoples and Local Communities in Governance of the Global Ocean Commons' (2018) 119 Marine Policy 104039; C Yow Mulalap et al., 'Traditional Knowledge and the BBNJ Instrument' (2020) 122 Marine Policy 104103, at 1 and 6.

scientific knowledge' and the degree of participation of traditional knowledge holders with regard to environmental impact assessments (EIAs) and marine protected areas.

The BBNJ Agreement considers as a general principle for its overall implementation 'the use of relevant traditional knowledge of Indigenous Peoples and local communities, where available'.[279] It makes both explicit and implicit reference to human rights. Its Preamble and one of its general principles refer to respecting, promoting, and considering the 'rights of Indigenous Peoples or of, as appropriate, local communities'.[280] It also provides more specifically for the respectful integration of Indigenous and local knowledge in its decision-making processes, subject to international human rights safeguards.[281]

In addition, BBNJ Parties are specifically required to take legislative, administrative, or policy measures to ensure that traditional knowledge associated with marine genetic resources in areas beyond national jurisdiction that is held by Indigenous Peoples and local communities is only accessed with their FPIC, approval, and involvement, on mutually agreed terms.[282] Parties are then required to collaborate and consult, as appropriate, with Indigenous Peoples and local communities in the development of proposals for area-based management tools (ABMTs). These proposals will be formulated on the basis of 'where available, relevant traditional knowledge . . . taking into account the precautionary approach and an ecosystem approach'.[283] Furthermore, Parties and the Secretariat are required to facilitate consultations with Indigenous Peoples and local communities with relevant traditional knowledge on ABMT proposals.[284]

Measures adopted on an emergency basis proposed by Parties or recommended by the Scientific and Technical Body must be based on the best available science and scientific data and 'where available, relevant traditional knowledge of Indigenous Peoples and local communities'[285] This requirement extends to the review of ABMTs by the Conference of the Parties, which can result in decisions or recommendations on the amendment, extension, or revocation of these tools.[286]

As part of EIAs screening, Parties are required to determine whether an EIA is necessary in respect of a planned activity under their jurisdiction or control, in a timely manner and on the basis of traditional knowledge, if available.[287] Parties are required to ensure that the impacts of planned activities, including cumulative impacts and impacts in areas within national jurisdiction, are assessed and evaluated using relevant traditional knowledge.[288] Traditional knowledge should also be relied upon to monitor the impacts of these activities. This monitoring helps to determine whether the authorized activities, under their jurisdiction or control, are likely to have adverse impacts on the marine environment, as well as considering the economic, social,

[279] BBNJ Agreement, Art 7(j).
[280] ibid, Art. 7(k). See also Framework Principles on Human rights and the Environment (n. 38), Framework Principle 15 and Morgera (n. 120).
[281] BBNJ Agreement, Arts 7(i)–(j).
[282] ibid, Art. 13.
[283] ibid, Art. 19(2)–(3) and 4(j).
[284] ibid, Art. 21(2)(c).
[285] ibid, Art. 24(3).
[286] ibid, Art. 26(5).
[287] ibid, Art. 31(1)(c).
[288] ibid.

cultural, and human health impacts, in accordance with the conditions set out in the approval of the activity.[289] In addition, the BBNJ Scientific and Technical Body may notify the Party that authorized the activity if it considers that the activity may have significant adverse impacts that were either not foreseen in the EIA or that arise from a breach of any conditions of approval of that authorized activity. It may make recommendations to the Party as appropriate, including on the basis of Indigenous Peoples' and local communities' relevant traditional knowledge.[290] The Scientific and Technical Body is then required to consider and may evaluate the matter based on relevant and available traditional knowledge.[291] Strategic Environmental Assessments[292] also involve consideration of broader human rights implications for Indigenous and local knowledge holders.[293]

Furthermore, the BBNJ Agreement integrates considerations of traditional knowledge in relation to capacity building and the transfer of marine technology through reference to 'information dissemination and awareness-raising . . . with respect to relevant traditional knowledge of Indigenous Peoples and local communities' in line with their FPIC.[294]

From an institutional perspective, the BBNJ COP is required to promote transparency in the implementation of this Agreement, including through the public dissemination of information and the facilitation of the participation of, and consultation with, Indigenous peoples and local communities with relevant traditional knowledge.[295] Representatives of Indigenous peoples and local communities may request to participate as observers in the COP meetings and meetings of its subsidiary bodies.[296] In addition, the Scientific and Technical Body will be composed of members serving in their expert capacity and in the best interests of the Agreement, nominated by Parties and elected by the COP, taking into account the need for multidisciplinary expertise, including relevant scientific and technical expertise and expertise in relevant traditional knowledge, gender balance, and equitable geographical representation.[297]

In addition, the BBNJ clearinghouse will provide links to relevant global, regional, subregional, national, and sectoral clearinghouse mechanisms and other gene banks, repositories, and databases, including those pertaining to relevant traditional knowledge, and promote, where possible, links with publicly available private and nongovernmental platforms for the exchange of information.[298] The special fund and the

[289] ibid, Art. 35.
[290] ibid, Art. 37(3)–(4).
[291] ibid, Art. 37(4)(c).
[292] Morgera et al., 'Addressing the Ocean-Climate Nexus in the BBNJ Agreement: Strategic Environmental Assessments, Human Rights and Equity in Ocean Science' (2023) 38 International Journal of Marine and Coastal Law 403; and M Strand et al., 'Reimagining Ocean Stewardship: Arts-Based Methods to 'Hear' and 'See' Indigenous and Local Knowledge in Ocean Management' (2022) Frontiers in Marine Science 886632.
[293] J Nakamura, D Diz, and E Morgera, 'International Legal Requirements for Environmental and Sociocultural Assessments for Large-scale Industrial Fisheries' (2022) 31 Review of European, Comparative and International Environmental Law 336, at 347. See also N Craik and K Gu, 'Strategic Environmental Assessment in Marine Areas beyond National Jurisdiction: Implementing Integration' (2022) 37 International Journal of Marine and Coastal Law 189, at 213.
[294] BBNJ Agreement, Art. 44(1)(b).
[295] ibid, Art. 48(3).
[296] ibid, Art. 48(4).
[297] ibid, Art. 49(2).
[298] ibid, Art. 51(3)(b).

Global Environment Facility trust fund are to be utilized in order to support conservation and sustainable use programmes by Indigenous peoples and local communities as holders of traditional knowledge.[299]

It remains to be seen, when the BBNJ Agreement enters into force, whether its implementation will effectively represent fair and equitable benefit-sharing from the integration of Indigenous and local knowledge in global ocean governance. Nonetheless, it stands as the most sophisticated expression within an international treaty regarding the recognition and integration of Indigenous and local knowledge at the international science-policy interface.

5. Fair and Equitable Benefit-Sharing with Local Knowledge Holders for Transformative Change

Intra-State and transnational benefit-sharing from the use of Indigenous and local knowledge, as well as intra-community benefit-sharing, remain largely untheorized. Such theorization, however, and considerations of different dimensions of justice—notably recognition of different knowledge systems and their distinctive contributions to sustainable development—can arguably be advanced by relying on the cross-fertilization of international biodiversity and international human rights law, as discussed in Chapter 3 with regard to Indigenous peoples. The recognition and integration of the distinctive ecological knowledge of non-Indigenous communities and rural women in decision-making affecting their lives contributes to: prevent discrimination; protect their rights to food, livelihoods, and culture; and ensure inclusion of their ecosystem stewardship in natural resource policies and practices to the benefit of everyone's human right to a healthy environment.

These forms of benefit-sharing are all crucial from the perspective of transformative change. IPBES[300] advocated for transformative change to address the intertwined global planetary crises. IPBES has referred to transformation as 'a fundamental, system-wide change that includes consideration of technological, economic and social factors, including in terms of paradigms, goals or values'.[301] It has also called attention to '[o]bstacles to achieving transformative change, including unequal power relations, lack of transparency, vested interests, unequal distribution of the costs and benefits of actions, tendencies for short-term decision-making, the psychology of losses and gains, the logic of market-driven processes, the lack of policy coherence and inertia'.[302] The key to transformative change is addressing inequalities, including regarding income and gender, which undermine the capacity for sustainability; inclusive

[299] ibid, Art. 31(1)(a)(ii).

[300] IPBES, 'Initial Scoping Report for Deliverable 1 (c): A Thematic Assessment of the Underlying Causes of Biodiversity Loss and the Determinants of Transformative Change and Options for Achieving the 2050 Vision for Biodiversity' (2021), available at https://ipbes.net/sites/default/files/Initial_scoping_transformative_change_assessment_EN.pdf, accessed 30 June 2023.

[301] S Díaz et al., 'Summary for Policymakers of the Global Assessment Report on Biodiversity and Ecosystem Services of the Intergovernmental Science-Policy Platform on Biodiversity and Ecosystem Services' (IPBES 2019),

[302] ibid, at 17.

decision-making, as well as the fair and equitable sharing of benefits arising from the use of biodiversity and its conservation; and the recognition and respectful inclusion of the knowledge and innovations of Indigenous peoples and local communities in environmental governance.[303]

Inter-disciplinary research has thus advanced the companion notion of transformative governance as a shift from 'the technocratic and regulatory fix of environmental problems to more fundamental and transformative changes in social-political processes and economic relations'.[304] Biodiversity scholars have called for transformative governance to be about co-developing transformative change by 'preventing a shifting of the burden of response onto the vulnerable; paying attention to social differentiation, through the lens of non-discrimination; and addressing issues of power and legitimacy'.[305] Transdisciplinary research is seen as a key component of transformative governance: the recognition of different knowledge systems and the inclusion of overlooked types of knowledge are seen as essential components of a process ensuring that solutions not only have sustainable impacts at various levels and sectors, but also empowers those whose interests and knowledge are currently overlooked but represent transformative sustainability values.[306] This is expected to enable learning, experimentation, reflexivity, monitoring, and feedback.[307] Co-production is understood in this context as 'social partnership and joint governance' that relies on the development of 'shared concepts of collaboration'.[308] These shared concepts could build upon the principles and requirements for resilience of socio-ecological systems, such as continuous learning, adaptive systems thinking, openness, and long-term monitoring and data sharing.[309] This in turn would require inter- and trans-disciplinary research to develop new, or adapt existing, scientific methods and tools, such as modelling, to the respectful and constructive integration of traditional knowledge, while international experience on the integration of Indigenous and local knowledge in global scientific assessments is being accrued.[310]

Ultimately, the international provisions on fair and equitable benefit-sharing towards Indigenous and local knowledge holders and rural women provide a legal basis not only to protect their human rights, but also to explore how the full realization of their human rights can support the development of transformative approaches to knowledge co-production and the co-development of sustainability solutions across cultures and worldviews. The normative argument advanced here is that fully

[303] ibid.
[304] IJ Visseren-Hamakers and MTJ Kok, 'Introduction' in I Visseren-Hamakers and M Kok (eds), *Transforming Biodiversity Governance* (Cambridge University Press, 2022) 3.
[305] ibid.
[306] ibid.
[307] ibid.
[308] B Nerlich, 'The Co-production Confusion' University of Nottingham blog post (20 March 2015) available at https://blogs.nottingham.ac.uk/makingsciencepublic/2015/03/20/the-co-production-confusion/ accessed 30 June 2023, indicating that this understanding is predominantly used in public policy but overlaps in part with science and technology studies.
[309] S Yadav and K Gjerde, 'The Ocean, Climate Change and Resilience: Making Ocean Areas beyond National Jurisdiction More Resilient to Climate Change and Other Anthropogenic Activities' (2020) 122 Marine Policy 104184, at 6.
[310] M Vierros et al., 'Considering Indigenous Peoples and Local Communities in Governance of the Global Ocean Commons' (2018) 119 Marine Policy 104039.

realizing the human right to science in this context can support transformative environmental governance 'that has the capacity to respond to, manage, and trigger regime shifts in coupled socio-ecological systems at multiple scales',[311] to the benefit of everyone's human right to a healthy environment. Such transformative governance, supported by fair and equitable benefit-sharing across the knowledge production chain from basic research to local and national environmental management and the global science-policy interface, can arguably lead to the co-development of solutions that have sustainable impacts across different scales and sectors, by integrating those whose interests are currently being overlooked and who represent values that contribute to sustainable development.[312]

[311] ibid. See also Yadav and Gjerde (n. 309), at 6.

[312] B Erinosho et al., 'Integrative and Inclusive Governance for Ocean Biodiversity' in Visseren-Hamakers and Kok (n. 304), 313.

5

Transnational Dimensions of Intra-State Benefit-Sharing

Business Responsibility to Respect Indigenous Peoples' Human Rights

1. Introduction

This chapter will analyse the role of international standards on fair and equitable benefit-sharing as part of the concept of due diligence in the context of business responsibility to respect human rights.[1] These are cases of transnational benefit-sharing, as they often involve multinational companies that are protected by international investment law. These standards related both to private sector-driven extractives and conservation in or near lands traditionally used by Indigenous peoples (discussed in Chapters 3 and 4 with a focus on intra-State benefit-sharing).

From an incompletely theorized agreement perspective, this chapter will provide a reflection on the current status of the progressive development of international law on the role of the private sector in respecting international law on human rights and the environment. It discusses the extent to which references to fair and equitable benefit-sharing in this context serve to illuminate the delicate line between obligations for public authorities and expectations based on the reach of private business actors. From a global law perspective, this chapter will provide an opportunity to discuss the role of (domestic) private law on contracts in the context of transnational benefit-sharing agreements, as well as the role of international benefit-sharing standards in influencing national and transnational practices.

From an environmental justice perspective, this chapter explores the role of private companies, including multinational corporations, in relation to distributive justice issues arising from the use of territories belonging to Indigenous peoples. Procedural justice issues are also explored in this context. The latter is particularly important as a number of domestic procedures for consultation and environmental assessments are effectively left in the hands of private businesses. Furthermore, issues of recognition arise in the context of ensuring culturally appropriate processes of communication and partnerships between private companies and Indigenous peoples. Contextual justice issues are also relevant depending on the support that Indigenous peoples receive from the State, and in cases of great power and information asymmetries, companies themselves may be called to support Indigenous peoples' capabilities to engage with them as partners.

[1] This chapter draws on E Morgera, *Corporate Environmental Accountability in International Law* (2nd edn, Oxford University Press, 2020).

Fair and Equitable Benefit-Sharing in International Law. Elisa Morgera, Oxford University Press. © Elisa Morgera 2024.
DOI: 10.1093/oso/9780198862130.003.0006

This chapter explains the emergence of international soft-law initiatives on business and human rights, and their respective references to benefit-sharing as safeguards for, or even a partnership model with, Indigenous peoples and other communities. The chapter concludes with a reflection on the different uses that can be made of these international standards in practice.

2. Business Due Diligence and International Law

Since the 1940s, multinational corporations have established themselves as major actors in the world economy through their ability to combine production factors around the world and achieve economic efficiency on a global scale.[2] The global reach of multinational corporations has significantly and rapidly increased their capacity to act at a pace and scale surpassing that of governments nor international organizations,[3] with various examples of adverse environmental and human rights consequences of corporate misconduct in the natural resource sector.[4]

Privatization of services related to the management of natural resources (such as water utilities) raises particular concerns. For instance, governments may not be able to adequately regulate multinationals to ensure fair prices for basic services and the proper consideration of environmental impacts. In essence, 'the internationalisation of production of goods and services by multinationals increases the likelihood of any related environmental damage to a greater number of countries and to a larger part of the world's environment'.[5]

In principle, multinationals are subject to the control of the State in which they operate (the 'host State'), both at the time of entry into its territory and during their operations. In practice, however, due to competition among host States to receive foreign investment, the bargaining strength of multinationals is at its highest at the time of entry[6] and host States may be severely limited by the terms of bilateral investment treaties they have entered into. After a multinational company is established, host States may have limited financial and human resources for effectively implementing and enforcing national environmental laws upon them, as well as limited information on the technology and the associated risks linked to the activities of these multinationals. Should damage occur, the so-called 'corporate veil' may prevent the host State from obtaining redress for victims. Multinationals have the ability to arrange

[2] KP Sauvant and V Aranda, 'The International Legal Framework for Transnational Corporations' in AA Fatouros (ed.), *Transnational Corporations: The International Legal Framework* (Routledge, 1994) 83, at 86; and A Perry-Kessaris, 'Corporate Liability for Environmental Harm' in M Fitzmaurice, D Ong, and P Merkouris (eds), *Research Handbook on International Environmental Law* (Edward Elgar, 2010) 361.

[3] Special Representative of the Secretary-General on the issue of Human Rights and Transnational Corporations and Other Business Enterprises John Ruggie, Interim Report, UN Doc E/CN.4/2006/97 (2006), paras 12 and 16.

[4] See Human Rights Committee (HRC), 'Report of the Working Group on the issues of human rights and transnational corporations and other business enterprises' UN Doc A/HRC/29/28 (2015), paras 89 and UN Doc A/HRC/26/25 (2014), para. 79.

[5] United Nations Conference on Trade and Development (UNCTAD), *Environment* (UNCTAD, 2001), at 7.

[6] e.g. M Sornarajah, *The International Law on Foreign Investment* (Cambridge University Press, 2010), chapter 2.

their company structure and financial assets in a way that limits the liability of the parent company thereby leaving a subsidiary with insufficient financial resources to compensate for damage, while the home State courts may lack jurisdiction over foreign entities, or be unable to enforce a judgment against them.[7] Furthermore, host country courts may be faced with significant conflicts of interest, as the host State may have authorized the foreign company's damaging operations, or even be directly involved in the business venture.

Control over multinationals can also be exercised by the State in which they are incorporated or have their headquarters (the 'home State'), through the extraterritorial application of home or international standards over multinational enterprises' (MNE) operations abroad.[8] Home State control, however, raises concerns regarding respect for the national sovereignty of foreign countries. It can lead to the application of different standards to MNEs operating in the same industry sector, depending on their country of origin; and faces major logistical, financial, and technical barriers. In addition, transnational litigation aimed at holding accountable parent companies in the home State[9] faces several challenges.[10] Home State courts often rely on their discretion to refuse to hear a case if the forum is inappropriate or inconvenient to the defendant (the doctrine of *forum non conveniens*). Furthermore, questions of jurisdiction have placed unfair obstacles in the way of foreign plaintiffs, thereby implicitly discriminating in favour of multinationals. In addition, home State judges may be unwilling to pierce the corporate veil, or might be concerned about affecting foreign relations between the home and host State. This adds to the extremely expensive and time-consuming nature of transnational litigation and to the high standard of proof expected from victims. Issues of enforcement in the host country of judgments issued in the home country are equally formidable.[11]

Against this background, an ongoing debate, which started in the 1970s, continues to haunt the international community in its efforts to come to grips first with de-colonization and now with globalization. This debate led, on 25 June 2014, to the Human Rights Council's decision to establish a process to elaborate an international legally binding instrument on transnational corporations and other business enterprises.[12] Significantly, the resolution was adopted by a majority vote with twenty countries in favour, fourteen against (including the United States and the European Union), and thirteen abstentions.[13] The proponents of the resolution emphasized that binding

[7] T Scovazzi, 'Industrial Accidents and the Veil of Transnational Corporations' in F Francioni and T Scovazzi (eds), *International Responsibility for Environmental Harm* (Graham & Trotman, 1991) 395.

[8] e.g. Sornarajah (n. 6), chapter 3.

[9] H Ward, 'Securing Transnational Corporate Accountability through National Courts: Implications and Policy Options' (2000) 24 Hastings International and Comparative Law Review 451.

[10] UNCHR, 'Interim Report of the Special Representative of the Secretary-General on the issue of Human Rights and Transnational Corporations, and other Business Enterprises', UN Doc E/CN.4/2006/97 (2006), para. 62.

[11] e.g. A Khokhryakova, 'Beanal v Freeport-Mcmoran, Inc.: Liability of a Private Actor for an International Environmental Tort under the Alien Tort Claims Act' (1998) 9 Colorado Journal of International Environmental Law and Policy 463.

[12] HRC Res 26/9 (25 June 2014).

[13] UNCHR, 'Council extends mandates on extreme poverty, international solidarity, independence of judges, and trafficking in persons' (26 June 2014), available at http://www.ohchr.org/en/NewsEvents/Pages/DisplayNews.aspx?NewsID=14785&LangID=E#sthash.oEXXs44o.dBWOFzwf.dpuf, accessed 29 June 2023.

international law already affords significant protection to foreign companies.[14] Multinationals benefit greatly from international investment law and can also obtain protection under international human rights law, but are not subject to corresponding international obligations in relation to the sustainable use of natural resources and human rights. Conversely, the victims of harmful corporate activities can only rely on international voluntary instruments. Those that voted against the resolution argued that international guidelines and national law, rather than an international treaty, are the most suitable approaches to address the matter.[15] The negotiating process is ongoing at the time of writing.[16]

The prolonged and ongoing international debate on corporate accountability is a stark illustration of the limitations of international law in effectively regulating the use of natural resources. This is also compounded by tensions among different bodies of international law. As Lorenzo Cotula has argued, while both international human rights and investment law set minimum standards and judicial review mechanisms with regards to the exercise of state sovereignty over natural resources, they are characterized by 'different historical trajectories, philosophical and conceptual approaches and different standards of protection'.[17] International investment law provides stronger protection to multinationals than international human rights law does to victims of corporate abuses, both in terms of substantive standards and in terms of accessibility and enforceability of remedies.[18] International environmental law is characterized even more by broad and flexible standards of protection and less stringent enforcement mechanisms.[19] This translates, at the local level, in stronger protection to large-scale, if not foreign, operators to the detriment of local actors, particularly Indigenous peoples and local communities, with little negotiating power and significant vulnerability to environmental degradation in the context of natural resource development.[20] At the same time, the international debate on corporate accountability shows how international law continually adapts, evolving gradually and in nuanced ways to address new challenges. It does so by forging synergies among human rights and environmental law, drawing upon their relative strengths to tackle new issues.[21] Notably, it could be considered an expression of equity *infra legem*. That said, it remains to be seen if this evolutive interpretation will suffice to counter the imbalances in international investment law as equity *contra legem*.[22]

[14] ibid.
[15] ibid.
[16] Updated draft legally binding instrument to regulate, in international human rights law, the activities of transnational corporations and other business enterprises (July 2023), available at https://www.ohchr.org/sites/default/files/documents/hrbodies/hrcouncil/igwg-transcorp/session9/igwg-9th-updated-draft-lbi-clean.pdf, accessed 9 February 2024.
[17] L Cotula, *Human Rights, Natural Resource and Investment Law in a Globalized World: Shades of Grey in the Shadow of the Law* (Routledge, 2012), at 39 and 65–78.
[18] ibid.
[19] See generally F Francioni, 'Environment' in A Cassese (ed.), *Realizing Utopia: The Future of International Law* (Oxford University Press, 2012) 443.
[20] Cotula (17), at 104, 129, and 151.
[21] E Morgera, 'Corporate Accountability' in E Morgera and K Kulovesi (eds), *Research Handbook on Natural Resources and International Law* (Edward Elgar, 2016) 109.
[22] See discussion in the Introduction of this book.

International soft-law initiatives have specified to some extent the international community's expectations on corporate accountability. They appear to indicate that the international community is no longer only concerned with the accountability of multinationals, but of other private companies too. It has thus become commonplace to start any discussion regarding business responsibility and related due diligence under international law with reference to the UN Framework and Guiding Principles on Business and Human Rights,[23] which have become the standard reference point due to their intergovernmental endorsement. This section will introduce these instruments and explain their significance in the context of a much longer history of attempts at the international level to define corporate responsibility. It will then introduce other international initiatives in the context of the United Nations, the Organization for Economic Cooperation and Development (OECD) and the International Finance Corporation of the World Bank family. These initiatives have also been relevant for clarifying benefit-sharing standards for private companies, with a particular focus on incorporating the main normative innovations of the UN Framework and its Guiding Principles on Business and Human Rights.

3. UN Framework and Guiding Principles on Business and Human Rights

The UN Framework on Business and Human Rights elicited intergovernmental support in 2008.[24] Its 2011 Guiding Principles were adopted by the Human Rights Council.[25] This was 'the first time the UN adopted a set of standards on the subject of business and human rights ... that governments did not negotiate themselves', in the face of the stagnation of 'traditional forms of international legalization and negotiation through universal consensus-based institutions' on this topic.[26]

The main normative contribution of the UN Framework was affirming that companies are expected to go beyond merely complying with the international obligations of host States as enshrined in their national laws. The Guiding Principles clarified that a 'global standard of expected conduct for all business enterprises wherever they operate', exists independently of States' abilities and willingness to fulfil their human rights obligations. This global standard operates 'over and above compliance with national laws and regulations protecting human rights', basically requiring business entities to take adequate measures to prevent, mitigate, and remediate adverse human rights impacts.[27] Political acceptability was ensured by placing these considerations as

[23] UN Special Representative on Human Rights and Business Enterprises, 'Protect, Respect and Remedy: A Framework for Business and Human Rights' UN Doc A/HRC/8/5 (2008) and 'Guiding Principles on Business and Human Rights to implement the UN Protect, Respect and Remedy Framework' UN Doc A/HRC/17/31 (2011).

[24] The Human Rights Council recognizing the need to operationalize the Framework: HRC Res 8/7 (18 June 2008), para. 2

[25] HRC Res 17/4 (6 July 2011).

[26] J Ruggie, 'Global Governance and "New Governance Theory": Lessons from Business and Human Rights' (2014) 20 Global Governance 5, at 5–6.

[27] UN Special Representative on Human Rights and Business Enterprises, 'Guiding Principles on Business and Human Rights to implement the UN Protect, Respect and Remedy Framework' UN Doc A/HRC/17/31 (2011), para. 11 (the Guiding Principles were adopted by HRC Res 17/4 (2011); see also

the second of three pillars: the duty of the State to protect against human rights abuses by third parties, including businesses; the corporate 'responsibility' to respect human rights; and the need for greater access to effective remedies.[28]

Under the second pillar, due diligence aims to avoid causing or contributing to adverse human rights impacts through companies' own initiatives and seek to prevent or mitigate adverse human rights impacts that are directly linked to their operations, products, or services by their business relationships, even if a business entity has not contributed to the impacts.[29] This aims to look beyond multinationals to supply chains and other business relationships. Under the third pillar—access to remedies—the Framework recognizes not only the role of States, but also the role of grievance mechanisms to be developed by private companies themselves,[30] as long as they are oriented towards redressing imbalances in expertise and access to information, and enabling effective dialogue with affected stakeholders.[31]

The UN Guiding Principles further clarify that the human rights due diligence process entails: (i) assessing actual and potential impacts in 'meaningful consultations' with potentially affected groups and other stakeholders at regular intervals; (ii) integrating the assessment findings in internal decision-making budget allocation and oversight processes; (iii) acting on those findings; (iv) tracking responses (including by drawing on feedback from affected stakeholders); and (v) communicating how impacts are addressed to right-holders in a manner that is sufficient for stakeholders to evaluate the adequacy of the company's response.[32] Companies are expected to prioritize the prevention and mitigation of the most severe impacts or those that a delayed response would make irremediable.[33] The reference to due diligence also benefitted from the notion being 'well-known to companies'.[34] John Ruggie, the author of the Framework and Guiding Principles, expressed that he successfully outlined the 'parameters and perimeters of business and human rights as an international policy domain' where international legal instruments provide 'carefully crafted precision tools' for the evolution of the international agenda.[35]

While undoubtedly a political success, the UN Framework and its Guiding Principles have also raised significant criticism from international human rights scholars and practitioners. In particular, critics have lamented that the emphasis on 'impacts', rather than 'violations', of human rights in the UN Framework points to 'a shift from a legal to a managerial conception of the responsibility of business' that

OHCHR press release, 'New Guiding Principles on Business and human rights endorsed by the UN Human Rights Council', 16 June 2011.

[28] The UN Framework was 'welcomed' with unanimous approval by the Human Rights Council and the need for its operationalization was recognized: HRC Res 8/7 (2008), para. 2.

[29] UN Guiding Principles, Principle 13.

[30] ibid, paras 93–95.

[31] ibid, para. 95.

[32] ibid, paras 17–21.

[33] ibid, para. 24.

[34] S Deva, *Regulating Corporate Human Rights Violations: Humanizing Business* (Routledge, 2012), at 108.

[35] J Ruggie, 'Hierarchy or Ecosystem? Regulating Human Rights Risks of Multinational Enterprises' in C Rodríguez-Garavito (ed.), *Business and Human Rights: Beyond the End of the Beginning* (Cambridge University Press, 2017), at 7–8.

responds better to corporate lobbying interests than to the long-standing demands of victims.[36] The Framework has been further criticized for falling short of proposing how to overcome barriers to hold corporations legally accountable at the national level, such as the *forum non conveniens* doctrine and the corporate veil.[37] This includes the criticism that the Guiding Principles are 'under-inclusive' regarding international human rights obligations. It has been argued that corporations already have certain legally binding human rights obligations and these obligations are not limited solely to the 'respect' category, or to the International Bill of Human Rights.[38] Ultimately, to gain political legitimacy, the UN Framework had 'steered clear of employing concepts cognate to international human rights law'[39] in a concerted effort to avoid the impression that companies are assimilated to States in terms of human rights protection. Thus, the UN Guiding Principles have been criticized for their limited critique of the protection of multinationals in international investment law, ignoring the power imbalances not only in the negotiations of bilateral investment agreements but also in host states' technical and financial support to home States/developing countries on regulatory reform that supports multinationals.[40]

From an institutional perspective, for instance, the intergovernmental endorsement of the UN Guiding Principles has led to a light-touch follow-up development: the 2011 decision by the Human Rights Council to establish a Working Group on the issue of human rights and transnational corporations and other business enterprises.[41] The mandate of the Working Group includes the promotion of the effective and comprehensive dissemination and implementation of the Guiding Principles and identifying, exchanging, and promoting good practices and lessons learned on their implementation. It is also to make recommendations on the basis of information from governments, transnational corporations, and other business enterprises, national human rights institutions, civil society, and rights-holders and to cooperate with other relevant special procedures of the Human Rights Council, relevant UN and other international bodies, the treaty bodies, and regional human rights organizations.[42] Arguably, the Working Group is meant to exert pressure from the bottom up, urging companies to continually improve the protection of human rights, but doubts were raised about its ability to do so in the absence of civil society participation in norm creation, revision, monitoring, and enforcement.[43] It remains to be seen if it will clarify benefit-sharing standards for companies.

[36] S Deva, 'Treating Human Rights Lightly: A Critique of the Normative Foundations of the SRSG's Framework and Guiding Principles' in S Deva and D Bilchitz (eds), *Human Rights Obligations of Business: Beyond Corporate Responsibility to Respect?* (Cambridge University Press, 2013) 78, at 86.

[37] Deva (n. 34), at 113.

[38] S Deva, 'Business and Human Rights: Time to Move Beyond the "Present"?' in Rodríguez-Garavito (n. 35) 62, at 63–64.

[39] M Karavias, *Corporate Obligations under International Law* (Oxford University Press, 2013), at 83 (and more generally at 81–83).

[40] P Simons, 'International Law's Invisible Hand and the Future of Corporate Accountability for Violations of Human Rights' (2012) 3 Journal of Human Rights and the Environment 5, at 19.

[41] HRC Res 17/4 (2011) and Res 26/22 (2014).

[42] The mandate was renewed until 2020: HRC Res 35/7 (2017).

[43] Rodríguez-Garavito (n. 35), at 23.

3.1 Business Responsibility to Respect Indigenous Peoples' Human Rights

The UN Framework on Business and Human Rights and its Guiding Principles do not identify specific environmental standards that are relevant to the private sector, leaving that to be determined on a case-by-case basis in line with the International Bill of Rights.[44] As such, the UN Framework avoids specifically mentioning environmental and human rights concerns regarding business conduct in the natural resource sector. Rather, the proposed 'common conceptual and policy framework' is expected to be further elaborated and adopted by all relevant social actors.[45] The Framework and Guiding Principles thus did not address the challenge for companies of identifying relevant international standards.[46] This appears even more surprising given that all previous UN initiatives had an environmental component that was largely convergent. Even at times when the focus shifted from regulating multinationals to facilitating foreign direct investment, there was broad consensus that it is appropriate and desirable to develop standards to guide or direct multinationals' conduct concerning environmental risks.[47]

Instead, while UN Special Representative on Business and Human Rights John Ruggie stressed the importance for the Framework of international policy coherence,[48] particularly with specific regard to 'prevailing social norms ... that have acquired near-universal recognition by all stakeholders',[49] he made no attempt to seek or acknowledge synergies between the UN Framework and relevant widely ratified international environmental agreements in the specific case of natural resource exploitation[50]—an area where serious corporate abuses of human rights have been documented.

Nonetheless, the Special Representative developed the procedural aspect of his proposed human rights due diligence process based on concepts and approaches[51] developed and tested in the environmental sphere. Notably, he drew from: (i) impact assessment; (ii) stakeholder involvement in decision-making; and

[44] Report of the Special Representative of the Secretary-General on the Issue of Human Rights and Transnational Corporations and Other Business Enterprises, 'Business and Human Rights: Towards Operationalizing the 'Protect, Respect and Remedy' Framework' UN Doc A/HRC/11/13 (2009), at 15.

[45] ibid, para. 107.

[46] Deva (n. 34), at 11.

[47] RJ Fowler, 'International Environmental Standards for Transnational Corporations' (1995) 25 Environmental Law Review 1, at 3.

[48] Report of the Special Representative of the Secretary-General on the issue of human rights and transnational corporations and other business enterprises, Business and Human Rights: Further steps toward the operationalization of the 'protect, respect and remedy' framework, UN Doc A/HRC/14/27 (2010), para. 52.

[49] ibid, 13.

[50] The UN Representative indicated that the scope of corporate responsibility to respect human rights is defined by the actual and potential human rights impacts generated by business, which can be identified on the basis of an authoritative list of international recognized rights including the 'International Bill of Rights', Conventions of the International Labour Organization (ILO), and depending on the circumstances human rights instruments concerning specifically Indigenous peoples and other vulnerable groups too: Report of the Special Representative of the Secretary-General on the issue of human rights and transnational corporations and other business enterprises, 'Business and human rights: Towards operationalizing the 'Protect, Respect and Remedy' Framework' UN Doc A/HRC/11/13 (2009), at 15.

[51] ibid, at 14.

(iii) life-cycle management. Equally, the UN Guiding Principles continued the self-referential trend of the UN Framework, with no specific reference to the relevance of multilateral environmental agreements. There was also no reference made to specific rights of Indigenous peoples, despite these rights providing one of the most tangible connections between human rights and environmental protection discourses.[52]

On the other hand, a plethora of international legal materials point to the applicability of socio-cultural and environmental impact assessments, free prior informed consent (FPIC), and benefit-sharing to business enterprises in the natural resource sector, albeit to different extents.[53] In particular, UN Special Rapporteurs and the UN Expert Mechanism on Indigenous Peoples' Rights have relied on Convention on Biological Diversity (CBD) materials[54] to argue that business responsibility in the extractives sector[55] includes benefit-sharing[56] and depends on companies facilitating Indigenous peoples' full access to information regarding potential financial benefits, even when this information is considered proprietary (in which case, it should be shared on a confidential basis).[57] On that basis, the UN Framework on Business and Human Rights and its Guiding Principles were referred to in the 2018 UN Framework Principles on Human Rights and the Environment.[58]

The interpretative work on extractive industries of UN Special Rapporteur on Indigenous Peoples' Rights James Anaya is particularly illuminating in this respect.[59] Anaya also devoted significant attention to the concept of fair and equitable

52 E Morgera, 'Environmental Accountability of Multinational Corporations: Benefit-sharing as a Bridge between Human Rights and the Environment' in B Boer (ed.), *Human Rights and the Environment* (Oxford University Press, 2015) 37.

53 S Seck, 'Indigenous Rights, Environmental Rights, or Stakeholder Engagement? Comparing IFC and OECD Approaches to the Implementation of the Business Responsibility to Respect Human Rights' (2016) 12 McGill Journal of International Sustainable Development Law and Practice 57.

54 Morgera (n. 52), at 37. CBD decisions are also routinely addressed directly to private operators, thereby providing an intergovernmentally adopted source of more specific corporate accountability standards, e.g.: Addis Ababa Principles and Guidelines for the Sustainable Use of Biodiversity, CBD Decision VII/12 (2004), Annex II, para. 1; CBD, Guidelines on Biodiversity and Tourism, Decision V/25 (2000), para. 2; Tkarihwaié:ri Code of Ethical Conduct to Ensure Respect for the Cultural and Intellectual Heritage of Indigenous and Local Communities, CBD Decision X/42 (2010), Section 6/3; and CBD, The Akwé: Kon Voluntary Guidelines, CBD Decision VII/16C (2004), Annex, para. 1 (albeit directed to parties and governments, these guidelines are expected to provide a collaborative framework for governments, Indigenous and local communities, decision-makers, and managers of developments: Akwé: Kon Guidelines, para. 3).

55 See generally UN Special Rapporteur on Indigenous Peoples' Human Rights James Anaya, Progress report on extractive industries, UN Doc A/HRC/21/47 (2012), and final study on extractive industries and indigenous peoples, UN Doc A/HRC/24/41 (2013), para. 62; and UN Expert Mechanism on the Rights of Indigenous Peoples, Progress report on the study on indigenous peoples and the right to participate in decision-making, UN Doc A/HRC/15/35 (2010) and 'Advice No. 2, Indigenous peoples and the right to participate in decision-making' (2011), paras 8–29.

56 UN Special Rapporteur on Indigenous Peoples' Human Rights James Anaya, Report, UN Doc A/HRC/15/37 (2010), paras 46 and 79.

57 Anaya, UN Doc A/HRC/24/41 (n. 55), paras 62, 66, and 72.

58 UN Special Rapporteur John Knox on the issue of human rights obligations relating to the enjoyment of a safe, clean, healthy, and sustainable environment, Framework Principles on Human Rights and the Environment, UN Doc A/HRC/37/59 (2018), para. 22.

59 UN Special Rapporteur on the Situation of Human Rights and Fundamental Freedoms of Indigenous People James Anaya, report, UN Doc A/HRC/12/34 (2009), Section E.

benefit-sharing, referring to the CBD work programme on protected areas as a helpful reference for the purposes of business due diligence.[60]

Anaya recommended that companies identify, fully incorporate, and make operative the norms concerning the rights of Indigenous peoples within all aspects of their work carried out within or in close proximity to Indigenous lands. In this connection, assessments are also expected to take into account Indigenous peoples' and local communities' rights over lands and waters traditionally occupied or used by them and associated biodiversity.[61] This raises issues of distributive justice. As part of their due diligence, companies should avoid endorsing or contributing to any act or omission on the part of the State amounting to a failure to adequately consult with the affected Indigenous community before proceeding with a project.[62] For their part, States still have to comply with their international human rights obligations when delegating to companies the execution of impact assessments and FPIC processes, considering the power imbalances and Indigenous peoples' lack of access to technical information about proposed projects.[63]

Anaya emphasized that social and environmental impact studies should be conducted according to the CBD Akwé: Kon Guidelines.[64] In addition, CBD guidelines call for adequate and balanced information from a variety of sources to be made available in accessible terms and Indigenous or local languages to ensure that all parties to a benefit-sharing agreement have the same understanding of the information and terms provided.[65] This raises issues of procedural justice. Anaya added that, in exercising due diligence, companies must identify, prior to commencing activities, all matters related to Indigenous peoples' rights and recognize their social and political structures, as well as their possession and use of land and natural resources.[66] This raises issues of recognition.

Anaya indicated that business enterprises should regard benefit-sharing '*as a means of complying with a right*, and not as a charitable award or favour granted by the company in order to secure social support for the project or minimize potential conflicts'.[67] He underscored the need to go beyond the usual model of natural resource extraction, whereby the initial plans for exploration and extraction of natural resources are developed by a corporation, with some involvement by the State, but little or no

[60] The CBD work programme on protected areas (CBD Decision VII/28 (2004), Annex) was referred to by the UN Expert Mechanism on the Rights of Indigenous Peoples, Progress Report on the Study on Indigenous Peoples and the Right to Participate in Decision-making, UN Doc A/HRC/15/35 (2010), para. 37.

[61] CBD Akwé: Kon Guidelines (n. 54), para. 57.

[62] Anaya A/HRC/12/34 (n. 59), Section E.

[63] Seck (n. 53), at 392

[64] Anaya A/HRC/12/34 (n. 59), paras 73–74.

[65] CBD, Mo'otz Kuxtal Voluntary Guidelines for the development of mechanisms, legislation or other appropriate initiatives to ensure the 'prior informed consent', 'free prior informed consent' or 'approval and involvement', depending on national circumstances, of Indigenous peoples and local communities for accessing their knowledge, innovations and practices, the fair and equitable sharing of benefits arising from the use and application of such knowledge, innovations and practices and for reporting and preventing unauthorized access to such knowledge, innovations and practices, CBD Decision XIII/18 (2016), para. 17(c)(iii).

[66] Anaya, A/HRC/15/37 (n. 56), para. 46.

[67] ibid, para. 79

involvement of the affected Indigenous peoples, with the result that Indigenous peoples are 'at best being offered benefits in the form of jobs or community development projects that typically pale in economic value in comparison to the profits gained by the corporation.'[68]

Similarly to States' benefit-sharing obligations, Anaya emphasized that companies should view benefit-sharing as separate from compensation,[69] as a tool to create genuinely equal partnerships with Indigenous peoples with a view to strengthening their capacity to establish and pursue their own development priorities and making their own decision-making mechanisms and institutions more effective.[70] Anaya argued that business due diligence would imply that companies set up specific benefit-sharing mechanisms based on international standards.[71] This implies moving away from an exclusive focus on damage prevention to a proactive and collaborative identification of benefit-sharing opportunities according to Indigenous peoples' worldviews.[72] To that end, Anaya envisaged that, if Indigenous peoples themselves do not wish or are unable to initiate resource extraction, they are entitled to participate in project decision-making *and* share in their profits through an agreement with outside companies (for instance, through a minority ownership interest in the extractive operations).[73] This highlights the value of benefit-sharing arrangements that simultaneously provide increased participation opportunities and income generation for Indigenous peoples, illustrating how procedural and substantive standards of distributive justice are interconnected.

Anaya did not refer to all the triggers for applying specialized standards to business due diligence. This was instead clarified by UN Special Rapporteur on Human Rights and the Environment John Knox, who identified two triggers. First, the use of Indigenous peoples' and traditional communities' traditional knowledge. Second, the extraction or other activities (including conservation) in relation to lands, territories, or resources (including genetic resources) that are traditionally owned, occupied, or used by Indigenous peoples and traditional communities. The latter includes lands they have had access to for their subsistence and traditional activities, and may not have formal recognition of property rights or delimitation and demarcation of boundaries.[74] Knox also clarified that the standards outlined for businesses and other

[68] Anaya, A/HRC/21/47 (n. 55), paras 68, 74, and 76.

[69] ibid, paras 89–91.

[70] UN Special Rapporteur on Indigenous Peoples' Human Rights James Anaya, Report on the rights of indigenous peoples, UN Doc A/HRC/66/288 (2011), para. 102; and Anaya, A/HRC/21/47 (n. 55), paras 52 and 62.

[71] Anaya, A/HRC/66/288 (ibid), paras 76–80.

[72] UN Expert Mechanism, Advice No. 4: Follow-up report on indigenous peoples and the right to participate in decision-making, with a focus on extractive industries, UN Doc A/HRC/21/55 (2012), para. 39(h) and implicitly UK National Contact Point, Final Statement on the Complaint from Survival International against Vedanta Resources plc, para. 73 (2009).

[73] Anaya, A/HRC/24/41 (n. 55), para. 75. These points have been reiterated by the African Commission's Working Group on Extractive Industries, Environment and Human Rights Violations in Africa, Final Communiqué on the National Dialogue on the Rights of Indigenous Peoples and Extractive Industries, from 7 to 8 October 2019, Nairobi, Kenya.

[74] Framework Principles on Human Rights and the Environment (n. 58), paras 53 and 48. See the comments in E Morgera, 'A reflection on benefit-sharing as a Framework Principle on Human Rights and the Environment proposed by UN Special Rapporteur John Knox (Part I)' BENELEX blog (April 2018), available at https://benelexblog.wordpress.com/, accessed 29 June 2023.

non-State actors in extractives are equally applicable for private operators involved in conservation.[75] The intergovernmental consensus achieved under the CBD on Indigenous and Community Conserved Areas was considered particularly instructive in this connection,[76] beginning with the need to recognize, respect, and support community-based approaches to conservation and the integration of communities in governance and management arrangements.[77]

Other relevant guidance can be found under the CBD, and should be considered relevant to understanding business responsibility to respect Indigenous peoples' human rights. This is the case of the CBD Mo'otz Kuxtal Guidelines, which emphasize that benefit-sharing 'may vary depending upon the type of benefits, the specific conditions and national legislation ... the content of the mutually agreed terms and the stakeholders involved' and benefit-sharing mechanisms 'should be flexible' and determined on a case-by-case basis.[78] A wider choice of benefits could enable a more tailored consideration of communities' needs, values, and priorities on a case-by-case basis, as required under international human rights law, on the basis of a more comprehensive understanding of opportunities within natural resource governance. Equally, however, the menu of benefits reveals the limitation of international biodiversity law: in the absence of specific procedural guarantees and indications of the minimum level of protection, benefit-sharing could be used to impose certain views of development upon Indigenous peoples that could endanger their cultural or physical survival. In effect, business-community benefit-sharing models can be far from beneficial for Indigenous peoples, as these models potentially entail unfair pricing and financial dependency.[79]

3.2 Practice of the UN Special Rapporteur on Indigenous Peoples' Rights

The role of the UN Special Rapporteur on Indigenous Peoples' Rights includes responding on an ongoing basis to specific cases of alleged human rights violations. To that end, Anaya established a practice of gathering, requesting, receiving, and exchanging information from all relevant sources, notably from Indigenous peoples and governments, and carrying out on-site visits to examine the issues raised with a view to providing observations and recommendations on the underlying human rights issues.

[75] UN Special Rapporteur on Human Rights and the Environment John Knox, Report on biodiversity and human rights, UN Doc A/HRC/34/49 (2017), para. 72.

[76] H Jonas, 'Indigenous Peoples' and Community Conserved Territories and Areas (ICCAs): Evolution in International Biodiversity Law' in E Morgera and J Razzaque (eds), *Encyclopedia of Environmental Law: Biodiversity and Nature Protection Law* (Edward Elgar, 2017) 145.

[77] CBD Decisions X/31/B (2010) para. 31, XII/19 (2014) para. 4(f), and X/33 (2010) para. 8(i) in relation to climate change (these recommendations are addressed to 'other/relevant organizations'); and XII/5 (2014) para. 11 (this recommendation is addressed to 'relevant stakeholders.')

[78] Mo'otz Kuxtal Voluntary Guidelines (n. 65), para. 24.

[79] L Cotula and K Tienhaara, 'Reconfiguring Investment Contracts to Promote Sustainable Development' (2013) 2011–2012 Yearbook of International Investment Law and Policy 281, at 293.

As several cases brought to his attention included infringements of the right to FPIC, especially in relation to natural resource extraction and displacement or removal of Indigenous peoples, and denial of their rights to lands and resources,[80] this practice has contributed to further clarifying international standards on benefit-sharing for businesses.

In a case concerning the Marlin mine project in Guatemala and Maya Indigenous communities, for instance, Anaya predominantly focused on the regulatory and administrative shortcomings of the State, but did not avoid noting that private companies had an influence on the conflicts with Indigenous peoples in that context.[81] He brought attention to procedural justice issues in this context. Anaya noted that the consultations undertaken by the company did not lead to an adequate understanding of the project's impacts on the communities, did not sufficiently take into account the community's concerns, and by all accounts should have involved the government more extensively. He thus called for a new consultation process focusing on mitigation measures, reparation of damage, the establishment of a formal benefit-sharing mechanism with full participation of the relevant communities, and the creation of a complaint and conciliation mechanism.[82] In his final recommendation, Anaya confirmed that the private enterprises' faults in due diligence could not be justified by the limitations of the host State's legal framework alone.[83] He recommended that private enterprises adopt internal policies on Indigenous peoples' rights and independent follow-up mechanisms, as well as permanent mechanisms for dialogue and grievance with the participation of State authorities.[84] It was in effect this monitoring activity that led Anaya to develop the guidance discussed earlier to give greater substance to the UN Framework on Business and Human rights with regard to Indigenous peoples' rights. He concluded that 'in its prevailing form, the model for advancing natural resource extraction within the territories of Indigenous peoples appears to run counter to the self-determination of Indigenous peoples in the political, social and economic spheres'.[85]

Following the adoption of his guidance, Anaya continued to investigate the conditions for fair and equitable benefit-sharing as part of business due diligence, with a focus on distributive justice issues. During a visit to Peru, he differentiated social funds as models that encourage the development of social investment projects specifically intended for Indigenous peoples as compensation for the negative impacts of private

[80] UN Special Rapporteur on the situation of human rights and fundamental freedoms of indigenous people James Anaya, Second International Decade of the World's Indigenous Peoples, UN Doc A/64/338 (2009), Section D.

[81] UN Special Rapporteur on the situation of human rights and fundamental freedoms of indigenous people James Anaya, Observaciones sobre la situación de los derechos de los pueblos indígenas de Guatemala en relación con los proyectos extractivos, y otro tipo de proyectos, en sus territorios tradicionales (observations on the situation of the rights of Indigenous peoples in Guatemala in relation to extractive projects and other kinds of projects in their traditional territories), UN Doc A/HRC/18/35/Add.3 (2011), para. 69.

[82] ibid, paras 69–70.

[83] ibid, paras 69–72.

[84] ibid, paras 89–93.

[85] UN Special Rapporteur on the situation of human rights and fundamental freedoms of indigenous people James Anaya, Extractive industries operating within or near indigenous territories, UN Doc A/HRC/18/35 (2011), paras 74–75 and 82.

companies from benefits in the form of 'jobs or community development projects, that typically pale in economic value in comparison to profits gained by the corporation'. He also emphasized that priority should be given at the outset to an alternative model for extractive activities in Indigenous territories consisting of Indigenous peoples themselves controlling the extractive operations, either through their own initiatives and enterprises, or through partnerships with responsible non-Indigenous companies with the necessary experience and funding to launch projects and with State support to build Indigenous peoples' capacity.[86] He addressed a recommendation directly to companies to ensure that Indigenous peoples participate directly in the distribution of fees or royalties, or in the earnings derived from the extractive operations.[87]

The successive Special Rapporteur, Vicky Tauli Corpuz, addressed business directly and indirectly in the majority of her country visit reports, in a varied manner, occasionally building upon the reports of the UN Working Group on Business and Human Rights. This served to make a clearer distinction between State obligations and business due diligence, with the latter including the expectation that private companies develop human-rights impact studies in accordance with international standards and the UN Guiding Principles on Business and Human Rights, in cooperation with Indigenous peoples.[88]

During a visit to Ecuador, for instance, Tauli Corpuz observed the absence of environmental rehabilitation, reparations, and adequate compensation for communities that for decades have suffered the impact of oil exploitation on their lands and territories, such as in the area affected by the operations of Chevron-Texaco. She also provided insights into benefit-sharing practices, noting that '[i]n the absence of State services, the companies provided basic social services which involved cronyism and paternalistic practices'.[89] This is indeed one of the main pitfalls in attempting to implement the international standard on benefit-sharing, as discussed also in relation to intra-State benefit-sharing in Chapter 3.

While on a visit to Mexico, Tauli Corpuz emphasized that companies' social and environmental impact assessments were approved before consultations were carried out with Indigenous peoples and did not adequately identify the real impacts that projects would have on them. She also reiterated the findings of an earlier mission by the UN Working Group on Business and Human Rights about competent authorities' limited capacity to examine these assessments and ensure proper oversight of their activities.[90] She further noted that contracts between large-scale wind power project proponents and communities were not necessarily concluded with representative authorities and had resulted in negative impacts on Indigenous land tenure, the

[86] UN Special Rapporteur on the situation of human rights and fundamental freedoms of indigenous people James Anaya, The situation of indigenous peoples' rights in Peru with regard to the extractive industries, UN Doc A/HRC/27/52/Add.3 (2014), paras 59–61.

[87] ibid, para. 72.

[88] UN Special Rapporteur on the situation of human rights and fundamental freedoms of indigenous people Victoria Tauli Corpuz, visit to Ecuador, UN Doc A/HRC/42/37/Add.1 (2019), para. 118; visit to Mexico, UN Doc A/HRC/39/17/Add.2 (2018), para. 108; and visit to Guatemala, UN Doc A/HRC/39/17/Add.3 (2018), para. 103(f).

[89] A/HRC/42/37/Add.1 (n. 88), para. 30.

[90] Tauli Corpuz A/HRC/39/17/Add.2 (n. 88), para. 38, also citing the UN Working Group on Business and Human Rights, UN Doc A/HRC/35/32/Add.2 (2017), paras 58–62.

environment, traditional economic activities, and community life.[91] In the course of a visit to Guatemala, Tauli Corpuz noted that despite having adopted a human rights policy under a coordinating committee of the agricultural, commercial, industrial, and financial associations, none of the participating companies had carried out human rights impact studies before engaging in activities that could affect Indigenous peoples.[92] She thus focused on procedural justice issues around benefit-sharing.

In the report of a visit to Brazil, a whole section was devoted to business responsibility where Tauli Corpuz highlighted the responsibility of businesses to ensure respect for Indigenous peoples' rights in their sugar, soy, timber, palm oil, and minerals supply chains, and to conduct adequate human rights due diligence. She also called on companies involved in mining, hydroelectric dams, transmission lines, or infrastructure projects to assess whether the State had complied with its duty to seek FPIC and had guaranteed that the projects would not impact Indigenous peoples' rights. She emphasized that companies, including banks, need to 'know and show' that they are not complicit in or contributing to human rights violations arising from the failure of the Brazilian authorities to adequately address Indigenous peoples' environmental concerns, provide them with effective remedies,[93] and implement previous recommendations by the UN Working Group on Business and Human Rights.[94] Her recommendations highlighted the independent nature of companies' due diligence obligations to respect Indigenous peoples' rights, including their land and consent rights, both for their own operations and for those in their supply chains. She also emphasized the need to participate in meaningful remediation processes in consultation with the concerned Indigenous peoples, using their leverage to prevent further rights violations and ensure appropriate remediation.[95] Companies' independent responsibility to respect Indigenous peoples' rights was also highlighted in her visit report to Honduras.[96] She noted that the Miskito community had relied on a 'biocultural [community] protocol', as recommended under the CBD, as a basis for the consultations on proposed hydrocarbon operations, which the government considered 'a basis for future consultations with Indigenous peoples on mining projects'.[97] The lack of consideration of community protocols by companies raised concerns regarding recognition around, but not directly on, benefit-sharing.

During her visit to Sápmi, Tauli Corpuz drew attention to the absence of provisions for benefit-sharing with Sámi communities when mines are located on traditional Sámi lands. She also noted the absence of any frameworks for dispute resolution between mining companies and affected Sámi communities, as well as the lack of cumulative impacts across different applications for exploration and exploitation

[91] Tauli Corpuz A/HRC/39/17/Add.2 (n. 88), para. 41.

[92] UN Special Rapporteur on the situation of human rights and fundamental freedoms of indigenous people Victoria Tauli Corpuz, Report of the visit to Guatemala, UN Doc A/HRC/39/17/Add.3 (2018), para. 43.

[93] UN Special Rapporteur on the situation of human rights and fundamental freedoms of indigenous people Victoria Tauli Corpuz, Report of the visit to Brazil, UN Doc A/HRC/33/42/Add.1 (2016), paras 77–78.

[94] ibid, paras 105 and 107.

[95] ibid, para. 104.

[96] ibid, para. 99.

[97] ibid, para. 54.

concessions.[98] She underscored that notwithstanding governments' endorsement of the UN Guiding Principles on Business and Human Rights and adoption of a national action plan for business and human rights,[99] deficient national regulatory frameworks created barriers for businesses to carry out their operations in a manner consistent with international expectations regarding the rights of Indigenous peoples.[100]

Overall, the Special Rapporteur on Indigenous Peoples' Rights has developed a practical understanding of the dividing line between business due diligence and State obligations, and with that, of the opportunities and risks in ensuring that businesses uphold the human rights of Indigenous peoples.

4. UN Global Compact

A different approach to developing international standards for business is the partnership model of the UN Global Compact.[101] It was launched by former UN Secretary-General Kofi Annan in 1999[102] and received an intergovernmental endorsement through General Assembly resolutions.[103] Almost 10.000 companies in over 160 countries participate in the Global Compact.[104] But reportedly 'growth in membership has been relatively moderate in recent years' and the Compact lacks 'a strategic vision for increased engagement of private companies'.[105]

The UN Global Compact has been widely publicized and criticized[106] due to its innovative approach according to which 'confrontation' with the business community has been replaced with 'cooperation'.[107] Its main aim is to build collaborative relations with the private sector on the basis of internationally agreed principles of good corporate citizenship (human rights, labour standards, environmental sustainability,

[98] UN Special Rapporteur on the situation of human rights and fundamental freedoms of indigenous people Victoria Tauli Corpuz, Report on the human rights situation of the Sami people in the Sápmi region of Norway, Sweden and Finland, UN Doc A/HRC/33/42/Add.3 (2016), para. 51.

[99] ibid, para. 35.

[100] ibid, paras 32 and 74 (reiterated in the recommendations).

[101] K Bruno and J Karliner, 'The UN's Global Compact, Corporate Accountability and the Johannesburg Earth Summit' (2002) 45 Development 3, at 34.

[102] UN Global Compact Office, 'United Nations Guide to the Global Compact: A Practical Understanding of the Vision and the Nine Principles' (undated) available at http://www.unglobalcompact.org/irj/servlet/prt/portal/prtroot/com.sapportals.km.docs/ungc_html_content/Public_Documents/gcguide.pdf, accessed 29 June 2023, 4 (hereinafter, United Nations Guide to the Global Compact); it was subsequently officially launched in July 2000, within the Economic and Social Council (ECOSOC).

[103] UNGA Res 62/211 'Towards Global Partnership' (2007), para. 9 and 64/223 'Towards Global Partnership' (2009), para. 13.

[104] See UN Global Compact, 'Participants' https://www.unglobalcompact.org/what-is-gc/participants, accessed 29 June 2023.

[105] UN Joint Inspection Unit, 'The UN System-private sector partnership in the context of the 2013 Agenda for Sustainable Development', UN Doc JIU/REP/2017/8 (2017), para. 181.

[106] For an overview of opinions on the Global Compact, see M Shaughnessy, 'The United Nations Global Compact and the Continuing Debate about the Effectiveness of Corporate Voluntary Codes of Conduct' (2000) Colorado Journal of International Environmental Law and Policy Yearbook 156; WH Meyer and S Boyka, 'Human Rights, the UN Global Compact, and Global Governance' (2001) 34 Cornell International Law Journal 501; and E Duruigbo, *Multinational Corporations and International Law: Accountability and Compliance Issues in the Petroleum Industry* (Transnational Publishers, 2003), at 150–153.

[107] Bruno and Karliner (n. 101), at 34.

and anti-corruption).[108] While the Global Compact environmental principles may be too vague to provide adequate guidance to companies per se,[109] they have provided a basis upon which the Global Compact has developed more specific guidance over time, which includes reference to benefit-sharing. Notably, the Global Compact has produced guidance on business responsibility to respect Indigenous peoples' rights,[110] bringing together different international sources, including the International Finance Corporation, as well as the cases of the Inter-American Court of Human Rights and African Commission on Human and Peoples' Rights.

This guidance refers to transparent benefit-sharing, and cautions against providing financial or other benefits in exchange for investment rights without first acquiring FPIC. It further calls for sharing benefits based on regular annual reviews of the activity and its profitability.[111] On the whole, the guidance focuses on compensation, indicating that businesses are expected to ensure that population increases caused by business activity do not strain natural resources, and do not otherwise disrupt the way of life for Indigenous peoples, including their access to food, water, medicinal plants, animals, and other resources.[112] In addition, business are further expected to provide compensation and restitution for damages inflicted upon the land, territory, and resources of Indigenous peoples, and the rehabilitation of degraded environments caused by any current or historic activities that did not obtain FPIC. Businesses are also to ensure that the allocated budget from activities covers all costs associated with closure and restoration, and includes sufficient funds to provide for potential future liabilities.

In what way, then, is the approach of the Global Compact distinctive in supporting these standards? It seeks to encourage the private sector to commit its support to these standards, expecting companies to integrate them into their core business operations, and pursue activities that advance their implementation, as well as other UN-related objectives, such as the Millennium Development Goals (MDGs) first[113] and the Sustainable Development Goals after 2015.[114] In that connection, the Global Compact can be considered as an advancement in the direct application of international norms to multinationals, by shaping global discourse, global governance methodology, and cultural expectations.[115]

Companies are free to adhere to any of the ten principles through a letter of intent. The 'opt-in' approach[116] of the UN Global Compact has been criticized with regard to companies' freedom to 'pick and choose' among the ten principles.[117] Adhering companies are further expected to post on the Global Compact website, at least once a

[108] ibid.
[109] Deva (n. 33), at 97.
[110] Global Compact Office, *The Business Reference Guide to the UN Declaration on the Rights of Indigenous Peoples* (United Nation Global Compact Office, 2013).
[111] ibid, at 70.
[112] ibid.
[113] UNDP, Millennium Development Goals Report 2015 (2015).
[114] UN Global Compact, 'The SDGs', available at https://www.unglobalcompact.org/sdgs, accessed 29 June 2023.
[115] K Miles, *The Origins of International Investment Law* (Cambridge University Press, 2013), at 249.
[116] As defined by Meyer and Boyka (n. 106), at 502.
[117] P Utting, 'The Global Compact: Why All the Fuss?' (2003) 40 UN Chronicle 1, at 2.

year, a report of the concrete steps taken, and lessons learnt on any of the principles. Under these conditions, business enterprises are free to publicize their participation in the UN Global Compact. This is meant to offer an incentive for companies to comply. In addition, engagement by the private sector also includes the commitment to work in a transparent and accountable manner, particularly by being prepared to respond to NGO observations and critiques on the Compact website.[118] One of the Global Compact's main features is thus multi-stakeholder involvement, through the encouragement of the 'spotlight effect' by voluntary monitoring undertaken by NGOs and the media.[119]

The UN Global Compact can be understood as a learning initiative through transparency, dialogue with stakeholders, and dissemination of best practices. Its learning approach has been praised for its potential to establish, through dialogue, 'broader, consensus-based definitions of what constitutes good practices … which will become a standard of reference source' through transparency, advocacy, and competition.[120] The approach also has the potential to 'lead gradually to a desire for greater codification benchmarking and moving from "good" to "best" practice', with 'laggards [having] a harder time opposing actual achievements by their peers than *a priori* standards'.[121]

The UN Global Compact makes it clear that it is not a substitute for effective action by governments nor does it supplant other voluntary initiatives. It is further specified that it does not endorse the companies participating in the initiative.[122] In time, however, it has become 'more sophisticated' in the interpretation of its principles, the guidance it provides to companies, and the reporting requirements.[123] Its key weaknesses, however, remain the lack of a gatekeeping function to screen participants[124] or substantively review their reporting and adherence to the principles: it relies on a global database to identify potential concerns and make enquires with local Global Compact networks.[125] Even if 'Integrity Measures' were introduced in 2005 to monitor companies' compliance with the reporting requirements and allow the submission of complaints regarding 'systematic or egregious abuses' of the aims and principles of the Compact to the Global Compact Office,[126] the procedure is not a compliance-based initiative, but essentially aims to safeguard the reputation and integrity of the Global Compact.[127]

118 United Nations Guide to the Global Compact (n. 102), 9.

119 Meyer and Boyka (n. 106), at 504.

120 J Ruggie, 'Theory and Practice of Learning Networks: Corporate Social Responsibility and the Global Compact' (2002) 5 Journal of Corporate Citizenship 26, at 32.

121 ibid, at 33 (italics in the original).

122 ibid, at 4.

123 P Simons and A Macklin, *The Governance Gap: Extractive Industries, Human Rights and the Home State Advantage* (Routledge, 2014), at 114.

124 UN Joint Inspection Unit, 'United Nations Corporate Partnerships: The Role and Functioning of the Global Compact' UN Doc JIU/REP/2010/9 (2010), paras 63 and 14 and comments by Simons and Macklin (n. 123), at 116–117.

125 ibid, at 117.

126 UN Global Compact Office, 'Note on Integrity Measures' (26 November 2007), available at https://unglobalcompact.org/about/integrity-measures, accessed 29 June 2023.

127 U Wynhoven and M Stausberg, 'The United Nations Global Compact's Governance Framework and Integrity Measures' in A Rasche and G Kell (eds), *The United Nations Global Compact: Achievements, Trends and Challenges* (Cambridge University Press, 2010) 251, at 262–263.

On the whole, it is difficult to gauge the significance of the Global Compact, either in terms of clarifying the role of benefit-sharing for business due diligence, or in creating a meaningful learning platform to identify and replicate businesses' good practices in respecting Indigenous peoples' human rights.

5. The OECD Guidelines on Multinational Enterprises

International standards for business have also been developed outside the UN, namely under the aegis of the OECD, which was created in 1961 with the understanding that 'the economically more advanced nations should co-operate in assisting to the best of their ability the countries in process of economic development' and in the recognition 'that the further expansion of world trade is one of the most important factors favouring the economic development of countries and the improvement of international economic relations'.[128] The OECD aims to achieve the highest sustainable economic growth and employment and a rising standard of living in member countries while maintaining financial stability and thus contributing to the development of the world economy through the expansion of world trade on a multilateral, non-discriminatory basis in accordance with international obligations.[129] It groups major capital-exporting States.

The OECD first approved its Guidelines for Multinational Enterprises[130] in 1976. The OECD Guidelines were adopted as part of the Declaration on International Investment and Multinational Enterprises,[131] which was designed to improve the international investment climate and to strengthen the basis for mutual confidence between enterprises and the society in which they operate. The OECD Guidelines were drafted solely as governmental recommendations formulated to directly address multinationals operating in adhering countries.

The Guidelines have been through various phases of evolution in their environmental content.[132] The early success of its activities on corporate accountability can be attributed to two factors. The first was the significantly limited membership of like-minded countries, as opposed to the United Nations.[133] Some viewed the birth of the OECD Guidelines as a strategy by developed countries to create their own framework for multinational activities in order to reinforce their negotiating position at the multilateral level.[134]

[128] Convention on the Organisation for Economic Co-operation and Development (OECD) (Paris, 14 December 1960, in force 30 September 1961), preamble.

[129] ibid, Art. 1.

[130] OECD, 'Guidelines for Multinational Corporations' (31 October 2001) OECD Doc DAFFE/IME/WPG(2000)15/FINAL.

[131] OECD, 'The OECD Declaration and Decisions on International Investment and Multinational Enterprises: Basic Texts' (9 November 2000) OECD Doc DAFFE/IME (2000) 20.

[132] III.5.a.

[133] Originally there were twenty Member States and currently there are thirty-five: Australia, Austria, Belgium, Canada, Chile, the Czech Republic, Denmark, Estonia, Finland, France, Germany, Greece, Hungary, Iceland, Ireland, Israel, Italy, Japan, Korea, Latvia, Luxembourg, Mexico, the Netherlands, New Zealand, Norway, Poland, Portugal, the Slovak Republic, Slovenia, Spain, Sweden, Switzerland, Turkey, the United Kingdom, and the United States, available at http://www.oecd.org/document/1/0,2340,en_2649_201185_1889402_1_1_1_1,00.html, accessed 29 June 2023.

[134] Sauvant an Aranda (n. 2), at 99.

Until States' backing of the UN Framework on Business and Human Rights, the OECD Guidelines were the only intergovernmentally endorsed corporate accountability instrument featuring a comprehensive subject matter and supported by an explicit commitment for States to ensure acceptable corporate conduct.[135] Fifty-one major home States, including non-OECD members, have adhered to the Guidelines.[136]

The Guidelines further translated the concept of business due diligence of the UN Framework as the process through which enterprises can identify, prevent, mitigate, and account for their actual and potential adverse impacts as an integral part of business decision-making and risk management systems. The process aims to avoid multinationals causing or contributing to adverse impacts on matters covered by the Guidelines through their own activities and address such impacts when they occur. In other words, due diligence can be included within broader enterprise risk management systems, provided that it goes beyond simply identifying and managing material risks to the enterprise itself, to include the risks of adverse impacts related to matters covered by the Guidelines. Potential impacts are to be addressed through prevention or mitigation, while actual impacts are to be addressed through remediation.[137]

The OECD Guidelines contain a specific and quite detailed chapter on the environment, which refers to general standards of environmental protection and to a list of specific tools for corporate environmental accountability.[138] Taking a pragmatic approach, the subsequent more detailed provisions list a series of tools for corporate environmental accountability: environmental management systems, communication and stakeholder involvement, life-cycle assessment and environmental impact assessments, education and training of employees, and contribution to public policies.[139] Certain elements also serve to delineate substantive dimensions, such as risk prevention and mitigation, and continuous improvement of corporate environmental performance. The most recent version also lists substantive areas such as climate change, biodiversity loss, degradation of land, marine and freshwater ecosystems, deforestation; air, water and soil pollution; and mismanagement of waste.[140]

The OECD Guidelines also elaborated on the extent to which their addressees extend beyond multinational corporations. They expressed the expectation for companies to seek to prevent or mitigate adverse human rights impacts even if they have not directly caused them, provided these impacts are linked to their operations, products, or services through a business relationship. Consequently, multinationals are to encourage, where practicable, business partners, including suppliers and

[135] The OECD Guidelines were negotiated and approved by national delegations, as highlighted in UNCHR Decision 2004/116; Office of the High Commissioner for Human Rights and Global Compact Office, 'Consultation on Business and Human Rights—Summary of Discussions' (22 October 2004).

[136] See OECD, 'National Contact Points', available at http://www.oecd.org/investment/mne/ncps.htm, accessed 29 June 2023.

[137] More practical information on business due diligence can also be found in the 2018 OECD Due Diligence Guidance on Responsible Business Conduct: see comments by C Shavin, 'Unlocking the Potential of the New OECD Due Diligence Guidance on Responsible Business Conduct' (2019) 4 Business and Human Rights Journal 139.

[138] OECD Guidelines for Multinational Enterprises on Responsible Business Conduct (OECD, 2023), Section VI.

[139] ibid, Section VI.1.

[140] ibid, chapeau of Section VI.

subcontractors, to apply principles of responsible business conduct compatible with the Guidelines.[141]

The human rights chapter of the OECD Guidelines, therefore, indicates that 'corporate respect for human rights is no longer exclusively anchored in host States' international obligations, but in international recognized human rights, irrespective of the country or specific context of [multinationals'] operations'.[142] It clarifies that multinationals are expected to uphold internationally recognized human rights for those affected by their activities,[143] meaning that they should avoid infringing on the human rights of others and should address adverse human rights impacts with which they are involved. It also entails engaging with relevant stakeholders to provide meaningful opportunities for their views to be considered in relation to planning and decision-making for projects or other activities that may significantly impact local communities.[144] It further entails providing or cooperating in legitimate processes in the remediation of adverse human rights impacts where they identify that they have caused or contributed to these impacts.[145]

While the OECD Guidelines do not mention benefit-sharing, implementation activities and sectoral guidance adopted under the OECD Guidelines in key sectors for corporate environmental accountability refer to benefit-sharing as part of business responsibility to respect Indigenous peoples' human rights.[146]

5.1 Business Responsibility to Respect Indigenous Peoples' Human Rights

The sectoral guidance under the OECD Guidelines on mining, textile, and agriculture refers to benefit-sharing,[147] as part of a model policy for companies based on a common set of intergovernmental expectations, which accompanies a five-step due diligence framework, suggested measures for risk mitigation and indicators for measuring improvement, and specific recommendations tailored to the challenges associated with particular supply chains.[148]

More relevant for present purposes are the OECD-UN Food and Agriculture Organization (FAO) standards of responsible business conduct in the agricultural supply chain, which followed the structure of the Due Diligence Guidance for Minerals but also integrated FAO international standards, such as the Principles for Responsible

[141] ibid, Section II.17.

[142] L Liberti, 'OECD 50th Anniversary: The Updated OECD Guidelines for Multinational Enterprises and the New OECD Recommendation on Due Diligence Guidance for Conflict-Free Mineral Supply Chains' (2012) 13 Business Law International 35, at 45.

[143] OECD Guidelines (n. 138), Section II.15.

[144] ibid, Section II.A.10–14.

[145] ibid, Section IV.6.

[146] OECD Due Diligence Guidance for Responsible Supply Chains of Minerals from Conflict-Affected and High-Risk Areas (OECD, 2013); and OECD-FAO Guidance on Responsible Agricultural Supply Chains (OECD, 2015).

[147] OECD Due Diligence Guidance for Responsible Supply Chains of Minerals from Conflict-Affected and High-Risk Areas (OECD, 2013); and OECD-FAO Guidance on Responsible Agricultural Supply Chains (OECD, 2015).

[148] OECD-FAO Guidance on Responsible Agricultural Supply Chains (ibid), at 41.

Investment in Agriculture and Food Systems,[149] and the Voluntary Guidelines on the Responsible Governance of Tenure of Land, Fisheries and Forests in the Context of National Food Security.[150] They have been considered a useful source of inspiration for national legislative initiatives,[151] as well as a 'standard of public interest which may affect national courts' decisions'.[152]

The OECD-FAO Guidance for Responsible Agricultural Supply Chains refers to operations involving Indigenous peoples' lands, resources, and knowledge.[153] They make benefit-sharing part of a broader commitment to ensure that operations are in line with the development priorities and social objectives of the host government.[154] Consequently, the Guidance calls for promoting fair and equitable sharing of monetary and non-monetary benefits with affected communities on mutually agreed terms in accordance with international treaties where applicable for parties to such treaties, for example when using genetic resources for food and agriculture.[155] This is an implicit reference to the Nagoya Protocol on Access to Genetic Resources and Benefit-sharing[156] and the International Treaty on Plant Genetic Resources for Food and Agriculture,[157] discussed in Chapters 1, 2, and 4.

The OECD-FAO Guidance makes no reference, however, to the need to respond to Indigenous peoples' views and preferences in this connection. It calls on companies to strive to identify opportunities for development benefits, such as through the creation of local forward and backward linkages and of local jobs with safe working environments; the diversification of income-generating opportunities; capacity development; local procurement; technology transfer; improvements in local infrastructure; better access to credit and markets, particularly for small- and medium-sized businesses; payments for environmental services; allocation of revenue; and the creation of trust funds.[158] These are largely based on CBD sources on monetary benefit-sharing, including not only profit-sharing through trust funds, but also licences with preferential terms, job creation for communities (which find resonance in the *Endorois* decision of the African Commission[159]), and payments for ecosystem services.[160] The Guidance

[149] Committee on Food Security (CFS), Principles for Responsible Investment in Agriculture and Food Systems (2014).

[150] Food and Agriculture Organization (FAO), Voluntary Guidelines on the Responsible Governance of Tenure of Land, Fisheries and Forests in the Context of National Food Security (VGGT), UN Doc CL 144/9 (C 2013/20) (2012), Appendix D.

[151] Liberti (n. 142), at 43.

[152] P Birnie, A Boyle, and C Redgwell, *International Law and the Environment* (Oxford University Press, 2009), at 328.

[153] OECD-FAO Guidance for Responsible Agricultural Supply Chains (OECD, 2016), para. 53 and fns 19–21 referring to CBD Akwé: Kon Guidelines (n. 54), para. 46 and IFC Performance Standard 7, paras 18–20.

[154] OECD-FAO Guidance (ibid), at 26.

[155] ibid, at 26.

[156] Nagoya Protocol Additional to the Convention on Biological Diversity 1992, on Access to Genetic Resources and the Fair and Equitable Sharing of Benefits from their Utilization (Nagoya, 29 October 2010, in force 12 October 2014).

[157] International Treaty on Plant Genetic Resources for Food and Agriculture (ITPGRFA) (Rome, 3 November 2001, in force 29 June 2004).

[158] OECD-FAO Guidance (n. 146), at 53.

[159] African Commission, *Endorois Welfare Council v. Kenya*, No. 276/2003 (4 February 2010), para. 297.

[160] Akwé: Kon Guidelines (n. 54), para. 46. See M Menton and A Bennett, 'PES: Payments for Ecosystem Services and Poverty Alleviation?' and I Porras and N Asquith, 'Scaling-up Conditional Transfers for

clarifies that benefit-sharing is separate (and may be additional) to compensation for unavoidable adverse impacts.[161]

OECD guidance on benefit-sharing for businesses has thus focused on distributive justice issues with a clearer distinction between benefit-sharing and compensation than the UN Global Compact.

5.2 Operationalization

Although the OECD Guidelines themselves are a voluntary initiative, they include an 'implementation procedure' that requires adhering countries to set up national contact points (NCPs).[162] In effect, the implementation procedure is considered the 'most visible sign of adhering governments' commitment to the Guidelines'.[163] As it is based on a legally binding act of the OECD (a Council Decision), it has been argued that this obligation may serve to hold a State internationally responsible if it fails to create an NCP. It could also lead to State accountability if the NCP does not carry out its role according to the goal of furthering the effectiveness of the Guidelines and fostering international cooperation, although pinpointing which international or national body would make such an attribution in a particular case could pose a challenge.[164] In addition, they have also made an impact at the national level: certain countries linked access to external trade assistance and export credit to the absence of findings against companies by the OECD National Contact Points.[165]

The activities of NCPs could contribute to clarifying the relevance of benefit-sharing in specific contexts where companies are facing challenges in respecting Indigenous peoples' human rights. And even when NCPs do not explicitly refer to the standard of fair and equitable benefit-sharing (as opposed to compensation), they can clarify how the intertwined safeguards of environmental and socio-cultural assessments and FPIC, as well as the reliance on community protocols, can provide a suitable context for business to share, fairly and equitably, benefits with Indigenous peoples.

For instance, the Norway NCP encouraged a company to work in a manner that more clearly promoted Indigenous peoples' rights and the implementation of the Guidelines. It noted that the actual implementation of the consultation process could have been better facilitated to foster mutual trust with a view to obtaining the Sámi village's consent. The NCPs also noted that the company went above and beyond

Environmental Protection and Poverty Alleviation' in K Schreckenberg et al. (eds), *Ecosystem Services and Poverty Alleviation: Trade-offs and Governance* (Routledge, 2018) 189 and 204 respectively.

161 OECD-FAO Guidance (n. 146), at 52.

162 J Huner, 'The Multilateral Agreement on Investment and the Review of the OECD Guidelines for Multinational Enterprises' in MT Kamminga and S Zia-Zarifi (eds), *Liability of Multinational Corporations under International Law* (Kluwer Law International, 2000) 197, at 200.

163 OECD Secretary-General, May 2004.

164 S Robinson, 'International Obligations State Responsibility and Judicial Review under the OECD Guidelines for Multinational Enterprises Regime' (2014) 30 Utrecht Journal of International and European Law 68.

165 R Cirlig, 'Business and Human Rights: From Soft Law to Hard Law?' (2016) 6 Juridical Tribune 228, at 243.

the Guidelines by covering parts of the Sámi village's outlays and travel expenses in connection with participation in consultation. It emphasized that this may be necessary in order to achieve genuine consultations where Indigenous groups are given an opportunity to promote and safeguard their rights. Furthermore, the NCPs viewed consultations as a continuing process that must be upheld and adapted so that new circumstances are also addressed, for example when it subsequently emerged that the impacts of the wind power development were greater than originally expected. All these specifications are in line with the international human rights law and international biodiversity law guidance on FPIC as an ongoing process.

The NCP also remarked that the company, being aware of Indigenous groups' vulnerability to more adverse impacts than assumed in the licence application, 'could have shown even more willingness to implement mitigating measures and adapt the scope of the project to a level where agreement could be reached, prior to the legal process and without waiting for decisions to be made by the court system'.[166] The NCP remarked that 'it would have benefited the process if the Sámi village had prepared a well thought-through plan for its use of the area. It would also have been beneficial if a coordinated process had been developed between Indigenous groups in the regions for how to deal with development project'.[167] The NCP recommended hiring an independent third party to assist in the consultation process and joint mapping of the impact of the project and/or monitoring of existing agreements, noting international expectations captured in 'A Good Practice Note', which has received support from the UN Global Compact's Human Rights and Labour Working Group.[168]

6. The Performance Standards of the International Finance Corporation

Another standard-setting initiative outside of the UN System can be found in the International Finance Corporation (IFC),[169] which is the largest multilateral source of financing for private sector projects in the developing world.[170] The IFC is the private-sector arm of the World Bank family.[171] Established in 1956, its functions also include assisting private companies in the developing world to mobilize financing in international financial markets and providing advice and technical assistance to businesses and governments. Its mission is to promote private-sector investment in developing

[166] Norway NCP, *Jijnjevaerie Saami Village v. Statkraft AS: Final Statement* (2016).

[167] ibid.

[168] ibid.

[169] Articles of Agreement of the IFC (20 July 1956, as amended by resolutions effective 21 September 1961 and 1 September 1965); C Mates, 'Project Finance in Emerging Markets: the Role of the International Finance Corporation' (2004) 18 Transnational Lawyer 165.

[170] IFC, https://www.ifc.org/en/home, accessed 3 August 2023. Note that the IFC provides both direct and indirect investments: in the latter case, the Performance Standards apply to financial intermediaries rather than to private companies carrying out projects in developing countries. See B Richardson, 'Financing Sustainability: The New Transnational Governance of Socially Responsible Investment' (2008) 17 Yearbook of International Environmental Law 73.

[171] A Kiss and D Shelton, *International Environmental Law* (Transnational Publishers, 2004), at 157–158.

countries, which will reduce poverty and improve people's lives.[172] In this light, the IFC can be described as an institution 'at the crossroads of the public and private sectors', as it is a public-sector institution committed to working with the private sector, sharing private-sector risks in making loans and equity investments without government guarantee of repayment.[173]

The International Finance Corporation's 2012 Performance Sustainability Standards relied on the CBD to include fair and equitable benefit-sharing as a key link between FPIC and due diligence. The implementation activities around the Performance Standards have also shed light on benefit-sharing as part of business due diligence. After introducing some specificities of the IFC, the following sections will discuss the normative clarifications and practical application of benefit-sharing by the IFC.

6.1 Introduction to the IFC and its Performance Standards

Although the IFC coordinates its activities with other institutions in the World Bank Group, it generally operates autonomously. It has its own legal and financial independence, governed by its own Articles of Agreement, share capital, management, and staff. This separation is motivated by the IFC's focus on generating profits from its investment, and it does not offer grants, unlike the World Bank. It also does not work directly with governments.[174] Nonetheless, there remain certain links between the Corporation and the Bank. First, the Bank's safeguard policies,[175] although drafted for public-sector projects, are deemed to apply by default to IFC-funded projects with the private sector when there are gaps in IFC's own policies and standards. Second, the Bank and IFC often cooperate when operating in the same country, thus in some instances the procedures of both organizations apply to a single project.[176] Third, the president of the World Bank Group also serves as the IFC president.

The IFC Standards are intended to apply throughout the life of an investment.[177] They are designed to provide 'guidance' to clients on how to identify risks and impacts and to 'help avoid, mitigate and manage risks and impacts as a way of doing business in a sustainable way'.[178]

[172] DL Khairallah, 'International Finance Corporation' in R Blanpain (ed.), *International Encyclopaedia of Laws (Intergovernmental Organizations—Suppl. 12)* (Kluwer Law International, 2002).

[173] C Lee, 'International Finance Corporation: Financing Environmentally and Socially Sustainable Private Investment' in S Schlemmer-Schulte and K Tung (eds), *Liber Amicorum Ibrahim F.I. Shihata* (Kluwer Law International, 2001) 469.

[174] B Saper, 'The International Finance Corporation's Compliance Advisor/Ombudsman (CAO): An Examination of the Accountability and Effectiveness from a Global Administrative Law Perspective' (2011) 44 NYU Journal of International Law and Policy 1280, at 1283 and 1285.

[175] L Boisson de Chazournes, 'Policy Guidance and Compliance: The World Bank Operational Standards' in D Shelton (ed.), *Commitment and Compliance—The Role of Non-Binding Norms in the International Legal System* (Oxford University Press, 2000) 281, at 297–302.

[176] As in the case of the Chad/Cameroon Pipeline and the Bujagali Hydropower Project in Uganda. Kiss and Shelton (n. 171), at 156 and G Hernández Uriz, 'The Application of the World Bank Standards to the Oil Industry: Can the World Bank Group Promote Corporate Responsibility?' (2002) 28 Brooklyn Journal of International Law 77.

[177] Overview of IFC Performance Standards (2012), para. 2.

[178] ibid, para. 1.

Because of a certain degree of international legal personality, international financial institutions are subject to duties under international law, which encompasses compliance with international environmental law. Any failure to comply with international environmental obligations may result in their international accountability as well as liability for damages.[179] The incorporation of such standards as conditions into loan agreements can make these international environmental standards for corporate accountability contractually binding on private companies. As opposed to the loan agreements between the World Bank and borrower governments that fall under the domain of the international law of treaties, the loan agreements of the IFC with private companies are usually concluded under the law of New York or English law,[180] thus may not be enforceable under international law.[181] Nevertheless, investment contracts can avoid mentioning IFC Standards or undermine them by placing restrictions preventing the host State from using domestic law to enforce investor compliance with IFC Standards on the basis of their agreement with the IFC or an Equator Bank.[182]

The relevance of the IFC Standards is broader than that. They have also set a trend for other international financial institutions, notably in the area of public participation[183] and commercial banks.[184] The Equator Principles are the best-known example,[185] but together with other socially responsible initiatives they are arguably 'a modest, niche sector of the financial economy only occasionally influencing the environmental practice of companies'.[186] In addition, all OECD export credit agencies claim that they apply the IFC Standards through the non-binding Common Approaches agreement,[187]

[179] P Sands and J Peel, with A Fabra and R MacKenzie, *Principles of International Environmental Law* (4th edn, Cambridge University Press, 2018), at 669.

[180] Private correspondence with IFC staff, dated 17 October 2006 (on file with author).

[181] Boisson de Chazournes (n. 175), at 290.

[182] S Leader, 'Human Rights, Risks and New Strategies for Global Investment' (2006) 9 Journal of International Economic Law 657, at 671.

[183] D Bradlow and M. Chapman, 'Public Participation and the Private Sector: The Role of Multilateral Development Banks and the Evolving Legal Standards' (2011) 4 Erasmus Law Review 91, at 92 and 95.

[184] This is the notable case of the Equator Principles, which were last reviewed in 2013 following the latest review of the IFC Performance Standards: http://www.equator-principles.com/, accessed 9 February 2024. C Wright, 'The Equator Principles' in T Hale and D Held (eds), *Handbook of Transnational Governance* (Polity Press, 2011) 229. And this is clearly an intention of the IFC itself: R Kyte, Director of the IFC Environmental and Social Development Department, 'The New IFC Standards' (2006) 12 CSR Asia Weekly (15 March) 13. L Ahearn, 'Environmental Procedures and Standards in International Transactions: Multilateral Models and Private Lending Practices' (1999) 27 International Business Lawyer 419.

[185] B Richardson, 'Financial Markets and Socially Responsible Investing' in B Sjåfjell and B Richardson (eds), *Company Law and Sustainability: Legal Barriers and Opportunities* (Cambridge University Press, 2015) 226, at 263–267. See also B Richardson, 'Socially Responsible Investing through Voluntary Codes' in PM Dupuy and J Viñuales (eds), *Harnessing Foreign Investment to Promote Environmental Protection Incentives and Safeguards* (Cambridge University Press, 2013), 383, at 412–414; D Ong, 'From "International" to "Transnational" Environmental Law? A Legal Assessment of the Contribution of the "Equator Principles" to International Environmental Law' (2010) 79 Nordic Journal of International Law 35; D Ong, 'Public Accountability for Private International Financing of Natural Resource Development Projects: The UN Rule of Law Initiative and the Equator Principles' (2016) 85 Nordic Journal of International Law 201.

[186] Richardson, 'Financial Markets' (n. 185), at 273.

[187] OECD, Recommendation of the Council on Common Approaches for Officially Supported Export Credits and Environmental and Social Due Diligence (TAD/ECG/(2015)5, 28 June 2012); Simons and Macklin (n. 123), at 132.

thereby facilitating access to capital markets because the IFC due diligence procedure reduces credit and capital risks.[188] The IFC has also started to control its financial intermediaries by imposing a review procedure on their activities if the project they finance with IFC support may have environmental and social impacts.[189]

6.2 Business Responsibility to Respect Indigenous Peoples' Human Rights

The IFC environmental standards clearly identify the responsibility of the private sector on the basis of international environmental principles, multilateral environmental agreements, and other international environmental law materials,[190] as well as of formalized dialogue with businesses and NGO representatives.[191] They comprise: a general, cross-cutting requirement for environmental self-assessment and management system (Performance Standard 1); a series of more specific environmental standards (Performance Standard 3 on resource efficiency and pollution prevention and Performance Standard 4 on biodiversity conservation and sustainable management of living natural resources), and other thematic standards that may concern the environment, such as Performance Standard 7 on Indigenous peoples and Performance Standard 8 on cultural heritage.[192] Furthermore, the IFC considers climate change and water, in addition to human rights and gender, as cross-cutting topics that are addressed across multiple Performance Standards.[193]

The International Finance Corporation's 2012 Performance Sustainability Standards built on CBD guidance on benefit-sharing. They identify as triggers: potential relocation of Indigenous peoples; impacts on lands and natural resources subject to traditional ownership or under customary use; and projects proposing to use cultural resources for commercial purposes.[194] These only partly overlap with those identified by UN Special Rapporteur on Human Rights and the Environment John Knox as the reference to traditional knowledge is limited to commercial use.[195] And while the IFC Standards make explicit reference to relocation in line with the UN Declaration on the Rights of Indigenous Peoples (UNDRIP),[196] they do not include

[188] M Langer, 'Key Instruments of Private Environmental Finance: Funds, Project Finance and Market Mechanisms' in Dupuy and Viñuales (n. 185), 161.

[189] ibid, at 163.

[190] As suggested in OECD, 'Key Messages' (OECD Workshop on Multilateral Environmental Agreements and the Private Sector, Helsinki, 16–17 June 2005).

[191] D Bradlow and A Naudé Fourie, 'The Operational Policies of the World Bank and the International Finance Corporation: Creating Law-Making and Law-Governed Institutions?' (2013) 10 International Organizations Law Review 3, at 24–26.

[192] The other Performance Standards focus on: labour and working conditions; community health, safety, and security; and land acquisition and involuntary resettlement (Performance Standards 2, 4, and 5). Due to the focus of this study, these standards will not be analysed.

[193] Overview of IFC Performance Standards (2012), para. 4.

[194] IFC 2012 Performance Standard 1, para. 35.

[195] Nagoya Protocol, Art. 8(a); E Morgera, E Tsioumani, and M Buck, *Unraveling the Nagoya Protocol: Commentary on the Protocol on Access and Benefit-Sharing to the Convention on Biological Diversity* (Martinus Nijhoff, 2014), at 179–184.

[196] UNGA Res 61/295 (13 September 2007).

projects adjacent to Indigenous peoples' lands or the storage of waste or hazardous materials on their lands, which UNDRIP specifically highlights.[197]

The IFC Standards further emphasize that FPIC and benefit-sharing are envisaged where the business entity 'intends to utilise natural resources that are central to the identity and livelihoods of Indigenous peoples and their use exacerbates livelihood risk'.[198] This should be understood in line with the concept of physical and cultural survival discussed in the Inter-American Court of Human Rights in relation to intra-State benefit-sharing discussed in Chapter 3:[199] either proposed development projects or conservation initiatives impacting natural resources that are *traditionally used* by Indigenous and tribal peoples; or the extraction of natural resources (notably minerals) that are not traditionally used by Indigenous peoples but are likely to affect other natural resources that are used by them.[200] This aligns with the view of ILO monitoring bodies that not only projects implemented in traditional lands, but also those having an impact on communities' life require a heightened level of protection.[201] The African Commission, in turn, emphasized the need to protect natural resources found on or under Indigenous land, rather than only those resources the extraction of which may have a negative impact on the group indirectly.[202]

In accordance with the 2012 version of the IFC Standards, private companies are called upon to put in place benefit-sharing by taking into account Indigenous peoples' laws, institutions, and customs.[203] Benefits may include culturally appropriate improvement of their standard of living and livelihoods and the long-term sustainability of the natural resources on which they depend.[204] The IFC further clarified that benefits associated with natural resource use 'may be collective in nature rather than directly oriented towards individuals and households', taking into account the ecological context.[205] This raises concerns related to recognition as a dimension of justice.

With specific regard to involuntary resettlement, IFC clients are expected to implement measures to ensure that communities relying on natural resource-based livelihoods maintain access to those affected resources or alternative resources with equivalent potential for earning a livelihood and are equally accessible.

With regard to continued access, according to the CBD Akwé: Kon Guidelines, proponents of development and associated personnel should respect the cultural

[197] Simons and Macklin (n. 123), at 135 based on Amnesty International, 'Public Statement a Missed Opportunity to Better Protect the Rights of those Affected by Business related Human Rights Abuses' (2011).

[198] IFC 2012 Performance Standard 1, para. 18.

[199] Inter-American Court of Human Rights (IACtHR), *Case of the Saramaka People v. Suriname*, Judgment of 12 August 2008 (Interpretation of the Judgment on Preliminary Objections, Merits, Reparations and Costs), paras 122–123; P Thornberry, *Indigenous Peoples and Human Rights* (Manchester University Press, 2002), at 282.

[200] IACtHR, *Case of the Saramaka People v. Suriname*, Judgment of 28 November 2007 (Preliminary Objections, Merits, Reparations and Costs), paras 155–158.

[201] S Errico, 'The Controversial Issue of Natural Resources: Balancing States' Sovereignty with Indigenous Peoples' Rights' in S Allen and A Xanthaki (eds), *Reflections on the UN Declaration on the Rights of Indigenous Peoples* (Hart, 2011) 348.

[202] G Pentassuglia, 'Indigenous Groups and the Developing Jurisprudence of the African Commission on Human and Peoples' Rights: Some Reflections' (2010) 3 UCL Human Rights Review 150, at 160.

[203] IFC 2012 Performance Standard 7, para. 19.

[204] ibid, paras 12–13.

[205] IFC 2012 Performance Standard 5: Land Acquisition and Involuntary Resettlement, para. 26.

sensitivities and needs of Indigenous peoples for privacy, especially with regard to important ritual ceremonies, and also ensure that their activities do not interfere with daily routines and other activities of those communities.[206] It should be noted that international human rights sources have not made reference to alternative resources, but only referred to the need for continued access. This is because providing alternative resources that offer equivalent potential for earning a livelihood may not ensure cultural appropriateness and may threaten the cultural survival of certain communities. This highlights the need for clearer differentiation within the IFC Performance Standards between the international standards of benefit-sharing and requirements of compensation,[207] as has been seen under the UN Global Compact. The lack of a clear distinction undermines the role of fair and equitable benefit-sharing in addressing distributive justice issues and represents a critical area of incomplete theorization of benefit-sharing in the context of corporate responsibility to uphold human rights.

6.3 Operationalization

Certain implementation activities around the Performance Standards have also focused on benefit-sharing. Complaints from those affected by IFC-financed projects can be filed before a compliance advisor/ombudsman (CAO), an independent oversight authority that reports directly to the President of the World Bank Group and that ensures the application of IFC Standards to companies involved.[208] The CAO 'attempts to resolve complaints through a flexible problem-solving approach and to enhance the environmental outcomes of the project' (ombudsman function).[209] Any person, group, or community affected, or likely to be affected, by a project is eligible, at any time in the project, to file complaints relating to any aspect of the planning, implementation, or impact of the project, without the requirement to specifically allege violations of particular IFC procedures and standards.[210] When the complaint is accepted, the CAO decides the best course of action. In addition to resolving issues for those directly or potentially affected by IFC projects, the CAO is also mandated to provide the IFC with policy and process advice on environmental and social performance, and conduct environmental and social audits and reviews to facilitate institution learning (compliance function). The CAO can thus decide to resolve a complaint by undertaking a compliance audit or exercising advisory functions rather than its ombudsman functions. In the latter cases, the complainant no longer controls the process.[211]

[206] Akwé: Kon Guidelines (n. 54), para. 33.
[207] IFC 2012 Performance Standard 5, para. 9.
[208] 2012 IFC Policy on Social and Environmental Sustainability, paras 54–57.
[209] ibid. See also the IFC CAO Policy (2021), available at https://www.ifc.org/content/dam/ifc/doc/2023/ifc-miga-independent-accountability-mechanism-cao-policy.pdf, accessed 3 August 2023.
[210] Centre for International Environmental Law (CIEL), 'A Handbook on the Office of the Compliance Advisor/Ombudsman of the International Finance Corporation and Multilateral Investment Guarantee Agency' (September 2000), at 5–6 (hereinafter, CIEL Handbook).
[211] ibid, at 8.

The ombudsman's modus operandi includes field visits to the site of contested projects and interviews with all parties involved: staff of the private company, local authorities, affected communities representatives, other relevant local organizations, and IFC staff. Complaints, reports of field missions, and recommendations are all published on the CAO website, together with updates on ongoing investigations.[212] Among these, the most important document is the assessment report, which serves both as the CAO's factual findings in relation to allegations contained in the complaint, and as an assessment of the 'ripeness' of any conflict or tension for resolution or management. Interestingly, after considering complaints, the CAO formulates recommendations not only to the IFC itself, but also directly to the private company involved, albeit such recommendations will then need to be endorsed by the IFC president. The latter would then transmit them to the private company and/or request the IFC to take the appropriate action.

In a particular instance, the CAO did engage in a detailed process of documentation of lessons learnt and of impacts not only at the community level, but also at national level, along with evaluating the CAO' practices on an international level. The CAO documentation is particularly enlightening with regard to the contextualization of the international standards of transnational benefit-sharing.

Following a series of complaints in 2000 concerning a mercury spill caused by the largest gold mining company in Peru, the CAO supported the establishment of a permanent roundtable for facilitating multi-stakeholder dialogue and resolving issues of concern between local communities and the mining company regarding the spill's aftermath and its long-term environmental impacts (*Mesa de Dialogo y Consenso*). The roundtable was designed to act in a proactive way, rather than being retrospective.[213] The *Mesa* eventually established itself as a formal legal entity and succeeded in functioning both as a forum for civil society dialogue and a mechanism for providing objective technical information on communities' concerns surrounding the company's environmental conduct (most notably, by producing a water quality and quantity assessment). The *Mesa* did not, however, represent a formal system of conflict resolution and its legitimacy was not recognized by local NGOs or local authorities. This was possibly due to the undisclosed relationships between members and the company's activities, whether direct or indirect.[214] Having provided financial and technical support to the *Mesa* since 2001, the CAO concluded its phased withdrawal from it in March 2006, recommending the continuation of the *Mesa*'s water monitoring programme and the establishment of transparent dispute resolution mechanisms.[215]

Nonetheless, the CAO continued to assess developments under the *Mesa*, culminating in the publication of three monographs assessing the impacts at different levels of four and a half years of work. In particular, from a standard-setting perspective,

[212] See CAO Ombudsman, available at http://www.cao-ombudsman.org/cases/, accessed 29 June 2023 where all the CAO documents cited below can be found.

[213] CAO, Exit Report regarding two complaints filed with the CAO in relation to Minera Yanacocha Cajamarca, Peru (February 2006).

[214] CAO, Report of the Independent Evaluation of the Mesa de Dialogo y Consenso CAO-Cajamarca, Peru (May 2005).

[215] CAO, Exit Report regarding two complaints filed with the CAO in relation to Minera Yanacocha Cajamarca, Peru (February 2006).

the CAO's assessment has unveiled the linkages between the implementation of the international standard of fair and equitable benefit-sharing and perceptions of risks, mediation training, as well as the independence, transparency, and monitoring of benefit-sharing arrangements.

First of all, the CAO linked the positive impacts of the *Mesa* with a combined vision of: commitment to scientific rigour and simultaneous recognition of the value and importance of local knowledge, its own growing expertise on environmental issues, and its understanding and practice of conflict resolution.[216] It then focused on the role of the platform in dealing with different perceptions of environmental risks from the project, arriving at the conclusion that the *Mesa* effectively managed the environmental hazard but was less able to compel the mining company to address community perceptions and emotions regarding risks. It thus noted the need for distinctive processes and solutions to engage with a discrepancy between perceived risk (such as negative impacts to water quality and quantity; loss of land, livelihoods, and traditional way of life; and eroding social cohesion) and perceived benefits (such as economic and educational benefits; improved standard of living; and improved infrastructure). To that end, the CAO recommended the establishment of dialogue platforms based on a 'situation assessment' that focuses on the history of the communities and their territories, a cultural context assessment to understand the distinctive ways that stakeholders approach conflict resolution (influence of power, rights, and interests, availability of social capital to obtain compliance with agreements), and corporate culture (its leadership, consistent messaging, and track record of compliance with community agreements).[217]

The CAO also assessed the role of mediation training in building capacity for dialogue, equipping communities with skills to advocate for the marginalized and bring about meaningful change. These skills were considered relevant for building trust and reciprocity within an iterative dialogue process that eventually evolved from a mechanism to prevent and resolve conflicts to an accountability mechanism that could assess the mine's operations and ensure the fulfilment of specific benefit-sharing commitments.[218]

Furthermore, based on the *Mesa* experience, the CAO investigated the conditions for ensuring independence and transparency in benefit-sharing arrangements. It noted the importance of a careful structure of governance arrangements that can be 'viewed by the majority of stakeholders as independent, even when the company is a major contributor' and are based on full disclosure and transparency. Additionally, this involved co-developed selection criteria for technical experts to support fact-finding or joint problem-solving; as well as regular communication on how independence is maintained.[219] This extends to co-developing monitoring and compliance approaches tied to benefit-sharing agreements with clearly defined lines of authority, incentives for all parties, and consequences for non- compliance. In practical terms, the *Mesa*

[216] CAO, The Power of Dialogue—Building Consensus: History and Lessons from the Mesa de Diálogo y Consenso CAO-Cajamarca, Peru (Executive Summary) (CAO, 2007).
[217] ibid, 5.
[218] ibid, 7.
[219] ibid, 8.

led to the development of a public system for tracking benefit-sharing agreements and the implementation of the recommendations arising from a water study and water monitoring programme, as well as specific claims of non-compliance brought by *Mesa* members. The tracking system was eventually used by the local branch of the national government's ombudsman office and supported external monitoring. The local ombudsman made public the results and conclusions from its analysis of the tracking results and then met with the mining company to evaluate progress and ensure follow-through with implementation.[220] This approach could be considered a practical method for viewing benefit-sharing as an ongoing partnership-building process that can also facilitate external oversight of the tangible distribution of benefits.

The *Mesa* also sparked a new benefit-sharing approach, with a view to involving the company in a more comprehensive development programme. As a result, the companies agreed in 2007 to allocate US$45 million over the next four years for development projects in the region under the aegis of a technical commission consisting of the regional government and the municipality and within the administration of the United Nations Development Program (UNDP).[221] The funding was used for social development projects (nutrition, education, and health), roads, water conservation programmes, tourism, strengthening institutions, and capacity building, as well as for feasibility studies (e.g. expanding the regional hospital, constructing a dam) and developing a comprehensive urban development plan. The CAO also underlined the 'pioneering independent participatory water study and the community water monitoring programmes' developed under the *Mesa* as the catalysts for a number of projects being implemented today.[222]

The *Mesa* also led to industry-wide benefit-sharing arrangements at the national level. In 2006, an agreement was reached between the government of Peru and the country's mining sector to make a voluntary payment of US$757.5 million over the following five years into an equity fund to fight poverty, malnutrition, and social exclusion in poor mining regions. The fund prioritized as beneficiaries, communities near mines, the poorest areas of mining regions, and the victims of political violence in those areas. The fund was to be co-managed by companies, beneficiary communities, and local and regional governments that would together allocate and administer the payments.[223] This shows the potential usefulness of documenting (and the need to independently research) the impacts of international oversight of corporate environmental accountability and responsibility standards across different levels.

Finally, through the assessment of the *Mesa* process, the CAO also identified lessons for its own ombudsman role. It emphasized the need for benchmarks to measure progress, the importance of developing clear exit strategies for interventions, and the challenges associated with independence and impartiality.[224] This particular case thus shows the CAO's role in proactively managing conflicts between companies and affected communities. First, it provided communities with a structured opportunity to

[220] ibid, 10.
[221] ibid, 11.
[222] ibid, at 12.
[223] ibid.
[224] ibid, 14.

be heard and supported in engaging in complex dialogue processes. Second, through that dialogue, it clarified the conditions for the applicability of international standards of corporate environmental accountability and responsibility. Third, this highlighted the capacity needs of private companies to take into account broader contextual and historical factors around project-specific benefit-sharing options. It also emphasizes the need for an iterative approach to fair and equitable benefit-sharing.

7. Business-Community Agreements

Whether on the basis of the international standards discussed in the previous sections or of their own initiative, business entities usually encapsulate benefit-sharing with Indigenous peoples in private-law contracts, such as business-community agreements. The use of contractual tools for incorporating benefit-sharing agreements between companies and Indigenous peoples, which is generally expected in the form for 'mutually agreed' benefits as referred to by international human rights bodies and under the CBD,[225] and which contains the written documentation of FPIC, is, however, fraught with complexities.

Contractual negotiations may in principle function as a dialogic partnership-building process between private companies and communities for a contextual application of benefit-sharing. However, there have been well-documented unequal disparities in negotiating powers, as well as information and capacity asymmetries.[226] These concerns are compounded by objective difficulties in reconciling communities' customary law within dominant legal systems,[227] including in connection with dispute resolution. In principle, benefit-sharing contracts may provide an opportunity to 'co-author' the terms of cooperation between companies and Indigenous peoples.[228] Contracts may incorporate community worldviews as principles of interpretation, and/or as elements determining the fairness and equity of benefit-sharing.[229] They may also incorporate reference to international human rights standards[230] to substantiate contractual obligations to respect community worldviews. This incorporation of different worldviews in contractual arrangements faces several practical challenges deriving from the limited opportunities for full and effective community engagement

[225] IACtHR, *Case of Kaliña and Lokono Peoples v. Suriname*, Judgment of 25 November 2015 (Merits, Reparations and Costs), paras 150 and 227–229. For a discussion, see A Lucas, 'Participatory Rights and Strategic Litigation: Benefits Forcing and Endowment Protection in Canadian Natural Resource Development' in L Barrera-Hernandez et al. (eds), *Sharing the Costs and Benefits of Energy and Resource Activity* (Oxford University Press, 2016) 339.

[226] E Morgera, 'Under the Radar: Fair and Equitable Benefit-sharing and the Human Rights of Indigenous Peoples and Local Communities connected to Natural Resources' (2019) 23 International Journal of Human Rights 1098, at 1105.

[227] For a reflection on the challenges of legal pluralism in the context of benefit-sharing from bioprospecting, see S Vermeylen, 'The Nagoya Protocol and Customary Law: The Paradox of Narratives in the Law' (2013) 9 Law Environment & Development Journal 185.

[228] N Craik, H Gardner, and D McCarthy, 'Indigenous—Corporate Private Governance and Legitimacy: Lessons Learned from Impact and Benefit Agreements' (2017) 52 Resources Policy 379, at 386.

[229] K Carpenter and A Riley, 'Indigenous Peoples and the Jurisgenerative Moment in Human Rights' (2014) 102 California Law Review 173.

[230] Cotula and Tienhaara (n. 79), at 302.

in contractual negotiations and potential conflict with the developer's commercial demands for expediency and cost-effectiveness.[231] A further layer of complexity arises from confidentiality clauses in benefit-sharing agreements, which limit cross-community communication of lessons learnt in negotiating benefit-sharing.[232] These fundamental challenges add to significant technical difficulties in accounting, calculating benefits, and ensuring environmental sustainability, which require significant administrative capacity.

An analysis within the Canadian context emphasized that despite their private law nature, business-community benefit-sharing contracts are designed to secure public benefits, as an indirect means for the governments to comply with international and constitutional obligations towards Indigenous peoples.[233] This justifies a role for the State in business-community agreement negotiations. From the government perspective, these contracts incorporate the findings of impact assessments, as well as provide for follow-up and monitoring obligations mandated by national law.[234] Special Rapporteur Anaya emphasized that 'the State remains ultimately responsible for any inadequacy in the consultation or negotiation procedures and therefore should employ measures to oversee and evaluate the procedures and their outcomes, and especially to mitigate against power imbalances between the companies and the Indigenous peoples with which they negotiate'.[235] To this end, domestic legislation is needed to ensure that benefit-sharing serves as a 'limit to contractual autonomy', on the basis of international human rights law.[236] In addition, consultations carried out directly by private companies with Indigenous peoples should be supervised by the State.[237] States must also verify that benefit-sharing agreements with extractive industries are crafted on the basis of full respect for Indigenous peoples' rights.[238]

There is evidence indicating substantive positive impacts when governments actively participate in negotiations between communities and companies.[239] However, it may be particularly complex for companies to respect international and national standards if communities prefer not to involve the government out of concern that the contract may become a source of external control (including the distribution of benefits within the community).[240] More generally, communities could find themselves in an adversarial relationship with the government, as different State entities may have a vested interest in the negotiations. One approach to address these concerns would

[231] Craik, Gardner, and McCarthy (n. 228), at 384.

[232] K Caine and N Krogman, 'Powerful or Just Plain Power-Full? A Power Analysis of Impact and Benefit Agreements in Canada's North' (2010) 23 Organization & Environment 76. See also M Langton, 'The Resource Curse Compared: Australian Aboriginal Participation in the Resource Extraction Industry and Distribution of Impacts' in M Langton and J Longbottom (eds), *Community Futures, Legal Architecture: Foundations for Indigenous Peoples in the Global Mining Boom* (Routledge, 2012) 23, at 29 and 38.

[233] See generally Craik, Gardner, and McCarthy (n. 228).

[234] ibid, at 383.

[235] Anaya, A/HRC/24/41 (n. 55), para. 62.

[236] F Francioni, 'Equity' in R Wolfrum (ed.), *Max Planck Encyclopedia of Public International Law* (Oxford University Press, 2010), paras 23–24 and 27.

[237] ibid.

[238] ibid, paras 88 and 92.

[239] Langton (n. 232), at 32.

[240] Craik, Gardner, and McCarthy (n. 228), at 385.

be relying on a national human rights ombudsman as semi-independent government entity that can mediate and facilitate negotiations between private companies and communities, including by signalling when proposals may be undermining existing human rights.[241]

Even more complexity surrounds community negotiations with private operators that are foreign investors. These negotiations may be constrained by the terms of an investor-State contract, which may limit the types of benefits to be made available, such as local employment and local business opportunities.[242] States could include in their agreement with investors an obligation for the latter to conclude a benefit-sharing agreement with communities, determining goals and minimum parameters below which the investor-community agreement cannot go.[243] This would allow the government to monitor and enforce possible violations of the investor-community benefit-sharing contract, including by sanctioning the violation of key terms of benefit-sharing contracts with the termination of State-investor agreements.[244]

Overall, the use of private and/or public instruments for encapsulating mutually agreed benefit-sharing remains a matter for further study in international environmental, human rights, and investment law. Much remains to be understood about the extent to which communities' worldviews can be expressed, understood, and realized within contractual, investment, and corporate legal tools and structures.[245] More research is also required regarding the necessary oversight of benefit-sharing agreements, including considering the integration of Indigenous procedural and substantive standards in this oversight.[246]

For these reasons, Anaya recommended that business' benefit-sharing contribute to 'genuinely strengthen the capacity of Indigenous peoples to establish and pursue their own development priorities and that help Indigenous peoples to make their own decision-making mechanisms and institutions more effective'.[247] *Support*-benefits should thus also be provided by private companies, with a view to enabling communities to play increasingly more significant roles in development projects.[248]

Some evidence has been accrued that business-community benefit-sharing arrangements can avoid paternalistic approaches and genuinely serve communities' vision for their economic participation and enterprise development, rather than mere accumulation and distribution of profit.[249] This situation might involve a genuine agreement on benefits involving access to and management of natural resources, heritage management, and decommissioning, which should be additional to ensuring the

[241] See generally P Marchegiani, E Morgera, and L Parks, 'Indigenous Peoples' Rights to Natural Resources in Argentina: The Challenges of Impact Assessment, Consent and Fair and Equitable Benefit-sharing in cases of Lithium Mining' (2020) 24 International Journal of Human Rights 224–240.

[242] Cotula and Tienhaara (n. 79), at 292.

[243] Albeit to the extent allowed by the State's bilateral investment treaties: ibid, at 303 and 294.

[244] ibid, at 303 and 293.

[245] ibid, at 293.

[246] C Kamphuis, 'Contesting Indigenous-Industry Agreements in Latin America' in D Newman and I Odumosu-Ayanu (eds), *The Law and Politics of Indigenous-Industry Agreements* (Routledge, 2019) 171.

[247] UN Special Rapporteur on Indigenous Peoples' Human Rights James Anaya, Report on the right of indigenous peoples, UN Doc A/66/288 (2011), para. 102

[248] Cotula and Tienhaara (n. 79), at 293.

[249] See generally M Langton, 'Introduction' in Langton and Longbottom (n. 232), 1.

right to engage in traditional activities[250]—the *control*-benefits discussed in Chapter 3 with regard to intra-State benefit-sharing.

8. Conclusions

The development of international standards under the aegis of the UN, the OECD, and IFC have started to clarify the role of fair and equitable benefit-sharing as part of business responsibility to respect Indigenous Peoples' human rights.

But much remains to be clarified about the kind of benefits to be shared and the safeguards to be put in place to avoid top-down and bad-faith practices that have resulted in disruptive and damaging impacts on communities. In addition, fair and equitable benefit-sharing and compensation are not clearly distinguished. Another great challenge surrounds the roles of private companies in taking into account the limited capacities of Indigenous peoples to engage in negotiations and put in place concrete measures to enhance communities' capacities, with a view to making benefit-sharing a genuine process of partnership building.[251] On the whole, transnational benefit-sharing as part of business due diligence is a major area of incomplete theorization, which has so far largely escaped the attention of the vast community of scholars on business and human rights.

Nevertheless, the international standards that have been developed so far help translate benefit-sharing as a benchmark of conduct for non-State actors, such as private companies, that are expected to act as partners with governments in the implementation of international human rights and environmental law.[252]

These international standards can be used in various configurations of global law. They can provide a 'template . . . that [is] intended to serve as common substantive reference points' for advocacy and litigation by victims of corporate abuse and NGOs, as well as for third-party benchmarking exercises.[253]

These standards can also guide national legislative developments to ensure that businesses are clear about their responsibility to ensure fair and equitable benefit-sharing with Indigenous peoples.[254] These standards can influence judicial practice.[255]

[250] K Doohan et al., 'From Paternalism to Partnership: The Good Neighbour Agreement and the Argyle Diamond Mine Indigenous Land Use Agreement in Western Australia' in Langton and Longbottom (n. 232) 232, at 244–246.

[251] Morgera (n. 1).

[252] V Lowe, 'Corporations as International Actors and International Law Makers' (2004) 13 Italian Yearbook of International Law 23, at 25 and 27

[253] For instance, the Global Reporting Initiative's standardized reporting developed by an NGO-led coalition, also including companies, academics, and accounting firms, was designed explicitly to complement the UN Global Compact:C Metcalf, 'Corporate Social Responsibility as Global Public Law: Third Party Rankings as Regulation by Information' (2010–2011) 28 Pace Environmental Law Review 145, at 148 and 154, who ultimately notes insufficient empirical research to determine whether this is an effective approach.

[254] UN Committee on Economic, Social and Cultural Rights, General Comment No. 24 on State obligations in the context of business activities (2017); Office of the High Commissioner for Human Rights, Report to the Human Rights Council: Improving accountability and access to remedy for victims of business-related human rights abuse, UN Doc A/HRC/32/19 (2016), Annex, paras 1.5–6 and 12.3–4, calling upon States to develop domestic public and private law regimes that 'communicate clearly the *standards* of management and supervision *expected*' of corporate entities for impacts associated with or arising from group operations and within their supply chains (emphasis added).

[255] Birnie, Boyle, and Redgwell (n. 152), at 327.

They can provide the basis upon which States may decide to hold corporations directly responsible by extraterritorial application of domestic law or as the basis for establishing some form of international jurisdiction.[256]

From an international investment law perspective, benefit-sharing standards can be integrated in international investment treaty-making (a reconceptualized bilateral investment treaty model) and dispute resolution (as interpretative tools), thereby potentially 'reorient[ing] the sole focus on investor protection that currently dominates international investment law'.[257] This may be facilitated by greater openness and accountability of international arbitration,[258] with a view to moving away from a 'narrow, asocial perception of investors' legitimate expectations concentrated on the conduct of the host country alone'.[259] For instance, benefit-sharing standards can contribute to delineate the 'fair and equitable treatment' that host States owe to foreign investors, to determine the poor judgement of an investor and its objectionable conduct as a defence for host States in international investment disputes.[260] States could also include in their agreement with investors an obligation for the latter to respect international corporate environmental accountability standards with communities, determining goals and minimum parameters to be respected in the investor-community agreement.[261] This would allow governments to monitor and enforce possible violations of investor-community contracts, including by sanctioning them with the termination of State-investor agreements.[262]

From the viewpoint of multinationals, international standards have a significant and growing commercial relevance. International benefit-sharing standards may enhance the process of project review by expanding the substantive criteria applicable to risk assessment and creating additional layers of corporate compliance beyond national law and possibly even beyond international treaties to which the host State is a party.[263] The increasing number of direct commitments of private companies to key provisions or goals of multilateral environmental agreements and their direct involvement in international standard-setting on corporate environmental accountability[264] helps companies in anticipating and preparing for future legal developments and thereby improve their reputation with consumers.

These standards can also influence the behaviour of private companies in their voluntary efforts. Arguably, ignoring global benefit-sharing standards would be 'contrary

[256] UN Special Representative on Business and Human Rights, Interim Report (n. 3), para. 65.

[257] Miles (n. 115), at 224–225 and 238.

[258] P Muchlinski, 'Corporate Social Responsibility' in P Muchlinski, F Ortino, and C Schreuer (eds), *The Oxford Handbook of International Investment Law* (Oxford University Press, 2008) 63, at 683. On the topic, see L Cotula, 'Expropriation Clauses and Environmental Regulation: Diffusion of Law in the Era of Investment Treaties' (2015) 24 Review of European Community and International Environmental Law 278.

[259] Muchlinski (n. 258), at 683.

[260] P Muchlinski, 'Implementing the New UN Corporate Human Rights Framework: Implications for Corporate Law, Governance, and Regulation' (2012) 22 Business Ethics Quarterly 145, at 172–173.

[261] Albeit to the extent allowed by the State's bilateral investment treaties: Cotula and Tienhaara (n. 79), at 303; and 294; and Morgera (n. 251), at 1120.

[262] Cotula and Tienhaara (n. 79), at 303 and 293.

[263] A Meyerstein, 'Global Adversarial Legalism: The Private Regulation of FDI as a Species of Global Administrative Law' in M Audit and S Schill (eds), *Transnational Law of Public Contracts* (Bruylant, 2016) 799.

[264] N Affolder, 'The Market for Treaties' (2010) 11 Chicago Journal of International Law 159, at 186.

to the requirement of due diligence under the UN Guiding Principles'.[265] As Miles highlights, 'the interplay of actors, instruments and differing forms of [corporate social responsibility (CSR)] implementation is also leading to the internalization of a CRS rationale within the business community—in other words, the normalization or mainstreaming of CSR within the private sector', as well as 'gradually altering the cultural environment in which transnational business is conduct'.[266]

International standards may also inform criteria of reasonableness at the domestic level in company law or tort law.[267] They can also guide commercial lawyers in their capacity as 'wise counsellors' to companies that are interested in engaging in collaborative and capacity-building approaches with subcontractors, rather than including 'boilerplate language' in the contracts and conducting top-down audits of their suppliers.[268]

A critical gap in international standard-setting initiatives discussed in this chapter, however, is the lack of sustained engagement with victims and right-holders 'before harm occurs, and in continual monitoring, agenda-setting, awareness raising and review processes'.[269] It has been emphasized that regional and local organizations that have direct experience of supporting victims of corporate human rights abuses linked to environmental degradation have not yet had adequate representation[270] in the process of learning from, assessing, or developing standards and their monitoring mechanisms discussed in this chapter. Even if a new treaty on business and human rights is adopted, the international standard-setting instruments and operationalization approaches discussed in this chapter are largely expected to continue being relevant,[271] but would need to further evolve to better respond to the expectations of the international human rights community. This may ultimately explain the significant incomplete theorization of fair and equitable benefit-sharing, as opposed to compensation, as part of business responsibility to respect human rights.

[265] R McCorquodale, 'Waving Not Drowning: Kyobel Outside the United States' (2013) 107 American Journal of International Law 846, at 848.

[266] Miles (n. 115), at 226 and 231.

[267] See also their relevance in domestic law: Muchlinski (n. 260), at 157–160.

[268] J Ruggie and J Sherman, 'Adding Human Rights Punch to the New *Lex Mercatoria*: The Impact of the UN Guiding Principles on Business and Human Rights on Commercial Legal Practice' (2015) 6 Journal of International Dispute Settlement 455; and D Baumann-Pauly, 'Bridging Theory and Practice through Immersion: Innovations for Teaching Business and Human Rights at Business Schools' (2018) 3 Business and Human Rights Journal 139.

[269] T Melish, 'Putting "Human Rights" back into the UN Guiding Principles on Business and Human Rights: Shifting Frames and Embedding Participation Rights' in Rodríguez-Garavito (n. 35) 76, at 84–85 and 88 (emphasis in the original).

[270] Rodríguez-Garavito (n. 35), at 37.

[271] ibid.

Conclusions

1. Introduction

This chapter reflects on the key findings of this book and the importance of the proposed mutually supportive interpretation of fair and equitable benefit-sharing with international human rights law. In particular, interpreting fair and equitable benefit-sharing in the light of everyone's human right to a healthy environment and human right to science, as well as Indigenous peoples' and peasants' human rights, serves to further its still incomplete theorization and shed light on potentially transformative ways to contribute to sustainability and equity.

This chapter also bring together various reflections on the status of fair and equitable benefit-sharing in international law, considering limited and qualified treaty bases, the debated relevance of authoritative interpretations, as well as arguments already put forward in specialist literature. The chapter will develop an argument about fair and equitable benefit-sharing as a general principle of international law and will consider its implications for the exercise of States' discretionary powers and for international organizations.

This chapter will ultimately identify research questions which arise from this body of research and that remain to be addressed, as to the extent to which fair and equitable benefit-sharing has already been interpreted to clarify the content of the duty to cooperate in international law, not only among States but also with human rights holders, civil society, and private companies.

2. Key Findings

Fair and equitable benefit-sharing is a complex and multifaceted phenomenon in international law that is still proliferating, incompletely theorized, and insufficiently operationalized. It relies on multiple global environmental law configurations and could potentially address numerous environmental justice dimensions, even if available empirical evidence indicates that it rarely contributes to its fairness and equity objectives. Although it has arisen in different areas of international law at different times and in different contexts, the main contention and starting point of this book is that advancing theorization, operationalization, and justice of benefit-sharing requires an interpretation that builds on general international law and rests on mutual supportiveness between international biodiversity law and international human rights law (Introduction).

Inter-State obligations of fair and equitable benefit-sharing are the cornerstone of the global regime on access to genetic resources and international bio-based

Fair and Equitable Benefit-Sharing in International Law. Elisa Morgera, Oxford University Press. © Elisa Morgera 2024.
DOI: 10.1093/oso/9780198862130.003.0007

innovation (the so-called 'ABS' regimes),[1] which comprises bilateral approaches and an increasing range of multilateral approaches. The latter have advanced the theorization of fair and equitable benefit-sharing by complementing treaty provisions with international funds and standardized private contracts. While a multilateral approach moves away from a mere logic of exchange, there still remains space for predominantly transactional interpretations, which have been considered a source of the continued ineffectiveness of international benefit-sharing regimes. This is because these interpretations inherently undermine the global benefits underlying specific benefit-sharing relationships, as well as increase the challenges for beneficiaries to exercise their agency in the context of power asymmetries. As a practical way forward, all the multilateral benefit-sharing approaches examined in this book have increasingly devised ways to facilitate and broker, and possibly also oversee and identify gaps or issues in, an otherwise ad hoc flow of non-monetary benefits, such as information sharing, scientific cooperation, and capacity-building activities. The main challenges that have emerged in the operationalization of these benefit-sharing mechanisms have thus proven the need for a concerted and iterative dialogue that can be supported by an institutionalized multilateral approach serving as a more profound level of global cooperation to realize relevant international objectives and beneficiaries' agency. As brought to light by the shared challenges across these regimes, in particular with regard to digital sequence information, iterative learning through some form of multilateral oversight or reflection on actual impacts on fairness and equity, and responsive redesign of multilateral benefit-sharing, has emerged as an essential approach to better understand how to generate and share global and local benefits in the achievement of international objectives of environmental protection, global food security, and global health security. A normative argument was thus developed about the need to move away from predominantly transactional interpretations and applications of international ABS regimes, towards interpretations of benefit-sharing that support effectiveness in the prevention of further global biodiversity loss and its negative impacts on the full enjoyment of human rights through iterative adaptation and oversight in treaty design and review (Chapter 1).

The sharing of scientific information, capacity building, and technology transfer have been identified as forms of inter-State fair and equitable benefit-sharing across different international regimes: the content of the duty to cooperate in this connection, and the underlying partnership model, however, remain vague. In the specific case of the law of the sea, the 2023 Agreement on Marine Biodiversity of Areas beyond National Jurisdiction (BBNJ) has developed clearer rules and an institutionalized approach to critically assess whether information sharing, capacity building, and marine

[1] Comprising: Convention on Biological Diversity (CBD) (Rio de Janeiro, 5 June 1992, in force 29 December 1993); International Treaty on Plant Genetic Resources for Food and Agriculture (ITPGRFA) (Rome, 3 November 2001, in force 29 June 2004); Nagoya Protocol Additional to the Convention on Biological Diversity 1992, on Access to Genetic Resources and the Fair and Equitable Sharing of Benefits from their Utilization (Nagoya, 29 October 2010, in force 12 October 2014); World Health Assembly Resolution WHA64.5 (2011) on Pandemic influenza preparedness: sharing of influenza viruses and access to vaccines and other benefits; and Agreement under the United Nations Convention on the Law of the Sea on the Conservation and Sustainable Use of Marine Biological Diversity of Areas beyond National Jurisdiction (New York, 19 June 2023, A/CONF.232/2023/4, not yet in force) (BBNJ Agreement).

technology transfer address equity issues in an iterative way. On the one hand, these developments reflect lessons learnt in earlier ABS regimes. On the other hand, this more explicit engagement with the challenges of fair and equitable benefit-sharing has the potential to avoid discriminatory results, prioritize the needs of the vulnerable, and factor in the need to protect against negative consequences of scientific research. To that end, a normative argument has been developed to interpret fair and equitable benefit-sharing through the lenses of the human right to science with a view to privileging models of mutual capacity building and technology co-development to take into account multiple dimensions of justice from the perspective of beneficiaries, as opposed to donor-dominated technology and capacity development processes. Moving away from the assumption that technology and capacity transfers are only possible from the Global North to the Global South not only unveils opportunities for mutual learning that are generally overlooked in this context, but fosters co-production of knowledge that can support transformative change (Chapter 2).

Intra-State benefit-sharing obligations in relation to the human rights of Indigenous peoples have emerged in the context of the regulation of extractive activities, nature conservation (such as the creation of protected areas), freshwater management, and climate change response measures that are situated, or may have impacts, on territories traditionally used by Indigenous peoples. In this context, fair and equitable benefit-sharing has gradually emerged as an inherent component of Indigenous peoples' human rights connected to traditional territories and natural resources in its interplay with impact assessments and free prior informed consent (FPIC). These safeguards basically focus on who gets to decide on the use of natural resources and under what conditions of participation, justification, and recourse. Fundamentally, however, they raise issues of recognition with regard to Indigenous peoples. This involves acknowledging them as self-identified and self-determined peoples; respecting their customary laws and traditional tenure; and understanding their knowledge systems, worldviews, and concepts of nature, well-being, and development in the face of historical and ongoing dispossession, displacement, and discrimination. So far, a mutually supportive interpretation of international biodiversity and international human rights law has emerged from various international and regional human rights bodies as a defensive approach that conceptualizes benefit-sharing as a procedural safeguard. This is significant because human rights standards helped identify the minimum requirements for States' benefit-sharing obligations owed to Indigenous Peoples, which had remained unspecified in international biodiversity law. This interpretation has effectively shed light on the limits to State discretion in the choice of means of implementation on intra-State benefit-sharing under the Convention on Biological Diversity, thereby enhancing justiciability. A normative argument was then developed to further advance this interpretation, shifting from a technocratic, damage-control approach, which is bound by a pre-determined set of development options, towards a potentially transformative collaboration across different worldviews and knowledge systems, with a view to addressing multiple dimensions of justice. The proposed interpretation emphasizes fair and equitable benefit-sharing both in its procedural dimension (Indigenous peoples' agency in the context of a concerned and iterative dialogue aimed at understanding and accommodating different worldviews) and its substantive dimension (the enhancement of Indigenous peoples' choice and capabilities) to collaboratively identify opportunities for the full realization of Indigenous peoples' human rights, not only their protection against negative impacts (Chapter 3).

Provisions on intra-State fair and equitable benefit-sharing with non-Indigenous communities, small-scale farmers and fishers, other legitimate tenure right holders, and rural women have also been developing internationally, but are significantly less articulated and theorized than those for Indigenous peoples. They can potentially provide a legal basis on which to develop and practice new approaches for the recognition of different knowledge systems and knowledge co-production, with a view to fully realizing the human right to science and support transformative governance. A normative argument was proposed to interpret intra-State benefit-sharing with non-Indigenous communities as a means of endorsing distinctive perspectives and vision of communities and groups characterized by socio-economic diversity and ecological culture. This was considered both essential to protect non-Indigenous communities' and rural women's continued control of their natural resources for the effective protection of their human rights to health, food, livelihoods, and culture, as well as in recognition of their ecosystem stewardship and contributions to everyone's human right to a healthy environment. For instance, a mutually supportive interpretation of fair and equitable benefit-sharing at the crossroads of international environmental law and international law on women's human rights would not only effectively prevent discrimination, but also nurture transformative change. This approach involves fully recognizing and fostering learning from women's distinctive ecological knowledge and their unique nurturing relationships with both humans and nature (Chapter 4).

The transnational dimensions of intra-State benefit-sharing were also analysed with regard to the use of Indigenous and local knowledge across national and international processes. This served to emphasize the challenge of ensuring knowledge holders' ongoing opportunities to govern and steward their knowledge, in line with their customary laws, while gaining more voice, recognition, and influence in decision-making processes that impact their lives and human rights. Ultimately, the justice dilemmas revolves around whose knowledge holds significance and determines environmental sustainability approaches. A mutually supportive interpretation at the crossroads of international environmental law and international human rights law was proposed on the basis of the human right to science, in order to support the agency of knowledge holders in co-identifying benefits and more equitable sustainability solutions. Such mutually supportive interpretation can serve to critically assess how and to what extent FPIC and fair and equitable benefit-sharing effectively ensure that Indigenous and local knowledge holders influence decision-making processes that are underpinned by the science base they have contributed to create. The normative argument was further developed by connecting the idea that transdisciplinary research should be seen both as a form of benefit-sharing and a precondition for transformative governance for sustainable development: the recognition of different knowledge systems and the inclusion of underrepresented types of knowledge ensures that solutions have sustainable impacts across different scales and sectors by empowering those whose interests are currently not being met and who represent transformative sustainability values[2] (Chapter 4).

The progressive development of international law on the role of the private sector in respecting international law on human rights and the environment provided a final area for the study of transnational forms of fair and equitable benefit-sharing. It revealed the delicate balance between public authorities' obligations and expectations placed on private business actors, who are often those driving developments affecting Indigenous peoples' and other communities' territories. In effect, business entities play a dominant role in the implementation of domestic procedures for consultation and environmental assessments in a context marked by significant power imbalances and unequal access to information. Overall, international standards on benefit-sharing for multinationals and other private companies have increasingly emerged to establish concrete measures to enhance communities' capacities to develop genuine partnerships with private companies when external engagement is locally identified as beneficial to communities' development aspirations. However, much remains to be clarified about the kinds of benefits to be shared and the safeguards to be put in place to avoid top-down and bad-faith practices that result in disruptive and damaging impacts on beneficiaries. The normative argument here was to draw connections between these international developments once again at the crossroads of international biodiversity law and international human rights law, which are still little known to the growing community focused on 'business and human rights'. This includes advocacy and litigation by victims of corporate abuse and NGOs, States' efforts to develop and enforce legislation, and international investment treaty-making and dispute resolution (Chapter 5).

In each case, the incomplete theorization of fair and equitable benefit-sharing is both a result of unresolved divergence in negotiating agendas and insufficient efforts to integrate learning from past experience in which benefit-sharing practices contributed to documented injustices. Nevertheless, incomplete theorization makes space for a mutually supportive interpretation of fair and equitable benefit-sharing across international biodiversity law and international human rights law, notably the human right to science and the human right to a healthy environment, that can clarify limitations to States' discretion and business due diligence, identify more genuine and specific cooperative approaches towards equitable sustainability solutions, and even illuminate a path towards transformative change.

3. Legal Status

In analysing a wide array of international legal materials on fair and equitable benefit-sharing, different conclusions may be reached on the status of benefit-sharing depending on whether it has emerged as an inter-State obligation or an intra-State one.[3]

[2] IJ Visseren-Hamakers and MTJ Kok, 'Introduction' in I Visseren-Hamakers and M Kok (eds), *Transforming Biodiversity Governance* (Cambridge University Press, 2022) 3.

[3] This section draw on, and further advances, arguments initially made in E Morgera, 'The Need for an International Legal Concept of Fair and Equitable Benefit-sharing' (2016) 27 European Journal of

For instance, inter-State benefit-sharing obligations related to mining in the deep seabed and bioprospecting, which are embedded in international treaty law and State practice, have led some scholars to consider them international customary norms.[4] On the other hand, it remains unclear if and how inter-State benefit-sharing relates to financial, technological, and capacity-building obligations under multilateral environmental agreements, as part of emerging practices of international institutions increasingly playing a proactive and brokering role. More recent treaty-making processes may shed light on this dimension of fair and equitable benefit-sharing: for instance the iterative approach now embedded in the 2023 BBNJ Agreement, and in the potential text on technology co-development in a new pandemic treaty under negotiation at the time of writing.[5]

With regard to intra-State benefit-sharing, limited and qualified treaty bases[6] have been increasingly complemented by authoritative interpretations put forward by international and regional human rights bodies of an adjudicatory and advisory nature, including by relying on international soft-law guidance adopted by consensus by CBD Parties. In addition, intra-State benefit-sharing requirements related to the use of natural resources and traditional knowledge have been increasingly reflected in international standards and guidelines. On the one hand, intra-State benefit-sharing obligations can be construed as interconnected with the prohibition of discrimination against Indigenous peoples on racial grounds.[7] This reveals the strategic advantage of relying on, among available human rights treaty bases, the Convention on the Elimination of Racial Discrimination,[8] which is the most widely applicable (179 Parties) in those countries that are not party to the Inter-American or African regional treaties and that have expressed limitations to their implementation of the UN Declaration on the Rights of Indigenous Peoples.[9] This could be an application of equity *intra legem* in international law. On the other hand, the connection between the human rights to which benefit-sharing is inherent and non-discrimination could support the argument that an international benefit-sharing obligation is an integral

International Law 353 and E Morgera, 'Under the Radar: Fair and Equitable Benefit-Sharing and the Human Rights of Indigenous Peoples and Local Communities Related to Natural Resources' (2019) 23 International Journal of Human Rights 1098.

[4] J Harrison, 'Who Benefits from the Exploitation of non-Living Resources on the Seabed? Operationalizing the Benefit-sharing Provisions in the UN Convention on the Law of the Sea' (2015), available at https://benelexblog.wordpress.com/2015/07/01/who-benefits-from-the-exploitation-of-non-living-resources-on-the-seabed-operationalizing-the-benefit-sharing-provisions-in-the-un-convention-on-the-law-of-the-sea/, accessed 8 February 2024, at 7–9; and R Pavoni, 'Biodiversity and Biotechnology: Consolidation and Strains in the Emerging International Legal Regimes' in F Francioni and T Scovazzi (eds), *Biotechnology and International Law* (Hart, 2006) 29.

[5] Art. 9(2) and Option 6(c).X of Option 12.B and Art. 11 (Option 11.B) in the draft pandemic instrument text (A/INB/X/X, 2023).

[6] CBD treaty provisions contains significantly qualified language and their legal weight has been contested: e.g. S Harrop and D Pritchard, 'A Hard Instrument Goes Soft: The Implications of the Convention on Biological Diversity's Current Trajectory' (2011) 21 Global Environmental Change 474.

[7] Inter-American Court of Human Rights (IACtHR), *Xákmok Kásek Indigenous Community v. Paraguay*, Judgment of 24 August 2010, Section 3.1 and n. 37.

[8] International Convention on the Elimination of All Forms of Racial Discrimination (New York, 7 March 1966, in force 4 January 1969).

[9] UNGA Res 61/295, 2007.

component of the customary international law prohibition of discrimination on racial grounds, which binds States even in the absence of applicable treaty bases and is considered *ius cogens*, thereby prevailing over other treaty provisions. This could be an application of equity *contra legem* in international law.

In addition, in understanding the common thread among multiple rights and multiple right-holders, the link between intra-State benefit-sharing and non-discrimination has been emphasized by UN Special Rapporteur on Human Rights and the Environment John Knox. He considered benefit-sharing as an additional measure to protect those who are most vulnerable to, or at particular risk from, environmental harm, with a view to complementing effective measures against the underlying conditions that cause or help to perpetuate discrimination. This applies to measures (such as mining and logging concessions) that have disproportionately severe effects on communities that rely on ecosystems, or that are likely to cause environmental harm reinforcing historical or persistent prejudice against groups of individuals.[10] Accordingly, using criteria for traditional occupation or use based solely on the larger society's understanding of continuity or patterns would be discriminatory. Intra-State benefit-sharing obligations also arise from the use of resources that are held without title[11] or for which communities unwillingly lost possession[12] and are therefore shared with the majority population. This sharing is justified as long as there is continuity in Indigenous peoples' terms of 'values' and 'shared mentality' related to these resources.[13]

In a broader range of cases with different beneficiaries including non-Indigenous communities and women, intra-State benefit-sharing obligations can be conceived as integral to the general principle of international law of effective consultation.[14] As such, it would affect the exercise of States' discretionary powers in relation to the development, interpretation, and application of international law even in the absence of an applicable treaty basis.[15]

Another common normative thread could also be explored—human dignity. This concept was mentioned explicitly by the Inter-American Court of Human Rights,[16] and scholarship on human dignity and the environment arguably provides a broader and more coherent framework for understanding benefit-sharing in the context of overlapping human rights of Indigenous peoples and local communities. Human

[10] J Knox, 'Report of the Special Rapporteur on the issue of human rights obligations relating to the enjoyment of safe, clean, healthy and sustainable environment' UN Doc A/HRC/37/59 (2018), para. 9.

[11] <IBT>African Commission on Human and Peoples' Rights (Afr. Comm.), *Centre for Minority Rights Development (Kenya) and Minority Rights Group International on behalf of Endorois Welfare Council v. Kenya* (4 February 2010) Case 276/2003, </IBT>paras 204–207.

[12] ibid, para. 209.

[13] African Court on Human and People's Rights, *African Commission on Human and People's Rights v. Republic of Kenya* (Ogiek decision), Judgment (Reparations) App. No. 006/2012 (23 June 2022), para. 185.

[14] G Pentassuglia, 'Towards a Jurisprudential Articulation of Indigenous Land Rights' (2011) 22(1) European Journal of International Law 165, at 176, reflecting on IACtHR, *Comunidad Garífuna de Punta Piedra y sus miembros vs Honduras* (Preliminary Exceptions, Merits, Reparations and Costs), 8 October 2015, para. 222.

[15] A Boyle and C Chinkin, *The Making of International Law* (Oxford University Press, 2007), at 222–225.

[16] IACtHR, *Kaliña and Lokono Peoples v. Suriname*, Judgment of 25 November 2015 (Merits, Reparations and Costs), paras 181 and 193 referring to the 'right to a dignified life ... connected with natural resources on ... traditional territories'.

dignity encompasses the interplay of self-determination (agency and autonomy in determining the course of one's life), subsistence (material dignity as the minimum conditions for physical and cultural existence), non-discrimination (the right to be acknowledged as equals against the background of historically entrenched and pervasive discrimination), and political participation (the opportunity for right-holders to preserve their identity and culture as part of broader society).[17] Human dignity is seen as a collective right (to be exercised as part of one's community and society) and as a collective obligation. From the latter perspective, it requires, on the one hand, not just protection, but also support from the State, which can be related to the various forms of non-monetary benefits identified under the CBD. On the other hand, a collective obligation also entails the efforts of everyone to respect the dignity of each other in ways that are contextual to a society's history and current challenges.[18] In this connection it could be argued that even on the basis of soft-law instruments on intra-State benefit-sharing, States are bound to respect their underlying obligations under the UN Charter[19] to 'protect human dignity, eliminate all forms of discrimination, promote the right to self-determination and progressively eliminate material obstacles that hinder economic, social and cultural development'.[20]

These interpretations, based on international human rights law, could also find support in the international human rights law principle *pro personae*. This principle suggests that when interpretating more general international human rights treaties, priority should be given to interpretations that are more beneficial to specific human rights holders. This prioritization of specific rights over general ones is central to this principle.[21]

Clearly, the meaning of fair and equitable benefit-sharing goes beyond a particular treaty regime in which it can be found, and is 'recognized by international law itself'[22] as a combination of engagement with benefit-sharing in international human rights case law and jurisprudence, and intergovernmental consensus in treaty- and international soft-law making.[23] Because of its flexibility, fair and equitable benefit-sharing has been able to adapt to different sectors and approaches in international law[24]

[17] <IBT>E Daly, *Dignity Rights: Courts, Constitutions and the Worth of the Human Person* (University of Pennsylvania Press, 2013) </IBT>at 5, 40, 59–60, and 119.

[18] ibid, at 119–121.

[19] Charter of the United Nations (San Francisco, 26 June 1945, in force 24 October 1945).

[20] F Francioni, 'The Peasants' Declaration: State Obligations and Justiciability' in M Albarese et al. (eds), *The United Nations Declaration on Peasants' Rights* (Routledge, 2022) 4, at 10.

[21] N Posenato, 'The UNDROP and the Case Law of the Inter-American Human Rights System' in Albarese et al. (n. 20), 237, at 243.

[22] R Wolfrum, 'General International Law (Principles, Rules and Standards)' in R Wolfrum (ed.), *Max Planck Encyclopedia of Public International Law* (2010; online edition), available at http://opil.ouplaw.com/view/10.1093/law:epil/9780199231690/law-9780199231690-e1408, accessed 8 February 2024, paras 28 and 33–36. See also P Birnie, A Boyle, and C Redgwell, *International Law and the Environment* (Oxford University Press, 2009), at 26–29; C Burke, *An Equitable Framework for Humanitarian Intervention* (Hart, 2014), at 3–4, 95, 115, 123, and 253; and I Saunders, *General Principles as Sources of International Law* (Hart, 2021) at 175 and 207.

[23] Note, however, various complexities in making this assessment and the differing views in international case law and the literature on these points: Saunders (n. 22), at 232–236.

[24] Being 'abstract', 'horizontally general', and representing a 'rapid legislative response to global issues' with transnational dimensions: Saunders (n. 22), at 221 and 272–274.

to address new problems in international law (such as bio-based innovation) as well as providing 'new ways of looking at old problems' (such as technological solidarity).[25] Its normative core shared by its inter- and intra-State dimensions of benefit-sharing (concerted and dialogic partnership-building in identifying and allocating economic, socio-cultural, and environmental benefits among States and non-State actors, with an emphasis on the vulnerable) can thus be considered a general principle of international law that represents the consistent consensus among developed and developing countries.[26] It is a general principle of international law that is derived from converging international—rather than national—legal developments.[27]

As a principle, it may affect the exercise of States' discretionary powers in relation to the development, interpretation, and application of international law in the absence of an applicable treaty basis.[28] In addition, as a general principle, fair and equitable benefit-sharing also applies to international organizations.[29] It exerts influence by providing 'parameters' (an objective to be taken into account and appropriate processes for doing so)[30] affecting the way governments, courts, and international organizations make decisions.[31] It provides a 'yardstick' contributing to 'the evolution of a new balance of rights and duties in many fields of international law' in the context of 'legal relationships of all kinds' and 'in a world deeply divided by conflicting ideologies as well as conflicting interests'.[32]

Going beyond the particular treaty regimes in which it can be found, fair and equitable benefit-sharing can be ultimately assessed as the manifestation 'recognized by international law itself',[33] across conflicting ideologies and interests, of the need for a new balance of rights and duties towards a global partnership for sustainable development.[34] In other words, it represents a specific expression of the broader principle of international law on equity that has arisen from the continuing and new environmental sustainability challenges facing the international community.

[25] Saunders (n. 22), at 275.

[26] Although general principles of international law and customary international law can be confusing, it has been argued that the former only requires *opinio iuris*, whereas the latter also requires consistent State practice: Birnie, Boyle, and Redgwell (n 22), at 28.

[27] Wolfrum (n. 22), paras 33–36, who calls for a comparison of relevant international materials to that end.

[28] Boyle and Chinkin (n 15), at 222–225.

[29] O De Schutter, *International Human Rights Law* (Cambridge University Press, 2010), at 55.

[30] Birnie, Boyle, and Redgwell (n 22), at 127.

[31] In accordance with Vienna Convention on the Law of Treaties (VCLT), Art. 31(3): Birnie, Boyle, and Redgwell (n 22), at 28.

[32] W Friedmann, 'The Use of "General Principles" in the Development of International Law' (1963) 57 American Journal of International Law 279, at 287 and 289–290.

[33] Wolfrum (n. 22), paras 28 and 33–36.

[34] Rio Declaration on Environment and Development 1992, UN Doc A/CONF.151/26 (1992), vol. 1, Annex 1. The argument develops the intuition expressed by P Sand, 'Cooperation in a Spirit of Global Partnership' in J Viñuales (ed.), *The Rio Declaration on Environment and Development: A Commentary* (Oxford University Press, 2015) 617; and a response to N Cooper and D French, 'SDG 17: Partnerships for the Goals: Cooperation within the Context of a Voluntarist Framework' in D French and L Kotzé (eds), *Sustainable Development Goals: Law, Theory and Implementation* (Edward Elgar, 2018) 271.

4. Research Agenda

All the manifestations of fair and equitable benefit-sharing in international law discussed in this book are under continuous evolution and increasing mutual influence, so continued research within each regime and from a general international law perspective is necessary. In addition, the international debate on the human right to a healthy environment, which has reached a new momentum in 2022,[35] will undoubtedly provide new insights for further theorization of fair and equitable benefit-sharing at the intersection of international environmental law and international human rights law. In addition, new methodologies and inter- and trans-disciplinary collaborations can shed new light on the international law analysis of fair and equitable benefit-sharing.[36] In fact research practices themselves[37] can and should provide a testing ground for understanding fair and equitable benefit-sharing in the continuum from knowledge co-production to sustainable governance.

[35] UNGA 'The Human Right to a Clean, Healthy and Sustainable Environment', Res 76/300 (1 August 2022); e.g. D Lupin (ed.), *A Research Agenda for Human Rights and the Environment* (Edward Elgar, 2023).

[36] E Mogera and L Parks, 'Reflections on Methods from an Interdisciplinary Research Project in Global Environmental Law' (2019) 8 Transnational Environmental Law 489; and E Mogera, L Parks, and M Schroeder, 'Methodological Challenges of Transnational Environmental Law' in V Heyvaert and LA Duvic-Paoli (eds), *Research Handbook on Transnational Environmental Law* (Edward Elgar, 2020) 48.

[37] E Morgera, K Kulovesi, and M Mehling, 'Global Environmental Law: Context and Theory, Challenge and Promise' (2019) 8 Transnational Environmental Law 405.

Selected Bibliography

Abseno, MM, 'The Concept of Equitable Utilisation, No Significant Harm and Benefit-Sharing under the River Nile Cooperative Framework Agreement: Some Highlights on Theory and Practice' (2009) 20 Journal of Water Law 86

Armeni, C, 'Participation in Environmental Decision-Making: Reflecting on Planning and Community Benefits for Major Wind Farms' (2016) 28 Journal of Environmental Law 415

Barrera-Hernandez, L et al. (eds), *Sharing the Costs and Benefits of Energy and Resource Activity* (Oxford University Press, 2016)

Baslar, K, *The Concept of the Common Heritage of Mankind in International Law* (Martinus Nijhoff, 1998)

Bavikatte, K and Robinson, DF, 'Towards a People's History of the Law: Biocultural Jurisprudence and the Nagoya Protocol on Access and Benefit Sharing' (2011) 7 Law Environment and Development 35

Bessa, A, 'Traditional Local Communities in International Law' (PhD Dissertation, European University Institute, 2013)

Bonfanti, A and Trevisanut, S, 'TRIPs on the High Seas: Intellectual Property Rights on Marine Genetic Resources' (2011) 37 Brooklyn Journal of International Law 187

Bouwer, K, 'Insights for Climate Technology Transfer from International Environmental and Human Rights Law' (2018) 23 Journal of Intellectual Property Right 7

Bouwer, K, 'Possibilities for Justice and Equity in Human Rights and Climate Law: Benefit-Sharing in Climate Finance' (2021) 11 Climate Law 1

Brand, U and Vadrot, A, 'Epistemic Selectivities and the Valorisation of Nature: The Cases of the Nagoya Protocol and the Intergovernmental Science-Policy Platform for Biodiversity and Ecosystem Services' (2013) 9 Law Environment and Development Journal 204

Broggiato, A, 'Marine Genetic Resources beyond National Jurisdiction—Coordination and Harmonisation of Governance Regimes' (2011) 41 Environmental Policy and Law 35

Broggiato, A et al., 'Fair and Equitable Sharing of Benefits from the Utilization of Marine Genetic Resources in Areas beyond National Jurisdiction: Bridging the Gaps between Science and Policy' (2014) 49 Marine Policy 176

Broggiato A et al., '*Mare Geneticum*: Balancing Governance of Marine Genetic Resources in International Waters' (2018) 33 International Journal of Marine and Coastal Law 3

Caine, K and Krogman, N, 'Powerful or Just Plain Power-Full? A Power Analysis of Impact and Benefit Agreements in Canada's North' (2010) 23 Organization & Environment 76

Cariño, J et al., *Nagoya Protocol on Access to Genetic Resources and the Fair and Equitable Sharing of Benefits Arising from Their Utilization: Background and Analysis* (The Berne Declaration, Bread for the World, Ecoropa, Tebtebba and Third World Network, 2013)

Chapman, A, 'Towards an Understanding of the Right to Enjoy the Benefits of Scientific Progress and its Applications' (2009) 8 Journal of Human Rights 1

Chiarolla, C, 'Plant Patenting, Benefit Sharing and the Law Applicable to the Food and Agriculture Organisation Standard Material Transfer Agreement' (2008) 11 Journal of World Intellectual Property 1

Clark, N, 'Institutional Arrangements for the New BBNJ Agreement: Moving beyond Global, Regional, and Hybrid' (2020) 122 Marine Policy 104143

Coolasaet, B and Pitseys, J, 'Fair and Equitable Negotiations? African Influence and the International Access and Benefit-Sharing Regime' (2015) 15 Global Environmental Politics 38

Craig, D and Davies, M, 'Ethical Relationship for Biodiversity Research and Benefit-sharing with Indigenous Peoples' (2005) 2 Macquarie Journal of International and Comparative Environmental Law 31

Craik, N, 'Process and Reconciliation: Integrating the Duty to Consult with Environmental Assessment' (2016) 52 Osgoode Hall Law Journal 632

Craik, N, Gardner, H, and McCarthy, D, 'Indigenous-Corporate Private Governance and Legitimacy: Lessons Learned from Impact and Benefit Agreements' (2017) 52 Resources Policy 379

Doyle, C, *Indigenous Peoples, Title to Territory, Rights and Resources: The Transformative Role of Free, Prior and Informed Consent* (Routledge, 2015)

Doyle, C and Gilbert, J, 'Indigenous Peoples and Globalization: From "Development Aggression" to "Self-Determined Development"' (2008/9) 7 European Yearbook of Minority Issues 219

Eichler, J, *Reconciling Indigenous Peoples' Individual and Collective Rights Participation, Prior Consultation and Self-Determination in Latin America* (Routledge, 2019)

Fedder, B, *Marine Genetic Resources, Access and Benefit-Sharing* (Routledge, 2013)

Frakes, J, 'The Common Heritage of Mankind Principle and the Deep Seabed, Outer Space, and Antarctica: Will Developed and Developing Nations Reach a Compromise?' (2003) 21 Wisconsin International Law Journal 409

Gilbert, J, *Natural Resources and Human Rights* (Oxford University Press, 2018)

Hiemstra, SJ et al., *Digital Sequence Information (DSI). Options and Impact of Regulating Access and Benefit Sharing—Stakeholder Perspectives* (University of Wageningen, 2019)

Humphries, F et al., 'A Tiered Approach to the Marine Genetic Resources Governance Framework under the Proposed UNCLOS Agreement for Biodiversity beyond National Jurisdiction (BBNJ)' (2020) 122 Marine Policy 103910

de Jonge, B, 'Towards a Fair and Equitable ABS Regime: Is Nagoya Leading Us in the Right Direction?' (2013) 9 Law Environment and Development Journal 241

de Jonge, B, 'What Is Fair and Equitable Benefit-Sharing?' (2011) 24 Journal of Agricultural and Environmental Ethics 127

Kamau, EC and Winter, G (eds), *Genetic Resources, Traditional Knowledge and the Law: Solutions for Access and Benefit Sharing* (Routledge, 2009)

Kamau, EC and Winter, G (eds), *Common Pools of Genetic Resources Equity and Innovation in International Biodiversity Law* (Edward Elgar, 2013)

Langton, M and Longbottom, J (eds), *Community Futures, Legal Architecture: Foundations for Indigenous Peoples in the Global Mining Boom* (Routledge, 2012)

Lawson, C and Downing, S, 'It's Patently Absurd—Benefit Sharing Genetic Resources from the Sea under UNCLOS, the CBD and TRIPS' (2002) 5 Journal of International Wildlife Law & Policy 211

Lawson, C and Rourke, M, 'Open Access DNA, RNA and Amino Acid Sequences: The Consequences and Solutions for the International Regulation of Access and Benefit Sharing' (2016) 24 Journal of Law and Medicine 96

Leary, DK, 'Bioprospecting and the Genetic Resources of Hydrothermal Vents on the High Seas: What is the Existing Legal Position, Where are We Heading and What are Our Options' (2004) 17 Macquarie Journal of International and Comparative Environmental Law 137

Leary, DK et al., 'Marine Genetic Resources: A Review of Scientific and Commercial Interest' (2009) 33 Marine Policy 183

Lodge, M, 'The Common Heritage of Mankind' (2012) 27 International Journal of Marine and Coastal Law 733

Louafi, S, *Reflections on the Resource Allocation Strategy of the Benefit Sharing Fund* (Swiss Federal Office for Agriculture, 2013)

McCool, S, 'Distributing the Benefits of Nature's Bounty: A Social Justice Perspective', Unpublished paper presented at the International Symposium on Managing Benefit Sharing in Changing Social Ecological Systems, Windhoek, Namibia, 2012

McDermott, M, Mahanty S, and Schreckenberg, K, 'Examining Equity: A Multidimensional Framework for Assessing Equity in Payments for Ecosystem Services' (2013) 33 Environmental Science and Policy 416

McIntyre, O, 'Benefit-Sharing and Upstream/Downstream Cooperation for Ecological Protection of Transboundary Waters: Opportunities for China as an Upstream State' (2015) 40 Water International 48

Mancisidor, M, 'Is There Such a Thing as a Human Right to Science in International Law?' (7 April 2015) ESIL Reflections

Marchegiani, P, Morgera, E, and Parks, L, 'Indigenous Peoples' Rights to Natural Resources in Argentina: The Challenges of Impact Assessment, Consent and Fair and Equitable Benefit-Sharing in Cases of Lithium Mining' (2020) 24 International Journal of Human Rights 224

Moeller, N and Stannard, C (eds), *Identifying Benefit Flows: Studies on the Potential Monetary and Non-Monetary Benefits Arising from the International Treaty on Plant Genetic Resources for Food and Agriculture* (FAO, 2013)

Morgera, E, 'Fair and Equitable Benefit-sharing at the Crossroads of the Human Right to Science and International Biodiversity Law' (2015) 4 Laws 803

Morgera, E, 'Justice, Equity and Benefit-Sharing under the Nagoya Protocol to the Convention on Biological Diversity' (2015) 24 Italian Yearbook of International Law 113

Morgera, E, 'The Need for an International Legal Concept of Fair and Equitable Benefit-sharing' (2016) 27 European Journal of International Law 353

Morgera, E, 'Fair and Equitable Benefit-sharing' in E Orlando and L Krämer (eds), *Encyclopedia of Environmental Law: Principles of Environmental Law* (Edward Elgar, 2018) 323

Morgera, E, 'Fair and Equitable Benefit-Sharing in a New International Instrument on Marine Biodiversity: A Principled Approach Towards Partnership Building?' (2018) 5 Maritime Safety and Security Law Journal 48

Morgera, E, 'Under the Radar: Fair and Equitable Benefit-Sharing and the Human Rights of Indigenous Peoples and Local Communities Related to Natural Resources' (2019) 23 International Journal of Human Rights 1098

Morgera, E, 'The Relevance of the Human Right to Science for the Conservation and Sustainable Use of Marine Biodiversity of Areas Beyond National Jurisdiction: A New Legally Binding Instrument to Support Co-Production of Ocean Knowledge across Scales' in V De Lucia et al. (eds), *International Law and Marine Areas beyond National Jurisdiction: Reflections on Justice, Space, Knowledge and Power* (Brill, 2022) 242

Morgera, E, Buck, M, and Tsioumani E (eds), *The 2010 Nagoya Protocol on Access and Benefit-Sharing in Perspective: Implications for International Law and National Implementation* (Martinus Nijhoff, 2013)

Morgera, E and Gillies, L, 'Realizing the Objectives of public International Environmental Law through Private Contracts: The Need for a Dialogue with Private International Law Scholars?' in D French, V Ruiz Abou-Nigm, and K McCall Smith (eds), *Public and Private International Law: Strengthening Connections* (Hart, 2018) 175

Morgera, E et al., 'Addressing the Ocean-climate Nexus in the BBNJ Agreement: Strategic Environmental Assessments, Human Rights and Equity in Ocean Science' (2023) 38 International Journal of Marine and Coastal Law 447

Morgera, E and Tsioumani, E, 'The Evolution of Benefit-Sharing: Linking Biodiversity and Communities' Livelihoods' (2010) 19 Review of European, Comparative and International Environmental Law 150

Morgera, E, Tsioumani, E, and Buck, M, *Unraveling the Nagoya Protocol: Commentary on the Protocol on Access and Benefit-sharing to the Convention on Biological Diversity* (Martinus Nijhoff, 2014)

Morris-Sharma, N, 'Marine Genetic Resources in Areas beyond National Jurisdiction: Issues with, in and outside of UNCLOS' (2017) 20 Max Planck Yearbook of United Nations Law 71

Nandan, SN, Lodge, M, and S Rosenne, *The Development of the Regime for Deep Seabed Mining* (Kluwer Law, 2022)

Newman, D and Odumosu-Ayanu, I (eds), *The Law and Politics of Indigenous-Industry Agreements, Natural Resources and the Law* (Routledge, 2021)

Nkhata, BA et al., 'A Typology of Benefit Sharing Arrangements for the Governance of Social-Ecological Systems in Developing Countries' (2012) 17 Ecology and Society 17

Noyes, JE, 'The Common Heritage of Mankind: Past, Present and Future' (2011–2012) 40 Denver Journal of International Law and Policy 447

Oberthür, S and Pozarowska, J, 'Managing Institutional Complexity and Fragmentation: The Nagoya Protocol and the Global Governance of Genetic Resources' (2013) 13 Global Environmental Politics 100

Oberthür, S and Rosendal, K (eds), *Global Governance of Genetic Resources: Access and Benefit Sharing after the Nagoya Protocol* (Routledge, 2015)

O'Faircheallaigh, C and Corbett, T, 'Indigenous Participation in Environmental Management of Mining Projects: The Role of Negotiated Agreements' (2015) 14 Environmental Politics 629

Oldham, P, Hall, S, and Forero, O, 'Biological Diversity in the Patent System' (2013) 8 PLoS ONE e78737

Paisley, R, 'Adversaries into Partners: International Water Law and the Equitable Sharing of Downstream Benefits' (2002) 3 Melbourne Journal of International Law 280

Parks, L, *Benefit-sharing in Environmental Governance: Local Experiences of a Global Concept* (Routledge, 2020)

Parks, L and Morgera, E, 'The Need for an Interdisciplinary Approach to Norm Diffusion: The Case of Fair and Equitable Benefit Sharing' (2015) 24 Review of European, Comparative and International Environmental Law 353

Paxson, E, 'Sharing the Benefits of Outer Space Exploration: Space Law and Economic Development' (1993) 14 Michigan Journal of International Law 487

Rogers, Alex et al., 'Marine Genetic Resources in Areas Beyond National Jurisdiction: Promoting Marine Scientific Research and Enabling Equitable Benefit-sharing' (2021) 8 Frontiers in Marine Science 667274

Rourke, M, 'Access by Design, Benefits if Convenient: A Closer Look at the Pandemic Influenza Preparedness Framework's Standard Material Transfer Agreements' (2019) 97 Milbank Quarterly 91

Rourke, M, 'The Pandemic Influenza Preparedness Framework as a "Specialized International Access and Benefit-sharing Instrument" under the Nagoya Protocol (2021) 72 Northern Ireland Legal Quarterly 411

Ruiz, M and Vernooy, R (eds), *The Custodians of Biodiversity: Sharing Access to and Benefits of Genetic Resources* (Earthscan, 2012)

Sadoff, CW and Grey, D, 'Cooperation on International Rivers: A Continuum for Securing and Sharing Benefits' (2005) 30 Water International 420

Salpin, C and Germani, V, 'Patenting of Research Results Related to Genetic Resources from Areas beyond National Jurisdiction: The Crossroads of the Law of the Sea and Intellectual Property Law' (2007) 16 Review of European Community and International Environmental Law 12

Schroeder, D, 'Benefit-Sharing: It's Time for a Definition' (2007) 33 Journal of Medical Ethics 205
De Schutter, O, 'The Right of Everyone to Enjoy the Benefits of Scientific Progress and the Right to Food: From Conflict to Complementarity' (2011) 33 Human Rights Quarterly 304
Scott, D and Berry, D, *Genetic Resources in the Age of the Nagoya Protocol and Gene/Genome Synthesis* (University of Edinburgh, 2016)
Sharman, N, 'Inter-State Climate Technology Transfer under the UNFCCC: A Benefit-Sharing Approach' (2022) 31 Review of European, Comparative and International Environmental Law 435
Simm, K, 'Benefit-Sharing: An Inquiry Regarding the Meaning and Limits of the Concept of Human Genetic Research' (2005) 1 Genomics, Society and Policy 29
Sing' Oei, K and Shepherd, J, 'In Land We Trust': The Endorois' Communication and the Quest for Indigenous Peoples' Rights in Africa' (2010) 16 Buffalo Human Rights Law Review 57
Singh Nijar, G, *The Nagoya Protocol on Access and Benefit Sharing: An Analysis* (CEBLAW, 2011)
Suiseeya, KRM, 'Negotiating the Nagoya Protocol: Indigenous Demands for Justice' (2014) 14 Global Environmental Politics 102
Swepston, L, 'New Step in the International Law on Indigenous and Tribal Peoples: ILO Convention No. 169 of 1989' (1990) 15 Oklahoma City University Law Review 677
Switzer, S, Burci, G, and Morgera, E, 'Biodiversity, Pathogen Sharing and International Law' in S Negri (ed.), *Environmental Health in International and European Law* (Edward Elgar, 2019) 271
Tladi, D, 'Genetic Resources, Benefit-Sharing and the Law of the Sea: The Need for Clarity' (2007) 13 Journal of International Maritime Law 183
Tobin, B, 'Bridging the Nagoya Compliance Gap: The Fundamental Role of Customary Law in the Protection of Indigenous Peoples' Resources and Knowledge Rights' (2013) 9 Law Environment and Development Journal. 144
Tobin, B, *Indigenous Peoples, Customary Law and Human Rights: Why Living Law Matters* (Routledge, 2014)
Tsioumani, E, *Fair and Equitable Benefit-sharing in Agriculture: Reinventing Agrarian Justice* (Routledge, 2021)
Tsioumani, E et al., 'Following the Open Source Trail Outside the Digital World: Open Source Applications in Agricultural Research and Development' (2016) 14 tripleC 145
Tvedt, M and Jorem, A, 'Bioprospecting in the High Seas: Regulatory Options for Benefit Sharing' (2013) 16 Journal of World Intellectual Property 150
Tvedt, MW and Young, T, *Beyond Access: Exploring Implementation of the Fair and Equitable Sharing Commitment in the CBD* (IUCN, 2007)
Vermeylen, S, 'The Nagoya Protocol and Customary Law: The Paradox of Narratives in the Law' (2013) 9 Law Environment and Development Journal 185
Vermeylen, S, Martin, G, and Clift, R, 'Intellectual Property, Rights Systems and the Assemblage of Local Knowledge Systems' (2008) 15 International Journal of Cultural Property 201
Vierros, M and Harden-Davies, H, 'Capacity Building and Technology Transfer for Improving Governance of Marine Areas both Beyond and Within National Jurisdiction' (2020) 122 Marine Policy 104158
Vierros, M et al., 'Considering Indigenous Peoples and Local Communities in Governance of the Global Ocean Commons' (2018) 119 Marine Policy 104039
Wilde, D et al., 'Equitable Sharing of Deep-sea Mining Benefits: More Questions than Answers' (2023) 151 Marine Policy 105572
van Wyk, E, Breen, C, and Freimund, W, 'Meanings and Robustness: Propositions for Enhancing Benefit Sharing in Social-Ecological Systems' (2014) 8 International Journal of the Commons 576
Wynberg, R, 'Biopiracy: Crying Wolf or a Lever for Equity and Conservation?' (2023) 52 Research Policy 104674

Wynberg, R and Hauck, M, 'People, Power, and the Coast: A Conceptual Framework for Understanding and Implementing Benefit Sharing' (2014) 19 Ecology and Society 27

Wynberg, R and Hauck, M (eds), *Sharing Benefits from the Coast: Rights, Resources and Livelihoods* (UCT Press, 2014)

Wynberg, R, Schroeder, D, and Chennells, R (eds), *Indigenous Peoples, Consent and Benefit Sharing: Lessons from the San-Hoodia Case* (Springer, 2009)

Xu, F and Su, J, 'Towards a Legal Regime of Benefits Sharing for Space Mining: With some Experience from the Area' (2022) 76 Resources Policy 102627

Yow Mulalap C et al., 'Traditional Knowledge and the BBNJ Instrument' (2020) 122 Marine Policy 104103

Index

For the benefit of digital users, indexed terms that span two pages (e.g., 52–53) may, on occasion, appear on only one of those pages.